A DIFFERENT FACE OF WAR

A DIFFERENT FACE OF WAR

Memories of a Medical Service Corps Officer in Vietnam

James G. Van Straten

Number 8: North Texas Military Biography and Memoir Series

Denton, Texas

10 9 8 7 6 5 4 3 2 1

Permissions:
University of North Texas Press
1155 Union Circle #311336
Denton, TX 76203-5017

The paper used in this book meets the minimum requirements of the
American National Standard for Permanence of Paper for Printed Library
Materials, z39.48.1984. Binding materials have been chosen for durability.

Library of Congress Cataloging-in-Publication Data

Van Straten, James G., author.
A different face of war : memories of a Medical Service Corps officer
in Vietnam / James G. Van Straten.

pages cm

Includes bibliographical references and index.

ISBN 978-1-57441-617-6 (cloth : alk. paper)
ISBN 978-1-57441-738-8 (paper : alk. paper)
ISBN 978-1-57441-621-3 (ebook)

1. Van Straten, James G.. 2. United States. Army--Officers--Biography. 3.
Health services administrators--Vietnam--Biography. 4. Health services
administrators--United States--Biography. 5. United States. Army. Medical
Service Corps--Biography. 6. United States. Army. Medical Service Corps--
History--Vietnam War, 1961-1975. 7. Vietnam War, 1961-1975--Medical care--
Vietnam. 8. Vietnam War, 1961-1975—Personal narratives, American. I. Title.

UH347.V36A3 2015 959.704'37--dc23 [B]

2015031937

The electronic edition of this book was made possible
by the support of the Vick Family Foundation.

A Different Face of War: Memories of a Medical Service Corps Officer in Vietnam
is Number 8 in the North Texas Military Biography and Memoir Series

For my loving wife, Patricia, and for my family. They make my life so much richer. For the spouses of American servicemen and women, wherever in this wide world they may reside. For they also serve. And for those American men and women whose names are inscribed on the Vietnam Wall. May they rest in peace.

TABLE OF CONTENTS

LIST OF IMAGES

ACKNOWLEDGEMENTS

I am hugely grateful to my good wife for saving all of the letters I wrote to her and our children while I was in Vietnam. Had she not done so, this memoir would not have been possible.

I would like to express my gratitude for the support so generously provided by our good friends Ken and Valda Lingle. Valda served as proofreader of the manuscript and Ken provided much appreciated support in my understanding the vagaries of electronic word processing and in the area of digitizing the almost fifty-year-old 35 mm slides and other images that appear in the book. Thanks also to my friend Lewis ("Bob") Sorley for his review of the draft manuscript and helpful suggestions.

Lastly, I want to thank our daughter, Kathryn, for her unflagging encouragement during the entire project. Without her spurring me on, the book would not have been written.

Acronyms and Abbreviations

APC	Aspirin, Phenacetin, and Caffeine (medication)
ARVN	Army of the Republic of Vietnam (our allies)
BX	U.S. Navy or Air Force Base Exchange
CID	Criminal Investigation Division
CNS	Catholic News Service
COLA	Cost of Living Allowance
CONEX	Container Express (shipping container)
CRS	Catholic Relief Services
DMZ	Demilitarized Zone
EMT	Emergency Medical Technician
G-I	General Staff Officer in the Area of Personnel
G-2	General Staff Officer in the Area of Intelligence
G-3	General Staff Officer in Area of Operations
G-4	General Staff Officer in the Area of Logistics
G-5	General Staff Officer in the Area of Civil Affairs
GP	General Purpose
Helipad	Helicopter landing pad
HQ	Headquarters
ICC	International Control Commission
I	I Corps Tactical ZoneCorps

LCDR	Lieutenant Commander
LTC	Lieutenant Colonel
LZ	Helicopter Landing Zone
MACV	U.S. Military Assistance Command, Vietnam
MARS	Military Affiliate Radio System
MEDCAP	Medical Civic Action Program
MILPHAP	Military Provincial Health Assistance Program
MP	Military Police
MSC	Medical Service Corps
Navy	U.S. Naval Support Activity Hospital, Da NangHospital
NCO	Non-Commissioned Officer
NCOIC	Non-Commissioned Officer in Charge
NSA	U.S. Naval Support Activity
NVA	North Vietnamese Army (the enemy)
PF	Popular Forces (district-level militia, our allies)
PIO	Public Information Officer
POL	Petroleum, Oil and Lubricants
POW	Prisoner of War
PX	U.S. Army & Air Force Post Exchange
RF	Regional Forces (regional militia, our allies)
Ruff-Puff	Regional Forces and Popular Forces (slang term)
SDO	Staff Duty Officer
SFC	Sergeant First Class
SP	Shore Patrol
SP-4	Specialist Four
TFO	Task Force Oregon (U.S. Army)
III	III Marine Amphibious Force (U.S. Marines)MAF
USAID	U.S. Agency for International Development
USARV	U.S. Army, Vietnam
USMC	U.S. Marine Corps
USOM	U.S. Operations Mission
VC	Viet Cong (the enemy)
VNAF	Vietnam Air Force (South Vietnam)
VOQ	Visiting Officers' Quarters

Image 1. Map of I Corps

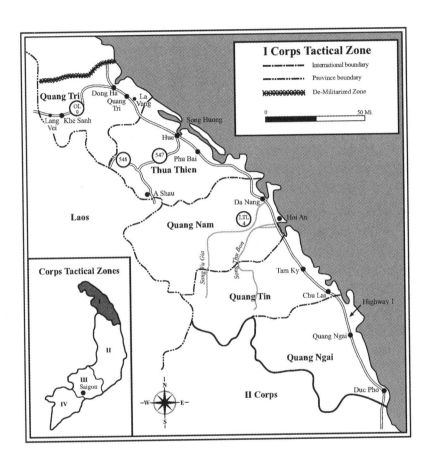

Courtesy of Mr. Alexander Mendoza

PROLOGUE

Memories of Vietnam seem to be inextricably woven into the very fabric of my soul. No day goes by that I don't think about the people or the events I experienced during the year I spent in that then war-torn country.

I went to Vietnam as a fairly young man, just two months beyond my thirty-third birthday. Now I'm an old man, 82 and a bit more. The years have not dimmed my memories of Vietnam. In many respects they are more poignant and deeply ingrained than most of the memories of my life. Why this is true, I cannot explain.

Relatively little has been written about those who advise foreign armies in the support services during time of war. This is especially true in regard to medical support. As the senior medical advisor to the Army of the Republic of Vietnam in the I Corps Tactical Zone, my geographic area of responsibility was roughly the northern quarter of the Republic of South Vietnam. It consisted of the five-province area from the Demilitarized Zone south to a point just below the coastal city of Quang Ngai.

During the year I was in Vietnam, I wrote 352 letters to my wife. Most were written between 0500 and 0630 hours in the morning or during the noon hour, those being the only times I could have access to the single typewriter in our office. My wife desperately needed constant reassurance of my safety and fidelity to family. Our year of separation was far more difficult for her than it was for me, a fact that will become obvious throughout this memoir. My almost daily letters became her lifeline.

In the writing of this memoir, I was most fortunate in that my wife retained all the letters I wrote to her and our children during the year I was away. The letters sat boxed-up in a closet for forty-five years. I read them for the first time during the summer of 2012. I am ever so grateful that my wife had the good sense to save them, as they provide an accounting not only of what happened on a day-to-day basis but also of my thoughts at the time. They also constitute an accurate chronology of events.

Many of the descriptions of people and events in the memoir are essentially extracts from the letters written to my wife. I had tried to describe as fully and accurately as possible the environment in which I worked; consequently, the language is sometimes graphic. This stark reality approach was at my wife's request; she wanted to know about the life I was living in Vietnam. She specifically asked that my letters be descriptive and specific, as she didn't want to be put in a position where she had to read between the lines.

My assigned duties while in Vietnam required extensive travel throughout the five-province area that comprised the I Corps Tactical Zone, commonly called I Corps and pronounced "Eye" Corps. Typically, I traveled to province capitals and remote villages and hamlets two or three days each week, which granted broad exposure to the country and its people. Few American soldiers had a comparable opportunity. In this respect I was most fortunate.

Introduction

Early in February 1966, cold north winds buffeted the campus of the University of Texas at Austin where I was studying under U.S. Army sponsorship. As I hurried to an early morning management seminar in the School of Business, my thoughts were elsewhere. Waiting anxiously for me to return home was my wife, probably cradling our very sick baby boy in her arms. We had to once again take our infant son to the military hospital at Bergstrom Air Force Base, located southeast of Austin. Born the previous June with a congenital lung disorder, the youngest of our six children had, on three occasions, developed pneumonia that threatened to take his life. On the first occasion, shortly after his birth, he was placed in the critical care unit of the hospital, and, upon advice of the attending physician, a priest was summoned to administer the Last Rites of the Catholic Church.

As I passed the building that housed the Army ROTC Detachment, a window opened and Major Ray Cook, a friend of mine and a faculty member in the Department of Military Science, yelled, "Hey, Jim, I see by the *Army Times* that you're on your way to Vietnam in July." That was my first indication of my next assignment.

As a career army officer, I expected to go to Vietnam upon completion of graduate degree requirements. However, the news jolted me because of the timing. I resolved to withhold the information from my wife until the crisis with our youngest son had passed.

Four weeks later, military orders arrived assigning me to the Military Assistance Command, Vietnam (MACV) with a departure date of 3 July

1966. The assignment to MACV was my first indication that I was to be an advisor to the army of the Republic of Vietnam. By the time I received the orders, the crisis with our son, Michael, had passed, and I was able to share the still disquieting news with my wife and children.

My wife and I had five months to prepare our six children and ourselves for a yearlong separation. We were resolved to do our best.

After I was awarded a graduate degree from the University of Texas in late May 1966, we rented an older but comfortable home in San Antonio, Texas and scheduled the move of our household goods from Austin to San Antonio. This was to be the eighth home we had occupied during our ten years of army service.

After getting settled in our new home, I took military leave and we packed up the six children and drove the 1,450 miles to our parents' homes in Wisconsin to say goodbye to family and friends. The discourse with both sets of parents was somewhat painful, as they simply couldn't understand why we had elected to have my wife, Patricia, and the six children spend the year in San Antonio rather than near family in Wisconsin. Despite our best efforts to explain the army support system, the availability of high quality medical services at Brooke Army Medical Center, and the nearness of the military commissary and Post Exchange in San Antonio, they were dubious about our decision.

My now deceased father had a habit with which I was very familiar. Whenever he had a serious matter that he wished to discuss with me, he would say, "Jim, I think I'll take a little walk and smoke a cigar. Do you want to come along?" This was not an invitation; it was a command.

He lit up his cigarillo, a little cigar that came in a box of six, and we were off on our walk. We revisited the subject of why we had decided to have Pat and the children stay almost 1,500 miles away from family, and I restated the reasons but never convinced him that it was the right thing to do. I stressed the fact that our youngest child needed to be near sophisticated medical support, but he was never convinced of the correctness of our decision.

Then came the subject of whether Pat and the children would be all right financially. I remember saying, "Dad, don't worry about that. I just got promoted to major and with the raise in salary, plus the extra $100.00 a month combat pay I'll be receiving while in Vietnam, I'll be making right at a $1,000.00 a month. I think I can live on $125.00 a month, or at most $150.00, so Pat and the children will have about $850.00 a month to live on." This seemed to satisfy him.

Finally he approached the big subject, the real reason he wanted me along on the walk, the "what if?" question. What if I didn't come home? As gently as I could, I assured him that Pat and the children would be alright; that they would receive a monthly stipend that would cover their basic living expenses. While not generous, the stipend would be adequate.

It was a quiet and somber walk back to my parents' home.

A few days later, after saying goodbye to our respective families and friends in Wisconsin, we started the long drive back to our new home in San Antonio. I was committed to spending much of the remainder of my time, prior to deployment, learning as much as I could about Vietnam, its people, and things that might confront me as an advisor to the South Vietnamese Army. Not knowing my specific assignment in Vietnam made the task difficult, but I did the best I could under the circumstances. Time not spent preparing myself for the assignment was used doing family-oriented things and getting settled in our new home.

Chapter 1

July 1966

Very early on Sunday morning, 3 July 1966, while the rest of the country was celebrating a long Independence Day weekend, I had the sad task of saying goodbye to my wife and children.

After hugging each of our six little ones and telling them how much I loved them, I kissed my wife goodbye and held her tightly. I then threw my military duffel bag and one small suitcase into the trunk of the waiting taxi and got in for the short ride to San Antonio International Airport. I had hired the cab, despite our tight budget, not wanting to subject my wife to saying goodbye at the airport and then having to drive home with all the children.

As the cab pulled away from our home I waved a final goodbye. There stood my wife on the front steps with tears in her eyes holding our fragile, one-year-old baby, Michael. Clinging to one of her legs was our two-and-a-half-year-old son, Steven, while five-year-old Laurie clung to the other. And clustered around their mother and younger siblings were six-year-old Kathy, nine-year-old Susan, and ten-year-old Leslie.

I remember thinking at the time that my wife's responsibilities while I was away would be, in many respects, far more daunting and challenging than mine in Vietnam. I also thought of the countless military wives around the country who saw their husbands off to war under similar or far more difficult circumstances.

It was a sad ride to the airport.

After several lengthy delays in California, another in the Philippines because of concerns that Mount Pinatubo was about to experience a volcanic eruption, and losing essentially a day because of time zone changes, we finally approached Vietnam on the afternoon of 6 July. It looked so peaceful from the air, with long sandy beaches punctuated by hundreds of little inlets and coves off the South China Sea, then high hills and mountains rising rather sharply beyond the coastal lowlands.

As we started our descent, evidence of war became visible. Air activity was great. Helicopters, fighter jets, and reconnaissance planes were below us and to our sides. When we neared Saigon, on a crystal clear day, we saw puffs of smoke on the ground. An older non-commissioned officer seated across the aisle from me peered out the window and told me artillery fire was causing the puffs of smoke. We were too high to see the actual artillery pieces.

Upon reaching the Saigon area, we were forced to circle for about 55 minutes before being cleared by air traffic control to land. We circled deep into the Mekong River Delta. It seemed to me as if much of the delta landmass was covered with a shallow sheet of water.

From the air, Saigon was beautiful. It looked like a big, lazily sprawling city with a river running through it. The captain warned us that the landing would be unlike any we had ever experienced. He was right.

Because of the danger of anti-aircraft fire from the ground, there was no lengthy, slow descent. When the word to land came, the captain put the plane in a fairly steep dive and descended very rapidly. The object was to get the plane on the ground as quickly as possible.

When we disembarked onto the sweltering tarmac of Tan Son Nhut Airport, temperatures were beyond 110 degrees. Once inside the terminal, the sorting process began. Those being assigned to U.S. Army, Vietnam over here; those going to Military Assistance Command, Vietnam over there; Air Force over here; Navy over there. After what seemed an interminably long time, the sorting and personnel accounting processes were over. The MACV contingent, of which I was a part, was about to board a bus for the trip to a downtown Saigon hotel when, unexpectedly, an old friend, Major John Bullard, slapped me on the back and said, "Jim, welcome to Vietnam. You're about to get your first glimpse of Saigon, the Paris of the Orient." He then told me that he'd pick me up at the hotel MACV used for in-processing at 1830 hours and we'd go out to dinner. He also told me that in all likelihood I'd be going "up country" to Da Nang. This was my very first indication of where I was being assigned.

The bus had no air conditioning. All the functioning windows in the bus were wide open and covered with heavy-gage mesh wire welded to the side of the bus. A Military Policeman, armed with a rifle, stood in the entrance well of the bus. He explained that the mesh wire over the windows was precautionary. On several recent occasions, terrorists riding on motorized bicycles had thrown grenades into the open windows of buses carrying troops, taking a number of lives and severely injuring many.

As our bus passed through the city, I couldn't help but notice the mounds of rotting garbage coupled with the overwhelming smell of diesel fuel. The garbage piles were twenty to thirty feet high, and rats scavenged in abundance, scurrying all over the mounds. There seemed to be one mound on each downtown city block. The guard aboard the bus explained that there was an ongoing strike by the garbage collectors' union. My weariness from the long journey and the stifling heat and humidity, combined with the stench of downtown, exceedingly odiferous and nauseating, made for an uncomfortable ride into the heart of Saigon.

Surprisingly, some sections of the city seemed unaffected by the garbage collectors' strike. They were clean and attractive. Outdoor dining seemed popular, not only on the sidewalks in front of fine restaurants but also alongside the plethora of eateries mounted on pull carts.

I quickly noted a major difference in the way commercially available products were displayed and marketed. There were two or three city blocks where nothing but plumbing fixtures were displayed and sold. Head-to-head competition was the norm. If you wanted a new toilet or a sink or a bath tub, you knew precisely where to go. Another section of the city was reserved for flowers and growing plants, while another concentrated on clothing and shoes. Birds and birdcages even had their own section of the city.

Bicycle repair shops seemed not to have adopted this marketing plan. They were everywhere. Men and boys dressed in shorts, tank tops, and sandals made from old tires, squatting with their knees to their chests next to a bicycle with a flat tire or a broken chain, were everywhere. It was so different from anything I had experienced in the United States or Europe.

Another thing that caught my attention was the absolute absence of obesity among the Vietnamese people. I made a point of looking for an obese person, and had great difficulty finding even one.

And then there were the gorgeous young Vietnamese women wearing ao dais, the traditional dress for the affluent woman of Vietnam. The absolute elegance of the garment was stunning. The ao dai is a very tight-fitting, long tunic, which is split up the sides to the waist and worn over pantaloons.

When we arrived at our hotel at about 1400 hours, the first step in the in-country processing was to draw our equipment and weapons. After that, we had a series of briefings and watched films to orient us to the country, its people, and some of their customs, traditions, and taboos. At about 1745 hours, we knocked off for the day, and I headed to my assigned room, which I shared with eight others. I was ready for a shower and a shave, followed by dinner with my friend, John Bullard. Although I was dead tired, I knew that it was best to "tough it out" until about 2200 hours and then try to get a good night's sleep to minimize the inevitably negative and sometimes prolonged effects of jet lag.

Still in duty uniform, John picked me up promptly at 1800 hours, and we rode to his downtown Saigon hotel in his assigned jeep. He grabbed a quick shower and changed into civilian clothes while I enjoyed a cold bottle of Ba Moui Ba, the local beer.

When John was finished showering and changing clothes, we enjoyed another Ba Moui Ba while he told me what he knew about my upcoming assignment to Da Nang. He then said that he wanted to treat me to the best French onion soup "in the whole wide world" and that the fastest way to get to the French restaurant that served it was by pedicab. A pedicab has a single seat mounted on the front of a tricycle that has two wheels in front and one in the back. It required two pedicabs to transport us to the restaurant.

We exited the front door of John's hotel, walked about a block along an incredibly boisterous and busy street, and there were the pedicabs--dozens of them--each with an entrepreneur owner hoping for a fare. John immediately got into one of them, and I started to do likewise when I thought I heard John say something to me. I walked over to him as he sat in his pedicab, and he told me that what he wanted to tell me could wait until we got to the restaurant. I then apparently got into a different pedicab than the one I had originally started to get into. The first driver became very agitated and angry, yelling at the driver of the second pedicab. Then the two drivers started shouting and shaking their fists at each other.

The cyclist powering my pedicab was exerting maximum energy trying to get away from the scene of the altercation. He kept looking back over his shoulder as he pedaled down the busy Saigon street. Suddenly, I sensed the other pedicab about to overtake us. I turned around, and there was driver number one brandishing a tire iron and looking furious. He jumped off his pedicab and smashed the driver of my pedicab in the head with the tire iron. Bleeding profusely from a deep scalp wound, the driver lost consciousness in the street. Almost immediately, a Saigon policeman was on the scene signaling for me to get the hell out of there, perhaps fearing that the growing crowd surrounding the injured driver was about to get out of control. John jumped out of his pedicab and quickly paid his driver. I threw some money onto the seat of my pedicab, and John and I sprinted down the street toward the French restaurant.

When we got inside the restaurant, soaking wet from perspiration, John smiled at me and said, "Jim, again, welcome to Vietnam."

***

Despite my best efforts to avoid it, jet lag plagued me upon arrival. The morning after the pedicab incident, I woke at 0230 hours and couldn't get back to sleep, so I got up and, after showering, shaving and getting into a fresh uniform, went down to the hotel restaurant and had an early breakfast. There were several other officers in there, so I can only assume that they, too, were afflicted with jet lag. After finishing my breakfast, it was still only 0400, and the first briefing of the day was not scheduled until 0800 hours. I had four hours to kill, so I boarded one of the Navy buses that operated around the clock, shuttling troops throughout the city on a prescribed route. The bus was due to return to our hotel at 0735 hours, which accommodated my schedule very nicely.

The activity level in the city, even at that early hour, can best be described as frenetic. Saigon showed only fleeting evidence of the once beautiful city that, by most accounts, it once was. Once again I encountered the mounds of decaying garbage populated by huge hungry rats with voracious appetites and bold dispositions. I concluded that rats must be nocturnal animals, for there were far more of them at night than there had been the previous day.

Never before had I seen such masses of people use such diverse means of transportation. At about 0630 the sidewalks and streets were full. Bicycles, cyclos, motorized bicycles, pedicabs, motor scooters, pushcarts, diesel fuel-spewing buses and trucks, taxis, military vehicles, armored personnel carriers, several tanks, a few privately owned passenger vehicles—the city was teaming with people and vehicles of all types. Refugees from the countryside had swelled Saigon's population to almost two million, over twice the population of the pre-war days. Children were everywhere. Many of the younger ones wore only shirts or tee shirts and flip-flops. Some of the street urchins were totally naked. I saw countless numbers of people sleeping on the street. Many homeless refugee families spent the night huddled in the entryways of stores.

Image 2. Street urchins, probably orphans, living on the streets of Saigon

Photo courtesy of the author

Craftsmen, mechanics, and artisans were everywhere, all looking for a way to earn a few piastres, the South Vietnamese currency.

All military buildings were fortified and guarded. Sandbagged defensive positions had been erected at all strategic locations: key intersections, important bridges, government buildings, train stations, etc. Saigon stood in stark contrast to cities I had seen throughout the United States and Europe. The early morning bus ride boggled my senses.

***

During my in-country processing and orientation, I lived in the Koepler Hotel, a facility in great need of maintenance. There were major plumbing problems that made occupancy interesting, to say the least. There was one small bathroom consisting of one small sink, one toilet, and one shower stall for each eight-to-ten-person room. Shaving and showering in the morning was a challenge. I was one of nine officers in the dormitory-style room to which I was assigned.

There was no potable water in the entire hotel except for bottled water that could be purchased in the hotel restaurant. To accommodate the absence of potable running water, two whiskey bottles, still with the Jim Beam and Seagram's labels attached, were placed in each bathroom. These bottles had been filled with potable water to be used exclusively for tooth brushing. Taped to the wall over the sink were instructions for brushing our teeth. We were instructed to take a small sip of water from one of the whiskey bottles, swish it around in our mouth, then spit it out and brush our teeth. After finishing the brushing process we were to take another small sip of water, swish it around in our mouth, and spit it out in order to rinse the toothpaste residue from our teeth and mouths. All nine occupants of our room used the same two bottles of water for this process. The bottles were re-filled once a day.

Showering was even more adventurous. Water seemed to be in very short supply. During my stay in the hotel, I never had the luxury of hot water. Frequently, the water simply stopped running right in the middle of a shower. Consequently, there was yet another sign taped to the wall near the shower, instructing us how to take a shower: Fill the nearby sink with water, get under the shower, wet down one's body, turn off the shower to conserve water, and then soap up and scrub one's entire body. We were then to turn on the shower once again. If there was water, we were able to rinse the soap off under the shower. If not, we had a sink full of water and a washcloth to complete the process.

The first morning I was a guest in the Koepler Hotel, I arose at 0230 because of jet lag. I tried to do everything according to the rules. I brushed my teeth without incident, and then got into the cold shower, wetted myself down, turned off the water, soaped and scrubbed my entire body, and then turned on the shower to rinse off. You guessed it: not only was there no running water, but I had forgotten to fill the sink. I rinsed off using a washcloth and a whiskey bottle full of potable water, thereby probably depriving others of the opportunity to brush their teeth.

I remember thinking as Spartan as this room in the Koepler Hotel was, it would probably be considered luxurious by the soldiers, marines, and navy corpsmen slogging around in the rice paddies and jungles.

***

The briefings presented during the two and a half days of in-country processing and orientation were excellent. I was surprised to learn that the U.S. troop strength had risen to 285,000 and even more surprised to learn that an anticipated 100,000 would be added during the coming year. Clearly a rapid buildup of U.S. forces was underway. President Lyndon Johnson had made a clear and seemingly unequivocal commitment to take the war to the enemy.

I decided on the first day to concentrate my attention on everything that was said about the customs, traditions, and taboos of the people, and on the tactical situation in the I Corps Tactical Zone, the region of the country where I would be serving. I learned almost immediately that no one referred to the area as the I Corps Tactical Zone, as most of the printed literature referred to it. Instead it was known simply as "I Corps." I Corps consisted of the five northern-most provinces of South Vietnam, each province being the political equivalent of a state in the United States.

I further learned something very disconcerting. Repercussions from the so-called "Buddhist Uprising" or "Struggle Movement" that had gripped

I Corps in May 1966, just two months prior to my arrival, were still being felt. We were told that the situation was "exceedingly tense and uncertain in I Corps," which was a Buddhist stronghold. The officers and non-commissioned officers presenting the briefings did not have in-depth knowledge about what had taken place, but they were very much aware of the fact that elements of the South Vietnamese Air Force, and perhaps the army as well, had joined the dissidents. Needless to say, I was concerned about what I would find upon my arrival in Da Nang. I had no idea if the military medical hierarchy in I Corps, the officers and non-commissioned officers I would be advising, had remained loyal to the established government or had joined the revolt. I would soon find out.

The HQ MACV orientation for newly assigned advisors ended at noon on Saturday, 9 July. During the last briefing, I was handed a note informing me that I was to be at the MACV Surgeon's office at 0700 on Monday morning for in-depth briefings on the medical situation in I Corps. I was also told that the Surgeon's office would arrange my transportation to Da Nang.

The MACV Surgeon's office was a beehive of activity when I arrived at about 0645 on Monday morning. The staff was scurrying around trying to untangle a logistical problem with the Saigon Port Authority. For reasons unknown, medical supplies shipped from the United States were not being off-loaded in a timely manner and, as a result, inventories of critically needed pharmaceuticals were running low throughout the country. I almost felt like an intruder as I sat there waiting to be briefed.

Eventually I received two helpful briefings, both making it very clear that at that point in time the I Corps area was the most active of the four corps areas in the country. Both officers who briefed me highlighted "lessons learned" by other corps-level advisors. The MACV Surgeon, Colonel David Eisner, interrupted halfway through the second briefing. He informed me that he had directed the officer I was replacing, Major Don Ross, to come to Saigon the next day to spend an hour or two briefing me on several areas that required immediate attention. I appreciated this greatly, for without Colonel Eisner's intervention, I would not have crossed paths with the officer I was replacing, as he was scheduled to depart Da Nang about two hours before I was to arrive. This change, of course, extended my stay in Saigon by an additional day.

Upon the conclusion of the two briefings, I was directed to report to the MACV Surgeon's executive officer, Lieutenant Colonel Darvin Patrick. I entered his office, saluted smartly, and stated, "Sir, Major Van Straten reporting as directed." Colonel Patrick returned my salute, then invited me to be seated and offered me a cup of coffee.

After exchanging a few pleasantries, he informed me that he was especially pleased to read in my file that I'd had assignments with both infantry and armor battalions.

"Those assignments should prove invaluable to your work in I Corps," he said. "I also noted that you just finished your doctorate in educational administration. I suppose because of that you were probably expecting to be assigned as the advisor to the Commandant of the Vietnamese Army Medical Service School here in Saigon. Ordinarily that would be the logical place to assign you, but these are not ordinary times. I want you to know that I personally made the decision to assign you to I Corps in Da Nang, at least initially. The need there is so much greater than it is at the service school in Saigon at this time. It may change later, but right now things are tense as hell in Da Nang. So that's how it is. If you want to complain to someone about not utilizing your civilian schooling, complain to me. I'm the guilty party. I wanted to look you in the eye and tell you that. I'm the guilty party."

I tried to assure him that I didn't want to complain to anyone, that I had no expectations whatsoever regarding where in Vietnam I would be assigned, and that I was looking forward to the assignment in Da Nang.

He then went on to tell me what I already knew: other than the U.S. Army Advisory team in the I Corps area, there were no U.S. Army forces in the I Corps Tactical Zone other than a small radio research unit.

Regarding U.S. ground forces, I Corps was Marine Corps territory. The U.S. Air Force had a huge presence, with the extremely active Da Nang Air Base, and there was a fairly large U.S. Navy and Seabee contingent as well, but there were no U.S. Army units other than MACV Advisory Team #1 and the radio research unit.

Colonel Patrick then asked if I had any questions. I thought for a moment, and then asked, "Sir, could I get a copy of the job description for a senior medical advisor at the corps level?"

He looked me in the eye and said, "Jim, I'll be totally honest with you. There is no job description. We tried to develop one, but we found that the job differs so markedly from one corps area to another that it was impossible to write a useful job description. To a very large degree, your duties will be dependent upon the rapport that you're able to establish with the Vietnamese physician assigned as the I Corps Surgeon. Some advisors are able to establish a good working relationship with their counterpart and others are almost totally unsuccessful in doing so."

Colonel Patrick then added, "I will say this, Jim, you can get involved in any aspect of medical support in which you feel competent, but please, please avoid advising on any aspect of clinical medicine. We've had advisors, non-physicians or nurses like yourself, who stupidly tried to modify the way Vietnamese physicians and nurses practice medicine. The physicians and nurses were rightfully resistant. In fact, some were indignant about this intrusion into their professional lives and complained to the MACV Surgeon. I think you will find that most Vietnamese physicians and nurses are quite well trained, many having been trained by the French. As a Medical Service Corps officer you can advise in so many different areas. Evacuation of casualties from the battlefields, inter-hospital transfers, and medical logistics are areas where they need help, as are field sanitation and malaria prevention. Keeping track of patients as they move from facility to facility seems to be a weakness. Balancing the workload among their hospitals is another area where they seem to struggle."

Colonel Patrick went on to say, "There are literally hundreds of areas in which you can get involved if—and this is a big if, Jim—if the I Corps Surgeon invites or allows your intervention. Just remember that you command nothing, not a single ARVN soldier do you command. Your power lies in persuasion. It depends on your ability to establish a meaningful relationship with your primary counterpart. If you can establish a trusting relationship your contributions can be enormous. Your success or failure is totally dependent upon the rapport that you're able to establish with your primary counterpart, the I Corps Surgeon. I've met the man and I consider him to be an officer of the highest quality."

He then concluded by saying, "Jim, there's one more thing. Make sure you take care of the MILPHAP teams that have been assigned in I Corps. Several of the province hospitals have been assigned a team and there is also a USAID sponsored team working at the city hospital in Da Nang. Those teams are doing such good and important work and a couple of them are way out there at the very end of the supply chain. MACV is responsible for making sure they receive the supply and maintenance support they need to accomplish their mission. Jim, I'm holding you personally responsible for seeing that the teams are supported. Is that clear?"

I responded, "Yes, sir."

He then looked me in the eye and said, "Good luck, Jim."

The meeting had ended. We shook hands. I saluted smartly and left Colonel Patrick's office. I didn't have the heart to tell him that at that point I didn't even know what a MILPHAP team was.

Major Don Ross, the officer I was replacing in Da Nang, was delayed by weather and arrived too late for us to get together on 12 July. Since there were important things happening in I Corps, Colonel Eisner, the MACV Surgeon, insisted that I delay my departure from Saigon for one more day to accommodate a meeting with Major Ross. I badly needed his insights regarding how to proceed, so I did not object. That gave me an entire day with nothing better to do than look around Saigon. I assuredly did not want to spend the day in the Koepler Hotel.

I found Saigon to be a very depressing city. It tore at my heartstrings to see the abject poverty and the homelessness of so many people. I was told that these conditions had arisen rapidly, within the past year or eighteen months at most, because of the tremendous number of refugees who had left their ancestral homes and flocked to the city for protection. The resulting contrast between "the haves" and "the have-nots" was stark and very visible. While "the have-nots" were trying to scratch out a living on the rat-infested garbage piles, "the haves" were going about their daily business wearing fine clothes, eating in fine restaurants, and more or less ignoring the poverty, the squalor, and the acrid smells of urine, feces and rotting garbage all about them.

I was amazed at the resourcefulness of the children. During my six-hour walk throughout the city, there was a very hard fifteen or twenty minute rain. It seemed as if half the poverty-stricken kids in Saigon under the age of ten, and there were a lot of them, took off their clothing and got a good bath during the downpour. A few had bars of soap, and those who were so blessed always seemed to share their bars with those not so fortunate.

At one point during my walk, I saw a little girl, probably five or six years old, who amazed me with her strength and resolve. She walked up to a community water spigot and filled two five-gallon cans. She then inserted a six- or seven-foot-long pole into the handles of the water cans—a can at each end of the pole—put her shoulder under the middle of the pole, and walked away. She appeared strong, tenacious in her determination to supply water for her family. I think of her often, the look of perseverance on her dirty, beautiful face.

***

During our eventual two-hour meeting the next day Major Don Ross gave me many insights into the Buddhist Uprising in I Corps. I came away from the meeting with a much better feel for what I could expect upon arrival. Major Ross was uncertain regarding what role, if any, my soon-to-be Vietnamese counterpart played in the uprising. He stated that, since the city of Da Nang was currently off limits, his contacts with him during the past few weeks had been limited.

At the conclusion of our meeting Major Ross casually mentioned that toothpaste and shampoo were in short supply in Da Nang. He recommended I go to the PX in Saigon and purchase some of each before departing for Da Nang in the early morning.

While at the PX, I ran into an old St. Norbert College classmate and friend, Major Joe Lutz. Joe was assigned to a Special Forces team and had been in country for several months. He seemed to know his way around Saigon and invited me to have dinner with him that evening. He said he had a jeep and would pick me up at 1900 hours at the Koepler Hotel.

That evening, prior to dinner, Joe showed me many interesting things in Saigon, primarily in the harbor area. I can't recall with certainty the name of the hotel where we enjoyed dinner, but I think it was either the Rex or the Caravelle. Joe suggested we eat alfresco in the rooftop restaurant of the hotel. By this time it was approaching 2030 hours, and the sun was starting to set. We sat there on top of the ten-story hotel, one of the tallest buildings in Saigon, with a cooling breeze making things very pleasant. We reminisced about our days in college, about playing football together, and about old friends while enjoying a couple of gin and tonics and listening to a small band with two excellent singers, one male and one female. Joe told me that Vietnamese singers have a reputation for being outstanding imitators. He was right. We listened as the male singer recreated Elvis Presley, Johnny Cash, Louis Armstrong, and others. Equally skillful was the young woman, who mimicked the work of Teresa Brewer, Patti Page, Janis Joplin, and even the late Kate Smith. The evening was beautiful, the entertainment was great, and our gin and tonics tasted better by the minute.

Eventually we ordered food. I chose lobster and was not disappointed. It was delicious. When we were finished with our entrées, we both ordered desserts and coffee. All the ingredients for a wonderful evening were present: tasty food and drink, classy entertainment, and spirited conversation with a good friend. By this time it was pitch dark. The war seemed so remote, almost non-existent. And then it started.

Whomp, whomp, whomp, a very unusual sound coming from what seemed to be the very edges of Saigon. *Whomp, whomp, whomp, whomp*, it continued.

I looked at Joe and asked, "Joe, what in hell is that noise?"

He said, "Come over here and I'll show you." We walked over to the edge of the roof and stood there peering over a four or five-foot wall guarding the edge. In the distance, I saw the flash of an explosion and then two or three more in rapid succession. Then there was a three or four second delay before the noise began again, *whomp, whomp, whomp*.

Joe said, "It's referred to as Arc Light bombing.[1] Our B-52s are conducting a bombing run."

I said, "Bombing run? I can't even hear the planes."

He then explained that the B-52s were flying at altitudes of 32,000 to 34,000 feet and that the planes were usually not detected by the enemy before the bombs exploded all around them. Joe also told me that the B-52 crews dropped their conventional 750 or 1,000-pound bombs from high altitudes with great precision, usually targeting enemy base camps, troop concentrations, and supply lines.

I said, "Joe, the explosions sound so close."

He said, "They're farther away than you might imagine, probably several miles outside of Saigon's defensive perimeter."

I asked, "Do they ever miss their primary targets?"

He answered, "Not very often, but when they do the results can be disastrous." Suddenly the hotel rooftop didn't seem as far removed from the war as it had moments before. It was a somber end to a memorable evening with an old friend.

The next morning, 14 July, I arose at 0200 hours, said goodbye to the Koepler Hotel and Saigon, and was transported by jeep to Tan Son Nhut Airport. While sitting in the crowded terminal awaiting my 0415 hours flight, I couldn't help but notice the bewildered, perplexed, and concerned looks on the faces of all the young soldiers, airmen, sailors, and marines in the terminal. I'm sure I looked equally perplexed and concerned. Despite the crowds of people in the terminal, I found it to be a very lonely place at 0300 in the morning.

I flew to Da Nang in the belly of a C-130 cargo plane. The seating consisted of four long rows of seats made of nylon webbing: a row against each side of the cabin and two back-to-back rows running down the middle. The soldiers and marines on board had their weapons cradled between their legs. News correspondents and camera crews were present in abundance. I interpreted this as a clear signal that something of significance was about to happen, or had just happened, either in Da Nang or somewhere else in I Corps.

On the way to Da Nang, we stopped in Pleiku to drop off about thirty soldiers. The landing was exceedingly rough because of crosswinds. Since there were no seat belts, several passengers were thrown violently from their nylon webbed seats. One cameraman was unable to hold onto his camera and tripod, and it smashed to the floor of the plane during the landing.

Upon our arrival at the Da Nang Air Base, we were discharged onto the tarmac. I was standing there waiting for my duffel bag and suitcase to be off loaded when suddenly an NCO approached, threw me a salute, stuck out his hand and said, "Sir, Welcome to Da Nang. I'm Sergeant First Class Sanders, your NCOIC."

I returned his salute, shook hands and said, "Sergeant Sanders, we'll make a helluva team."

He smiled and said, "You've got that right, sir. We'll make a helluva team, but only for six weeks. I go home about the first of September." Even though Sanders was a "short-timer," I immediately liked him.

While SFC Sanders transported me to my assigned room to drop off my duffel bag and suitcase, I quizzed him about my counterpart. He assured me that he seemed like a fine officer, but told me that he didn't have much contact at that level. I then asked him point blank if the I Corps Surgeon and the Commander of Duy Tan General Hospital had remained loyal to the South Vietnamese government or had joined or sympathized with the insurrectionists.

He looked me in the eye and said, "Sir, in all honesty I don't know with certainty, but it is my strong feeling that both remained loyal to the government."

After we dropped off my gear, SFC Sanders drove me to the I Corps motor pool where I signed for my jeep. I then followed him to I Corps HQ. He introduced me to my new boss, LTC Fred Mabra, a black officer, who served as the senior advisor to the I Corps G-4. My first impression of Colonel Mabra was very positive and that impression proved to be accurate. He was a fine officer and gentleman.

I spent about two hours with Colonel Mabra, during which he laid out his expectations concerning my job performance. After this orientation-type meeting, he escorted me up to the office of the commander of MACV Advisory Team #1 where I met Colonel Arch Hamblen, the commander, and Colonel John Beeson, the deputy commander.

After LTC Mabra introduced me to my new bosses, we exchanged handshakes, and then Colonel Hamblen smiled, slapped me on the back, and said, "Welcome to Da Nang and to the number one MACV advisory team in the Republic of Vietnam." I was then seated and offered a cup of coffee. Colonel Mabra excused himself, stating that he had an important meeting to attend.

Colonel Hamblen started the conversation by asking if I had been assigned an adequate room and if I had transportation. He also checked to be certain I was aware that downtown Da Nang was strictly off limits. I assured him that I was well taken care of and that I had been made aware that Da Nang was off limits.

For the next thirty minutes the conversation was most instructive. Almost immediately Colonel Hamblen launched into a discussion of the Buddhist Uprising and its negative impact on the pacification program that had been gaining momentum in I Corps.[2]

Colonel Hamblen asked, "During your orientation in Saigon what did they tell you about the situation in I Corps?"

I responded, "Well sir, they told me that things were tense as a result of the Buddhist Uprising."

He then asked, "Did they tell you that our whole pacification program has come to a standstill during the past three months?"

"They implied as much, sir, but didn't state it outright," I responded.

Colonel Hamblen then said, "I assume you know that some elements of the South Vietnamese Army and Air Force joined the insurrectionists. They became rebellious, much to our chagrin. It really pissed off the young U.S. Marines. How widespread this insurrection was among the ARVN and VNAF, we do not know for certain, but it was substantial and troubling. Were you aware of that?"

I replied, "Yes, sir, it was touched upon during the briefings I received in Saigon."

Colonel Beeson then jumped into the conversation and asked, "What did they tell you about the causes of the uprising?"

I answered, "Not a whole lot, sir, but as I understand it the Buddhists felt they should have a stronger voice in the direction of the country. Since they comprised a solid majority of the population, they felt they ought to have a louder voice."

Colonel Hamblen then said, "That's essentially correct. Although the Catholics were in the minority in the country, they somehow gained power and pretty much ran the country, cutting the Buddhists out of the dialogue, frequently not even consulting with them on important matters. No wonder the Buddhists decided to rise up. If the government officials in Saigon had reached out a conciliatory hand and listened to what the Buddhists had to say, we wouldn't be in the damned mess we're in today. At least that's my feeling."

Colonel Hamblen went on, "I assume you know that blood flowed in the streets of Da Nang during the April and May uprising. About 300 lives were lost during the fighting. It shocked the hell out of the people of Da Nang and Hue. For the most part the casualties that have been sustained since the very beginning of the war have come from the villages and the countryside. The people in the cities, with a few exceptions, have been spared. This was a wake-up call for the city-dwellers. Things in Da Nang and Hue have pretty much come to a halt during the past few months. The already fragile economies of both cities took a big hit. Businesses are just now getting back to where they were before the uprising started."

I then said, "But, sir, I was told in Saigon that the Buddhists were demanding not only a louder voice in government but also an end to the war and the immediate withdrawal of all United States forces. I can't see the South Vietnamese government agreeing to those kinds of demands."

Colonel Hamblen responded, "I can't either, but I firmly believe that if Premier Ky and Chief of State Thieu had left General Thi in command of I Corps he would have successfully defused the uprising. You know that Chief of State Thieu is a figurehead, do you not? Ky has all the power. Thieu jumps when Ky tells him to do so. Did they tell you in Saigon that General Thi is Buddhist, as are the majority of the people in I Corps? General Thi is also anti-Communist, strongly so in fact. He's also a great commander and a good and honest man. Premier Ky felt threatened by General Thi and relieved him under the false pretense of his having a medical problem. Now he's in exile in the United States. The people up here in I Corps, for the most part Buddhists, greatly respected General Thi and resent the fact that he was forced into exile. They would have listened to General Thi. They admired him and trusted him. Exactly why Premier Ky felt threatened by him I do not know."

Colonel Beeson then asked, "Are you aware that I Corps has had three different commanders since General Thi was exiled to the United States just a few months ago?"

I replied, "Sir, the briefings I received in Saigon mentioned that, but didn't paint it as a negative."

Colonel Beeson went on to say, "First we had General Chuan, who was relieved of command by Ky because he thought Chuan wasn't forceful enough in his attempts to regain control of Da Nang. Then Ky appointed General Dinh. Progress, as far as calming the situation, was being made under General Dinh, but Ky fired him too. I guess he thought the situation was calmed because of Dinh's strategy of appeasement, and he couldn't tolerate that. Then Ky ordered in his airborne troops and took control of Da Nang by brute force, by fighting in the streets. The people of the city were furious. And now we have General Lam, who seems like a capable commander, but only time will tell if he's up to the task. It's been a revolving door insofar as commanders are concerned. It's been very frustrating for all of us, especially for General Walt, the U.S. Marine commander and senior advisor to the Commander of I Corps, whomsoever the commander happens to be on any given day."

Colonel Hamblen interjected, "We need a little stability if we're going to get on with the difficult tasks of pacification and winning the war."[3]

As that introductory meeting with my commander and his deputy was ending, Colonel Hamblen and Colonel Beeson again welcomed me to Da Nang and to MACV Advisory Team #1. Colonel Hamblem told me that I would "sense the tension in the air of Da Nang."

I asked him if he had any information regarding the loyalty of ARVN medical officers. I wanted to know if they had remained loyal to the government or had joined the insurrectionists. He stated that he was uncertain and that I should "tread lightly and make my own assessment of the situation." With that bit of advice the meeting ended. I returned to my office and found that LTC Mabra was ready to depart for the day. I got in my newly assigned jeep and followed him through the tense streets of Da Nang to the MACV Officers' Club, where I enjoyed a cold bottle of American beer and my first of many meals in that facility.

On 15 July, my first full day in Da Nang, I spent another hour or two with my new boss, LTC Mabra, getting oriented on operating procedures within I Corps HQ. I then squared away my desk in the office I shared with Colonel Mabra and Specialist Behner, our clerk-typist. When this was completed, I telephoned my Vietnamese counterpart, Major Pham Viet Tu, a physician who was serving in a dual capacity as the I Corps Surgeon and acting commander of Duy Tan General Hospital.

Although I was concerned about the distinct possibility that Major Tu or members of his staff could have been part of the insurrectionist movement within the South Vietnamese Army, I asked if he had time for us to meet. He said he would "make time available." I interpreted his response as a positive sign. He suggested we meet at Duy Tan General Hospital, where he typically spent much of his day.

We met for the first time at 1400 hours that day, my first full day in Da Nang. He greeted me enthusiastically and welcomed me to Da Nang. I liked him from the moment we met. I knew that our relationship was going to be open and professional.

Prior to having one of his subordinate officers present an overview briefing on the medical situation in I Corps, Major Tu offered me a cup of coffee or tea. I accepted coffee, while he enjoyed tea. I was surprised and relieved when the briefing officer openly discussed the Buddhist Uprising and its impact on I Corps and its medical treatment facilities.

At the conclusion of the briefing, Major Tu asked if I would like to see Duy Tan General Hospital, the largest and most sophisticated treatment facility in I Corps. An ARVN military physician, Captain Tran Tan Phat, commanded the 1,000-bed facility, but he was in Saigon and would be gone for a period of time, so I readily accepted Major Tu's offer to show me the hospital. He then told me that he had a meeting to attend and that the deputy commander of the hospital would escort me through every part of the hospital except the wards, which Major Tu wanted to personally show me when he rejoined us at the conclusion of his meeting.

The hospital was a large, sprawling, one-story cantonment-style facility. I asked hundreds of questions of the deputy commander as we toured the facility, gleaning as much information as possible, not only about the hospital but also about how the available Vietnamese military medical resources were distributed throughout the five-province area that comprised I Corps.

At about 1545, Major Tu rejoined us, and we started walking through the many wards of the 1,000-bed hospital. All the wards were full. There wasn't an empty bed anywhere. Some beds contained more than one patient. The wards were clean and orderly. All lights were turned off so as not to generate unnecessary heat. All windows were open, allowing a cooling breeze to offer some relief to the patients and staff. There was no air conditioning; it simply didn't fit in the budget. The outside temperature was right at 100 degrees.

Major Tu comprehensively answered every question I asked as we proceeded through the wards. He did not apologize or complain about the over-crowded conditions and the lack of air conditioning. At one point he looked at a patient for a moment, went over to the bedside, reached for the man's wrist to take his pulse, and then gently covered his face with the bedsheet. The man had died.

This scenario repeated itself a little later during our tour of the hospital's wards—gently reach for the wrist, verify death, and cover the face with the bedsheet. It was done respectfully. He then signaled a nurse, I assume to have the body removed from the ward. By the very manner that Major Tu approached the task, I could tell that it happened often. At the conclusion of our walk through all the wards of the large hospital, I asked Major Tu what the hospital census was. He stated that as of that morning, it was 1,328, although the hospital was staffed to care for for a maximum of 1,000 patients.

As we walked back to my jeep, Major Tu told me that he welcomed me in his office at any time and that he would always give my recommendations serious consideration. He also told me that I should meet Captain Phat, the commander of Duy Tan Hospital, as soon as he returned from Saigon. I felt good about that first meeting with my primary counterpart.

Sergeant Thong, an ARVN soldier, was attached to the G-4 advisor's office as the interpreter for the Medical Civic Action Program (MEDCAP) and for general support. He knew the city of Da Nang well and was an experienced driver. Colonel Mabra's duties rarely required that he be away from the I Corps compound, whereas my duties required that I spend the majority of my time in the field. Therefore, almost by default, Sergeant Thong became my driver and interpreter. LTC Mabra infrequently required his support.

I found Sergeant Thong to be invaluable in regard to my carrying out my assigned duties. In addition to being my driver, he spoke passable English and was eager to learn more. He was like a sponge. I would use a word he didn't understand, and immediately he would ask me to define the word and use it in a couple of sentences. Although not formally trained as an interpreter, he seemed to have a knack for communicating precisely what I wanted to say to the many non-English speaking Vietnamese persons I came in contact with on a daily basis. We became a team. He was at my side practically every day I was in Da Nang except Sundays, his day off duty. I sometimes took him with me when I traveled to remote sites. I appreciated his services greatly.

***

Image 3. The author's ARVN counterpart and trusted friend Major Pham Viet Tu

Photo courtesy of the author

The second evening I was in Da Nang, I had dinner at the MACV Officers' Club and returned to my hotel room at about 2030 hours. I was unpacking my duffel bag when suddenly there was a knock on the door. I opened it and was startled to see a Vietnamese woman, perhaps thirty-five years old, standing in the entryway with a huge smile on her face.

She handed me a typewritten note that introduced her as Bá Tran Thi Vy and went on to state that she would like to work for me, doing my laundry and taking care of my room. Just as I was reading the note, another American officer, whom I had not yet met, walked by and greeted the woman by name. He then explained to me that there were no laundry and room cleaning services available in the hotel. He said all of the officers and NCOs who were assigned as advisors hired a person for a nominal monthly wage to do these tasks. He further stated that Bá Vy, which translates to Mrs. Vy, worked for several other officers in the hotel and was very good, totally reliable, and trustworthy. I hired her on the spot and never regretted doing so, as she was a delightful person and the quality of her work was exceptional.

The fourth day after I arrived in Da Nang, Sunday, 17 July, I called the commander's office of the U.S. Naval Support Activity Hospital[4] and requested an appointment to see him. I was scheduled for 1100 hours the next day.

We met in his office and, after introducing myself, I told him that I welcomed his ideas regarding how I could best interface with the hospital he commanded. He told me that he had known my predecessor, Major Don Ross, but while Major Ross interfaced with his staff from time to time, he personally had had little interaction with him. He then made a phone call and asked another person to join us in his office. I believe it was either his Deputy Commander or the Chief of Professional Services.

Immediately upon discovering the nature of our meeting, the second physician said, "I'll tell you what you can do to help us. You can serve as a liaison between this hospital and the ARVN hospital across the river."

To make certain that I knew what hospital he was referring to, I asked, "You mean Duy Tan General Hospital?"

He nodded his head in agreement, and then went on to explain that when casualties came in from the battlefields they were occasionally inter-mixed. The U.S. Marine helicopters would land on the U.S. Navy hospital's helipad and, upon off-loading, they would find one or more Vietnamese casualties, usually ARVN soldiers but sometimes civilians, inter-mixed with the wounded U.S. Marines. Conversely, on a few occasions, U.S. Marines ended up being evacuated to Duy Tan General Hospital. After discussing this problem in more depth, I readily agreed to accept this liaison responsibility.

After the meeting concluded, the commander asked that someone give me a brief tour of the facility before lunch in the hospital's dining facility. The hospital was built using a series of Quonset and prefabricated buildings partially interconnected by covered walkways. The hospital provided all the basic services of a modern American hospital, although its exterior was Spartan at best. The person conducting the tour described it as "not pretty but functional."

Several physicians and the hospital administrator joined us for lunch, a wonderful opportunity for me to meet some of the hospital staff. Among those I had lunch with was Dr. John Henry Giles, a highly skilled general surgeon from North Carolina and a remarkable man. I liked him from the moment we met. When we finished our lunch Dr. Giles asked if I could spare a few minutes. We stayed in the dining facility as the others said their good-byes and returned to their duties.

Over a second and then third cup of coffee, Dr. Giles told me that as a general surgeon he wanted to stay busy. He said that unless he spent time at the operating table his skills eroded. At one point he said, "You're too new in Vietnam to know this, but war is episodic in nature. There is a certain ebb and flow to war. For a few days or a week we'll be intensely busy with U.S. Marine casualties, then things quiet down and we'll see virtually no new casualties for several days. Frankly, I get bored during the down time, and, of greater importance, my surgical skills get rusty. I'm wondering if you could help alleviate my frustration and at the same time do some good by bringing to me Vietnamese civilians who have deformities that I might correct. My commander is supportive; in fact we've set aside two small rooms where Vietnamese patients, along with a family member caregiver, can be accommodated."

He then went on to explain the types of deformities I might look for in my travels throughout I Corps. He emphasized the fact that he had no means of transporting anyone to the hospital or back to their homes after their surgery but was hoping that I might figure out a way to do that.

The meeting turned out to be a godsend. The good that Dr. Giles and his colleagues did cannot be overemphasized. There were many other physicians, nurses, and technical staff who assisted greatly in the effort, but Dr. Giles spearheaded the program. He was my primary point of contact in Project Help—sometimes referred to as Project Harelip. I wish I had an accurate accounting of the number of surgeries that he and his colleagues performed to correct the deformities of poor Vietnamese children, young adults, and on a few occasions, adult men and women. I feel certain that the number of harelip repairs he performed numbered between seventy and 100, and in addition, Dr. Giles and his colleagues corrected clubbed feet, hammer toes, twisted limbs that were set incorrectly or not at all after a fracture, and myriad other conditions. They removed exterior growths and internal tumors. They even performed a minor surgical procedure to help a poor man reinsert a glass eye. They literally transformed lives; they were angels of mercy, and all was done in their discretionary time without neglecting, in any way, their primary duty to take care of American military men and women, casualties of war.

After the meeting, I returned to my office to study the map and a staffing chart that my predecessor had hung on the wall next to my desk. He had taped a note to it saying that the staffing document was up-to-date as of his departure from Da Nang.

***

The map at the beginning of this book depicts the five provinces that comprised the I Corps Tactical Zone. This was my area of medical advisory responsibility. The provinces were further divided into districts, the Vietnamese political equivalent of our counties. The map also shows the major cities and the Demilitarized Zone that separated the Republic of Vietnam from Communist North Vietnam. In the lower left corner of the map is a smaller index map showing I Corps in relation to the other three corps areas in the Republic of Vietnam.

As a Medical Service Corps officer with the rank of major, I was responsible for overseeing and coordinating the medical advisory effort in the entire I Corps area. The MACV staffing document for I Corps recognized three additional commissioned officer positions. An MSC officer in the rank of captain was authorized as the medical advisor for the ARVN 1st Infantry Division. This division was headquartered in the northern city of Hue, which was in Thua Thien Province. The 1st Division's subordinate units were spread throughout Quang Tri and Thua Thien Provinces. The ARVN 2nd Infantry Division, which was headquartered in Quang Ngai City in Quang Ngai Province, was also authorized an MSC officer in the rank of captain. The 2nd Infantry Division had subordinate units located in Quang Ngai and Quang Tin Provinces. The final officer position authorized was an MSC captain to serve as advisor to the commander of the ARVN Medical Depot, located in Da Nang. This depot had logistical responsibilities throughout the entire I Corps area.

The MACV staffing document also authorized a number of enlisted medics to operate dispensaries in Quang Tri, Hue, Da Nang, Hoi An, Tam Ky, and Quang Ngai. These small dispensaries were established to provide basic medical support to all members of the MACV advisory teams located throughout I Corps. Each dispensary was typically staffed with only one or two NCOs or specialists. These highly skilled medics also assisted in medical training to upgrade the skills of ARVN medics.

Lastly, and of great importance, one medical NCO or specialist was authorized for each sub-sector advisory team. In MACV parlance, a Vietnamese province was referred to as a "sector." Vietnamese provinces were further subdivided into districts, also referred to as "sub-sectors." A five-person advisory team was assigned to each sub-sector. An officer of the rank of major or lieutenant colonel typically headed these small teams. One of the team members was always a medic, either an NCO or specialist. The medic provided medical support for his team members and worked with the Vietnamese medics who were part of the Regional Forces and Popular Forces, typically referred to informally as the "Ruff/ Puff." These Vietnamese Forces were somewhat the equivalent of our National Guard or Reserve forces, although not nearly as well trained or equipped.[5]

On Thursday, 21 July, I returned to the Navy Hospital. The place was buzzing with the news that a U.S. Navy pilot, shot down and declared missing in action on 1 February, had been rescued by a USAF helicopter crew and evacuated to the Navy Hospital. LTJG Dieter Dengler had been a prisoner of the Pathet Lao in Laos for five months before he escaped. He had been on the run for 23 days before being rescued.[6] Dr. Giles took me into a ward where I saw Dengler propped up in bed asleep. His ribs stood out all over. He was emaciated and dehydrated, but Dr. Giles said he would recover fully.[7]

On Saturday morning, 23 July, after the 0900 staff meeting, Colonel Arch Hamblen asked LTC Mabra and me to come with him to his office. When we arrived, he closed the door, looked at me, and said, "You're going to Khe Sanh."[8]

I said, "Sir, with all due respect, where in the hell is Khe Sanh?" It was the name of a place I had not heard of to that time. Together we walked over to a map he had taped to the wall of his office, and he pointed out Khe Sanh, way up in the northwest corner of South Vietnam. Laos was just four miles to the west, and the DMZ just twelve miles to the north.

Image 4. LTJG Dieter Dengler, weighing just 98 pounds, upon arrival at the
U.S. Naval Support Activity Hospital, DaNang

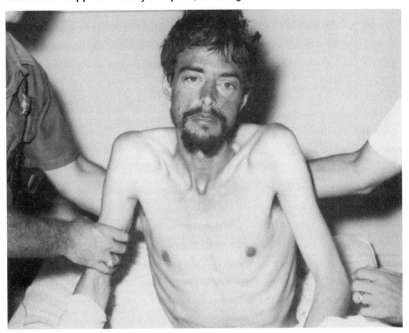

Photo courtesy of the U.S. National Archives, Photo No. 428-N-711506

I asked, "What's going on, sir?"

He said, "I can't tell you much about the situation for security reasons,
but let's just say that Khe Sanh is of great importance to General Walt
and General Westmoreland."

I said, "Sir, why am I going up there?"

He then said, "General Lam, the I Corps Commander, is about to direct
his corps surgeon to send a preventive medicine team up there to try and
figure out why malaria rates have gone up so dramatically. Those rates,
if they persist, could become problematic in the future. We want you to

go along with the team to make sure they don't get crossways with our Specials Forces units operating in the area. We don't want a problem."

After two attempts to get into Khe Sanh failed because of bad weather, the team and I finally got in late during the following week, and the malaria survey was completed without incident. That was my introduction to Khe Sanh.

***

On the second Sunday I was in Da Nang, 24 July, I went to my office early, typed a letter to my wife, then went to the Officers' Club for breakfast prior to going to church services. I was still the new guy on the advisory team, and when I entered the dining room I knew not a single person. I spotted a four-person table with three officers sitting at it and asked if I could join them. We enjoyed our breakfast and then one man invited all of us to "come on up to the bar and I'll buy a round of Bloody Mary's." I politely declined, stating that I was going to Mass. He then asked what time the service started. When I told him that Mass started at 9:00 A.M., he said, "You've got plenty of time. Come join us for a drink." I again declined, stating that I wanted to receive Holy Communion and that required fasting from all food and drink for one hour prior to receiving. He then said, "You're really into that Jesus crap, aren't you?"

My first inclination was to show my indignation and reply sharply. But I thought better of it and simply said, "Yes, I am."

I never saw the man again, but one of the other two officers seated at the table with us came to me after breakfast and apologized for the officer's comment and told me how inappropriate he thought the man's remarks had been. Several weeks later, the man who offered the apology came to me again in the dining room and stated that he was a fallen away Catholic and that he wanted to come back to the church. He asked if we might talk about how to go about this. He said that when he heard me say, "Yes, I am," it had gotten him thinking about how much he missed the church.

I can't help but think that, had I responded sharply and shown my indignation to the boorish officer, this may not have happened. I'll never know with certainty, but I do know beyond a shadow of a doubt that example is more powerful than strong words.

I spent the afternoon of 27 July in Quang Ngai. My return flight was delayed for mechanical reasons, so I didn't get back to my office until about 1900 hours. Lying in the middle of my desk was a rice paper envelope with an invitation inside. Paper-clipped to the envelope was a note from our clerk-typist, Specialist Behner. The note read: "Sir, this invitation was hand carried to our office at about 1730 hours and I couldn't get it interpreted for you because the interpreter wasn't in his office."

I decided it could wait until morning, so I didn't bother to take the invitation upstairs to an interpreter that evening. The next morning, I arrived at the office at about 0500 hours and immediately took the invitation to an interpreter. He told me that he would get to it just as soon as he finished interpreting a document for the G-3. At about 0730 he brought the interpreted invitation back to our office. I was on the telephone at the time, and not wishing to interrupt, the interpreter caught my attention and then laid the invitation on my desk. The phone call was lengthy, and I didn't look at the invitation until about 0750. When I finally looked at it I panicked. General Lam, the I Corps commander, had invited me to a breakfast honoring the ARVN Surgeon General, commencing at 0730.

I jumped in my jeep and hurried over to Duy Tan Hospital, only to learn that the breakfast was just then concluding and that the Surgeon General had not arrived as scheduled. His plane had been delayed by weather, and he was now scheduled to arrive in about thirty minutes. I made my apologies about missing the breakfast and waited for the Surgeon General to arrive and present his speech. As it turned out, the Surgeon General was accompanied by a delegation of twenty-two persons. The breakfast honoree came not as the Surgeon General but as the Deputy Chairman of the Vietnamese Political Advisory Committee to the Republic of Vietnam's government. The total committee, we were told, consisted of eighty influential men and women charged with steering overall Vietnamese policy until a parliament could be duly elected.

Yes, there I was, involved in a blatantly political meeting in a city that only two and a half months earlier had been engulfed in insurrection and violence, a city where the Struggle Movement had been crushed with arms and where blood had flowed on the streets of Da Nang and Hue. I looked around the room and, as far as I could tell, I was the only American there. Why had I been invited? I didn't have a clue, but there I was.

At the conclusion of the speech, after the applause had subsided, my counterpart, Major Tu, graciously introduced me to the Vietnamese Surgeon General, who welcomed me to Vietnam. We exchanged a few pleasantries. Throughout the brief encounter, I thought he looked at me rather strangely, frequently glancing at my shoulders and neck.

I drove back to the I Corps military compound and, as I entered my office, SP4 Behner looked at me and asked, "Sir, where's your brass?" Yes, I had forgotten to pin on my insignia of rank and my corps emblem. No wonder the Surgeon General had looked at me so strangely.

At the suggestion of my immediate boss, LTC Mabra, I then went up to the office of the commander of our advisory team, Colonel Hamblen. I reported to him that I had been involved in a blatantly political meeting, through no fault of my own, and that I thought he should be aware of it. He looked at me and said, "Let's hope there are no repercussions."

***

The principal civilian hospital located in Da Nang served the health care needs of the people living in the city and, to a limited degree, the villages and hamlets throughout Quang Nam Province. A team of volunteer U.S. physicians, nurses, medical technicians and administrators, working for the U.S. Operations Mission (USOM), which was a part of the United States Agency for International Development (USAID), supplemented the hospital's Vietnamese staff. The team was headed by an American physician and operated in much the same manner as the military's MILPHAP teams. Most Americans referred to this facility as either the USOM or USAID Hospital. I preferred to call it the USAID hospital.

The telephone call from an American physician at the USAID Hospital came to me early on the morning of 29 July. Could I possibly obtain the use of a helicopter to transport a Vietnamese peasant family from a refugee camp just outside of Da Nang to the USAID Hospital? Time was of the essence. They had tried other avenues but no helicopter seemed available. The need was urgent. It was a life and death situation.

I told him I'd call back as soon as I could check it out. I hurried upstairs to the office of Colonel Hamblen and explained the situation as best I could with the fragmentary information that was available. He asked the extent of the family's injuries, and of course I didn't have a clue.

I said, "Sir, I don't know the extent of the family's injuries, but I do know the physician who called. If he says the need is urgent, I believe the need is urgent."

Colonel Hamblen made two phone calls. After he hung up the phone, he looked at me and said: "All right, you've got your helicopter. It's now 0812. The helicopter will be on our helipad at 0830 hours. I need it back on our helipad NLT than 0930 hours. You've got one hour to get that family to the hospital and get that ship back to me. Is that clear?"

I saluted and said, "Yes, sir. I'll do my best."

I raced back to my office and called the physician I had spoken to earlier. I told him that we'd have a helicopter at the USAID Hospital at 0840 hours and that he had to have someone at the helipad who knew precisely how to get to the refugee camp. If he could get a set of map coordinates, that would be great. If not, we needed a person who knew the area. I also told him that the refugee family had to be ready to go immediately upon arrival of the helicopter, because we had a very tight window. He said he'd do his best.

At 0832 hours, I leapt into the helicopter and, when we arrived at the USAID Hospital helipad, an American physician was waiting with a map in his hand. An "X" marked the spot of the refugee settlement. I gave the map to the co-pilot, who gave me the thumbs up. He knew the area. We were in luck.

When we arrived at the camp, the family was ready and waiting. Here's what we found: the young family of four had been the innocent victims of a bombing attack on a small hamlet, a known Viet Cong safe haven. The family's only daughter, three years old, had been killed in the attack. Their five-year-old son had had his left foot almost blown off just above the ankle. It was heavily bandaged. The father had what appeared to be a closed fracture of the left leg and a nasty head wound, and the mother had multiple penetration wounds of her chest and abdomen. The parents had buried their daughter near their home on Tuesday, put a crude tourniquet on the boy's leg, and for the past two and a half days had been making their way toward Da Nang carrying their little boy. The boy had lost a lot of blood and was unconscious, with a very weak pulse. The USAID physician aboard the helicopter said the mother had, in all likelihood, significant internal injuries, and the father's probable broken leg was grossly swollen and blackened. When we lifted them into the helicopter, there wasn't even a whimper. In fact, there was a slight smile of gratitude on the mother's face. I've often wondered how I would have reacted had I been a part of that family. Would I have had the strength to hold the family together in the face of such adversity?

We transported the family to the USAID Hospital and off-loaded them as quickly as we could. I got the helicopter back to the I Corps helipad not at 0930 hours as ordered but at 0948 hours. I hurried up to Colonel Hamblen's office and told him the story then apologized for missing his imposed deadline. He looked at me and said, "Don't worry about it." And I didn't.

***

During the I Corps staff meeting held on Saturday morning, 30 July, General Walt and General Lam spent considerable time telling the staff that we had to put the Buddhist Uprising behind us. The message was that we had to get on with prosecuting the war while gaining the allegiance and support of the people. The generals did not minimize the difficulty of the tasks confronting us.

At the conclusion of the meeting, in keeping with military protocol, General Lam, the Vietnamese commander of I Corps, General Walt, the III MAF commander, and Colonel Hamblen and Colonel Beeson, the commander and deputy commander of MACV Advisory Team #1, rose to exit the classified conference room while all other attendees stood at attention. I was standing next to the exit aisle. As they passed, Colonel Hamblen spotted me and said, "General Lam and General Walt, I'd like you to meet our recently assigned senior medical advisor, Major Van Straten."

General Lam put out his hand to shake mine and said a few words of welcome. General Walt looked me in the eye for a long moment and, while shaking my hand with his huge right hand, asked in a gruff voice, "Where'd you come from, Major?"

I said, "Sir, I came from the University of Texas Graduate School."

He responded, "Did you learn anything?"

I responded, "Yes, sir."

Then he said, "What do you know about pacification?"

I responded, "Not nearly enough, sir."

He said, "Good answer. None of us knows enough, but we're learning what works and what doesn't. This you can be sure of, though, keeping their babies alive is a damned important part of the process."

And with those words he moved on, looking every bit the offensive and defensive lineman he once was for Colorado State University. As the months moved on, I gained a tremendous respect for the man. He had a big heart, and he cared deeply about his marines and the Vietnamese people.

***

Operation Hastings was raging in Quang Tri Province. The U.S. Marines had launched Hastings on 15 July to clear the area near the DMZ of Viet Cong.[9] It was the largest and most costly operation of the war to that point, involving about 8,000 U.S. Marines. The ARVN launched a supporting operation, Lam Son 289, to the south, involving over 3,000 ARVN soldiers.[10] Casualty tolls were mounting. Tri Phuong Station Hospital in Hue, where practically all the seriously wounded Vietnamese soldiers from Lam Son 289 were taken, was way beyond capacity. The hospital was staffed and equipped for a maximum of 400 patients. On the morning of 31 July, it had 564 patients, with more being admitted by the hour. The surgery backlog was mounting, as was the in-hospital death rate.

The other two ARVN hospitals in I Corps, Duy Tan General Hospital in Da Nang and the First Field hospital in Quang Ngai, both had unused capacity on 31 July. Why wasn't the corps surgeon, my counterpart, taking active steps to arrange an inter-hospital transfer of patients? I had pushed him hard during two previous meetings to take steps to alleviate the pressure on Tri Phuong Hospital, but he had taken no action. On 31 July, I decided the issue was of critical importance and had to be addressed once again.

I sat down with Major Tu and told him that I simply couldn't understand his reluctance to order the movement of patients from one hospital to another. I told him that the U.S. military gave patient regulating and evacuation policies a very high priority and that in our military hospitals those policies were established in writing and rigorously adhered to. Major Tu started talking about the constraints on their system and why he was reluctant to move patients. He told me that when young men were conscripted into the Army of the Republic of Vietnam they underwent initial basic training. Then, insofar as possible, they were assigned to a military unit located in the region from which they were conscripted. Many had families to support, and moving soldiers considerable distances from their homes caused great family difficulty and low morale. Most soldiers served in the same unit during their entire time in uniform.

If an ARVN soldier was wounded or contracted a disease that required hospitalization, every attempt was made to admit him to the hospital closest to his home of record. During hospitalization, in most instances, a family member, usually a mother or spouse, provided basic nursing support. The Vietnamese military hospitals did not have sufficient staff to provide this support without family assistance. Bathing, feeding, laundry services, help with toilet, exercise, and in some instances the changing of dressings and bandages was seen as a family responsibility. To move the soldier to a hospital located a great distance from his home served to destroy this system of family support.

Typically, when a soldier was admitted to a hospital, he stayed in that facility until he either recovered sufficiently to be moved to a convalescent center, was placed on convalescent leave at home with his family, or died while hospitalized.

In addition to not having sufficient staff to provide basic nursing support, Major Tu also pointed out that the ARVN did not have the capability to move patients out of the country, a very significant advantage of the U.S. medical support system. In the U.S. system, if it were adjudged that a patient admitted to a hospital for wounds or disease would not be able to return to duty within 30 days, the patient was evacuated to Japan, Okinawa, Hawaii, or the United States. In the ARVN medical systems, all patients had to remain in country for the duration of the war.

CHAPTER 2

AUGUST 1966

Each U.S. advisor worked very closely with a Vietnamese officer who occupied a senior position within the Vietnamese military hierarchy. The Vietnamese officer was referred to as the American advisor's "primary counterpart." My primary counterpart was Major Pham Viet Tu, the I Corps Surgeon. At the time I served as his advisor, Major Tu was a thirty-seven-year-old physician with a family similar to mine. He and his wife had four girls and two boys. His wife delivered their second son only a couple of months prior to my arrival.

I also worked closely with Captain Tran Tan Phat, commander of Duy Tan General Hospital. He was not, however, my primary counterpart. Captain Phat's responsibilities extended only to Duy Tan General Hospital, whereas Major Tu's responsibilities were much broader, encompassing ARVN medical activities throughout all of I Corps.

At about 1600 hours on 2 August, an invitation was placed on my desk. I was invited by Captain Phat to a dinner party to be held the very next evening in honor of three military physicians who were being transferred to new assignments.

Since I had been told that all business establishments in the city of Da Nang were off limits to U.S. military personnel, I was about to call Captain Phat and politely express my regrets. Before doing so, however, I mentioned the invitation to my boss, LTC Mabra.

He said, "Jim, you better run the invitation by the command element and see what they say." I did so and was surprised when informed by Colonel Hamblen that I should attend. He said that General Walt felt strongly that, if duties permitted, advisors should accept all social invitations extended by their Vietnamese counterparts. Not to do so caused them to lose face and was detrimental to a sound relationship between advisor and counterpart. Colonel Hamblen went on to tell me that procedures were in place to accommodate the acceptance of invitations.

In order to attend I had to do three things: 1) get permission from the commander of MACV Advisory Team #1 (which I already had), 2) provide the Military Police the name and address of the restaurant and the starting time of the event, and 3) notify the Military Police when the dinner party was over and I was safely back in my room. It was a cumbersome procedure, but that's the way it was.

The dinner party proved to be delightful. It gave me the opportunity to see aspects of the Vietnamese culture that were probably hidden from most Americans. About twenty officers attended the event. All were physicians except me. The party started at 2000 hours with beer, roasted peanuts, and something similar to pretzels. We were in a small room by ourselves. The conversation was jovial and lively. All members of the group spoke passable English except one. All in attendance did their very best to refrain from speaking Vietnamese, which they knew I did not understand. They included me in the conversation as much as possible.

After about an hour, Dr. Phat rose and dinged his beer glass with a chopstick to get the group's attention. He started his remarks by warmly welcoming me to Vietnam and to Da Nang. He then turned his attention to the departing physicians and, in the military tradition, roasted the officers with great enthusiasm. After a pause to let the laughter subside, he offered generous and heartfelt praise of the performance of each of the departing officers. He ended his remarks by presenting each with a beautifully enameled black box. Each box had a mother of pearl depiction of Duy Tan General Hospital inlaid on the cover.

The party then moved to the dining room. As we were about to be served the first course, Dr. Phat turned to me and asked that I rate each course of the seven-course meal by inscribing the menu with one, two, or three stars for each course. According to his rating scale, one star meant that I wasn't wild about the dish but could tolerate it; two stars were to be given to those dishes that I considered quite good; and three stars were to be awarded to those I felt were superb. If I couldn't stomach a dish it was to receive no stars.

The food was exceptionally good with one exception. I simply could not stomach the hard boiled eggs that had been submerged in oil-laden charcoal and allowed to sit for four to five months. The charcoal and oil turned the eggs pitch black. The blackened eggs, I was told, are a Vietnamese delicacy. I simply couldn't eat the one placed before me. I was polite and sampled it, but I must admit that I did not like it. In view of the dish being considered a delicacy, and not wishing to offend, I generously gave it a one star rating.

Since the eggs were the very first course served, I thought I was in for a long evening. I was wrong. All subsequent courses were superb. I especially liked the lobster dish. The meat was removed from the shell and served in little balls along with cooked celery, which complimented the lobster in a most unusual and palatable way. The fried rice was also superb.

I clumsily used the chopsticks, to the delight of the Vietnamese. The host had placed a fork alongside my dinner plate as a courtesy, but I never touched it. Dr. Phat demonstrated the proper use of chopsticks for me before the meal began, and I was resolved to be a good sport and do my best with the chopsticks, which I did throughout the year I was in Vietnam.

I was pleased that I had attended the party, for it gave me the opportunity to meet key physicians from Duy Tan Hospital, the largest and most sophisticated hospital in I Corps and, according to the MACV Surgeon, perhaps the best in the entire country. I know the officers in attendance appreciated my being there.

***

During the Buddhist Uprising in Da Nang, scores of innocent civilians got caught in the crossfire between the warring factions. One four-year-old girl, Phan Thi Tuyet, whom I had seen near my hotel on several occasions, was struck in the axilla of her right arm with a fairly large chunk of shrapnel. The wound healed, but the arm was left totally nonfunctional. It just hung at her side, and the dead weight was starting to deform her right shoulder and collarbone. Despite the problem, she always had a smile on her face. She tried to play with the other children as best she could, but was having great difficulty keeping up with them. She tore at my heartstrings.

With difficulty, my interpreter Sergeant Thong, who also served as my driver, located the little girl's mother, a peasant-class woman. I told Sergeant Thong to tell the mother that perhaps we could help the little girl and to ask her permission to take her daughter to the Navy hospital for an evaluation. At first the mother was dismissive, telling Sergeant Thong that the little girl's injury was not a problem. We were finally able to convince her that her daughter would have a better life if the injury could be corrected. She reluctantly gave her consent for an evaluation after telling Sergeant Thong that she was concerned about the Viet Cong. I asked Sergeant Thong to explain her concern. He informed me that many people feared that if they cooperated with the Americans in any way, the Viet Cong would interpret their cooperation as a sign of political allegiance. Therefore, the people would rather remain neutral than provoke the Viet Cong.

Dr. Hogan, an American surgeon at the USAID Hospital, agreed to see the little girl to evaluate the injury. We transported mother and child to the hospital in my jeep. As luck would have it, a U.S. Navy neurosurgeon happened to be in the hospital at the very time we brought the little girl in for Dr. Hogan's evaluation. Whereas a general surgeon would probably not have taken on the case, the neurosurgeon looked upon it as a challenge. He agreed to personally perform the operation when his schedule allowed. The mother, after having been apprised of the risks and the relatively low chance of total success, consented to the surgery. She said, according to my interpreter, "Anything doctor says, I do."

Because of the hospital's surgical backlog, the surgery had to be postponed for several weeks. I was concerned that during the long delay the girl's parents would change their minds and not consent to the surgery. Finally, the day for the surgery arrived. The little girl passed the pre-op physical exam, and the U.S. Navy neurosurgeon, Dr. Paul Pitlyk and Dr. Hogan, performed the surgery in early September. They were able to rejoin two of the three major bundles of nerves that control the arm.

Both the mother and the father were in the hospital waiting room during the surgery. After several days in recovery, the little girl was ready to be discharged. Sergeant Thong, both parents, and I went to the hospital to pick the girl up and return her to her home. Prior to discharge, the doctor spent considerable time trying to convince the mother and the father, through my interpreter, of the absolute necessity of rigorous exercise. He told them that the girl's arm had to be exercised for at least two hours each day for an entire year starting in about two weeks, after the surgical site had healed. He stated that it would initially be very painful for the little girl, that she would cry and beg them to stop. He emphasized that if the muscles in her arm were not exercised, they would further atrophy and wither away while the nerves were mending. If the muscles were not exercised, he told them, the operation would be a complete failure.

Two weeks later we returned the girl and her parents to the hospital for a post-surgical evaluation. The doctor was satisfied that the surgical site was sufficiently healed to begin moderate exercise. He then demonstrated for the parents how they were to exercise the arm. The little girl screamed while he did so. The parents looked shocked, but seemed to understand and promised to do their best. The doctor asked Sergeant Thong to have the parents explain back to him what they were to do. While the parents explained, as best they could, Sergeant Thong repeated their explanation in English. The doctor was satisfied that they understood and hopeful that they would follow through. I am convinced that the parents did indeed follow through, for I saw the little girl on several occasions during the next ten months, and the arm was slowly but steadily improving. The doctor told the parents their daughter would never regain full mobility of her arm, but it should be greatly improved if they followed through as he had demonstrated. I think of that little girl often.

***

On 5 August, I experienced the Medical Civic Action Program for the first of many times. MEDCAP, along with other civic action programs, was a very important part of our attempts to pacify the people in the region, especially in the small villages and rural areas. The U.S. military, as well as the ARVN, established MEDCAP teams that visited selected villages and refugee centers more or less on a scheduled basis.[1]

I accompanied a U.S. Navy team operating out of Da Nang. We drove to a small village located 8-10 miles from Da Nang. Immediately upon arrival, the Navy team, supplemented by ARVN trainees, off-loaded its equipment and supplies and established an outdoor clinic. There were perhaps 150 to 200 Vietnamese men, women, and children awaiting our arrival. I was asked to help in the triage effort, separating the sick and the injured into four categories as established by the U.S. Navy physician who served as the team chief. You cannot imagine, in your wildest dreams, the types of things the team was confronted with. Many of the children had "mattery" eyes, probably due to an outbreak of pinkeye, which the flies and the gnats simply couldn't let alone. Runny noses and pus coming out of partially healed wounds again presented targets of opportunity for the gnats and flies. Head lice galore. Large boils that needed lancing. Obvious malnutrition. Lots of diarrhea.

Scars of all varieties. Scar tissue that pulled on an eyelid, making it impossible to close the eye when the person was trying to sleep. Scar tissue that made it impossible to straighten out an arm or a leg or the fingers on a hand. Horrible scars. Smashed fingers and toes. Lots of cuts and abrasions, some infected. One navy corpsman did nothing but gently scrub with soapy water the wounds, scars, noses, scraped knees, feet, smashed fingers and hands of those seeking treatment. The team worked hard for about four hours.

Image 5. ARVN trainees pass out supplies during U.S. Navy MEDCAP operation

Photo courtesy of the author

It was more or less assembly line medicine. Many medications were dispensed, especially salves, germicides, fungicides, and Kaopectate.

Quite a number of cuts were stitched up. Many bars of soap and bottles of shampoo were given out. Everyone was seen. And around the perimeter stood several young men wearing the omnipresent black pajama-type garb and toting rifles. Who they were, nobody seemed to know. They could have been government loyalists, the so-called Regional Forces, or they could have been Viet Cong. The MEDCAP team members had learned not to ask. It was quite an experience for me. Before departure, it was announced that the team would be back in that village in two weeks. Each MEDCAP team seemed to have a regular cycle of villages that they visited and took care of. To a degree, this enabled them to get to know the people on a personal basis.

In early August, I spent two days in Quang Tri Province, spending the night with the U.S. Navy MILPHAP team in the city of Quang Tri. One day, while near the DMZ, I had the opportunity to watch and interact with an International Control Commission team attempting to make an assessment of an alleged incident involving the establishment of an ammunition storage point inside the DMZ. The team was attempting to determine culpability. The facts were murky, as they usually were, so I doubt they were successful. The ammunition was definitely there, but who had put it there could not be determined.

Way up in the northern part of Quang Tri Province, near the DMZ, the people appeared hardier than those further south. They seemed to be somewhat larger in stature and stronger. I watched with amusement a group of women woodchoppers, all stripped to the waist. The wood chips were flying, and there were other things flying as well. There seemed to be a different code of modesty in the remote areas of the country. I was told by a public health official that just because a peasant-class woman had bare breasts didn't mean that she was being immodest. Some of the bare-breasted women were actually wearing scapular medals, as worn by adherents of the Catholic faith. It looked unusual, to say the least.

***

On my wife's thirty-first birthday, 12 August 1966, I attempted to surprise her with a phone call using the Military Affiliate Radio System. MARS was the only means of transoceanic communication available, other than sending letters or tape recordings, which typically took six to ten days. It was a cumbersome and unreliable system and, because of the weather, I was unsuccessful in reaching her. I was, however, able to get through on two later occasions during our yearlong separation. It was special to be able to hear her voice and the voices of the children, and to be reassured that they were doing all right.

The MARS system worked as follows: I had to go to the MARS station at 1300 hours on the day I wished to make a call. The station was located at the far end of the Da Nang Air Base runway. It was housed in a metal cargo box called a CONEX container. I had to fill out a form that provided the radio operator with the name and phone number of the person I wished to call. The completed forms were kept in the order they were received, and the calls were made in that order. Based on my placement in the queue, I was then given an approximate time when I had to return to the MARS station, the CONEX container, to make my call. All calls were made in the late afternoon, from 1630 to 1830, or at night starting at about 2300 hours and going until 0230 the next morning. As a point of reference, when it was 2330 hours in Da Nang, it was 1130 in the morning in San Antonio.

Each night, approximately fifty-five to sixty of the thousands of American service men and women in Da Nang were able to call home. We stood in line outside the metal box waiting to be called in. On my wife's birthday, I stood in line for 45 minutes in a driving rainstorm only to be told that the connection with California had been lost. When the system was working properly, the radio operator called service members into the CONEX container, one at a time, after having already made radio contact with a MARS station operator located in California. The operator in California was then given the phone number. The California operator placed a long distance phone call from California to the number being called in the United States. If the phone call was answered, the service member got to talk to his loved ones for three minutes. The conversation was transmitted by phone line between California and, in my instance, San Antonio, and by radio transmission between California and Da Nang. At the end of three minutes, the operator abruptly signaled that the call had to be concluded so the next caller could be accommodated. The charge for the long distance call from California to San Antonio, in my instance, was then billed to my wife's phone bill.

The radio operators in Da Nang and in California were able to listen to the entire conversation. A record of the calls was kept to make certain that people didn't abuse the privilege by calling too frequently. It was recommended that we not call more often than once every four months.

Sometimes the connections were excellent and at other times they were poor or non-existent. During the call, it was imperative that only one person speak at a time because of the time delay in transmission. When I called, at the end of each of my comments, I was instructed to say "over." My wife was then to pause briefly before making her reply. At the end of her comment she, too, was supposed to say "over." As cumbersome as this system was, we cherished it. I frequently think about how rapidly the world of communication has changed. With Skype, FaceTime, email, Twitter, Facebook and a host of other modalities, deployed military men and woman can now communicate almost instantaneously and at length with their families and friends located anywhere in the world.

***

On Saturday, 14 August, I played the role of the Good Samaritan. As usual, I attended the weekly I Corps staff meeting. After the meeting, a sergeant in our office told me that a Major Aske (an American) had called and said that a 9-year old Vietnamese boy had been bitten by a confirmed rabid dog four days earlier. He had been taken to the USAID Hospital shortly after being bitten. They immediately started the anti-rabies vaccine. That very morning the boy was taken back to the hospital for his fourth of fourteen daily injections, only to be told that there was no more vaccine. The USAID Hospital had run out of this critically needed vaccine. I got on the phone and, on my fourth call, located some vaccine at a U.S. Air Force dispensary. I drove to the dispensary, explained the situation and obtained enough vaccine for the boy to receive all fourteen doses. Sergeant Thong and I then went to the refugee hamlet on the edge of Da Nang where the boy's family lived, found the boy after an hour's search, and transported him and his mother back to the USAID Hospital for his fourth shot. I explained the situation to an American physician on staff. He promised to control the vaccine in a small refrigerator in his office and to personally administer the ten additional daily injections. I felt good about being able to help since rabies is a killer. The little boy was very brave. He climbed onto the treatment table and didn't even utter a whimper when the reportedly painful injection was being administered.

**

In mid-August, I became embroiled in a project that drew the attention of the International Control Commission. The ICC was a twenty-two-person commission set up in 1954 to enforce the Geneva Accords. The commission was comprised of representatives from anti-Communist Canada, Communist Poland, and neutral India. Each of those countries supplied one-third of the membership of the commission. The chairman of the ICC was from India.[2] Although I could not see a connection between the Geneva Accords and the project I'm about to explain, the ICC had chosen to get involved. In all likelihood some individual or group had asked the ICC to take a look at the project.

At the time I became involved with the project, it had already been the subject of several negative articles in the Vietnamese press. The etiology of the problem began with the irrefutable fact that all Vietnamese hospitals that I worked with, both military and civilian, were under-staffed. Additionally, the total number of Vietnamese civilian physicians was grossly inadequate to meet the burgeoning needs of a country at war, a war that was producing significant numbers of civilian casualties. Therefore, Vietnamese military physicians, those serving as commissioned officers, were encouraged to "moonlight," *i.e.*, to have a civilian practice in addition to their military duties so as to help meet the health care needs of the people of the country. Because of the great shortage of nurses, technicians, and ancillary support staff, family members of hospitalized patients were expected to provide the patients with most of their non-medical, hygienic care. A large percentage of the military and civilian patients in I Corps were fed, bathed, clothed, assisted with toilet, shaved, etc. by members of their own families, usually wives or mothers.

When the wives of wounded or diseased soldiers came to a military hospital from their outlying village to care for their husbands, many brought their children with them. They had no alternative. The problem surfaced when family members providing basic nursing support and hygienic care in the military hospitals during the daytime had nowhere to live at night. They could not live in the hospitals, because they were already overcrowded. The logistics of providing sleeping space, equipment for cooking, bathrooms, garbage disposal, and all of the other necessities were too formidable for the hospital to take on without a huge infusion of resources, which was not forthcoming. Therefore, military hospital commanders, for the most part, simply barred family members from the military hospital grounds from 1800 hours, after the patients were fed, until 0600 hours the next morning. As a result, ghettos sprung up around the hospitals. Sanitary conditions in these ghettos became unbelievably bad. From a preventive medicine and communicable disease perspective, they were dangerous.

Long before my arrival, the commander of Duy Tan Hospital, who recognized the hospital's ghetto as being a significant problem, took a group of sympathetic American doctors, ministers, priests and rabbis through the ghetto in the hope that they could help. I was told that the members of the American group were appalled by what they saw. The conditions so horrified them that they hastily promised aid in the form of food, beds, bedding, toilet articles, cleaning supplies, and $140,000 to help build quarters to house up to 800 transient persons. The manner in which this generous act was put into action turned out to be a disaster. The American humanitarians worked with an existing Vietnamese group that called itself the Social Service Welfare Committee. This Vietnamese committee decided to name the new facilities that were to replace the ghetto the "Social Service Center." Outwardly, the members of the group appeared responsible. Upon getting the pledge of support from the Americans, the committee announced that they had gotten an additional pledge of support from wealthy Vietnamese Buddhists. Unbeknownst to the American donors, this pledge of additional funding was earmarked to build a pagoda. When I arrived in Da Nang, the construction of the pagoda was about to begin.

To make matters even more complicated, the Social Service Welfare Committee was headed by two Buddhist monks, one of whom was in jail in Saigon for the role he had played in the anti-government, anti-American Buddhist Uprising that had occurred in April and May. The other Buddhist monk remained in Da Nang and continued to head the Social Welfare Committee. He stated openly that the pagoda was to be the centerpiece of the new Social Service Center. He tried to convince everyone who would listen that the pagoda would be "non-sectarian and available to all." But those statements flew in the face of the reality that twenty-two Catholic, seven Protestant, and two Cao Dai families had been refused permission to sleep in the Social Service Center the week prior to our first meeting. There seemed no way that the project could ever be viewed as non-sectarian under the current leadership. I got involved in this brouhaha when my commander appointed me as the only U.S. representative in a working group charged with recommending a solution to the problem. The American donors looked to me to protect their interests. Also, since it was American "seed money" that got the project started, the commander of MACV Advisory Team #1 felt that I, as the senior medical advisor, had to be involved "so the whole thing doesn't blow up in our face." Further complicating matters was the fact that practically all of the I Corps military hierarchy was Buddhist. They were reluctant to challenge the leadership of the Buddhist monk heading

the Social Services Welfare Committee. The Catholic, Protestant, and Cao
Dai minorities were loudly demanding justice. Cao Dai, I soon learned,
is a monotheistic religion that has its roots in Vietnam. It was founded
in 1926 in Tay Ninh, a small city several hundred miles south of Da
Nang. I knew little about the religion, except that we had to work with
its adherents as best we could to resolve the problem.[3]

One day, Captain Phat, who had recently returned from temporary duty
in Saigon, requested that the monk heading the Social Service Welfare
Committee meet with him in his office to discuss a potential solution that
would be acceptable to all parties. I was present at that meeting. Captain
Phat treated the man with great respect, doing everything he could to put
him at ease and to assure him that his opinions were respected. After the
initial greeting, during which the monk seemed cordial, an abrupt change
took place. The monk's response to every question that Captain Phat
asked, or statement that he made, was stony silence. The monk stared
straight ahead, his eyes unblinking and his expression unchanging. I was
seated across from him, and it appeared he was staring right through me
at some distant object. His demeanor was very disconcerting, and it also
bothered Captain Phat. The meeting ended without the monk making
a single statement about the project.

I later attended two meetings with Captain Phat and several secular
community leaders appointed to come up with a solution to the problem.
Since the transient quarters were directly related to Duy Tan Hospital,
and since Captain Phat commanded that hospital, the community leaders
were insistent that he should draft a proposal for solving the problem. He
was reluctant to do so, pointing out that the Social Service Center was
not a part of the hospital and that he had no command authority over it.
Technically, it was a part of the city of Da Nang and not the hospital. The
community leaders pushed hard, and Captain Phat eventually accepted
the task and started drafting a proposal. He told me that just as soon as
he had a first draft, he wanted to sit down with me and get my reaction
to the document.

The Buddhist leadership in the community, including the head of the Social Service Welfare Committee, became aware that Captain Phat was drafting a proposal. Immediately, they requested a meeting with him, to be held in their conference room. Without requesting their permission, he invited me to accompany him to the meeting.

As we entered the room the monks looked startled by my presence. They whispered to each other behind raised hands. When their initial surprise dissipated, they shifted their complete attention to Captain Phat, totally ignoring my presence. There was much smiling, bowing, and clasping of hands in front of chests on the part of the Buddhist monks. It was very obvious that they were attempting to curry the favor of Captain Phat, knowing that he was in the process of formulating a proposal for the future of the transient quarters. They treated him almost reverentially, while ignoring me. The dialogue was entirely in Vietnamese. Not a word of English was spoken, even though several of the monks were fluent in the language. The meeting itself was an unforgettable experience for me. Since I was not involved in the discussion, I could sit back and study the surroundings and listen to the sing-song rhythm of the dialogue as they tried to convince Captain Phat of their point of view. Clearly, they wanted to maintain Buddhist control of the Social Service Center.

After the proposal was drafted, Captain Phat showed me the document and, true to his word, it was balanced in its approach. While making some concessions to the Buddhists, he was not about to give them control. He had built into the proposal a series of checks and balances and an appropriate level of community oversight. I agreed with what he was about to propose.

Since the International Control Commission had inquired about the project earlier, the working group charged with finding a solution to the problem thought it prudent to brief the members of the ICC on the proposal to assure they had its support before presenting the document for final approval. This was done, and the ICC interposed no objection to the document.

As the working group was in the process of finalizing the document for approval by city government officials, yet another problem arose. Catholic Relief Services officials in Da Nang became irate over the activities of the center. Peter Cannon, the CRS director in Da Nang, told our working group that, just three days prior, CRS had provided the Buddhist monk in charge of the center with enough food to feed 600 people for an entire month. That food had disappeared. When confronted with this information, the monk could not show us any of the many bags of rice and bulgur wheat or the bottles of cooking oil the CRS had given to the center. Mr. Cannon had personally helped deliver the food. The monk in charge would say nothing, only maintain a stony unemotional silence. He just sat and stared at Mr. Cannon. He made no attempt to explain or defend himself. Mr. Cannon said he hesitated to cut off future food donations from CRS because the need was so desperate.

When I departed Da Nang many months later, the transient quarters adjacent to Duy Tan Hospital were still a matter of concern. The truce that had been brokered was uneasy at best.

***

On 15 August, I Corps celebrated the anniversary of its founding. Why the ARVN made such a big deal of it, especially during wartime, I do not know. It started at 0900 hours with a two-hour outdoor ceremony in the I Corps compound. Among the notables attending were U.S. Ambassador Henry Cabot Lodge, Premier Ky, Head of State Thieu, the I Corps commander General Lam, General Westmoreland's deputy General Hinges, and seemingly every senior officer in I Corps. As a field grade advisor, I was invited to sit on the huge platform with all the notables, along with my fellow field grade advisors. Practically all the dialogue was in the Vietnamese language, so I understood very little of it. The ceremony seemed to follow Buddhist tradition. There was the burning of incense, the lighting of dozens of joss sticks by some of the dignitaries, and the release of hundreds of balloons of many colors. This was followed by the presentation of military awards to about fifty Vietnamese military officers and non-commissioned officers. After those so honored received their military decorations, pretty young Vietnamese women placed rings of flowers around their necks.

That evening, commencing at 1830 hours, all field grade officers serving on MACV Advisory Team #1 were invited to an anniversary reception. It was quite elegant and apparently enjoyed by all. Some of the Vietnamese officers brought their wives, which was quite unusual. They were charming women, well dressed and well mannered. The reception was held in a huge circular building that I found to be most attractive. The drinks flowed freely, and the food was excellent. There was lots of seafood, which I really liked. The reception ended at 2000 hours, but we were told that after a 30-minute break there would be an open house to celebrate the recent approval of a new ARVN Officers' Club. There would be a dance band, and we were all invited to stay, so we did.

At the open house the Vietnamese really "let their hair down." Three of my fellow advisors and I were assigned a small four person table not too far from the dance floor, so we got a firsthand look at all the action.

At about 2100 hours, we were sitting there, enjoying yet another of their excellent drinks, a tropical concoction with coconut and mangos in the gin, when suddenly a stir went through the crowd, followed by dead silence. In walked Premier Ky with his stunningly beautiful wife and a very large party. In the party were three or four other officers, their wives, about twenty unescorted lovely young women, and about fifteen to twenty secret service men.

Premier and Madame Ky and General and Madame Lam occupied a four-person table adjacent to the dance floor, right in front of the one where we were seated. Madame Ky was known as one of the loveliest women in Asia, or so we were told by Vietnamese officers in attendance. The premier seemed as cavalier and cocky as I had envisioned him. During the morning ceremonies, he had worn a black Air Force flight suit, a black baseball-style cap with military gold "scrambled eggs" on the bill, and a bright magenta scarf around his neck. He was a dashing figure indeed. At the evening social event, all of the men except Premier Ky wore coats and ties, while the women wore the traditional ao dai. Premier Ky showed up in a guayabera-style embroidered white shirt and dark slacks. He looked more comfortable than we did in the tropical heat.

When the music began, most of the officers who had brought their wives moved to the dance floor, including General and Madame Lam. Many of the Vietnamese bachelor officers danced with the pretty young women who had entered with Premier Ky and his party. Premier Ky and his wife never danced, nor did any of the Americans in attendance. When not engaged in conversation with General and Mrs. Lam, it was obvious that Ky was watching the pretty young women on the dance floor. Without doubt, he had a roving eye. Occasionally, he leaned over and said something private to his wife, but for the most part he just stared at the young women.

At about 2215 hours Madame Ky got up from the table and Premier Ky rose and kissed her hand, after which she departed the scene with two or three secret service men. This was the last we saw of the beautiful Madame Ky.

Within five minutes of Madame Ky's departure, Premier Ky nodded his head toward a lovely young woman about nineteen or twenty years old who was on the dance floor with a partner. She was one of the many girls who had entered with the Ky party earlier in the evening. As soon as the music stopped, a secret service man walked over to the girl and obviously told her that Ky wanted her company. She was very nervous as she was seated at Ky's table. The decorative fan in her hand was working overtime to keep her forehead dry. She was not what he wanted. After about five minutes, she was discharged. The winnowing process went on. Four girls were summoned from the dance floor, one at a time, until he finally found one that met his favor. She was a tall, slender, dark-eyed beauty, apparently his precise cup of tea. After a brief conversation with the girl, he signaled a secret service man, whispered something in his ear, and then got up, said goodnight to General and Mrs. Lam, and left the event along with several secret service men.

Within five minutes after Ky's departure, the girl he had selected was discreetly whisked away by three of Ky's assigned secret service entourage. I asked an English-speaking secret service man, who remained at the event, what would now happen to the girl. He unabashedly told me, "Premier Ky is going to honor her great beauty by taking her to his bed. After he has taken his pleasure, she will be given a bracelet or a necklace as a token of remembrance of her good fortune at having been selected by the premier. She will then be delivered to her home and Premier Ky will be taken to Madame Ky or, if he wishes, back to this celebration."

I was told that, while Vietnamese wives did not approve of this type of interaction, they felt somewhat powerless to do anything about it. Most wives seemed to be subservient to their husbands. Whether or not this type of behavior was commonplace among the elite I do not know, but I suspect it was not.

***

On 16 August, an ARVN MEDCAP team was scheduled to be in a small village north of Da Nang. I decided to go along because I had received a disturbing report that an ARVN non-commissioned officer had been demanding money prior to providing treatment during MEDCAP visits to that village. This was strictly forbidden. All treatment was to be extended without cost to the patient.

After spending about thirty minutes observing the interaction of the team with the villagers who presented themselves for treatment and seeing no cause for concern, I noticed a young woman with her right hand up to her mouth, looking in the rear window of the village's small one-room dispensary. I looked at her and smiled. She immediately withdrew from the window. It struck me as being odd. A moment later, she was back at the window, peering at those receiving treatment. This time I saw the reason for her discomfort. An ugly harelip extending well into the nostril of her nose had turned this eighteen-year-old woman into a recluse. She avoided contact not only with me but also with the people of the village.

Through my interpreter I was able to gently speak to her and calm her enough that she would listen to what I had to say. In the privacy of my jeep, because the villagers' prying eyes were making her a nervous wreck, I explained through Sergeant Thong that maybe we could have her hare lip corrected. I told her that after surgery she would still have a scar but the void would be filled with flesh. She then went home to get her father. Reluctantly, he gave his consent for Sergeant Thong and me to take his daughter to the U.S. Navy Hospital for an evaluation. She was evaluated on Tuesday of the following week, and on Wednesday Dr. Giles did the repair. I went to the hospital on Friday afternoon to pick her up and return her to her village. When she saw me, her face lit up; she bowed deeply and clasped her hands in front of her chest in a prayerful gesture. She was most grateful.

Dr. Giles and I had our first disappointment regarding Project Harelip on 17 August. Sergeant Thong and I had taken two children in for evaluation on that day. Their mothers accompanied us to the hospital. One child passed the physical exam and the surgery was scheduled for later that same day. The other, sadly, could not be scheduled. During the physical examination that always preceded general anesthesia and surgery, it was discovered that the three-year-old boy had advanced tuberculosis, even though outwardly he looked healthy. It was especially difficult for me to take the little boy and his mother back to their home. After the boy's parents had gotten their hopes up, they were confronted with the sad news that the lip could not be repaired and that the child had a life-threatening disease. The chances of a peasant-class family getting tuberculosis successfully treated in Vietnam at that time were not good.

***

On the evening of 17 August, a tragic terrorist bombing occurred in Hue. It seemed as if the NVA or VC could strike almost anywhere at any time. They blended in so well that it was impossible to tell friend from foe. It seemed to me the typical Vietnamese citizen was ambivalent about which side to support, which side of the political fence to get behind. Over twenty-five people were killed and well over 100 badly injured in the attack. I talked to Captain Bob Helton the next morning, and he sounded discouraged. I could appreciate his feelings. He told me the death count had risen to forty-six and over 100 were injured, many of them critically.

It was such a senseless taking of human life. The bomb went off at a gathering similar to a county fair. There were no political overtones to the gathering that should have caused the VC or NVA to carry out the terrible act. It was sheer terrorism. The explosion itself was bad enough, but the ensuing panic made it even worse. Captain Helton told me that many slightly injured children were literally trampled to death by the fleeing crowd. The people of Hue were in despair.

On 18 August, I visited the city of Tam Ky with an infectious disease specialist who had been dispatched to evaluate an outbreak of bubonic plague. While the physician was deciding upon a course of action to quell the outbreak, I observed him as carefully as possible and asked many questions so as to learn from the experience. It was the first of many times I was to see the victims of Black Death, as the disease had been called during the Middle Ages. The painful nodules under the arms and in the groin area of its victims, which I had read about in chronicles of the Middle Ages, probably looked just as frightening to me as they did to Europeans writing about them six centuries earlier. It became clear to me, as I interacted with the physician as he went about his work, that the disease could be prevented if the rat population were controlled.

I was eventually to get more directly involved in trying to slow the tide of this killing disease. When we had an outbreak in I Corps, I was sometimes asked to serve as a courier to deliver the live attenuated vaccine to the city or village where it was needed. The vaccine was produced at the Pasteur Institute in Saigon and then shipped to Da Nang by air. When it arrived at the Da Nang Air Base, I was called upon to pick it up and, as expeditiously as possible, get it to the site where it was needed, in an attempt to quell the outbreak of the disease. Typically, it arrived at the CIA's Air America terminal. The CIA had a fleet of very fast aircraft that they flew all over the Republic of Vietnam on a more or less scheduled basis.[4] The Air America pilots seemed to recognize the urgency of getting the vaccine to the right place as quickly as possible, making them ideal carriers. Even though the vaccine was refrigerated, it still had a relatively short shelf life.

***

Head lice were prevalent among the peasant population of Vietnam. Whenever I was among the poor, I saw many little girls with their heads bowed down, their mothers squatting before them, attempting to pick the lice off their daughters' scalps. When the mothers determined that most of the lice had been removed, they bowed their own heads, and their daughters reciprocated by picking the lice from their mothers' scalps. Probably because of their short hair, males did not seem to be affected to the degree that females were. Also, many of the young boys shaved their heads, thereby controlling the lice. The problem of lice infestation seemed especially acute among very old ladies. They seemed to help each other rid their scalps of lice. I felt so sorry for them.

***

On 22 August, there was a mandatory meeting of all members of MACV Advisory Team #1. During the meeting, it was announced that until the Vietnamese national elections, scheduled for 11 September, were over, we had to be in our rooms by 1930 hours each evening. This was very disruptive to our daily advisory schedules. If we wanted to eat an evening meal, we had to curtail our activities in time to rush to the Officers' Club, order and eat dinner, then get to our rooms before the imposed deadline. The local authorities were expecting a significant increase in terrorist activity from that point until the elections were over. Political rallies and occasional fights had already started in Da Nang. So, as to preclude advisors' getting trapped in highly emotion-charged, pre-election rallies, the curfew had been established. It was probably a prudent move, but it was also a painful adjustment for the advisors, as there wasn't much to do while sitting in a barren room alone. As a further irritant, my hotel was without running water and electricity for the first four days of the curfew.

***

Murphy's Law states that "Anything that can go wrong, will go wrong." I would add to the law, "and at the worst possible time." On the morning of 23 August, I got to my office very early and almost immediately received a call from the MILPHAP team in Tam Ky. They had run out of liquid suspension tetracycline, the drug of choice for treating those who had bubonic plague. The need was acute.

I started making phone calls. The U.S. Air Force Dispensary didn't have any of the medicine to spare. The U.S. Naval Support Activity Hospital had some, but not nearly enough. I checked with the ARVN Medical Supply Depot in Da Nang when the commander arrived at about 0700 hours and was told that, while the depot was showing a zero balance for the item, he felt certain that some was available at the Red Beach port area. Most military medical supplies for I Corps were received at this port. After several calls to Red Beach, which was about ten miles north of the Da Nang Air Base, I was able to ascertain that they did in fact have liquid suspension tetracycline in the quantities required. Due to the extreme circumstances presenting themselves at Tam Ky, they were willing to issue some to me as the senior medical advisor. I told the person that I was talking to on the phone that I'd get to Red Beach as soon as possible and asked him to please set the tetracycline aside.

Then I started working on transportation to Tam Ky. How was I going to get the much-needed antibiotic to Tam Ky in a timely manner after I picked it up at Red Beach? I found out that an Air America flight was scheduled to depart Da Nang at 1100 hours and was assured that if I got the medication to their terminal before departure they would transport it to Tam Ky.

I looked around the office and asked, "Where's Sergeant Thong? I've got to go to Red Beach, and I need him to come along."

SP-4 Behner, the clerk-typist for our office, said, "Sir, Sergeant Thong is sick with the flu. We have a replacement driver for the day." The replacement driver, whose name I can't recall, spoke no English. Also, he had arrived at our office unarmed. It became obvious that he would have to drive the jeep while I rode shotgun.

Shortly before departure for Red Beach, I got a call from an NCO in our MACV dispensary. The NCO said he had heard I was going to Red Beach and asked if I could bring back some supplies that were awaiting pickup. I had the replacement driver attach a trailer to my jeep to accommodate the medical supplies. We then departed Da Nang for Red Beach. I had driven the route many times previously, so I was familiar with the roads. Every time Sergeant Thong and I traveled outside of Da Nang, I would point out danger zones and potential ambush sites. I would also instruct him regarding how to react if we came under fire. He understood, and I'm confident that if the need had arisen, he would have reacted appropriately. My guidance had always been as follows: if we start to take fire when you're driving down a road, the best thing to do is put the accelerator to the floorboard. Do not, under any circumstances, stop or try to turn the vehicle around.

The replacement was a competent driver. He did not, however, know the route. Because he spoke no English, I had to frequently tap his shoulder and then use hand signals to indicate which way to go.

Suddenly it happened. Before I even heard the crack of the enemy rifle, a bullet shattered the top of the windshield between the driver and me. A small piece of glass hit the driver on the bridge of his nose. Blood ran down his face. He panicked, hit the brakes, and then attempted to turn the jeep and trailer around on the fairly narrow road, a difficult task even under ideal conditions. I was screaming at him, to no avail. He understood not a word and continued with the task of turning the jeep around. More shots rang out, but not a single one struck the jeep, the driver, or me. Two hit the trailer. How very lucky we were. I couldn't help but think of my addition to Murphy's Law. Assuredly it was "the worst possible time," as I had a replacement driver who spoke no English and who had never been given instructions on what to do if he came under fire while driving a jeep.

We retreated to Da Nang, where I called Red Beach and told my point of contact what had happened. He said, "Well, you're in luck. We've got to make a run into Da Nang to deliver some spare parts to NSA. We'll swing by I Corps HQ and deliver the tetracycline to your office at about 1430 hours."

I then called the Air America terminal and told them I would not be able to get the medication on the 1100 flight. Luck was with me again, as I was informed that another flight to Tam Ky was scheduled for departure later in the day. The liquid suspension tetracycline, although a few hours late, was delivered as promised.

***

My home for the year I spent in Da Nang was on the third floor of a very small rundown hotel. My quarters consisted of one room, three paces wide and three-and-a-half paces long, approximately 9' by 10' in size. The only light in the room was one bare bulb hanging from an electrical cord positioned more or less over a very small, single pedestal, wooden desk. There was a wooden chair at the desk and an upholstered easy chair in one corner. A twin bed, very narrow, was situated in one corner. Over the head of the bed was a small cork bulletin board, apparently placed there by a previous occupant. The room had a two-drawer chest for my folded clothing plus a wooden pole suspended from the ceiling by two wires on which to place my hanging clothing. The one small window overlooked an unimpressive courtyard. The dominant feature of the courtyard was an open well with a bucket suspended from a rope. Bá Tran Thi Vy, my hired maid, pulled buckets of water out of the well to wash my clothing by drenching them with water, soaping them down and then beating them on the cement slab surrounding the well.

There was no plumbing in the room, but immediately across the narrow hallway was a bathroom I shared with two other officers. It had a sink and a shower, but no hot water. Under the sink was a five-gallon water can on which was painted my name. There were identical cans for the other two officers sharing the bathroom. The water in the cans was for drinking and brushing one's teeth.

While taking my daily shower (when there was water), I noted that if I cupped my hands and filled them with water, squiggly little red worms were swimming furiously about in the water. This observation gave the five-gallon water can under my sink new relevance. The can had to be re-filled from a water trailer near my office in the I Corps compound. After I observed the worms, the five gallons of water didn't seem nearly as heavy as I lugged the container up to the third floor after refilling it about once a week.

There was one telephone in the hallway to meet the needs of the occupants of the rooms located on the third floor. It rang frequently, and when it did, it was typically between 0100 hours and 0300 hours, causing someone to have to get up and pad down the hall to answer it, then try to rouse the person for whom the call was intended.

The hotel had no lobby. The only place suitable for a small group of officers to socialize or enjoy a cold beer or a soft drink was the small balcony overlooking a busy street. When the six occupants of the rooms on the third floor got together, each would grab the desk chair from his room and bring it out to the balcony. On stifling hot nights, the balcony provided some respite from the humidity and heat. There was no air conditioning in the hotel, so some officers slept out there when the fans in their rooms were not working as the result of a power outage.

There were sandbagged defensive positions at the front and rear of the hotel. ARVN soldiers guarded the hotel 24 hours a day. Our jeeps were parked as close to the guards as possible to preclude their being booby trapped during the night.

In each of the hotel's rooms, there was an overhead fan in the center of the ceiling. These fans moved almost no air. They had only two speeds, slow and slower. But the fan in my room had one redeeming grace, for on its blades a little gecko had decided to make its home. It was a funny little creature, and over time it became my friend. When I entered the room, it always jumped from blade to blade on the fan, as if genuinely pleased to see me. The gecko was with me for the entire year, looking down at me in the morning as I got dressed for the day, greeting me in the evening when I came home, and seemingly watching over me as I slept. It also kept my room free of mosquitoes, a genuine blessing in the tropics. Of even greater importance, the little gecko helped to relieve the boredom and loneliness during the long evenings and nights. It was nice to have another living creature in the room with me.

Although the room was Spartan by all accounts, I did not complain. I realized full well that to the young soldiers, marines, and navy corpsmen slogging around in the rice paddies, triple canopy jungles, or mountains, being shot at frequently, my room would seem like paradise. I thought of them, and prayed for them, every day.

***

By late August the tempo of commercial activity in Da Nang was starting to pick up. It seemed as if there were far more people on the streets than just a few weeks prior. The bakery shops, outdoor vegetable, fruit and meat markets, and mobile restaurants all appeared to have an abundance of customers. The stifling effects of the Buddhist Uprising on the economy of Da Nang seemed to be a thing of the past.

Especially was this true of the fish market. The fishing boats would come in off the South China Sea and then move up the Han River until they reached the area set aside as the outdoor fish market. It appeared as though the boats, laden with fish, docked at the market two or three times a day, five or six days a week. The women of the city seemed to know precisely when the boats would arrive. They flocked to the wharf area, carrying wicker baskets on their hips or heads, with determined looks on their faces, each hoping to buy the choice fish of the lot.

They got the fish right off the boat, pointing out which ones they wanted and conversing in an animated and joyous manner with the fishermen, all of whom seemed to wear only shorts, tank tops, and flip-flops made of old tires. I watched this activity on several occasions and could never quite figure out how the women paid for the fish they bought. It appeared that no money exchanged hands until the women were about to depart from the market. How the fish merchants kept the finances straight, and how they compensated the owner of each individual boat, I do not know. They apparently had an accounting system of some type, but I couldn't figure it out. But since fish was such a major component of the Vietnamese diet, the women's frequent trips to the market were important and serious events.

**

In mid-August, my mother sent me a newspaper clipping informing me that Captain Duane Miller, a friend and former high school classmate, was stationed in Da Nang. The news clipping stated that he was an Air Force officer who flew the HU-16 Albatross, used to rescue downed American pilots from the South China Sea. The Albatross, a two-engine plane, had very high wings and was equipped to land on the water near a downed pilot and pick him up.

After several attempts to reach Duane, I was finally successful on 24 August. He told me that he had a 72-hour break from flying, so I decided to pick him up and show him a little bit of Da Nang while I went about my duties. It was a real treat for him, because although he had been in Da Nang since April, this was the very first time he'd been off the Da Nang Air Base, except when he was flying. He had never seen the city of Da Nang except from the air. Duane was with me for about three hours during the late afternoon of that day.

I took him many places. Wherever my assigned duties took me, he came along. The last place we visited was an ARVN Convalescent Center.

As we entered the building, I could see a look of disbelief and shock come over his face. Almost 50 percent of the patients were amputees. He couldn't believe it. He told me later that the experience had almost made him ill. Initially, he started interacting with the patients in the same manner in which I did, trying to make them feel as if they had a future by shaking their hands, smiling at them, ruffling their hair, patting them on the back, and so on, but he couldn't take it. He was almost overcome and asked me if we could leave. I found this to be a fairly typical reaction of non-medical people when taken into an ARVN treatment facility, especially a convalescent center.

After leaving the convalescent center, we went to a promotion party thrown by a couple of NCOs. The ribald humor, coupled with raucous laughter and a couple of cold beers, helped Captain Miller forget, at least temporarily, that which he had witnessed that afternoon. During the next ten months, I always felt it served a purpose to seek out opportunities to expose non-medical American servicemen to an ARVN treatment facility in that it provided them with an object lesson on the tragedies of war.

By late August, I was becoming physically and emotionally drained. I was working long hours, typically 12-13 hours a day, trying to get on top of the job and understand its complexities and many facets. Few days had gone by that I had not been exposed to heart-rending trauma. The victims were soldiers and civilians alike, men, women, and lots of children. This was a new and frightening experience for me. I had seen virtually no trauma before arriving in Vietnam. The moaning of the children in the province hospitals as they had their burns dressed, bones set, and wounds debrided, cleaned, and stitched, tore at my heart. So did the anguish and helplessness in the eyes of their parents.

Image 6. Severe burns covering much of child's body

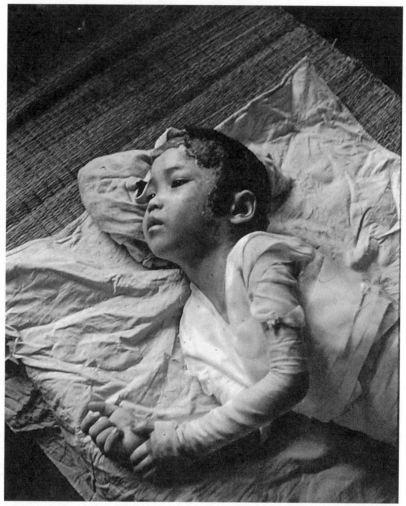

Photo courtesy of the author

I was also very troubled about the rapidly approaching monsoon season.[5] Based on the intelligence estimates I listened to every Saturday morning during the I Corps staff meetings, it seemed inevitable that the rapidly approaching monsoon was going to be particularly rough for I Corps. The enemy had large troop concentrations in both Quang Tri and Quang Ngai Provinces. He operated well in foul weather, whereas we did not. We had the advantage of air and vehicular mobility, far superior weaponry, and many other technological advantages, but bad weather drastically diminished their impact. I felt a moral obligation to do everything I could to insure that the ARVN medical units were ready for the worst. I discussed my concerns and apprehensions about the upcoming monsoon season with my counterpart, Major Tu, and he readily agreed with my assessment. Together we put together a plan whereby we would personally visit medical units throughout the corps area to stress the importance of training and maintenance and to make an assessment of each unit's readiness to respond.

On 26 August, Major Tu, Captain Nhan and I started visiting ARVN medical units. We decided to begin in Quang Tri Province, since intelligence estimates indicated that this was the most likely area of attack. I picked the two of them up at Major Tu's office at 0630 hours that morning and transported them to the Air America Terminal on the Da Nang Air Base. We then flew to the city of Quang Tri on an Air America C-45, a plane equipped with instrumentation that enabled it to fly in pretty nasty weather.

We were on the ground in La Vang, a small village with an airstrip about two or three miles south of Quang Tri, by 0800 hours. Sergeant Yates, a medic, met us with a jeep and drove us into the city of Quang Tri. By 0830, we were sitting down with the commander of an ARVN clearing company for a cup of the omnipresent orange tea, served piping hot and never with sugar. Major Tu, Captain Nhan, and I inspected the unit. I may have seen a medical unit in worse shape somewhere in the world, but I certainly couldn't recall it. This one was abysmally bad. Their equipment was dirty, there was virtually no maintenance of vehicles, their supply system was in shambles, maintenance and training records were either non-existent or fabricated, and there was no training whatsoever taking place. The commander of the unit spoke no English, so I could openly converse with Major Tu regarding my observations. I suggested that as a test he ask the commander to have two of his best enlisted medics demonstrate how to put on a standard piece of equipment used to splint a fractured leg. Major Tu did so. As expected, the two selected corpsmen, supposedly the best in the unit, floundered badly as they tried to splint the imaginary fracture of another soldier's leg. If it had been an actual casualty with a fractured femur, the injury would have been worsened by the experience. The commander, an ARVN lieutenant, was embarrassed, as well he should have been. Major Tu upbraided him pretty harshly, not in front of his subordinates, but in the confines of his office. He told the lieutenant that he or one of his subordinates would be back in one month to re-inspect the unit and if it hadn't shaped up he would recommend the lieutenant be relieved of command. That would be the end of his military career and cause him and his family to lose face.

We also noted that the clearing company had an unusually high number of malaria cases on its wards. It was very difficult to watch the victims, covered with blankets, shiver and shake. Sweat was pouring off them. Even though the outside temperature was right at 100 degrees, they were shivering uncontrollably.

By 1000 hours, we were at the Quang Tri Province Hospital where Vietnamese civilians received treatment. Dr. Tu was especially interested in going to this hospital in order to see an old friend, Doctor Tung. I had been at the hospital on several previous occasions during my efforts to support the U.S. Navy MILPHAP team that worked there.

As was typical, before looking over the hospital, we had to drink more orange tea with Dr. Tung and another physician. Upon completion of this traditional ritual, we accompanied Dr. Tung through the hospital. On the maternity ward, I was amazed at the efficiency, skill and professionalism of the midwives. We watched the birth of two beautiful babies, born within minutes of each other.

We then came to a ward for those recovering from burns, some inflicted as a result of war and some by household accident. The screams of one severely burned little boy, as they attempted to change his dressings, still resonate through my brain. Some sounds, like the wail of the siren in the movie of Anne Frank's life, seem never to leave. This may be one such sound for me. Some of the burns were horrible beyond description. One woman, her breasts almost burned off as a result of a household accident involving scalding hot water, and a child whose face was just one massive, excruciatingly painful blister, were particularly difficult for me to observe. It was tough to keep from tearing up.

And then came something seemingly even more tragic. My heart bled for the poor child, but I could do nothing. Just as we entered the surgical department they wheeled in a fourteen-year-old girl. She was silently crying. Her parents accompanied her. Two American physicians from the MILPHAP team and one Vietnamese doctor examined her and then explained to us that she had been purposely shot by the VC the night before because they thought her parents were cooperating with the ARVN. She was shot to provide a lesson for her parents and the people of the village in which she lived. The bullet had entered on the outside of her left knee. At the point of entry, the hole was very small. But at the point of exit, you could put your entire hand into the cavity. There was no chance. The leg had to come off if her life were to be saved. The head of the tibia was smashed beyond repair, and the threat of gangrene was always present. Her parents were torn, but when told that if the leg was not removed the girl might die, they gave permission for the amputation. The poor girl was pleading and praying that the doctors not remove her leg. In her pleading, she always seemed to repeat the same words. I asked Dr. Tu what she was saying. He told me she kept repeating, "Oh, no, please no. What man will ever love me and marry me with only one leg? I'll never have children. I'll never have a man to call my own. Oh, no, please no. Don't let them mama and papa." May God help her was my silent prayer.

The number of civilian casualties produced by the war was appallingly high. As a younger man, I had so wanted to become a physician, but exposure to trauma of that magnitude convinced me that I was not emotionally equipped to handle it. Sometimes I got mildly depressed. I was encountering heart-rending trauma almost on a daily basis.

Major Tu, Captain Nhan and I flew back to Da Nang on a C-130, a much larger aircraft than the C-45 we had flown up in. On the trip back to Da Nang, we shared the cargo compartment with a front-end loader, a huge piece of engineering equipment that was tethered to the floor and sides of the plane. At one point during the flight, I climbed into the seat of the front end loader and pretended to drive it off the rear ramp. It gave everyone a good laugh, which we all needed after a rather joyless day.

On Sunday, 28 August, I went to an early morning Mass followed by breakfast at the MACV Officers' Club. After breakfast, I joined a group of officers in the barroom for a Bloody Mary. The discussion was all about the upcoming election of a new Constitutional Assembly for the Republic of Vietnam and the heightened level of political activity, not only in the city of Da Nang, but throughout the countryside.

During the I Corps Saturday morning staff meeting, held the day before, it had been announced by the I Corps G-2 that between three and four hundred Viet Cong soldiers were in Da Nang for the explicit purpose of disrupting the elections by sabotage and terrorism.

An American officer stationed in Saigon was a part of the barroom discussion. He stated that the conventional wisdom in Saigon was that the Ky-Thieu government was feeling a great deal of pressure. Either they got out the vote or they would be seriously weakened, even though they might win the election. Most of the Saigon pundits said that unless Ky and Thieu could garner three million votes they would "lose face" with the Vietnamese people. The thinking seemed to be that if the people stayed home from the polls and didn't vote, they were voicing their dissatisfaction with the Ky-Thieu government.

After leaving the Officers' Club, I decided to drive the three or four miles to my office to see if I had any mail and if there was anything urgent going on. I was utterly amazed by the level of political activity as I passed through the city. Thousands of people were milling around in the streets. Several different political rallies were in progress. It seemed to me as if most of their campaigning was going on in the streets, somewhat similar to the United States in the 1920s and 1930s.

I saw firsthand that it was very difficult for a candidate to project his or her image and get his message out to the electorate without broadcast media. The people seemed to demand an opportunity to hear the candidates speak and were unwilling to rely solely on newspapers to help them make up their minds. They wanted to be able to see the person. Based on my two-month exposure to the people and the country at that time, I predicted there would be a reasonable voter turnout in the major cities but a miserable turnout in the countryside. Why did I come to that conclusion? Because I felt that peasant-class people, especially those who lived in the countryside, would be reluctant to take sides. A vote in the election might put them and their families at risk. The people in the cities felt safer and hence more willing to cast a vote.

***

During the morning of 30 August, I experienced something that was quite interesting. While in the Old Imperial City of Hue, one of Captain Helton's NCOs took Sergeant Thong and me to a small village about ten miles north of Hue to observe an ARVN MEDCAP team in action. Upon arrival, I started asking the people awaiting treatment a series of questions through my interpreter. I asked them what they thought of MEDCAP, and as expected they lavished praise on the program. I decided to probe a little deeper, and told them that I was most interested in hearing how we could do things better. Reluctantly they started talking. They talked not specifically about MEDCAP but about American aid in general. They pointed out that, while there were helpful American projects and programs, and while the Vietnamese people appreciated the assistance, they would be even more grateful if the Americans gave support to some of their existing projects and programs instead of always starting new ones.

I asked for an example of Vietnamese self-help projects that needed support. An elderly man, who identified himself as a Buddhist, stepped forward and asked that we follow him. He led us through the village to a small metal-roofed building. Outside the door was a Catholic nun in full habit. Inside the building were about forty-five to fifty children ranging in age from two to five years old. All were clean, wore decent clothing, and were seated in a circle on straw mats eating their noon rice. About five other nuns were bustling about while the children worked their chopsticks at full speed. They held glass bowls right up to their chins, more or less shoveling the rice into their little mouths.

Through my interpreter, I determined that, while many of the children were orphans, some were children whose mothers had died. In order to allow the widowed fathers to continue working, the nuns took care of the children during the day. The Buddhist man then told me that the nuns were always short of funds to keep the project going and asked why we couldn't help them. He also told us that the nuns accepted children from Buddhist as well as Catholic and Protestant families and that everyone in the village respected the program. I thought it utterly amazing that a Buddhist man would show us this project as an example of a Vietnamese-initiated project deserving of American support. I made a mental note to discuss it with Captain Bob Helton in the hopes that he could steer some assistance to the project.

After completing the MEDCAP, Sergeant Thong and I were scheduled to return to Da Nang on an Air America flight at 1600 hours that same day, 30 August. We were at the airport at 1530 hours when a violent thunderstorm hit the area. We could see the Air America plane circling over the airport, but the pilot apparently decided it was too risky to land. The crosswinds were ferocious. At the time I remember feeling that the pilot was probably being overly cautious, but five minutes later we watched a small, single engine L-19 try to land. The plane was buffeted violently by the winds and then came floating to the ground. The pilot and passenger got out unharmed, but the incident gave me new respect for the decision the pilot of the Air America aircraft had made. We did not return to Da Nang until the next day.

After returning from Hue on 31 August, I transported two little girls to the Navy Hospital for harelip repair. I had lost track of the number of harelips that Dr. Giles had corrected since my arrival, so I asked him if he had kept count. He responded, "I don't know how many, but I know there are more out there. I want you to keep me busy." Then he smiled and said, "I think it's been about thirty."

While I was there, I noticed two other toddlers who were ready to go home after having their lips repaired. They had been operated on three days previously and, although the stitches were out, there was still a great amount of swelling. It was not a pretty sight. It took eight to ten days for the swelling to disappear and for the children's faces to take on a semblance of normalcy. It always seemed to shock family members when the child was reintroduced into the home just a few days after surgery. Through Sergeant Thong, I always tried to assure the families that the swelling would go down soon and that they must be patient. It would have been helpful to keep the children in the hospital a few days longer, but in most instances this was not possible because of the tempo of the war.

While at the hospital I spoke with Dr. Giles about scheduling an operation to correct two clubbed feet, both on the same nine-year-old boy who lived in Tam Ky. The boy had never sought medical attention for his deformed feet. Several members of the MILPHAP team had noticed him struggling around the streets of Tam Ky and alerted me to his plight. When I watched the poor boy walk, it appeared as if he were walking on his ankles or on the sides of his feet. The prognosis for total relief, according to Dr. Giles, was very good. Dr. Giles told me to tell the parents that after surgery, the boy's lower legs and ankles would have to be in casts for about three months and that after the casts were removed, it would take at least that long, maybe even longer, for the boy to learn to walk normally. Every time I met with Dr. Giles, I came away admiring his basic human goodness. In my mind, he was a miracle worker.

CHAPTER 3

SEPTEMBER 1966

On 1 September, I participated in the inspection of an ARVN medical unit in Quang Ngai and uncovered the fact that the unit had not pitched some of its larger tents in seven years. I told the commander, an ARVN officer, that I would be surprised if the unit could even get its large tents in the air, and if they did, I could almost guarantee him that dry rot or mildew would have made them totally unusable. The commander of the unit, a lieutenant, and his senior NCO seemed unconcerned when I talked to them about my concerns. The lieutenant smiled at me and said that since the tents hadn't been used to support combat in the past seven years, he doubted they would be needed in the next seven. He explained that either U.S. Marine or occasionally ARVN helicopters evacuated most of the casualties from the battlefields directly to hospitals, frequently bypassing his unit altogether. He said he believed the big tents would never be needed and the smaller ones were enough to meet the unit's needs. Therefore, he wasn't concerned about dry rot or mildew having destroyed the large tents. When I pointed out that helicopters sometimes can't fly in monsoon rains and that the monsoon season was but a few weeks away, he shrugged his shoulders, smiled and said in pidgin English, "I take my chance that there be break in rain when sun shine and helicopter fly."

On the morning of Saturday, 3 September, I kept thinking of my daughter Kathy. It was her sixth birthday, and it was tough to be away. The day proved to be frenetic, to say the least. Bubonic plague had broken out yet again, this time in both Quang Tin and Quang Ngai Provinces. The Vietnamese preventive medicine people were desperately trying to insure that the outbreak didn't turn into an epidemic. I had been in Quang Ngai the day before, spending time with the soon-to-depart medical advisor to the ARVN 2nd Infantry Division. Upon returning to my office, I found a note on my desk informing me that 21,000 doses of plague vaccine had arrived at the Da Nang Air Base and that my newly assigned NCOIC, SFC Davis, had picked the shipment up at the Air America Terminal and delivered it to Duy Tan General Hospital for storage. The boxes containing the vaccine were addressed to "MACV Senior Medical Advisor, Da Nang, for delivery to Duy Tan General Hospital." Officials at the Pasteur Institute in Saigon, where the vaccine was produced, addressed the boxes in that manner because they knew it was difficult for Duy Tan Hospital personnel to gain access to the Air America terminal located on the Da Nang Air Base.

The instructions accompanying the shipment stated that part of the shipment was to go to Tam Ky, the capitol of Quang Tin Province, and part to Quang Ngai. On the morning of 3 September, after the Saturday morning staff meeting, I was able to secure a helicopter to deliver the vaccine. After getting confirmation of the availability of the helicopter, I called Duy Tan Hospital to tell the Staff Duty Officer that I would be at the hospital in about an hour to pick up the vaccine. About thirty minutes later, the duty officer called me back to tell me that the vaccine was no longer at the hospital. He was told that the hospital did not have sufficient refrigeration, so the vaccine had been taken to the ARVN Medical Depot in Da Nang for storage.

I tried to call Captain McLain, the American advisor to the commander of the medical depot, but he was not available. Nobody at the facility, on that Saturday morning, spoke English. I rushed down to the depot and, through gestures and loud talk, convinced the duty officer that I had to have the vaccine immediately because a helicopter was waiting to transport it to Tam Ky and Quang Ngai. With a great deal of trepidation the duty officer showed me where it was stored and allowed me to sign a disbursement receipt for the vaccine. He and I then took all 21,000 doses, about 700 vials, out of the refrigerator and re-packaged it in ice for shipment before I rushed the vaccine to the helipad. Within minutes, the helicopter was airborne and on its way to Tam Ky and then Quang Ngai.

While in flight, the pilot received a call instructing him to proceed immediately to Hoi An to pick up another officer who needed transportation to Tam Ky. We picked up the officer and had just gotten airborne when another radio call came in, telling the pilot to proceed immediately to the field headquarters of a U.S. Marine tank battalion to pick up a severely wounded Vietnamese civilian. After picking up the injured man, the pilot had to return to Hoi An to deliver him to the province hospital. Before even leaving the ground at Hoi An, the pilot received yet another call ordering him to return to the field headquarters of the tank battalion to pick up a friendly Vietnamese district chief who urgently needed to get to Tam Ky for the funeral of a family member. We returned to the tank battalion's field headquarters, picked up the district chief, and finally proceeded to Tam Ky and then on to Quang Ngai to deliver the life-saving vaccine and the passengers. From Quang Ngai, we flew back to Da Nang. As we flitted around the sky from one destination to another on that Saturday morning, I felt like a gnat in a windstorm.

***

I arose at 0630 hours on 4 September, much later than usual because it was a Sunday, and I didn't have any pressing obligations. I went to Mass at 0730 hours, then after services, drove out to my office to see if I had any urgent messages. While driving back to my hotel room, I skirted a political rally of some sort, curious but not wishing to get too close. Suddenly, I saw a little Vietnamese girl dash into the street where a small car hit her and threw her little body about fifteen feet. She landed on the adjacent sidewalk. The driver of the car that hit her did not stop.

I felt morally obligated to stop, despite the risk of getting entangled in a pre-election crowd of people. By the time I got to the little girl, her older sister was kneeling alongside her. Her sister appeared to be about eighteen years old and spoke some English. She tearfully told me that she worked as a custodian at the U.S. Navy Hospital and asked if I would be so kind as to transport her and her unconscious little sister to that hospital. I readily agreed to do so. We carefully lifted the little girl into the back seat of my jeep and drove the three or four miles to the hospital. During the trip, the girl regained consciousness and started to cry.

Upon arrival at the hospital, I noted that the older girl was well known and respected at the hospital. Without any questions concerning why the girl hadn't been taken to the civilian hospital in Da Nang, the emergency room physician took the little girl to an examining room. The ensuing examination revealed that she was not seriously injured. As a precaution, the physician ordered x-rays of her head, right shoulder, and rib cage. No fractures or other abnormalities were revealed. The doctor then dressed a few minor cuts and scrapes on the side of her face and right shoulder and released her.

I breathed a sigh of relief as I returned the two girls to their home. The older girl was exceedingly grateful that I had stopped to help. She wanted me to meet her parents, but I declined because it would have meant parking my jeep on the street, in an unfamiliar area, and walking through a maze of little houses to their home. From a security point of view, this would not have been a good idea, and besides that, I was now in a hurry to get to a dedication ceremony for a new all-faiths MACV chapel scheduled for 1130 hours.

The chapel dedication ceremony was well attended by civilian and military dignitaries, both Vietnamese and American. However, the

Buddhists were conspicuous by their absence. The Archbishop of the Da Nang Diocese, the Most Reverend Peter Chi, presented the dedicatory address. I found him to be a very charismatic man, intelligent, witty, and well informed. Everyone in attendance, Catholics, Protestants, and Jews, seemed very impressed by the man. Vietnamese Catholics in attendance told me that it was felt that Archbishop Chi might be elevated to Cardinal some day. Had this happened, he would have been the first person from Vietnam to be so honored.

Another person who impressed me at the dedication celebration was a priest by the name of Father O'Connor. Unfortunately, I didn't get his first name. I talked with him for quite some time during the reception that followed the ceremony. Father O'Connor was a member of the Columban Fathers, a missionary order named after Saint Columban. He was born in Ireland and, for the past twenty-two years, had been in charge of the Asian branch of Catholic News Service, the Catholic Church's equivalent of United Press International. I told him I would enjoy spending an evening with him over a couple of beers and a good meal, for I found him to be a fascinating man with many stories to tell. He told me that he had been based in Asia during his entire twenty-two years with CNS. Until 1956, he was in North Vietnam, but with the Communist takeover there, he was moved to the south. He promised to look me up if he got back to Da Nang before my tour of duty ended. I told him that I would show him several projects in and around Da Nang that were being supported by U.S. tax dollars that would "do his heart good." During our discussion, it became very obvious that he had a soft spot in his heart for the Vietnamese people, especially the impoverished.

Before going to dinner, I returned to my office to type a letter to my wife. Sitting in the office by himself was my boss, LTC Fred Mabra. He was in a pensive mood and, shortly after I entered, swiveled in his chair and said to me, "Jim, we need to talk." We then proceeded to have a minor argument about the way I was handling my job. He expressed his feelings that I was traveling too much and needlessly putting myself at risk by doing so. He said, "Jim, I get the impression that when you leave Da Nang on your many trips throughout I Corps, you're not even sure how you're going to get back." He was, of course, correct. That was the very nature of non-priority air travel in Vietnam.

He then went on to tell me that he also thought I sometimes delegated responsibilities to my NCOIC when I was away from Da Nang that were beyond his scope of competence. I told him that I thought he was wrong and that I didn't intend to change my modus operandi unless he gave me a direct order to do so. I told him that I couldn't do justice to the position without traveling extensively throughout I Corps. He countered by repeating that he thought I was carelessly exposing myself to unnecessary danger. I then told him that I thought I was capable of assessing risk and that I would be very careful not to do anything stupid. I respected LTC Mabra greatly, and I knew in my heart that he in turn respected me. I told him that I didn't think he had a good feel for what my job entailed, that I was charged to advise and assist the I Corps Surgeon and other Vietnamese medical authorities throughout I Corps to the best of my ability, and that I intended to do just that. I also told him that in some areas my knowledge and skills were lacking but that I was doing my very best to learn as quickly as possible. We ended the conversation with a rather uneasy truce.

I then sat down and typed a letter to my wife telling her how much I wished that she and I could experience together some of the things that I had been experiencing alone. I wrote, "I know that you enjoy new and unusual experiences as much as I do. And I love you so deeply that having you to share the experience would make it even more meaningful for me. All I can do is tell you in my letters what I'm experiencing." I then told her that it was "difficult for me to understand why many of my fellow American officers complain that they have little to tell their wives in their letters home." Such was not my problem. I had so much that I wanted to tell her that it became a matter of picking from a plethora of experiences those that were most poignant and compelling.

When I finished typing the letter, Colonel Mabra was still in the office. He looked at me, smiled, and said, "Let's go get a beer before dinner." I knew then that I was still in his good graces.

***

On 6 September, I wrote to my wife, mildly complaining that we had had no electricity in our hotel for four of the past five nights. It was frustrating because without electricity, it was almost impossible to sleep. Without some movement of air, it became unbearably hot and uncomfortable. A few of the officers in our hotel moved their beds to the porch overlooking the street, but then the mosquitoes pestered them all night. It was one of life's little problems, but when I compared our lives as advisors to the far more dangerous and uncomfortable lives of all of those young Americans who were constantly in harm's way, it seemed petty and juvenile to complain. I decided then and there to be grateful for what I had and to overlook the minor discomforts. For the most part I was able to do so.

We had a beautiful view from the balcony of our humble hotel. It overlooked Doc Lop Street, one of the main streets of Da Nang. The Da Nang Cathedral was only a couple of blocks up the street, and we were only two blocks from the Han River, which ran parallel to our street. We had a huge rain flower tree in the front of the hotel, and when the moon shone off the water of the Han River and the moon rays came through the rain flowers, it was a beautiful sight. I enjoyed sitting on the balcony at night devouring the sights, sounds, and unusual smells of Vietnam.

In my 6 September letter to my wife I also relayed the news that, commencing on September 9th, three days from the date of the letter, the entire MACV Advisory Team was to be restricted for four days, either to our rooms or to the I Corps compound. We were to stay off the streets on the following Friday, Saturday, Sunday, and Monday, and possibly longer. This was the critical period leading up to the Vietnamese parliamentary election. General Walt wanted to make absolutely certain that there would not be an incident whereby we could be accused of interfering with or taking sides in the election.

In that same letter I informed my wife that Captain King, a newly assigned American officer in Tam Ky, and I had lined up two children with harelips from Tam Ky to admit to the U.S. Navy Hospital in Da Nang for corrective surgery. He had to do quite a selling job on both sets of parents in order to convince them that surgery was the right thing to do. Many Vietnamese peasants seemed to cling to the disheartening notion that God sends a deformed child into the world to punish the parents for their sins and that to correct the deformity is to tamper with the relationship between man and God. Both sets of parents in Tam Ky seemed to cling to that archaic belief. Reluctantly, the parents finally agreed to the surgery.

Captain King personally accompanied the two children and their mothers on the airplane trip to Da Nang, a frightening experience for the mothers who had never before even been near a plane. Sergeant Thong and I met the five-person group at the Da Nang Air Base with two jeeps to transport them to the Navy Hospital. Upon arriving at the hospital, we were told that they could not be admitted at that time because the hospital commander had been directed to suspend all elective surgery and to have 200 beds available by nightfall. It was easy to deduce what that directive meant: either a major military operation, with the expectation of large numbers of casualties, was about to commence, or there was growing concern over the likelihood of problems surrounding the Vietnamese election. It was exceedingly difficult for Captain King and me to explain to the two mothers, through Sergeant Thong my interpreter, what was going on. Sadly, we had to arrange transportation for the group back to Tam Ky and hope that we could convince them to let us try again at some time in the future.

Such was life in Vietnam. You won some and you lost some. In the letter to my wife, I wrote, "I just wish I could get my emotions under better control at the time of a setback." The case mentioned above really bothered me. I couldn't help but wonder what those two mothers were thinking as we returned them to the Da Nang Air Base for the trip back to Tam Ky. Upon getting to their homes, how do you suppose they explained to their husbands what had happened? Would we see them in the future, or would the two children spend their lives handicapped by a highly visible, though easily correctable, deformity? God only knows.

***

I always found Da Nang to be very interesting in the early morning hours. The route between my hotel and the I Corps compound ran past a large pond and a number of rice paddies. On several occasions, very early in the morning, I saw a completely nude woman sitting on a rock in the middle of the pond taking a bath. She was very old, and her teeth were stained pitch black from betel nut. Her lips and mouth were bright red, also the result of chewing betel nut, a stimulant much like the caffeine in our coffee or tea that stains a user's teeth jet black and their lips and mouth a bright red. Many poorer people in Vietnam were users. When the woman saw me passing, she always smiled broadly and waved. She seemed to have more wrinkled skin on her frail body than flesh, but appeared happy.

The city awakened very early. It seemed as though many of the people, perhaps most, bought and ate their breakfast meal on the streets. The sidewalks were lined with little mobile restaurants. Large numbers of women prepared food in their homes and carried it to a location many people passed on their way to work or school. Typically the food was carried in big metal pots suspended by ropes at the ends of a "don ganh," a bamboo pole or slat of wood with ropes at both ends carried on the shoulder. The pots seemed to be piping hot, casting off steam and aroma as the women who carried them shuffled through the crowds of people. I was told they shuffle to keep their load in balance and not spill the food. Their feet barely left the ground. They more or less slid along the surface of the street at a fairly good pace. When they got to their desired locations, the pots and a number of small bowls were positioned on a cloth placed on the sidewalk, where they were ready for their first customer.

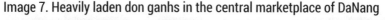

Image 7. Heavily laden don ganhs in the central marketplace of DaNang

Photo courtesy of the author

Other merchants, perhaps the more affluent, had their businesses on wheels. Little glassed-in boxes on carts were used to display their wares. People of all social classes seemed to purchase from these street vendors, the full spectrum from the very poor to the very rich. Where the poor got the money to make a purchase, I do not know.

It was very common to see a woman eating a meal while sitting or squatting on the sidewalk and at the same time nursing her baby. One day I saw a woman eating her breakfast while nursing two babies. The tiniest one, a newborn baby, was cradled in one arm and tugging at a breast while a toddler, perhaps fifteen-months old, was standing in front of his mother with her other nipple in his mouth. Life was difficult for the poor. The rate of childhood mortality was estimated by public health officials to be near 50 percent. This meant that half the newborns in the entire country didn't live to see their twelfth birthday. Based on my observations, I felt certain the mortality rate was much higher in the countryside than it was in the cities.

***

In the last few days leading up to the parliamentary election, pre-election fervor built to a fever pitch. To me the situation appeared to be so tense that if one shot were to be fired in anger it could have incited a bloodbath. I prayed that this would not happen. Electioneering seemed similar to that which I experienced as a boy in the late 1930s and early 1940s. Posters, all pretty much the same in design, were everywhere. Sound trucks passed throughout the city blaring out popular Vietnamese music followed by the political message of the candidate. Crowds gathered to listen to speeches presented by the candidates or their representatives. Banners strung across the streets typically showed a picture of the candidate and contained a few inspirational words about the man or woman. Mass media seemed almost nonexistent. So few of the peasant-class were literate, very few of them had radios, and almost none had television. Reaching the electorate was very difficult for the candidates.

On Friday, 9 September, the restriction to our rooms or the I Corps compound began. The election was scheduled for Sunday, 11 September. I chose to stay in the compound and provide coverage for the G-4 advisory effort. I had a folding canvas cot with an inflatable rubber mattress, so I was reasonably comfortable at night. I had C-rations to eat and plenty of water and soft drinks to drink. I was the only one in our office. The rest of the G-4 advisory staff remained in their living quarters, located in leased properties throughout the city. Each staff section had to designate one person to stay in the office in order to remain somewhat operational for the period leading up to the election. I volunteered to cover the office for the G-4 because I thought it would be far more interesting in the office than in my lonely room. Additionally, the office gave me access to a typewriter.

Friday and Saturday remained relatively peaceful in Da Nang, but a phone call from Captain Bob Helton in Hue informed me that there had been a minor problem up there. The patients in the military hospital, Tri Phuong Station Hospital, had staged a hunger strike. It lasted only a couple of days. Ostensibly they had struck because of the poor quality of the food in the hospital, but Bob Helton felt certain there were political overtones in the decision to strike. During the Buddhist Uprising the hospital had been one of the insurrectionists' strongholds.

On Saturday, my counterpart, Major Tu, called to tell me that downtown Da Nang was a beehive of pre-election activity and that the ARVN were taking a very active role in providing tight security for the election. Major Tu told me that on Friday, as a precautionary measure, tanks, armored personnel carriers, and machine gun emplacements were located at strategic points throughout the city. He said the NVA and VC desperately wanted to disrupt the election and perhaps the best way for them to do so was to create a wave of terrorism just prior to the opening of the polls. Vietnamese officials would not then have time to reassure the people that things were under control and it was safe to leave their homes and go to the polls. There were 127 polling places located throughout Da Nang. The expectation was that several would be hit hard.

The night before the election, I was invaded by termites; at least I think they were termites. I was sitting at my desk reading a book at about 0200 hours when suddenly I became aware of other living creatures. The room was alive with swarming flying insects. Apparently, the light on my desk had attracted them. By morning they were seemingly all dead, lying all over the room, on top of the desks and filing cabinets, just covering everything. I was never able to determine where they came from or what made them die. It was a strange phenomenon of nature.

The night was occasionally interrupted by gunfire. Fortunately, the incidents in and around Da Nang seemed ill-planned and poorly executed.

Early on Sunday morning, the actual day of the election, all persons in the HQ got a summary report that there had been seventeen separate Viet Cong- or NVA-initiated incidents in Da Nang from 2000 hours on Saturday until 0600 hours on Sunday. The polls opened as scheduled at 0700 Sunday morning and remained open until 1600 hours in the afternoon. During the daylight hours Da Nang remained calm and the election was conducted without serious incident.

Major Tu told me that the election polling places were all bedecked with yellow and red flags, the flag of the Republic of Vietnam They used hundreds of flags to make certain the polling places could be readily identified and to stimulate a sense of nationalism among the people. I was told that there were ten armed ARVN soldiers at each polling place during the election to provide security. Although it was difficult to have a free and open election under conditions of war, the fledgling country seemingly did its best.

During the period I was restricted to my office, I was somewhat bored. On the second day, I decided to write a lengthy letter to my wife telling her more about Vietnam and its people. I wrote that one thing that had struck me as being very strange was the almost total absence of cats. I don't think I saw more than five or six cats during my entire year in Vietnam. This surprised me greatly. For some reason I had always pictured most Asian nations as having great cat populations.

While there were few cats, dogs were everywhere. And sicker looking dogs, I had never seen during my entire life. It struck me that about 80 percent of the dogs looked as if they should be put out of their misery. Most had mange, with their hair falling out in big chunks. Most were emaciated, sadly undernourished. I was told by the U.S. Army veterinarian stationed in Da Nang, Major Ed Eckermann, that quite a number of the dogs were rabid. Dogfights in the street of Da Nang were common, and the fights usually attracted large numbers of cheering spectators. It seemed cruel and sadistic to me. Children gathered quickly whenever two or more of the hungry beasts snarled at each other. It frightened the hell out of me to see two or more angry, mangy beasts with gnashing teeth fighting to the death, with fifty or sixty little children forming the arena for battle and cheering them on.

Children of the poor, primarily the boys, but quite a few girls as well, seemed to smoke from the age of six or seven on. Their parents were seemingly not disturbed by this destructive activity. Tobacco wasn't readily available to the children, so they smoked all types of weeds and reeds, anything that would stay lit. They also bummed cigarettes from American marines and soldiers whenever possible. "Hey, GI, you give me cigarette?" was heard frequently. I could only imagine what their lungs must have looked like. If there was a single widely practiced human habit that repulsed me in Vietnam, it was little children smoking. Young children in more affluent families seemed not to smoke. Their habits seemed to parallel ours.

Head lice seemingly inhabited the heads of all of the poor who had hair. Many solved the problem by simply shaving their heads; however, hair seemed to be a bit of a fetish for many adults and adolescents. It was not at all uncommon to see women and teenage girls with hair to their waists. Some people who were badly infected with lice refused to shave their heads because of this fetish. I always carried lice powder with me, but I was reluctant to distribute it because the instructions on the metal cans were in English. Since I didn't speak the language and couldn't explain how to use the powder, it easily could have been misused. I envisioned a poor family using it as a food seasoning. When Sergeant Thong was with me and could carefully instruct the mothers regarding how to use it, I distributed the powder in great quantities.

Another aspect of Vietnam that bothered me was the number of young women who drifted into prostitution. I was told that, in Vietnam, once a prostitute, always a prostitute. In that society, at that point in time, a girl or young woman who decided to become a prostitute wasn't especially looked down upon. But once she made the decision to prostitute herself, she had to abide by that decision for life. Vietnamese friends told me that

September 1966

97

such a girl would never be able to marry because of societal demands that she adhere to the lifestyle she had chosen, that of a prostitute. Despite this severe limitation, many girls willingly accepted prostitution as a way of life. Why? Because it provided them with the material things they craved and could otherwise not afford. During the war, prostitutes did well financially and were able to buy for themselves things that only the very rich were otherwise able to afford. Materialism seemed to be a tremendous inducement for a young woman to become a prostitute, especially for those who had nothing. Materialism probably lost its motivational power as the girl grew older and began to realize that living a happy and complete life was not dependent on acquiring nice things. But by the time this realization hit them, it was already too late. When their feminine charms and physical attributes started to wither and fade they were left with only a closet full of sexy clothing and a bedroom full of useless junk. It was tragic, but far too often true.[1]

In our country the right to choose your own occupation or profession is deeply ingrained. This was not the case in Vietnam. Usually a son did what his father did. If the father was a peasant farmer, the son became a peasant farmer. If the mother worked as a domestic, the daughter automatically worked as a domestic. It pained me to see little girls carrying heavy loads on their don ganhs at construction sites just because that's what their mothers did. It pained me, not because I feared it would hurt the girls physically, although it might, but because I feared once they picked up the don ganh at a construction site they would never be able to put it down. They would forever be trapped in that occupation. Girls of ten years old already looked and acted much like their mothers. The idea of doing something different with their lives did not seem to enter their consciousnesses. Children seemed bound to the lifestyle of their parents. To me, that seemed very sad, as their true potential would be forever unknown and unrealized.

***

Late on Sunday afternoon, shortly after the polls had closed, those Americans restricted to the I Corps HQ compound were summoned to a briefing. It was reported that things had gone amazingly smoothly throughout the entire Republic of Vietnam. In Da Nang there were some difficulties the day and night before the election, but on Sunday there had been virtually no trouble other than a few incidents of small arms fire in the early morning and the detonation of two small explosive devices in the afternoon. Casualties were minimal. There were a few injuries, but no one was killed. It was reported that an estimated 70 percent of the eligible voters in I Corps had actually cast a vote.

After the briefing was over, I continued writing a letter to my wife. In it, I expressed my doubts.

> I have a strong feeling that there was government coercion involved in the high turnout. I looked at the voter registration certificate of one of the ARVN enlisted men in the HQ and noted that after he voted his certificate was punched with a star in the upper right corner. He told me that anyone having a certificate that was not punched would be "open to suspicion." It troubled me to hear that sort of thing. I'm sure tomorrow's headlines will trumpet the smashing victory of the Ky-Thieu regime. I have my doubts about the election, based on my conversations with scores of ARVN officers and enlisted men. But then again, I could be wrong. This region of the country is definitely not pro-government. Maybe Ky and Thieu enjoy more support in other regions of the country than I'm aware of.

On Monday, 12 September, the members of U.S. Advisory Team #1 couldn't get over the election results. It was the buzz of the I Corps compound. The Vietnamese press reported that nationally more than 80 percent of the registered voters had cast ballots. The Vietnamese seemed very pleased. They contended that it was the most open and free election they had ever had. Reportedly, there was little or no coercion regarding for whom to vote. The only coercion centered around the decision to vote or not to vote. Five-hundred thirty-two candidates had competed for the 117 seats to be filled in the Republic of Vietnam's Constitutional Assembly.[2] I still had my doubts.

***

I had a lengthy meeting with my counterpart, Major Tu, at Duy Tan Hospital during the afternoon of 12 September. At the conclusion of the meeting, he somewhat reluctantly asked if I would feel comfortable going to Hue with him to make an assessment of the situation at Nguyen Tri Phuong Station Hospital, where the pre-election hunger strike had taken place, and to give him my recommendation regarding an appropriate course of action. Specifically, he wanted to know if he should intervene as the I Corps Surgeon. A senior non-medical Vietnamese commander in Hue felt the strike was politically motivated and the hospital commander was ineffective and should be relieved of his command. Major Tu believed otherwise. He contended that the patients' complaints about the quality of the food were very real and not politically motivated. He pointed out that the hospital was given thirty-seven piastres (about 30 cents) per patient per day to buy food. He pointed out that eggs cost 10 cents each, fish were quite high, rice was high, sugar was very high, everything was high.

Major Tu questioned how the commander could possibly provide a nutritious meal for the patients with such a measly food allowance. I agreed to go with him and told him that, while we were in Hue, I would also discuss the situation with Bob Helton, a very capable officer and trusted military colleague of mine. I was certain that he would have insights into the matter. I told Major Tu that after we completed our work in Hue I needed to fly up to Quang Tri to deal with a situation involving two American NCOs whom the Navy MILPHAP team commander insisted be transferred for repeated inappropriate actions involving Vietnamese female workers at the hospital. Both had received Article 15-type punishment, but the behavior persisted.

When I got back to my office, I was informed that an American advisor, an NCO, had been bitten by a rat. The NCO had crawled into his bed in the early morning hours after spending the entire weekend on duty and was greeted by a big, probably frightened rat. The rat bit him two times, once on his right foot and once on his left leg below the knee. Before the man could react, the rat was gone. The NCO had been taken to the Navy hospital. Colonel Hamblen asked me to get a report on how the man was doing. I drove over to the hospital and met with the doctor who had seen the soldier in the emergency room. The doctor told me that, as a precaution, he had started the man on rabies vaccine. The doctor said that contracting rabies from a rat bite was rare, which surprised me, but that it had happened on a few known occasions. He decided to go ahead with the vaccine, reasoning that it would be imprudent to take a chance with a man's life. On the way back to my office, I noted that the rain flowers were all gone and recalled that it had been dark and gloomy for the past three or four days. I couldn't help but think that the monsoon season was just around the corner.

***

With only a few exceptions, my travel from Da Nang to other cities throughout I Corps was by air. The roads, for the most part, were unsafe to drive. The risk of ambush was too great, unless traveling in a convoy of vehicles. Practically all air transport was unscheduled. It was catch-as-catch-can and not unusual to get "bumped" at the last minute by a higher-ranking officer or a person with a more urgent flight requirement.

On the morning of 13 September, Major Tu and I flew to Hue on an Air America flight. We dealt with the situation at Nguyen Tri Phuong Hospital and concluded that the hospital commander was correct. The patients had a legitimate complaint. The food was inadequate.

While in Hue, I witnessed a funeral procession that was very moving. Vietnam, during the war years, had a plethora of funny little buses that looked very much like slightly enlarged Volkswagen campers, a vehicle that was popular in the United States in the 1960s and 1970s. Somehow, the Vietnamese managed to jam twenty-five to thirty people into these buses. All the vehicles seemed very old and dilapidated. Most were on their last leg. But, during the war, the Vietnamese continued to repair them, wire and duct tape them together, and somehow make them work. The people desperately needed public transportation during those tragic days. Only the very wealthy had private automobiles. There were no trains. The buses were vital for meeting the transportation needs of the masses.

When people died, their bodies had to somehow be transported to their places of burial. There were no hearses *per se.* The very rich, I was told, hired a professional funeral arranger and that person provided a burial wagon of some sort to transport the remains of the deceased to his or her grave. The poor people either hand-carried the casket, placed it on a bicycle and wheeled it, or hired one of the old, previously mentioned buses to transport the remains of a loved one to the gravesite. On the day I'm writing about, I saw a very elderly man walking slowly in front of a funeral procession, crossing a bridge over the Perfume River in Hue. The old man was carrying a cluster of some type of slow-burning dried vegetation. It did not appear to be the traditional joss sticks that were seen so frequently, but instead a type of reed or weed. The vegetative cluster exuded large quantities of smoke. There were no flames, just smoke.

This old man was followed by an orderly row of five or six mourners. And then came the old, dilapidated bus. Inside were eight women, all veiled and dressed completely in white. They sat four on each side of the wooden casket, which was painted bright red. Candles burned on both sides of the casket. All the women in the bus were weeping. Behind the bus came the remaining mourners. All were wailing or crying softly. This procession wound its way slowly toward the final resting place of the deceased. I took a series of pictures, but they did not turn out well because they were shot from a considerable distance. Out of respect for the deceased and the mourners, I did not want to take a photograph when the procession was at close range.

Later that same day, Major Tu returned to Da Nang, while I flew on to Quang Tri on a USMC Chinook helicopter. When I finished my work at the province hospital in Quang Tri, I got a jeep ride to the airfield at Dong Ha, a small city north of Quang Tri. I had been told that there would be an Air America flight departing Dong Ha for Da Nang at about 1500 hours. That flight was canceled.

It appeared I was going to have to find a ride back to Quang Tri and spend the night with the U.S. Navy MILPHAP team stationed there, when suddenly a Vietnamese Air Force helicopter swooped in and landed. I inquired and was told that the helicopter would be departing shortly for Da Nang and that there was room for another passenger. As I sat there waiting for the flight to depart, I noted that the pilot was wearing a magenta scarf, similar to the one worn by Premier Nguyen Cao Ky when he was in military uniform. I thought to myself, I'm going to be flying with a "hotshot" pilot.

Suddenly, an enlisted crewman gestured for me to get into the helicopter. He pointed to where he wanted me to sit, and I buckled myself in. Just before the blades started to turn for the start-up of the helicopter, a jeep pulled up alongside, and two young women scrambled out and climbed into the cabin of the Huey. They were dressed unlike any that I had seen in my travels throughout I Corps. In fact, I had seen no one similarly dressed since leaving Saigon. Both were wearing white, very short, short shorts, long black mesh stockings, and spiked high-heeled shoes. One was wearing a purple and the other a bright green halter-top. As they giggled and chatted with each other, all I could speculate was that they were the pilot and co-pilot's entertainment for the evening.

Soon the helicopter was airborne and headed for Da Nang. We had just cleared Quang Tri city and were headed along Highway 1, the so-called "Street Without Joy," when trouble erupted. The helicopter was flying very erratically. I looked at the cockpit. It appeared that both the pilot and co-pilot were desperately fighting the controls in attempts to keep the bird in the air. Suddenly, after conferring with the pilot on his headset, the enlisted crew chief unbuckled himself, leaned into the back of the cabin area, and grabbed a can of hydraulic fluid and a can opener with a built-in spout. He punctured the can with the opener, opened the sliding door of the helicopter, and gingerly stepped onto the skids while the helicopter was in full but erratic flight. While holding on for dear life with one hand, he proceeded to pour the hydraulic fluid into the tube leading to the hydraulic fuel reservoir with the other. Almost immediately, the helicopter started flying normally and we proceeded to Da Nang without further difficulty.[3]

***

Early in September, Colonel Hamblen called me to his office and told me in no uncertain terms that I was to become a teacher for the Vietnamese-American Association in their evening continuing education program. I tried to beg off by telling him how much I already had on my plate, but he insisted that I teach for one semester.

I met with my class for the first time on the evening of Tuesday, 13 September. I was provided a copy of a book containing a series of lessons in the subject area of conversational English. There were twenty-six students in the class, fourteen boys or young men and twelve girls or young women. One of the women was twenty-nine years old, but most of the students were between fifteen and twenty years of age. Most spoke very little English, although they were supposedly intermediate English speakers. I had hoped that they would have mastered about 1,000 English words, but such was not the case. It appeared as if most had learned only a couple of hundred words at best, mostly nouns.

Most of the students were very meek, almost bashful. All were very respectful of me, the teacher. The first night of classes was spent by candlelight. Yes, the power in Da Nang was off once again. It seemed strange to be teaching by candlelight, but to the students it seemed commonplace, as if it happened all the time. No one seemed very concerned. A portion of one lesson was on the snows of Mount Everest, and I was looked upon with considerable awe when I revealed to them that I had grown up in the snow and ice of Wisconsin's winters. Overall, I was pleased with how things went on the first night, although a little disappointed at their level of prior learning. I assigned a pretty heavy dose of homework, which seemed to startle them. I asked that they learn sixty additional English nouns and twenty verbs by the next time we were scheduled to meet, which was on Thursday, only two days away.

***

On Wednesday, 14 September, I spent most of a frustrating day trying to understand the vagaries of the medical logistics and blood supply systems at Duy Tan General Hospital. Late in the afternoon, I was scheduled to transport three Vietnamese people to the U.S. Navy Hospital for evaluations, one at the request of our commander, Colonel Hamblen. Unfortunately, one of those needing help did not show up at the prearranged point for pickup. A little boy with a clubfoot, easily operable according to the surgeon, was absent. His parents had promised to have him at the I Corps Headquarters main gate at 1630 hours. Sergeant Thong and I waited thirty minutes and, when they still hadn't arrived, I had Sergeant Thong instruct the gate guards to call my office and leave word with Sp-4 Behner if they showed up later, but no call came. I thought I had convinced the parents that surgery was in the best interests of the child, but I had apparently failed. Later, we found out that a Buddhist sorcerer, with his deck of cards, had convinced the parents that they should not allow the child to be operated on. This bothered me greatly.

The other two persons who were scheduled for evaluations arrived at the prearranged pickup point on time. The first was Madame Truong Thi Tuc, wife of the I Corps Assistant G-3, a mother of seven children, thirty-seven years old. The entire right half of her face was suddenly and inexplicably paralyzed on 24 August. Her hearing was also adversely impacted. Vietnamese doctors had seen her, but were not able to come up with a definitive diagnosis or provide any relief. Colonel Hamblen asked that I take her to a neurologist at the U.S. Navy Hospital for an evaluation. After spending about twenty minutes with Madame Tuc, the doctor stated that without question she had Bell's palsy. The diagnosis, according to the doctor, was clear-cut and unambiguous. She could not wrinkle her forehead, could not wrinkle her nose, could not close her left eye completely, and could not feel any sensation on the left side of her tongue. Apparently, all of these things are classic symptoms of Bell's palsy. According to the neurologist, the chances were about fifty-fifty that the palsy would clear up by itself, perhaps a bit less than fifty-fifty because of her age. Naturally, she was very upset, because the palsy had misshapen her once beautiful face and twisted it to one side. Although it was not as noticeable to others as she imagined, it was terribly discomfiting to her.

The second evaluation was conducted on Miss Nguyen Thi Quang, an eighteen-year-old girl with what had been diagnosed by a Vietnamese doctor as a very advanced cataract in her right eye and a left eye that had a less advanced cataract. Her Vietnamese physician had told Miss Nguyen that her prognosis was poor unless the cataracts could be removed very soon. The operation was deemed beyond the capabilities of the Vietnamese doctor. Upon evaluation by an ophthalmologist at the U.S. Navy Hospital, it was determined that Miss Nguyen had an ulcerated cornea in one eye and a cataract in the other. Sadly, the ulcerated cornea required a replacement cornea. The ophthalmologist patiently explained that corneas were very difficult to come by in Vietnam and that he had no idea where one could be obtained. He then went on to tell her, with the translation assistance of Sergeant Thong, that the eye with the cataract was operable and he would schedule her for surgery as soon as possible. He assured her that she would have normal vision in one eye.

Both patients seemed very appreciative of American efforts to help, as were the elder woman's husband and children and the younger women's parents. Even though the outcomes were not the best, they were both given the priceless gift of hope. The four-year-old child with the clubfoot, however, bothered me all the while I was in Vietnam. I saw him frequently, dragging his foot and walking on his ankle. His parents never relented. I still think of the boy and wonder how his life is now unfolding as a middle-aged adult.

On Thursday evening, 15 September, I met my conversational English class for the second time. When I arrived I was surprised to learn that I had three new students, two younger girls, twelve and thirteen years old, and a Buddhist monk perhaps fifty years old. He had a shaven head and wore a flowing orange robe and sandals. He sat in the front row and stared at me. I knew it was going to be an interesting ten weeks.

During the ten-minute break that occurred half-way through the two-hour session, the director of the continuing education school, Barry Ballow, approached me and told me, much to my chagrin, that I had to accept compensation for my work. He insisted on paying me 200 piastres (about $1.75) per hour for teaching. Mr. Ballow, an American, claimed that experience had taught him that if the students did not pay a nominal fee for their instruction, they were less motivated and more likely to drop out. According to him, when the students paid for a course, they wanted to get their money's worth, so they studied harder. I decided to accept the piastres and donate them to the leprosarium on Marble Mountain.

I was led to believe that the students would know and understand far more English than they actually did. The lesson plans that I was provided were way beyond their capabilities. I had to start pretty much at the bottom rung of the English ladder. This was especially true regarding their understanding of concepts. About all they seemed to grasp were proper nouns, people, places, and things. During the second session, I tried to get them to understand the concept of "comparing one thing to another." I approached it from several different angles. Finally, one student got it and quickly explained it to the other students in their native language. When they finally understood, they all smiled and bowed toward me.

***

On 16 September, I got to my office at about 0430, an hour earlier than usual. I couldn't sleep because of a bad cold, so I decided that, rather than toss and turn in bed, I might as well drive to the office and type a letter to my wife. Just as I was starting to type, a little gecko fell from the ceiling fan onto my desk. Geckos seem to be everywhere in Vietnam, perhaps as they are in most Asian countries. They are an interesting little creature, looking much like a small lizard or salamander. Their normal habitat seemed to be the ceilings and walls of homes and offices. They have a terrific suction apparatus built into the bottoms of their feet, enabling them to cling to the ceiling. They are very fast as they dart about. Most people living in Vietnam, I was told, appreciated having them in their homes because they are living mosquito and fly traps. If you have a gecko in your bedroom, as I did, mosquitoes and flies will not bother you. I noted that the most fashionable restaurants, in both Saigon and Da Nang, seemed to have fifteen or twenty of them running around their walls and ceilings. They were not in the least bit offensive. In fact, I rather enjoyed having the one in my room.

***

Duy Tan General Hospital had a fairly extensive building program about to commence in September 1966. Thirteen new wards were being added, as well as a new mess hall, an incinerator for disposing of medical waste, five new latrines, and a new morgue to replace the one then in use. During the entire afternoon of 16 September, I reviewed the plans and the timeline with Dr. Tu and several of his staff members. At one point during this lengthy session, Dr. Tu asked me to go with him to the morgue so he could graphically explain to me why a change in the plan for the new morgue was necessary.

When we approached the morgue, I noted that the remains of eleven ARVN soldiers were aligned before two altars built into the exterior walls of the morgue. There were nine flag-draped caskets before the Buddhist altar and two before the Christian altar. The smell of incense and burning joss sticks was heavy in the air. A few mourners were squatting before several of the caskets, all draped with the yellow and red flag of the Republic of Vietnam.

As we entered the morgue through a side door, I immediately noted that three men were just starting to prepare a newly arrived corpse for eventual burial. First, the boots of the deceased soldier were unlaced and removed from his feet, and his stockings were taken off. Then, all clothing was either removed intact or cut off using large scissors. The corpse was bathed with soapy water, rinsed with clear water, and then dried with white towels. A burial shroud was then put on. The shroud was snow white and covered the corpse from neck to ankles. The head and the feet were left exposed. The attendants then gently laid the body on a flat pallet in the center of the room and covered it with a white sheet.

A young woman in a white ao dai, apparently the spouse of the deceased soldier, was then invited into the room. Dr. Tu and I respectfully moved to a far corner of the room when the woman entered. She knelt on the floor, removed the sheet covering the deceased's head, and tearfully kissed her husband on the forehead. She grasped his right hand and softly kissed it, then repeated some type of verbal mantra three or four times. After that, she was given several sheets of red crepe paper by one of the attendants. She gently wrapped the red crepe paper around the head of her deceased husband, then got to her feet and, almost reverentially, was ushered from the room.

The attendants then placed the corpse in a red casket. Several large pails of sand were poured into the casket on both sides of the corpse. Lime was liberally sprinkled onto the shrouded corpse and the surrounding sand. The casket was nailed shut and then carried outside and placed before the Buddhist altar.

On the way back to his office, Dr. Tu told me that the sand served two purposes. It prevented shifting of the remains in the casket and also absorbed body fluid seepage. The lime was used to lessen the odor of decaying flesh and to partially control flies, maggots, and other insects. For me, this was a very poignant although sad experience. I thanked Dr. Tu for giving me the opportunity to witness it.

***

The senior U.S. military officer assigned to I Corps during most of my tenure was Lieutenant General Lewis Walt, USMC. He attended the Saturday morning staff meetings quite routinely, although not always.

General Walt wore many hats, among them those of Commanding General of III Marine Amphibious Force, I Corps Coordinator, and Senior Advisor to the commander of I Corps. He and the I Corps Commander, Lieutenant General Hoang Xuan Lam, along with the commander of Advisory Team #1, Colonel Arch Hamblen, were always seated together in the first row of chairs in the briefing room. Each principal staff officer was given an opportunity to brief. General Walt was very interactive with those presenting the briefings. Sometimes he comprehended fully what they had to say, while at other times he sought more in-depth information. Quite often he disagreed with the conclusions of the briefer.

As an officer serving in the relatively low rank of major, I felt privileged to be able to attend these Saturday morning staff meetings at I Corps HQ. Typically, I was among the most junior officers in attendance. Precisely why I was included in these high-level briefings I do not know, but inexplicably I was.

On Saturday morning, 17 September, the I Corps G-2, an ARVN colonel, was presenting the "Intelligence Estimate." He projected vu-graph after vu-graph on the screen in front of the room, showing known and suspected enemy locations, strengths, weaponry, etc., then went on and on about what the enemy—the Viet Cong and the NVA—wanted to do to punish and defeat our forces.

I could tell that General Walt was becoming agitated. He kept asking questions about enemy forces, strengths, morale, equipment, flow of replacements, weaponry, and a host of other topics. The briefer danced around the questions as best he could with the information he had available, but he did not satisfy General Walt.

The briefer kept repeating the same mantra, "This is what the enemy *wants* to do. This is where he *wants* to attack to insure the defeat of our combined forces. We have solid intelligence that tells us that this is what he *wants* to do."

All of a sudden General Walt, an ex-football player at Colorado State University and a bear of a man, exploded. He jumped out of his chair, pointed his large index finger at the Vietnamese colonel presenting the briefing and said, "I don't give a rat's ass what the enemy *wants* to do. I know what he *wants* to do. You're being paid to tell me what he's *capable* of doing. What are his capabilities? If you don't know the answer, sit down and get somebody up there who can give me the information I need." The room went silent. Nobody breathed until General Walt said, "Next briefer."

***

When the Saturday morning staff meeting ended, I returned to my office and found a note that led to a rather interesting and unusual experience. The note stated that a person had called to tell me that Madame La Boq would like to see me at the earliest opportunity. If possible, I was to please come by today. Madame La Boq would be home all day. No need to call in advance. The caller was not Madame La Boq, but an employee in her home.

I recognized the name. Shortly after I arrived in Da Nang, I had attended a reception and was introduced to Mr. La Boq, the French consular officer in Da Nang. He was about sixty-five years old. I found him to be very personable, witty and jovial. In short, during our brief meeting, we hit it off well. But I had had no further contact with him since that meeting.

I obtained the address of the La Boq home and, because Mr. La Boq was a member of the diplomatic community, decided I'd better respond as soon as possible. The La Boq residence was a rather pleasant old French-style villa, one of many in Da Nang. I proceeded through the entry gate to the front door. I was surprised that there was no security. The door was wide open, as were many doors in Vietnam. There was no doorbell or knocker, so I simply called, "Hello," in a rather loud voice. Soon, an English-speaking servant appeared. I introduced myself and explained that Madame La Boq had requested that I stop by the home. The servant asked that I write my name on a slip of paper. I did so and gave it to her. She excused herself, and I continued standing in the entry foyer.

In a moment, who should appear but a striking thirty-five or thirty-six-year-old woman. A very fetching blond, she was wearing a tight-fitting, light blue, jersey top and tight-tight, white slacks. She introduced herself as Madame La Boq and invited me into her formal French sitting room. My surprise must have shown, because the first thing she asked was, "You are surprised by my youth, are you not?" I admitted that I was. She explained that she had "fallen madly in love" with Mr. La Boq, "a dashing diplomat," when she was eighteen years old, talked him into marrying her, and they had lived a very happy and complete life ever since.

She then said that the reason she wanted to see me concerned her husband's health. A Vietnamese friend at Duy Tan Hospital had recommended she talk to me. Her husband had a hernia that was causing him much discomfort, but he refused to have it taken care of because of what he considered to be "inadequate Vietnamese hospitals and surgeons." She asked, "Is there any chance that it can be repaired at the U.S. Navy hospital?" I told her that, while I was uncertain regarding Navy regulations concerning such an operation on a foreign diplomat, I would check it out promptly and let her know the outcome.

She thanked me and, as I got up to leave, asked me, "Would you jeep me up to the French School?" She explained that the nun who taught her six-year-old son had a rule that the children could go "pee pee" only during the break periods, and that her son had wet his pants for the past three days. It was causing him and her much emotional distress, and she felt the need to talk to the teacher. She jumped in the jeep and off we went to the French School.

That whole experience was interesting but disarming. Who would have expected Consular Officer La Boq to have such a young and beautiful wife?

***

On Sunday evening, 18 September, I witnessed a troubling event while on my way to a reception that General and Madame Lam hosted to honor the newly elected members of the constituent assembly. As background, it seemed to me that mental illness and drug addiction went virtually untreated in Vietnam in those days. I suspected that that was probably the case in most third world developing nations.

What I witnessed, however, was both pathetic and tragic. Right in the very heart of Da Nang, at one of its busiest intersections, there was a police stand, a small box about three feet square and eighteen inches high, upon which a policeman stood to direct traffic during busy times of the day. On Sundays, the traffic stand was not manned.

As I approached the intersection in my jeep, I noticed that a large crowd had assembled. A loudspeaker was blaring Vietnamese music into the air for all to hear. Instinctively, I tried to shy away from the intersection, because large crowds could be very dangerous for an unarmed American in an open vehicle. I was considering making a U-turn and going the other way, but there was too much traffic to safely do so.

Suddenly, I noticed the reason for the large crowd. On the traffic stand was a woman who appeared to be about forty years old. She was either mentally ill or high on drugs, I can't be certain which. She was standing on the police stand and slowly dancing to the blaring music while at the same time removing her clothing. By the time I passed through the intersection, she had removed everything on top and was stepping out of her pajama-like bottoms. All that remained on her body was her soiled underwear.

There was no laughter or hilarity. I think everyone recognized how tragic and pathetic the poor woman was, but no one offered help. I considered doing so myself but decided I couldn't risk it because of the obvious danger. I could envision myself parking my jeep, walking to the center of the intersection to try and get her to step down from the stand, only to have her refuse. Soon the crowd would be jeering me for interfering in their internal affairs. And a jeering crowd could quickly degenerate into an angry, anti-American mob. It was difficult for me to drive away without trying to help, but I simply had to do so. Such was life in war-torn Vietnam.

And speaking of Vietnamese music, it is quite different from Western music. During the period leading up to the parliamentary elections, music blared from sound trucks all over the city and in small villages throughout I Corps. I was told that their music is composed using only five discrete notes, whereas western-style music has several more.

The reception hosted by General and Madame Lam was a very nice affair. After all the invited guests passed through a formal receiving line, drinks were served on the patio. After the cocktail hour, the newly elected government officials were introduced one at a time. After each newly elected official was appropriately introduced and applauded, we enjoyed a sumptuous buffet-style meal, heavy on seafood, which I appreciated.

It was heartening for me to hear the generous applause given to the newly elected Montagnard assemblymen. I was told by my counterpart that the Montagnards faced considerable discrimination in Vietnam. They are physically a very small people, considerably darker in color than the typical Vietnamese person. They were fiercely loyal to the Americans during the entire Vietnam War.

As usual at this type of gathering, women were somewhat conspicuous by their absence. I think there were five or six women and about seventy-five men at the event. The women were very deferential to their husbands. They were rarely introduced to anyone and almost never joined in the conversation. The one notable exception was Madame Lam, the general's wife, who was undeniably a very beautiful woman. She interacted freely with those in attendance, in much the same manner as an American woman would do at a reception. She was seemingly liked and respected by all in attendance.

***

On Tuesday, 20 September, my boss, LTC Mabra, departed for Bangkok on a much-needed five-day period of R&R. Just before departing the office for the airport, he told me that I would serve as the acting G-4 senior advisor during his absence. He stated that I was "not to leave Da Nang under any circumstances." Although LTC Mabra had an assistant, Captain Stephens, the officer was so new to the job that he was unaware of many of the logistical balls that were in the air at that time.

Upon receiving this direct order, I immediately called Major Tu, my counterpart, and told him I would not be able to accompany the ARVN preventive medicine team to Lang Vei, near the DMZ and the Laotian border, as previously agreed. I recommended he find an ARVN officer who spoke very good English to accompany the team. I explained that I was very concerned about possible communication problems arising between the ARVN Preventive Medicine Team and the U.S. Marine and Army Special Forces teams operating in the area. The Regional Forces and Popular Forces had a full-scale malaria outbreak going on in Lang Vei and were struggling to contain it. It was seriously degrading their fighting strength and limiting their ability to repel VC and NVA attacks. Major Tu agreed to try to find an officer with the requisite language and interpersonal skills to accomplish this potentially sensitive task. Fortunately, as things turned out, during their work in the area, the ARVN malaria experts had only brief contact with one U.S. Special Forces "A" Team, and there were no problems.

***

On Wednesday, 21 September, I drove to Duy Tan Hospital to see Captain Phat, who had recently returned to Da Nang after an extended period of temporary duty in Saigon. After our business was completed, he unexpectedly asked me to be the judge of a patient art contest. What did I know about art? Each patient in the hospital had been given the opportunity to submit an original piece of work. There were sculptures, paintings, and drawings using many different mediums. One patient's work was exceptional. A psychiatric patient submitted a drawing of a legendary Vietnamese hero named Le Loi, about whom I knew nothing. I declared his drawing to be the overall winner of the contest, and there seemed to be overwhelming consensus that it was a proper choice. Many of the art objects were very good, but his was without doubt the best. I told the young soldier, through Captain Phat, that I thought his work was worthy of hanging in any art gallery in the world. This seemed to please him immensely. He proudly posed as a photographer took his picture with Captain Phat and me standing alongside.

For some unknown reason, hospitalized soldiers seemed to want their pictures taken. They moved in front of the camera whenever I was getting ready to take a photograph. It seemed as though they considered it an honor to be photographed. In fact, most of the peasant people seemed eager to have their pictures taken. This appeared true for people of all ages, except young, unmarried women. They typically hid their faces when a camera appeared. Captain Phat told me that "only the man a young woman intends to marry is supposed to possess a likeness of her." To preclude anyone else having such a likeness, the girl or young woman simply avoided being photographed. I always respected their wishes. The poor, especially young children and elderly men and women, got in front of the camera at every opportunity, as did the injured soldiers in the ARVN hospitals and convalescent centers.

Image 8. Two girls who insisted on having their picture taken with the author

Photo courtesy of the author

On the night of 21 September, I had a rather frightening experience. The Navy Hospital was on the same road as a known VC stronghold near Marble Mountain. At about 1800 hours, I arrived at the Navy hospital to meet with Dr. Giles concerning scheduling two children from Quang Tri Province for surgery. After our meeting, we enjoyed dinner and a couple of drinks. Time slipped away, and soon it was pitch dark. As I drove back along the sandy, unpaved road taking me to the bridge over the Han River, I suddenly had a blowout of a front tire on my jeep. I soon discovered that my lug wrench was missing. In all likelihood it had been stolen. I was all alone out there in an uninhabited no man's land. I didn't want to ruin the wheel by running on the flat, nor did I want to simply abandon my jeep and start walking. It was about a mile to the bridge and a little over a mile back to the Navy Hospital. After about fifteen minutes of anxious waiting, an ambulance from the Navy Hospital came by. I was able to flag down the driver. The lug wrench in the ambulance didn't work on my jeep's wheel. The driver said he had a buddy in the maintenance section of the hospital who could help me. He proceeded to the hospital in the ambulance, and about fifteen minutes later, a sailor showed up with a lug wrench that worked on my jeep. He quickly changed the tire for me. I thanked him profusely and told him I would buy him a beer the next time I was at the hospital. He laughed and soon was on his way back to the hospital. Needless to say, I was greatly relieved when I crossed the bridge over the Han River on my way to the relative safety of my room.

***

Thursday evening, 22 September, I was asked to attend a meeting of the faculty of the Vietnamese-American Association's Continuing Education Center. We met prior to the start of classes. After the short meeting was concluded, we had about fifteen minutes before the evening's classes were to commence. Mr. Ballow asked if we had any questions we wanted addressed. I asked him why so many young girls were asking me if I would give them a ride home in my jeep to meet their parents. I told him that I always refused these requests by telling the girls that I was a married man with a family.

Mr. Ballow laughed out loud and told us that the girls' intentions were completely honorable. He said that in Asia, especially in Vietnam and China, teaching was among the most honorable and respected professions. According to Mr. Ballow, the girls would bring great honor to their families by having their professor come to their private homes to meet with their parents. I felt rather foolish for imagining that it was my charming manner or excellence as a teacher that had provoked the invitations. Barry then asked the other American members of the faculty if they had experienced the same thing. All had. We laughed about our misunderstanding of the girls' intentions. Mr. Ballow encouraged us to accept at least one student's offer just for the experience. One American teacher asked why the boys in their classes never extended similar invitations. Mr. Ballow didn't know the answer to that question.

***

On 23 September, I was shocked by the news that three of the most trusted nurses at Duy Tan General Hospital had been picked up as agents of the Viet Cong. The nurses had been transmitting precise casualty data, KIA as well as WIA, to the VC for months before they were detected. The Viet Cong knew exactly how many officers and non-commissioned officers and soldiers had been killed or wounded, as well as the units from which they came. From these data, they could extrapolate how badly they had hurt the ARVN. The news of these special agents greatly shocked Captain Phat, commander of the hospital. It seemed virtually impossible to know who among the populace was the enemy.

On that same day, we were also informed that the old battleground where Operation Hastings had been fought, just days after I had arrived in country, was once again under attack. Hastings had been the largest operation of the war to that point. On the morning of 23 September, two U.S. Marine companies had been cut off and, with their backs against the

DMZ, their ability to maneuver was severely impaired. The battle raged much of the day and into the night before reinforcements arrived.[4]

I arrived at my office rather late on the morning of Saturday, 24 September. I apparently didn't hear my alarm clock and overslept. As soon as I entered the office, Captain Stephens, LTC Mabra's recently assigned assistant, informed me that I had to brief General Walt on the ARVN medical situation in I Corps at the conclusion of the staff meeting. The meeting was to commence in two hours. I hurried over to Duy Tan Hospital to talk to Major Tu and Captain Phat in order to make sure my facts were in order, then hurried back to my office to type a few notes for the briefing.

When the staff meeting was concluded, and most attendees were excused, General Walt looked at me and said, "All right, you've got fifteen minutes to tell me everything I need to know about the medical situation in I Corps as it impacts the ARVN. Let's go." I did my best not to violate his imposed time limitation, but he asked quite a number of questions, so I went a few minutes over the limit. That was the first time I had ever briefed a three-star general.

I made sure he knew the medical situation in I Corps gave me cause for great concern. In addition to the ARVN hospitals being severely understaffed and full beyond listed capacity, we had a plague outbreak in Da Nang, malaria in epidemic proportions in Lang Vei, malaria throughout Quang Tri Province, and a cholera outbreak in Tam Ky. Additionally, the medical supply pipeline, especially as it related to whole blood and certain pharmaceuticals, presented cause for grave concern. At the end, I highlighted my concern about the number of civilian casualties being generated by the war. General Walt gruffly complimented me on my briefing, then closed by saying, "You're not the only one who loses sleep over civilian casualties." And with that, he shook my hand and hurried out of the classified conference room.

At that time, there was a rumor circulating throughout our advisory group to the effect that General Walt would soon be promoted to four-star level and replace General Westmoreland as the overall U.S. commander in Vietnam. This, of course, proved to be false. I have no idea where that rumor came from, or whether it had any basis in fact, but I was very much aware of the fact that General Walt and General Westmoreland had very divergent views regarding how to prosecute the war. Although I never heard General Walt criticize General Westmoreland by name, I heard him, on multiple occasions, question his strategy for conducting the war.[5]

The morning of 25 September, a Sunday, I attended Mass and then went to my office to see if I had any mail. A rice paper envelope was lying on my desk. In it was an invitation from Madame Lam, the I Corps commander's spouse, inviting me to attend the opening ceremonies of the Mid-Autumn Festival the very next day. I was also asked to assist her and others in distributing gifts to the children of deceased ARVN soldiers gathered from throughout I Corps.

I handed the invitation to my boss, LTC Mabra, who was also in the office checking his mail and said, "Sir, this is getting to be a bit much. If I accept this invitation it will mean an entire afternoon away from my job." As he was reading the invitation, our commander, Colonel Hamblen, poked his head in the door and asked, "What are you two doing in here on a Sunday?" Without saying a word, Colonel Mabra handed him the invitation.

As he was looking at it, I said, "Sir, these invitations are getting to be a bit much. It seems I'm getting more than my fair share."

He looked at me and said, "Stop your whining."

I responded, "Sir, I'm not whining. I'm just concerned that these social events are taking me away from my job. I just don't understand all of this socializing when there's a war going on."

He exploded. "What do you want them to do, hunker down in their homes and adopt a siege mentality? That's the last thing we want. That would spell certain defeat."

I said, "No, sir, that's not what I want, but this is a bit much. It will take me away from my job for almost a half a day. I had things planned."

He calmed down and asked, "Why don't you look upon these invitations as a part of your job and not as an add-on? One of our primary purposes as advisors is to show the Vietnamese people that there is a good life out there awaiting them if only they, with our help, can keep the VC and the NVA away from their throats. We want life to go on normally. Isn't it wonderful that they have the courage to go ahead with some of their cherished customs and traditions even in the face of war? I think it's wonderful and you should too."

I said, "Sir, I hadn't thought of it in that light, but it still seems as if I'm getting more of these invitations than I should. I must admit that I enjoy many of the events, but I'm having guilt feelings because my fellow officers on the advisory team aren't getting nearly as many invitations as I am."

He said, "Get over it. They'll invite whosoever they damned well please." With that he walked out of the office. I dutifully called and accepted Madame Lam's invitation to the Mid-Autumn Festival.

The next morning, Monday, 26 September, there was a handwritten note, sealed in an envelope, from Colonel Hamblen lying on my desk. It simply said that he would attempt to shield me from an excessive number of invitations to social events, but doing so would not be easy. He explained that I was perceived by the Vietnamese to be a part of two professions they respected greatly, medicine and education. He also asked that I try to respond positively to all invitations I received. When I felt it absolutely necessary to turn down an invitation, I was to let him know in advance. He wanted to do everything in his power to maintain a positive relationship between the MACV Advisory Team and the I Corps hierarchy.

On that same Monday morning, the Vietnamese officer whose wife had Bell's palsy came to my office as I was about to leave for lunch to

tell me that his wife was "somewhat improved" and to present me with a
thank-you gift. He gave me a gift-wrapped tablecloth with eight dinner
napkins. It was quite attractive, made of high quality cotton cloth with
a design woven into it, pure white in color. Colonel Mabra was in the
office at the time the gift was presented. After the Vietnamese officer
left the office, I asked Colonel Mabra if I could legitimately keep the gift.
I was concerned about the ethics of accepting it. He promised to check
it out with Colonel Hamblen. I had considered refusing the gift when
it was offered, but thought better of it. It would have been demeaning
for the officer presenting the gift to have it refused. Additionally, the
officer said the gift was from his wife, although she wasn't present. It
was a very thoughtful gift, though unnecessary. Colonel Hamblen told
me to keep the gift, and I did.

That afternoon, I attended the opening event of the Mid-Autumn
Festival. The festival seemed similar to our Halloween. As I understood it,
26 September is always the date of the event, but the celebration seemed
to go on all week long. Why it was called the "Mid-Autumn Festival,"
when it was held in very early autumn, I do not know.

The official hostess, Madame Lam, had acquired a large theater for
the opening event. She filled it with about 3,000 children who had lost
their fathers during the war. Only the children of soldiers who had been
killed in action were invited. The younger children, those six years old
and under, were accompanied by their mothers. About fifty Vietnamese
and American officers and non-commissioned officers were invited to
help Mrs. Lam distribute gifts to the children. I was among that group.

The theater was very ornate. Promptly at 1500 hours, the I Corps
military band started playing and the children started singing. They
ranged in age from two-year-old toddlers to fourteen or fifteen years old.
We were told that there were representatives from every single South
Vietnamese military unit in I Corps.

Madame Lam gave a brief speech in Vietnamese, obviously aimed
at the children, and then the gift giving started. It was organized so

that five children at a time approached each of the fifty gift presenters. Each child received an armful of gifts, at least six or seven in number. It tore at my heart to see the little ones come forward for their gifts. Montagnard children, barefooted and wearing turbans wrapped around their little heads; tiny little black-haired children with fear and gratitude both reflected in their pretty dark eyes. This went on for over an hour, until all the children seated in the lower level of the theater had been given multiple gifts. Then the entertainment began.

The lights in the cavernous theater were totally extinguished. Nothing but the sound of a big drum filled the pitch-dark theater for about two minutes. Suddenly the lights were turned on, and a troop of about twenty men, all very small in stature and quite old, entered via the back door of the theater. Each was wearing a tight white tee shirt, black pants, and a red flowing sash around his waist. Immediately behind them were two men carrying a huge drum made in the shape of a wooden barrel. A man doing a slow, rhythmic dance was beating the drum and dancing at the same time. Then came a big dragon, spitting fire with eyes flashing. I had seen such dragons in pictures, but in reality they were even more colorful than I had assumed. The head of the dragon, with one man inside it, was about twenty feet in circumference. Behind the head came the trailing body, consisting of four or five men completely covered with the silk train. They were good, in fact very good. All their movements seemed perfectly coordinated and designed to excite and shock. The dragon danced ferociously and worked the children into an absolute frenzy.

Eventually, the dragon made its way to the stage of the theater, where it continued its wild dance. Suddenly, a knight in armor stepped out from the curtains and seemingly slew the dragon as the children gasped. But soon the dragon was resurrected. It came back to life and started to dance again. Two men then came onto the stage, each carrying a pole about twenty-five feet long. One end of each pole was placed on the floor, and the other extended toward the ceiling. The poles were distanced about four feet apart. The head of the dragon was then pushed up the space between the two poles by the human chain inside the tail. Soon the head of the dragon was at the very top of the poles, spitting fire, eyes flashing, snarling, growling and glaring down at the children in the theater. The children were howling; they were in an absolute frenzy. Even the toddlers were into it, not in the least fearful of what was going on. The knight in armor then came forward again, swung his mighty sword and cut off a part of the dragon's tail. This infuriated the dragon. He spit fire and screamed at the top of his lungs. Suddenly, his head swooped down, as if to devour the knight. The brave knight, seeing his opportunity, drove his sword into the very depths of the dragon's brain. The dragon was done. The people were saved. Good had prevailed over evil. The theater lights were then extinguished, and the dragon disappeared into the darkness.

After the dragon's demise, more gifts were distributed, this time to those in the balcony of the theater. Eventually, every child left with six or seven gifts—dolls, trucks, airplanes and other toys. I couldn't help but think that in some respects it was sad, a token gesture for the years of loneliness and deprivation that most of the children would probably face. But then again, I thought, it was at least something that would brighten their lives for the moment.

Later, there was more entertainment, Asian dancers and sword dancers. The children, including the toddlers, seemed to love it all. By chance, when it was my turn to present gifts, I had the privilege of giving them to twelve little Montagnard children. I hugged each one of them, as if they were a part of my family. At that moment, I missed my six children more than ever.

***

On the evening of 27 September, I decided to act upon the recommendation of Barry Ballow and accept an invitation, if extended, to meet the parents of one of my students. As soon as class was over, a petite young woman named Phan Thi, about fifteen years old and among the prettiest girls in the class, shyly asked if I would consent to take her home and meet her parents.

I answered, "Yes, I will be most pleased to meet your parents."

She smiled and demurely said, "Thank you." She daintily climbed into the passenger side of my dirty old jeep and within five minutes we were outside her modest French-style home. She was very shy and seemed nervous. I parked the jeep, and as we reached the entryway to her home, the door opened, and her father, a local businessman, met me with a wide grin, a bow, and a handshake. He ushered me into his home and introduced me to his wife. We exchanged pleasantries, they thanked me for my willingness to serve as a "professor" in the Vietnamese-American School. We smiled at each other a lot and spoke briefly about Da Nang, their family, and the school his daughter was attending. They asked about my family, we drank a cup of tea, and the brief meeting was over.

It was as simple as that. It was all over in less than thirty minutes. The young girl disappeared just as soon as we entered the house, and I didn't see her again during the entire visit. I thought it remarkable that the Vietnamese apparently had so much respect for education and the teaching profession that they were willing to go through this ritualistic visit with each new teacher that their children experienced.

***

On 28 September, I was informed by a phone call from the MACV Surgeon's office in Saigon that I needed to go to the Air Base at 1130 hours and pick up a Captain Leonard Schumacher. He was being assigned as the medical advisor to the ARVN 2nd Infantry Division, headquartered in Quang Ngai. Len was a Notre Dame graduate with about nine years in the army, and I was delighted to have him on the team. The position in Quang Ngai had been vacant for almost a month. Why I hadn't received advanced notification of his assignment I do not know. He spent one day in Da Nang getting oriented, and I then arranged transportation for him to get to Quang Ngai.

***

Meanwhile, the Mid-Autumn Festival continued for five or six days. On Thursday evening, 29 September, I had a rather frightening experience related to it. The Continuing Education Center where I taught was right across the street from a soccer stadium. Many of the Autumn Festival celebrations were held there. The stadium was noisy and boisterous. About 20,000 people, seemingly all Vietnamese, jammed the darkened stadium. Most carried lanterns with a burning candle inside. A few carried gasoline torches instead. The rhythmic beat of a drum made it difficult for me to fully concentrate on teaching conversational English. This was especially true when the traditional dragon dance reached its climactic peak. Many of the Vietnamese worked themselves into a frenzy, and when the dragon was slain a deafening cheer arose from the people in the stadium.

There were twelve Americans who taught in the program. Our jeeps were parked inside the Polytechnic High School grounds. A closed metal gate guarded the entryway to the parking lot. When the evening session was over, we went to our jeeps to return to our quarters, but the crowd of people leaving the stadium wouldn't allow us to open the outward-swinging gate. They pressed against it, chanting slogans that we could not understand. The impasse lasted for about thirty minutes. Finally, three ARVN Military Police arrived in three separate jeeps, brandished their weapons, and ordered the crowd to move away from the gate. The MPs then formed a convoy with one MP jeep leading the way and two in the rear, slowly escorting us through the unruly crowd.

I felt very insecure as we inched our way through this sea of people, feeling that all it would take was for one person to throw a rock or jerk one of us out of our jeep and suddenly we would have a full-scale anti-American, anti-Vietnam War riot on our hands. I was very concerned about VC or VC-sympathizers in the crowd, a pretty high likelihood in Da Nang after the Buddhist Uprising. I felt very vulnerable sitting behind the wheel of my jeep. As I slowly made my way through the crowd, numbering in the thousands, I was determined to make eye contact with no one. Fortunately all went well. My concerns were in vain.

***

On the very last night of the Mid-Autumn Festival, several children's parades, each headed by a dragon similar to the one described earlier, were winding their way through the city when I drove back to my room after having dinner at the Officers' Club. I stopped briefly to watch one of them passing through a residential area. The dragon leading the parade stopped at a home and playfully knocked on the front door. An entire family came to the door. The dragon apparently asked for money. The children in the family all pointed to the roof of the home. The dragon looked up, summoned two men with poles as described earlier, got pushed to the roof of the home between the two poles, retrieved the money, came back down, thanked the family, and then proceeded on down the street with hundreds of children following. I discussed this experience with Major Tu and he told me that the people are expected to reward the dragon's performance. Some people put money in the dragon's hand, but the more adventurous placed it on their rooftop in order to watch the dragon go up the poles. I couldn't help but wish I could share some of these experiences with my wife and children.

***

On Saturday, 30 September, I drove to the Da Nang Air Base to pick up and orient two newly assigned U.S. Army physicians, Dr. William Williams and Dr. Janos Voros. Both were recently commissioned and also newly married. They had left Fort Sam Houston and the Basic Officer Course just two weeks prior to arriving in Vietnam. One was assigned to Hue, the other to Quang Ngai. I remember thinking that I could now breathe a little easier knowing that we had medical coverage for members of the MACV Advisory Teams in those two cities. Hue had not had an American physician for several months. The MACV Advisory Team in Hue had relied totally on enlisted corpsmen, many of whom were very good, but the more advanced training and skills of a physician we definitely needed.

By late September, the monsoon rains and winds had started. Daily high temperatures unfortunately still hovered around 100 degrees, making life rather miserable. The strange thing about Vietnam was that, once the rain stopped and the sun came out, even for ten or fifteen minutes, there was dust everywhere, red dust that permeated everything.

The monsoon favored the VC. Our mobility was greatly diminished while his remained essentially the same. Our helicopters and fixed wing aircraft frequently couldn't fly, our jet aircraft were somewhat limited in their effectiveness, and our trucks and tracked vehicles were slowed considerably. But the VC continued to slog along at essentially the same pace. The rains and winds seemingly reduced our combat forces' mobility almost to the level of the enemy. The effectiveness of our superior technology in weapons systems and detection devices was also greatly diminished, putting us at a distinct disadvantage because we relied so heavily on technology. General Walt felt strongly that there would be a major monsoon offensive on the part of the VC and NVA starting almost anytime.

For some unknown reason, there seemed to be a great deal of pessimism concerning the war setting in among the members of our Advisory Team by the end of September 1966. Most seemed to be of the opinion that this was going to be a very long, protracted conflict. There didn't seem to be a way to move it along any faster. The members of Advisory Team #1 were beginning to fully realize that our Communist enemies had hit on something extremely advantageous to them when they decided to fight the type of war that had evolved. It was exceedingly frustrating for American fighting men to not be able to identify friend from foe. The United States had never fought a war even remotely like this in recent times. The closest parallel that I could think of was the war in the Philippines at the turn of the 20th century.

Our two most recent wars, WW II and Korea, had been totally different. In those wars, we fought a uniformed enemy who could readily be identified. Gains could be assessed by territory taken and secured. Those parameters for measuring success didn't work during the Vietnam War. Some Americans felt exceedingly helpless. The day seemed to belong to us, but the night belonged to the enemy. We would fight for a piece of terrain today and relinquish it tomorrow. I couldn't see that we were making much progress. When we were with the people in the villages and hamlets, protecting them and helping them move toward a better life, they loved and respected us. When we moved out, the enemy moved in, and the allegiance of the people rapidly shifted toward the enemy, probably because of fear and intimidation.

Alternative courses of action seemed extremely limited. We didn't have the manpower to establish a presence in all the populated areas of the country. Frustration was setting in. I expressed these feelings to my wife in several letters but always cautioned her to "please keep these thoughts to yourself. They may seem somewhat heretical to some." The truth was I didn't see many good options.

***

On the very last day of September, I experienced an event that was very gratifying. Major Tu had pointed out to me, about ten days prior, an elderly man who lived near Duy Tan Hospital and asked if an American ophthalmologist might take a look at him. He explained that Vietnamese doctors could not help him. The man had had an eye gouged out in some type of accident many years ago. At the time of the accident, he was fitted with a prosthetic eye, but for the past five years, he had been unable to wear it. The ceramic eye irritated the socket so badly, he simply couldn't wear it. Most people avoided eye contact with the man, because the empty socket was so difficult to look at. The man had become somewhat of a social recluse.

I loaded him into my jeep and took him to see Dr. Leonard, an ophthalmologist at the Navy Hospital. After examination, Dr. Leonard told my interpreter to tell the old man that he could fix his problem, but he would need his full cooperation. Upon hearing this, the man smiled and nodded his head repeatedly, his promise to be a good patient. That very day, Dr. Leonard took him into one of the treatment cubicles and performed a relatively simple procedure whereby he removed hardened scar tissue from the eye socket. He then inserted into the empty socket something called a plastic "ellipse." This ellipse was slightly larger than the socket itself, thereby stretching the socket. The man was to wear this ellipse for two weeks, after which time I was to take him back to the hospital, and Dr. Leonard would insert a slightly larger ellipse, which would then stay in place for two or three weeks. This procedure was to repeat itself at least two and maybe three more times. Dr. Leonard told his patient that he was certain that at the end of the process, the prosthetic eye would fit properly in the socket.

Even with the ellipse in place, the man looked much better than he did previously. After the ellipse was inserted, Dr. Leonard gave the man a small mirror. He looked at himself, and a beautiful smile crept over his face. My interpreter told Dr. Leonard that the old man was "most happy."

When I drove him back to his home, I found out just how elated he really was. Typically the Vietnamese were very slow to show even the slightest bit of affection toward spouses in public, but upon seeing his wife, the old man embraced her warmly. He showed her the ellipse and brought her to me where she bowed in gratitude and shook my hand for helping her husband. It was a very poignant moment.

When I left Da Nang, all clinical visits to Dr. Leonard had been completed, and the delighted old man was again proudly wearing his ceramic eye.

CHAPTER 4

OCTOBER 1966

Lang Vei and Khe Sanh are remote mountain villages near the DMZ and the Laotian border, both located in the far northwest corner of South Vietnam. The villages were populated primarily by Montagnards, staunch allies of the United States during the war.

I accompanied Major Tu, the I Corps Surgeon, on a liaison and fact-finding visit to these two villages in early October. When we arrived at Lang Vei by plane, it was nearing lunchtime. We were met by a Montagnard officer in the Regional Force or Popular Force. He approached us, saluted, and asked Major Tu if we would honor their unit by having lunch with them. We accepted the invitation. To do otherwise would have been a social affront.

We entered a small building, presumably their Officers' Club, constructed primarily of bamboo poles and thatched vegetation with a tin roof. There were open spaces for windows but no glass. In the front of this one-room building was a roughly constructed wooden table approximately fifteen feet long and four feet wide. This table, the head table, was facing six or seven smaller tables, each with a few chairs. Seven or eight crudely constructed wooden chairs were sitting along one side of the head table. On the table, in front of each chair, was a barely opaque water glass, a thirty-two-ounce bottle of warm Coca-Cola, a small pitcher of water, and a bottle of whiskey. There was also a not-so-clean dinner plate, knife, spoon, and set of chopsticks.

With considerable elan and a huge smile on his face, our host seated Major Tu and me at the head table. He then gestured at the array of drinks and suggested that we indicate our choices. Knowing that the water was probably not safe, I pointed at the Coca-Cola. Our host barked an instruction, and a diminutive man appeared out of nowhere, removed the cap from the bottle and filled my not-so-clean glass with cola. The same procedure was followed for each of the persons seated at the head table.

When all the glasses were filled, the host got up and proposed a toast to something or someone. Everyone smiled, and we drank. Major Tu then nodded at me, seeming to indicate that it would be appropriate for me to propose a toast. I stood and said simply, "I propose a toast to our good and loyal friends, the brave Montagnard peoples of Vietnam." Major Tu translated my remarks for the assembled group and there were even broader smiles on the Montagnards' faces before the toast was drunk. Each person at the head table eventually proposed a toast. Many in attendance were drinking the whiskey and not the cola or water.

Then, with considerable expectation in the air, the door to the club was opened, and a procession of small Montagnard enlisted men proudly carried the food into the dining room. The first man was carrying what was obviously chicken. I say obvious because the scrawny head and a few neck feathers were still attached to the body of each bird, as were the legs with the feet intact. The second was carrying some type of green vegetable dish, something like collard greens. But the large bowl carried by the third man, especially interested me. Immediately upon seeing it, I thought of my dear mother and a rice pudding she made that my six siblings and I enjoyed immensely while growing up. My mother's rice pudding contained brown sugar and raisins in addition to white steamed rice. The dish the third man was carrying looked exactly like my mother's rice pudding. I was looking forward to tasting it to see if it was similar to hers. But my appetite went away when, with a flourish, the soldier sat the bowl on the table in front of me, and all the "raisins" flew away. The pudding had been covered with flies.

Image 9. Montagnard home in village of Lang Vei

Photo courtesy of the author

On Sunday, 2 October, Da Nang woke up to the dramatic news that the Chief of Surgery at the Naval Support Activity Hospital, Captain Harry Dinsmore (a navy captain rank being equivalent to an army, marine corps or air force colonel), had removed a live sixty millimeter mortar round from inside the body of an ARVN soldier. Dr. Giles told me that the round had hit the soldier in the left shoulder, penetrated the skin, and, for reasons unknown, failed to explode. The young soldier had been medically evacuated off the field of battle and, when he was brought into the Navy hospital, was conscious and holding what looked like a big lump on his left side. When they took an x-ray, they were astounded to see the live mortar round lodged between the soldier's rib cage and skin at the level of the floating ribs.

Dr. Dinsmore cleared the operating room of everyone except a navy operating room nurse, an enlisted demolition expert, and himself. At Dr. Dinsmore's direction, a chest high barrier of sandbags was built around the operating table. Standing behind this barrier, Dr. Dinsmore made a long incision and, with the assistance of the nurse and demolition expert, carefully removed the potentially lethal round from the man's body.

It was a dramatic act, and Dr. Dinsmore and his two assistants deserved the accolades of true heroes. Dr. Giles told me that two or three younger surgeons had offered to remove the round, but Dr. Dinsmore, as the Chief of Surgery, felt the awesome, life-threatening responsibility was his. He was not going to endanger the lives of his subordinates and was adamant in refusing their help. He also took all steps possible to protect the surgical nurse, the demolition expert, and himself by having the sandbag barrier constructed before the surgery commenced. The ARVN soldier not only lived but returned to active duty in the South Vietnamese Army.[1]

On that same Sunday morning, right after Mass and Communion, I took the elderly man with the artificial eye to the hospital to allow the ophthalmologist to see how the elliptical stretching of the eye socket was progressing. As we arrived at the hospital, I noted a large group of people standing in the rain outside one of the Quonset buildings that housed an operating room. It turned out they were mostly news reporters and film crews. There were representatives from *Time*, *Life*, ABC and NBC News, and several foreign news agencies, all clambering for the story about the removal of the live mortar round.

Image 10. X-ray showing live mortar round between the skin and ribcage of
ARVN soldier Nguyen Van Luong

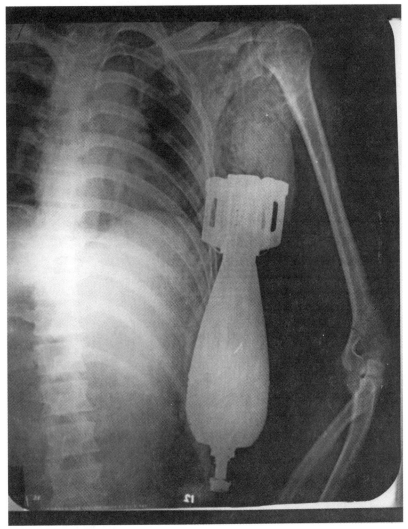

Courtesy of the U.S. Navy Bureau of Medicine and Surgery Archives

Image 11. Captain Harry "Hal" Dinsmore and navy medical colleague with patient after the dramatic surgery

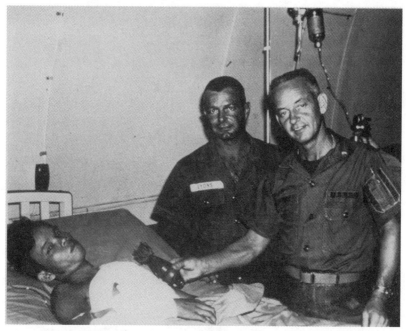

Courtesy of the U.S. Navy Bureau of Medicine and Surgery Archives

In order to get to the Quonset building that housed the ophthalmology clinic, the elderly man and I had to go through the group of reporters and camera crews. A reporter told me that NBC News would have given $20,000 for film footage of the actual operation. Dr. Giles told me that three or four Navy hospital staff members had offered to film the removal of the mortar round, but Dr. Dinsmore had refused. His logic was that it would be senseless and less than ethical to endanger an additional person just for the sake of film footage.

***

Monsoon rains and winds continued to pound Da Nang all Sunday afternoon. Since my hotel was again without electricity, I decided to go to

the Officers' Club in mid-afternoon. The club was busy. I joined a group
of officers at the far end of the bar for a rather raucous dice game called
"horse." There was a great deal of hilarity and good-natured banter, but
then someone brought up General Walt and the problems he seemed to
be having executing the war in I Corps. Almost immediately, the dice
game stopped and the mood turned reflective.

"I wish General Krulak would stay the hell out of the war and let
General Westmoreland run it. Krulak's always butting in and muddying
the water. Poor General Walt doesn't know which way to turn. One
minute he's getting directions from Krulak in Hawaii and the next
minute General Westmoreland is giving him orders from Saigon," said
a lieutenant colonel.

A newly assigned army captain asked, "Who's General Krulak?"

"He's the Commander of Fleet Marine Force, Pacific, headquartered in
Hawaii. Krulak thinks he runs the war in I Corps. He flies to Da Nang,
or summons General Walt to Hawaii, about once a month," answered
the first officer.

"Does he have command authority over General Walt?" asked another.

The first officer said, "I'm not sure, but he sure as hell acts like he does.
The chain of command is somewhat murky.[2] I've heard that Krulak's a
big favorite of President Lyndon Johnson. Rumor has it that the president
finds General Krulak's vision of how to fight the war pretty compelling,
but Secretary McNamara leans more toward General Westmoreland's
strategy. Poor General Walt gets his marching orders from Krulak and
then General Westmoreland steps in and turns them around. Between
the two of them, Westmoreland and Krulak, they've got General Walt's
testicles in a ringer. He doesn't know to whom to respond. Krulak and
Westmoreland both wear four stars and they both give General Walt
directions, and the directions are frequently not compatible. In fact
they're often contradictory. Krulak pushes a strategy of pacification,

while Westmoreland pushes a tactic of search and destroy which amounts to a strategy of attrition."[3]

Someone else chimed in, "Sounds to me as if President Johnson and Secretary McNamara have a command and control problem. If Westmoreland's the overall commander in Vietnam, he should be demanding that Secretary McNamara order General Krulak to butt out."

A major then retorted, "President Johnson and Secretary McNamara better address the problem soon or it will come back to bite them in the ass."

"Krulak's the general who developed the ink blot strategy," added another. "He believes that if you pacify and protect one village, then spread the blot to the adjoining village or hamlet, and then to another and so on you'll eventually pacify and protect the people of an entire region of the country."

"That sounds good in theory, but it takes a lot of time and a lot more manpower than General Walt has available," replied the lieutenant colonel. "In the meantime General Westmoreland keeps pushing his search and destroy tactics and his strategy of attrition. He believes the quickest and least costly way to end the war is by taking the fight to the enemy. Kill as many as possible. Destroy their equipment. Disrupt their lines of supply and communications, find their ammunition caches and destroy them."

"Sounds good if we knew who the enemy was. How the hell do you identify the enemy? He might be a farmer by day, but a Viet Cong fighter or sympathizer by night," quipped a major.

"What a strange war this is," another added.

I then asked, "How many of you support General Westmoreland's strategy on how to fight the war?"

One officer of the seven or eight in the group indicated that he supported the attrition strategy.

"I know this for certain, General Walt does not believe that the war can be won if we rely on search and destroy tactics. He does not believe in a war of attrition. In a recent staff meeting I personally heard him angrily exclaim, 'They want me to go after the enemy more aggressively, to pull my marines out of the villages and hamlets and chase the VC and NVA all over the damned countryside trying to get the VC and NVA to stand and fight. If I do this, everything we've gained will be lost. If those people in Saigon think we can kill our way out of this war, they're wrong,' " I said. "I don't believe that General Walt fully accepts General Krulak's theories either. I think he has serious doubts about the ink blot strategy. But I know this for certain, he firmly believes the war will be lost if we fully adopt search and destroy tactics and a strategy of attrition. The VC and NVA know exactly what's going on. They know the box they've got us in. They purposely try to bait the U.S. Marines and the ARVN into moving into the remote areas, the mountains and jungles, in order to pull them out of the villages and more populated areas. If the Marines and ARVN take the bait the people in the villages are then essentially unprotected. Just a few acts of VC terrorism, the assassination of a popular district chief or the maiming of a defenseless child, would serve to convince the people that they'd better not take sides in the struggle."

Another officer angrily retorted, "That's bullshit! The only way to defeat terrorism is by brute force."

Another interrupted, saying, "I think General Walt is right. There's no way we can kill our way out of this war. They will keep coming at us, and if they run out of manpower they'll throw their women at us, and if they run out of women they'll ask the Chinese for help. I think General Walt is correct. We can't kill our way to victory. We've got to find another way."[4]

And so the argument went during that rainy, windy October day in Da Nang. The only thing we could absolutely agree on was the inescapable fact that the lines of command authority in regard to I Corps were ambiguous at best, and that if President Johnson and Secretary McNamara failed to promptly address the problem it was at our country's peril.

***

While driving to work on Monday morning, 3 October, I was startled by the sound of gunfire. I soon saw what was happening. Several Vietnamese men were in the process of killing a large water buffalo not too far from I Corps Headquarters. They were shooting the poor beast in its belly. I couldn't understand why they didn't just shoot the poor animal in the head and put it out of its misery. I later found out that the animal was probably crazed. Captain Phat told me that there are many instances where a buffalo goes berserk and attacks a person, many times a child. He said a berserk buffalo must be put down.

Despite monsoon rains, Da Nang was exceedingly hot for October. There was again no electricity in my room making conditions somewhat miserable. I got up many mornings soaking wet from perspiration. It was almost eighty degrees at 0515, with high humidity from the constant rain. With no overhead fan to at least circulate the air, I was not in a very good mood upon getting up. Adding to my frustration was the continuing problem with mold and mildew. By happenstance, I looked at my leather belt, hanging along with my clothing on the bamboo pole suspended from the ceiling. It was green with mold as was my only pair of non-military leather shoes sitting in a box on the floor. Everything reeked of mold and mildew, including my clothing.

***

I spent several hours on 3 October wrestling with logistical problems. As the senior medical advisor, I had been taking a lot of heat from the MILPHAP and sub-sector advisory teams over our inability to keep them adequately supplied. They were trying to do their best, but without a reliable stream of medical supplies, it was difficult to provide the indigenous Vietnamese population with the support they so badly needed. Both MEDCAP and MILPHAP were very important programs in the pacification strategy that General Walt was pushing so hard. Without these two programs, the people living in the hamlets, villages, and rural areas had very limited medical support.

The day of Monday, 4 October, was rather hectic and not very productive. Colonel David Eisner, the MACV Surgeon, had arrived for his quarterly visit to I Corps the evening before and was with me all day. I had elaborate plans to take him to Quang Ngai and then to Hoi An, two cities he had expressed interest in visiting. At 0730 hours, our small fixed-wing plane finally took off after a thirty-minute delay because of an intense thunderstorm. We had gotten halfway to Quang Ngai when we started getting buffeted around so badly by a storm that the pilot decided to head out to sea and try and go around it. We got out about forty-five miles, a long way from land for a light aircraft, and still couldn't get around the storm. The pilot then tried to find an opening, but every time we got into the heart of the storm, the little aircraft became almost uncontrollable. The pilot then attempted to get under the storm. He dipped down to about the 100- to 150-foot level, dangerously low in a storm, and was flying along quite well when suddenly, the plane caught a downdraft that almost took us into the water. The pilot finally decided he simply had to abort the flight and return to Da Nang.

When we arrived back in Da Nang, Colonel Eisner asked if he might visit a couple of U.S. medical units while we were waiting for the storm to pass. I scrambled around trying to line up short visits to the U.S. Navy Hospital and the Air Force Casualty Staging Facility at the Da Nang Air Base. As might be imagined, neither unit commander was overly thrilled to accommodate us on such short notice. Both knew full well that Colonel Eisner lived in close proximity to General Westmoreland. Rumor had it that they talked frequently. Naturally, the medical unit commanders would have liked a little more warning before a visit by the MACV Surgeon. Be that as it may, the U.S. Navy Hospital didn't get much warning, twenty minutes at most. I called the hospital from my office and told the person who answered the phone that Colonel Eisner would be on his way to visit the hospital in a few minutes. Both visits went fine, however, and I'm sure when we left the commanders of the two units breathed a sigh of relief.

We then went to the Officers' Club for lunch and, after eating, since it was raining harder than ever, I could see no alternative other than to take Colonel Eisner to my office or to my room to wait out the storm. He opted for my office when I explained how Spartan my room was. Colonel Eisner, LTC Mabra, and I had a pleasant conversation, but accomplished nothing of substance during the hour and a half that we talked. At 1430, the rains subsided, and I was able to line up a helicopter flight to Hoi An. Just as we boarded the helicopter, the monsoon rains started again, preventing our taking off. At about 1500 hours, the pilot was finally able to get the helicopter in the air. Twenty minutes later, we were in Hoi An. The commander of the MILPHAP team gave Colonel Eisner a very comprehensive briefing and tour of the hospital. He also gave him an earful about the lack of medical supplies and maintenance support that the MILPHAP team was receiving.

And so it went during a wet, soggy day when I was striving mightily to execute a "fly by the seat of your pants" contingency plan to replace the primary plan aborted because of bad weather. I was very happy to see Colonel Eisner climb aboard the C-130 at 2230 hours that night, still in a downpour, for the flight back to Saigon. He was thoroughly soaked, tired, and a bit disgruntled, but I had done my damnedest to accommodate his wishes.

***

On the morning of Wednesday, 5 October, I arrived at my office about 0515 hours. Lying on the middle of my desk was a handwritten note that read, "See the staff duty officer immediately." I hurried up to the command suite where the staff duty officer said, "Major Van Straten, an ARVN Airborne Task Force, operating above Dong Ha in Quang Tri Province, got caught in the open last night during heavy monsoon rains and was cut to ribbons by NVA or VC mortars. The mortars rained down on them for several hours and after that there was a ground attack. The ARVN task force apparently has been decimated. Casualties are expected to be very high. As of now, none have been evacuated from the battlefield because of the weather."

I hurried back to my office and tried to call Captain Bob Helton, medical advisor to the ARVN 1st Infantry Division headquartered in Hue. His advisory responsibilities extended throughout Quang Tri and Thua Thien Provinces. Captain Helton was unavailable. I was told that he was on his way to the airport to catch a ride to Dong Ha.

I then went over to my counterpart's office. Major Tu had not yet arrived. While waiting for him, I made several calls to try to get more definitive information about the number of casualties. Casualty estimates were still not available. All that was known for certain was that the Airborne Task Force had not been dug in for the night as they should have been. The enemy had been relentless in dropping mortars on the ARVN paratroopers as they writhed around in the mud trying to escape shrapnel from repeated mortar explosions. When the mortars ceased, the VC or NVA followed up with an immediate ground attack, essentially destroying the Airborne Task Force. Meanwhile, torrential rains continued, making the battlefield a quagmire.

I then started making calls to inquire about the availability of air transport, should the number of casualties overwhelm the system in Quang Tri Province. It didn't look good. All the C-130s seemed to be committed to hauling ammunition and other supplies and shuttling troops into the embattled area.

When Major Tu arrived at his office, I passed on the fragmentary information I had. He and I then went up to the operations center and received an update from the G-3. It was known that casualties were very high, but there were still no firm estimates regarding numbers. It was decided that I would go to Dong Ha, and Major Tu would remain in Da Nang to assist in coordination of the flow of casualties.

At about 1030 hours, I departed Da Nang on a C-130 resupply aircraft headed for Dong Ha. Upon arrival, a scene that could have been taken from *Apocalypse Now* greeted me. The airstrip was absolute bedlam. I found Captain Helton at a landing zone marked by a huge fabric red cross staked to the ground. That marking enabled the pilots of approaching helicopters, carrying the dead and wounded, to pick out the casualty reception LZ as they prepared to land.

Captain Helton gave me a quick rundown on the situation, telling me that he still did not have a good casualty estimate. The process of clearing the battlefield, delayed because of torrential rains, had now begun but was going very slowly. U.S. Marine H-37 helicopters were the primary aircraft being used to evacuate casualties. Occasionally a larger H-46 cargo helicopter was made available to fly a mission. The ARVN 1st Infantry Division, to which the ill-fated Airborne Task Force was attached, had only six or eight H-34 helicopters in its total inventory, and all were being used for troop shuttle and re-supply missions. It was decided that none could be made available for the evacuation of casualties. This decision caused Captain Helton great consternation. He expressed his dissatisfaction openly and repeatedly to ARVN officers who had made the decision.

As Captain Helton and I were talking, a U.S. Marine H-37 helicopter landed on the LZ. When the doors opened, ARVN medics on the ground started off-loading the dead and wounded. The dead were wrapped in their ponchos. The wounded were either lying on a poncho or on the floor of the helicopter. There were no stretchers. As I recall, there were nine or ten dead and ten or eleven seriously wounded ARVN soldiers in the helicopter.

The U.S. Marine pilot must have identified me by the MACV patch and medical caduceus I was wearing. He signaled for me to come over to the window of the cockpit. So as to save precious time, the helicopter was not totally powered down. The rotor was still spinning, and there was considerable noise. The pilot was fuming mad. He screamed at me, "I'll not go back onto that battlefield one more time unless you can get those stupid bastards to give priority to the wounded. I've been out there three times, and each time I end up transporting as many corpses as wounded soldiers. I'll be damned if I'll put my ass on the line to transport the dead off a hot LZ and let the wounded lie in the rain on the battlefield. The wounded yes, I'll go back for them. The dead—no way. Nobody can help them. They can wait. Goddammit, do something about it! You advise the ARVN, don't you? Do something about it."

I could appreciate his comments, for the H-37 was terribly slow and difficult to maneuver, especially when operating on a hot LZ. By this time, the process of off-loading the dead and wounded was over and the pilot was given a signal to take off.

I turned my attention back to Captain Helton. It was his turn to be fuming mad. The number of reporters, camera crews, civilians from the nearby village of Dong Ha, and ARVN and U.S. military officers and non-commissioned officers surrounding the LZ was so great that the helicopters were having difficulty landing. Because of the crush of humanity, ground ambulances couldn't get to the LZ to transport the casualties from the helicopters to the triage and stabilization area. Captain Helton was screaming at the people to get out of the way. He and I actually joined hands and pushed our way through the crowd to clear a path for departing ground ambulances.

At one point, it became so bad that Captain Helton recommended to the ARVN medical company commander that he place an armed guard at the entrance point to the LZ and not let anyone in who was not authorized. The ARVN officer accepted this recommendation, and an armed guard was posted at the entrance to the LZ. Despite the guard, Captain Helton and I continued to fight a losing battle in regards to crowd control for much of the afternoon. The number of people attempting to observe the off-loading and movement of the dead and wounded was so great that lives were being jeopardized.

Captain Helton angrily referred to the large numbers of military officers and non-commissioned officers crowding the LZ as "Saigon Cowboys." He expressed his feeling that many were "desk jockeys" who flew to

Dong Ha from Saigon and Da Nang when reports of the battle started reaching those cities. He said they wanted to "feel as if they were a part of the action."

It then became apparent that many lives were going to be lost unless we could transport large numbers of casualties requiring surgery from Dong Ha to the ARVN hospitals in Hue and Da Nang by a means other than ground ambulance. The distances were too great, the road too dangerous, and the injuries too severe to consider using ground ambulances. We needed air transport support to move the casualties. My counterpart back in Da Nang, Major Tu, and I spent at least an hour on the phone trying to convince South Vietnamese Air Force or USAF officials, or both, of the criticality of C-130 support. We eventually got a commitment that three C-130s would be made available. Bob Helton and I then shifted our attention to coordinating projected flight arrival times with getting the casualties to the loading point on the tarmac. Major Tu was coordinating projected arrival times at the Hue and Da Nang landing points to ensure that the planes could be rapidly off-loaded and the casualties placed in ground ambulances for transport to Tri Phoung Station Hospital in Hue or Duy Tan General Hospital in Da Nang.[5]

I was most thankful that an officer of Captain Helton's ability was on the scene at Dong Ha. Without him, I am convinced the loss of life would have been much greater than it was. He was superb in advising and assisting the ARVN medical authorities and in helping coordinate the movement of casualties resulting from that tragic event.

At about 2145 hours, I boarded a C-130 carrying the last group of casualties to Da Nang. When we landed, I disembarked the aircraft, assured myself that there were adequate personnel and ambulances to transport the casualties to Duy Tan Hospital's operating rooms and wards, and then drove to my hotel. Though I was bone weary, sleep would not come. At about 0200, I got out of bed and ate a candy bar, suddenly realizing that it was my first food in about 18 hours.

I subsequently discussed with several ARVN officers the tendency of the Vietnamese to evacuate the dead before the wounded. Respect for the dead and ancestry worship, they explained, were deeply ingrained in the Vietnamese culture, and especially in those adhering to the Buddhist faith. While the pleas for help from the wounded were heard, the culturally-imposed mandate regarding the dead trumped the requirement to remove the wounded from the battlefield.

Early the next morning, I drove to Duy Tan Hospital to assess the situation with Doctors Tu and Phat. There was still a backlog of wounded soldiers awaiting surgery. Several had died while being transported from Dong Ha to Da Nang, and several more were in critical condition in the hospital's intensive care unit following surgery. Fortunately, it appeared the tactical situation would not generate additional casualties over the weekend. We could all breathe a little easier.

During the I Corps staff meeting the following Saturday morning, an after action briefing was presented. It revealed that three NVA regular battalions had rained mortars on the ARVN Airborne Task Force for three or four consecutive hours. The monsoon rains had rapidly turned the battlefield into a quagmire. All the exposed soldiers could do to try to escape the deadly shrapnel was wallow in the mud. In the first hour of the battle, it was estimated that there were 200-250 ARVN casualties. Help could not be gotten to the unit because of the intensity of the rains and winds.

On Sunday morning, 9 October, it was still raining. I had never in my lifetime seen it rain so hard for such a prolonged period of time. It had rained for at least seven to ten hours during each of the past ten days.

***

Colonel Hamblen asked me to attend a briefing presented by a U.S. Air Force meteorologist at the Da Nang Air Base on Monday, 10 October. The briefing was on the subject of what we could expect during the monsoon. I couldn't believe what I was hearing. He told us that the full fury of the monsoon would not strike for another ten days. There was a high pressure area over China at that time that, when it moved south, would signal the start of about two-and-a-half to three months of rain. The winds would get to about forty knots. It would rain almost every day, sometimes for all of the day. We were also told that it would get much colder, with temperatures occasionally in the low to mid-forties. Because of the winds and the rains, it would feel like the temperatures were in the high twenties to low thirties. I knew without question that under these conditions, the tactical advantage would shift to the VC and the NVA. I dutifully passed the meteorologist's information on to our commander and to anyone else who would listen.

***

My fellow advisors and I relied on one-day laundry service, but now it was taking three days and sometimes four days. Our uniforms simply would not dry. The poor maids squeezed as much water out of our clothing as they possibly could with their hands, then hung them all over the hotel, but the humidity was so high that they would not dry. Everything came back smelling slightly of mildew or mold.

On 11 October, I received a newspaper clipping from my mother, taken from a Seymour, Wisconsin, newspaper, informing me that the Seymour Jaycees had honored my old high school friend, Air Force Captain Duane Miller. I was pleased and happy for him. As an HU-16 Albatross pilot, his job was to rescue downed pilots, usually from the South China Sea. He flew his aircraft over water most of the time and any malfunction could be perilous. While all flying in combat carried its risks, this was especially true of medical evacuation flights. It was reported in the I Corps staff meeting that during the month of September 1966, medevac flights constituted 7.5 percent of all helicopter flight time in I Corps, but those same flights accounted for 46 percent of all downed helicopters in the entire corps area. It was a dangerous job.

***

On the way to my office on 12 October, I noted a group of women wading in a pond that was covered with green algae. They were carefully dipping out the algae with woven baskets. I had noticed this activity before. Later that day, I asked Major Tu what was going on. He told me that algae was eaten in Vietnam. He said it was quite tasty and an excellent source of protein. The algae seemed to replenish itself almost overnight. I made a mental note to some day sample it.

On that same day, I received a letter from my wife chastising me for not telling her that I had been in a helicopter that had been hit by ground fire. She was partially incorrect. It was not a helicopter but a fixed wing aircraft that had been hit. Upon reading that part of her letter, however, I couldn't help but wonder how she had received that information, because I thought I had withheld it.

The letter went on to explain that I had sent her two boxes of thirty-five millimeter slides, and in one of the boxes were two pictures of a bullet hole in the roof of an aircraft. My wife added that she "had a premonition" that I was a passenger in that plane. I had meant to remove those two slides before sending the rest but had forgotten. The bullet hole was in the roof of the cockpit of an Air America C-45. I had been in the co-pilot's seat when we were landing at Quang Ngai, always a dangerous airport. The round tore through the floor of the cockpit as we were in the final approach for landing, right between the pilot and me. We were very lucky. The bullet passed through the pilot's flight manuals, then through the roof, but we were untouched. I whispered a silent prayer.

On Thursday, 13 October, Secretary of Defense McNamara was in I Corps HQ for a part of the morning.[6] He flew from Da Nang to Dong Ha later that same morning. We were informed that he was in I Corps to review a request from General Walt that he be given more manpower. There was great concern that the VC and NVA were massing their forces in the northern part of Quang Tri Province, between Dong Ha and the DMZ, for an all-out assault on the city of Quang Tri. The feeling was that the enemy badly needed a significant victory. Taking and holding Quang Tri City, according to intelligence reports, was their objective. After Secretary McNamara departed, I heard a rumor that a U.S. Army division would soon be moving into the southern part of I Corps to free up the marines to move farther north. This rumor proved to be accurate. A few months later, it was announced that the U.S. Army 23rd Infantry Division, also known as the Americal Division, would move into the Chu Lai area.

While Secretary McNamara was in I Corps HQ, I was summoned for a medical emergency that occurred in an office near mine. Colonel Cach, the Vietnamese Civil Affairs Officer, known in the military as the G-5, had collapsed at his desk. He was forty-six years old, a nice man, hard working, married, nine children, and very, very nervous. Right after he fell, he vomited a large amount of red blood. I was almost certain he had a perforated ulcer. His blood pressure was dangerously low. I read it at fifty-five over thirty-three. I thought he was very close to going into shock. I asked that he be transported to Duy Tan General Hospital as quickly as possible. While he was on his way, I called Captain Phat to alert him about his condition and expected arrival time. I couldn't help but reflect on how much faith the officers in our HQ, both American and Vietnamese, had in my very limited medical abilities. To them I was always known as "Doc."

***

During the afternoon of 13 October, while in a small coastal village near Da Nang, I witnessed yet another water buffalo being put down. The poor animal had been shot several times and staggered all over the street before finally collapsing onto its front knees. The beast was frothing at the mouth and throwing its head around wildly. Some of the Vietnamese, not the majority, seemed to get a weird sense of pleasure out of watching the animal suffer. It nauseated me. The pleasure the few experienced was probably somewhat similar to that experienced by persons who cheer at a dogfight as one dog tears into the flesh of another, or at cockfight when one angry rooster destroys another.

Another example of this seemingly perverse sort of pleasure involved the trapping of rats. I witnessed that which I'm about to describe on three or four occasions while in Vietnam. A box consisting of a wooden frame covered by wire mesh was constructed with a built-in trap door. The box was then baited. When the unwary rat entered the box through the door to get at the bait, the trap door slammed shut. Then, instead of simply killing the captured rat quickly, some of the trappers would pour gasoline on the poor creature, throw a lighted match at it, and then gleefully watch the immolation. Sometimes, crowds of people gathered for "the burning." I didn't like it one bit, but the only way I could demonstrate my disapproval was by shaking my head disgustedly and walking away. The bystanders seemed to get the message.

On the evening of 13 October, I was invited to a dinner party hosted by Dr. Tu. It was held in an upscale downtown restaurant, so I had to again go through the cumbersome procedure of getting my commander's approval and then notifying the Military Police of the event. Our party of about twelve persons was seated at a big round table. While we awaited the arrival of our food, an American construction worker walked into the restaurant holding the hand of a little eight- or nine-year-old Vietnamese girl. The American was not in the military. He probably worked for RMK-BRJ, a huge conglomerate of U.S. construction companies that did work under contract with the Department of Defense.[7] There were hundreds, maybe thousands, of such workers in Da Nang. They made a handsome wage, over $1,000 per month, all of which was tax-free. In addition, their lodging and food were provided at no cost.

A lower-ranking U.S. Marine, by contrast, was paid only about $150 a month. There was always tension between the enlisted marines and the construction workers, and sometimes fights broke out. The construction workers were allowed free reign of the city, whereas marines were restricted from entering any place of business. The marines were laying their lives on the line daily. Construction workers were not. It was easy to see why there was tension between the two groups. I report this only as background information.

The worker that I am about to describe was perhaps forty-five years old and had a bad case of what I diagnosed as "laps disease," the condition in which the belly laps over the belt. He was unkempt, loud, and at least moderately under the influence of alcohol. The little girl, the only child in the restaurant, was dressed in a brand new blue silk dress that was at least three sizes too large for her. It hung almost to the floor. She was wearing shoes with moderately high heels, totally inappropriate for her age. Upon observation, it became apparent that the little girl was severely retarded. It appeared to the members of our dinner party as though the worker had taken pity on her and was attempting to help her, probably buying her the large dress and inappropriate shoes she was wearing.

In all likelihood, according to the Vietnamese officers I was with, she was an abandoned child living on the streets before meeting the man who befriended her. The man and girl were seated at a table, a rather unusual couple in the upscale restaurant. He ordered from the menu for both of them. A glass of cola was soon placed before the young girl and a bottle of beer and a glass before him. In her attempts to take a drink, the little girl lost control of the glass and spilled the soda all over the front of her new dress. The waiter bustled around with a napkin trying to soak up the soda. Eventually, their food arrived, but the little girl absolutely refused to take a single bite. The man got angry and slapped her across the face. She started to cry, and soon there were several wait staff members around the table trying to settle things down. Incredibly, they seemed to be paying far more attention to the man than to the child. She was more or less ignored by the waiters. I'm not sure what the dynamics were, but it bothered me greatly to observe what was going on. Eventually the man and little girl left the restaurant, but to this day I occasionally think of the child and wonder what eventually happened to her.

***

I always enjoyed sitting on our hotel balcony and watching the activity on the street below. Asian stick music frequently filled the air and always intrigued me. Although I had occasionally experienced this type of music prior to going to Vietnam, while in Da Nang I listened to it frequently. A man or a boy always seemed to be the musician. I never witnessed a woman or girl playing the bamboo sticks. The music was produced by two heavy pieces of bamboo, each about seven to eight inches in length, one held in each hand. The musician simply banged them together at different angles and intensity. The partially hollow bamboo then filled the air with musical sounds. The musical sticks could be heard from considerable distances, at least a couple of city blocks. The sound was somewhat eerie, but in a pleasant sort of way. Sometimes, the musicians sang along with the rhythmic knock-knock of the sticks. Little boys were frequently seen playing them while walking along the street. Occasionally, merchants used them in attempts to call attention to their wares.

Bread salesmen, usually young boys, were also amusing to watch. Each salesman had a large burlap bag with an attached strap that went over the shoulder of the salesman. The bag was full of hot, French-style breads that were absolutely delicious. As the salesmen wove their way through the crowds of people on the sidewalks, they repeatedly sang something at the top of their lungs that sounded like "chooie hooie." The sound of their voices rose and fell and filled the air with an unmistakable sound. From our hotel balcony, we could hear the bread sellers coming for at least five minutes before they actually arrived in front of our hotel. We frequently watched them from the balcony and sometimes went down to the street and bought a loaf of bread.

***

On 14 October, I received a distressing letter from my wife informing me that once again our fragile baby son had developed a very bad cold. I immediately fired off a letter cautioning her to be careful. If he started running even a low-grade fever, I wrote, "get him to see a pediatrician as quickly as you can. We simply can't take a chance on yet another bout with pneumonia." As I walked the letter to the mail drop, I couldn't help but think how futile my cautionary remarks were, as it would take the letter a minimum of five to six days to reach my wife.

***

By mid-October, malaria was seriously eroding the strength of several ARVN battalions operating in I Corps. The fighting effectiveness of these battalions was heavily impacted. Through my reference book on tropical diseases, I learned that Vivax malaria had been largely eliminated through World Health Organization measures. Falciparum malaria, however, was running wild in I Corps. There really wasn't much that the ARVN preventive medicine people could do to slow it down beyond what they were already doing. The mosquito that transmitted falciparum malaria was present in large numbers, and it simply was not feasible to spray all of Vietnam. The human reservoir was present, people who had had the disease and now carried it in their bodies, and it was impossible to treat all human carriers. They probably numbered in the hundreds of thousands.

Consequently, the only thing that could be done was to try to keep healthy soldiers from being bitten by mosquitoes. Repellant sprays, netting over beds, clothing with long sleeves, and tucked-in pant legs were all measures employed and emphasized, but maximizing the effectiveness of these controls depended on troop discipline. The ARVN also pushed the use of chloroquine-primaquine, a preventive drug that was reasonably effective. In early October, one ARVN battalion in I Corps had 235 of its 500 soldiers incapacitated by malaria. I took a lot of heat from my commander about those high rates of malaria, but was rather helpless to do anything about it.

Also in mid-October, the big bombers, the B-52s, repeatedly pounded the area a few miles south of Marble Mountain. At times, the war seemed so far away from the city of Da Nang, but at other times it was so very close. Every time I saw a flash of light, followed by a slight delay, and then heard an explosion, I thought of my conversation with Major Joe Lutz on the rooftop restaurant of a Saigon hotel about Arc Light bombing. I couldn't help but wonder how many innocents the bombs killed or maimed. I knew in my heart that that was not the way I was supposed to think, but I had no control over the thoughts that entered my consciousness.[8]

***

I have reflected on the experiences I'm about to describe many times during the past forty-nine years, and I simply do not understand them. All I can speculate is that deep-seated cultural difference caused wounded soldiers from different countries and cultures to react in widely diverse manners.

During the period from the beginning of September to mid-October 1966, I witnessed five situations wherein large numbers of casualties, fifteen or more, arrived at a hospital within a fifteen-minute period. I saw this on two occasions at the ARVN Duy Tan General Hospital in Da Nang, once at the ARVN Nguyen Tri Phuong Station Hospital in Hue, and twice at the U.S. Naval Support Activity Hospital in Da Nang. The casualty reception, assessment and initial treatment processes were essentially the same at all three hospitals.

However, I was struck by the vast differences manifested in the behavior of the wounded. While the severity of the wounds among the U.S. Marines and ARVN soldiers seemed very similar, the reactions of the wounded were vastly different.

Wounded ARVN soldiers spoke virtually not at all. Their behavior could best be described as stoic. The noise level in the large room where casualties were assessed and treatment initiated was very low; in fact, it seemed to me almost eerily so. Physicians, nurses, and technicians moved about the room in the processes of removing all ammunition from the casualties, taking off boots and clothing, assessing the extent and severity of the injuries, taking the vital signs, starting IVs, administering medications for pain, treating for shock, stopping bleeding, insuring airways were open, initiating medical records, making decisions about the urgency of surgery, ordering x-rays, and discussing treatment options almost silently. All these important procedures proceeded quietly and without much interaction with the patients. There was an occasional question addressed to a patient, but most of the interaction was one health care provider talking to another in a low voice. While all of this was going on, the patients themselves were relatively still and relatively quiet. The noise level in the room could perhaps best be described as subdued. There was the limited conversation between health care providers, coupled with low-intensity painful moaning on the part of the patients. Most were relatively still, although there was some writhing and gritting of teeth because of intense pain.

To compare and contrast the above-described Vietnamese casualty reception area with American casualties I witnessed at the Naval Support Activity Hospital is like comparing night with day.

The noise level in the casualty reception and triage area of the American hospital was extremely high. Some wounded marines and navy corpsmen were praying, begging God for help. Others were asking for their mothers. A few were swearing at the doctors and nurses. Many were pleading for help. "Help me, help me," was heard frequently, as were prayers to Jesus and his Blessed Mother. Practically all the marines, except those who were unconscious, were loudly vocal. Additionally, many were writhing around on the treatment table or stretcher, and some were trying to get off their stretchers, making it difficult to take vital signs and initiate IVs. Many of the health care providers were actively communicating with the patients, unlike the providers in the two Vietnamese hospitals.

To this day, I do not understand the vast differences that manifested themselves in the described settings. All I can attribute them to are the very different cultures in which the wounded were born and raised.

***

After the I Corps staff meeting on Saturday morning, 15 October, I had to hurry down to the MACV Officers' Club for a luncheon meeting with a Mr. McMahon, the U.S. Agency for International Development's advisor for civilian law enforcement. Colonel Hamblen had asked that I serve as our advisory team's representative on a committee Mr. McMahon headed. He was working on a plan to initiate a Disciplinary Control Board for I Corps. He explained that it was anticipated that some of the cities in the I Corps area would be placed "on limits" in the near future. This meant that American servicemen and women would, in certain cities, be able to go into the business districts, eat in the restaurants, drink in the bars, shop in the stores, and so on. If and when that happened, we had to be ready, and a Disciplinary Control Board would become a necessity.

This board would have the authority—the power, if you will—to declare certain business establishments "off limits." This would enable U.S. military authorities to exert at least a modicum of control over vices such as prostitution, gambling, illegal drugs, price gouging, and many other things. The threat of placing an establishment off limits, it was thought, would cause a lot of businesses to clean up their acts. They knew, it was thought, that doing business with marines and sailors could be very lucrative, so they would be willing to modify their practices in order to stay in the good graces of the Disciplinary Control Board.

***

While in Quang Ngai on Monday, 17 October, I had a very sad and unusual experience. I was at the Quang Ngai Province Hospital to discuss ongoing supply and maintenance problems that the MILPHAP team was experiencing. As I was walking through one of the crowded wards with the American commander of the MILPHAP team, he discreetly pointed out a twenty-year-old girl who was dying. He told me that, at best, she had only a few hours of life left. As we walked past her bed, she wanly smiled, so I returned her smile. I then stopped by her bedside. Through an interpreter, I told her that she was a very lovely and courageous woman. She thanked me and said she was grateful for my comment. She then went on to tell me that she was dying, but she was not afraid. She was ready to die. I raised my hands in a prayerful gesture, and we parted. About an hour later, I had to return to the same ward to talk to one of the technicians and look at a defective piece of equipment. As I passed the young woman's bed, she reached up her hands to me. I stopped and took her hands in mine. She said something that obviously was very important to her, but I'll never know what it was, for the interpreter was not with me and the American technician spoke only a few words of Vietnamese.

She died peacefully as we stood at her bedside. I'll never know what she was trying to communicate to me, but I think about it often.

Later that same day, after I had returned to Da Nang, I happened to see a little boy with a harelip playing with a group of children alongside his school. School was over for the day. Rather boldly, I entered the school seeking a teacher who spoke English. I found one, and together we walked onto the playground. I pointed out the boy and asked if she thought his parents would consent to an operation to repair his abnormality. The teacher told me that the boy's family lived near the school and that she would be willing to go with me to the home and serve as an interpreter. She got into my jeep, and we drove to the home. The mother was there alone. At first she seemed very uneasy about having an American soldier in her home, but the teacher was able to calm her. The teacher then communicated the purpose of our visit, and, surprisingly, the mother told me to return that very evening when her husband would be home from work.

At 1900 hours that evening, Sergeant Thong and I went back to the home. Within about twenty minutes, Sergeant Thong and I were able to convince the mother and father that it was in the best interests of the eight-year-old child to go ahead with the surgery. They were naturally concerned about the risks. I told them that, while there were risks related to general anesthesia and post-operative infection, they were low. Sergeant Thong and I were always pleased when these efforts to help turned out well. He seemed to have as much emotional capital in a successful outcome as did I.

***

I always marveled at the young entrepreneurs in Da Nang. On the way to my office, I had to pass by several roadside ponds. On the afternoon of 18 October, I noted that a young man had set up a car and truck washing business adjacent to one of the ponds. He had a small gas engine attached to and powering a pump with a long hose. He was working on a jeep as I passed, and there was another waiting. He had a big smile on his face as he stood before his hand-lettered sign that read: WASH JEEP FOR SELL—FAST—VERY CHEAPER. He probably made a decent living during the duration of the war.

That evening, I was back in the classroom after a week's absence because of yet another Vietnamese holiday. I was having great difficulty getting the students to understand certain abstract concepts such as: 1) accurate, 2) serious, and 3) lonely. To ascertain whether they understood, I asked questions and had them write their answers on the chalk board.

I asked, "Are you lonely?" Twenty-six of the thirty-two students wrote, "Yes, I be lonely" or something similar. Then I asked, "Why are you lonely?" One wrote, "I lonely because I alone. Parents live in Hanoi." Another wrote, "I lonely because wife die three years ago." Clearly, those two understood the concept of loneliness. But another answered, "I lonely because I do not have much money." And yet another wrote, "I be lonely because I have very nice friend." I found out that teaching was challenging but, although mentally fatiguing, also emotionally rewarding.

Classes that evening had to be dismissed at 2000 hours because of the rain. It wasn't the rain, *per se*, but rather the accompanying noise. The downpour pounded on the metal roof and sides of the building so hard and so relentlessly that no one could hear. It was impossible for the students to hear me, and even more difficult for me to hear them because so many of them, especially the females, were soft spoken. When I left the classroom that evening, it was raining so hard that I had great difficulty navigating. Finding my hotel was a challenge.

During the two-mile drive to my room, I found out how little my jeep protected me from the weather. It didn't have side curtains or doors. By the time I got home from school, my trousers were absolutely soaked, and I had to pour water out of my boots. To make matters worse, there was zero chance of drying out my boots before I had to wear them again. I only had two pairs, so I rotated on a daily basis during the entire monsoon season, But neither pair ever completely dried out during that two-and-a-half-month period. I constantly had to guard against mold and mildew, which developed very quickly. The U.S. Air Force meteorologist put out a statement on the Armed Forces Radio Network to the effect that the monsoon in the northern part of South Vietnam was far more intense than that encountered in Saigon and the Delta. The monsoon for those living in Saigon and the delta region was already over, whereas ours was just beginning in October. Theirs was known as a southwester, ours as a northwester.

I saw some very unusual rain gear during the monsoon. Perhaps the most notable was that worn by the very poor, who wove a cape out of rice straw. It looked just like a thatched roof, and surprisingly it seemed to shed most of the water. Many homes in Da Nang were standing in water on the morning of 19 October. I marveled that the poor had the courage and tenacity to face the monsoon season year after year. I couldn't help but think of the soldiers and marines in combat units who were out in the weather much of the time. I had great empathy for them, and I must admit that I sometimes felt guilty when I saw them coming in after an operation just caked in mud. Compared to them, my life was easy. Compared to the average citizen in the United States, it was not. While many of my friends at home were looking forward to a big weekend of football and partying, I looked forward to trying to dry out my boots. Sometimes life didn't seem fair.

Colonel Hamblen called me up to his office on 20 October and told me that Madame Lam, General Lam's wife, had requested an English tutor and that my name was being forwarded to General Lam for his approval. I voiced my displeasure and asked Colonel Hamblen to please withdraw my name. I reminded him that I was already teaching two nights a week for the Vietnamese-American Association. Reluctantly, he agreed to withdraw my name. I was off the hook.

***

I spent a part of 21 October in Phu Bai with an ARVN preventive medicine officer. The ARVN had a training center near Phu Bai where the trainees were having continuing problems with dysentery. When we

landed at the small airport, I chuckled over the U.S. Marines' active sense
of humor. Right alongside the runway, they had posted a highly visible
sign with an arrow pointing toward the United States. Under the arrow,
printed in bold lettering, was the following: CHICAGO — 10,657 MILES.

The return trip was a rough one. When we were about thirty miles
from Da Nang, we got caught in a severe monsoon squall that really gave
us a ride. The pilot headed out to sea, but couldn't get around it. Next,
he tried to duck under it, but to no avail. Finally, he had no recourse
other than crashing right through it, because the weather behind us
was worsening by the minute. Several people got airsick during the
flight. Flying was becoming more and more problematic as the monsoon
intensified. I knew that my time away from Da Nang was going to be
seriously curtailed by the weather.

***

I was always amused by the manner in which animals were transported
around the country or to market. Transportation in Vietnam was in very
short supply. All public transportation was typically very crowded. The
small passenger buses that scurried around the country on all available
roads also carried animals, especially squawking chickens and hogs. Pork
and chicken were two staples of the Vietnamese diet, a primary source
of protein. Both were transported to market in baskets. The baskets were
frequently placed inside or on top of buses. At other times, a person,
usually a woman, carried as many as twenty to thirty chickens to market
in two baskets, one basket at each end of her don ganh. Pigs, on the other
hand, were somehow coaxed into oblong woven baskets approximating
their own size. All movement of the pig was restricted by the woven
basket. For reasons unknown, the pigs seemed content in these baskets.
They struggled very little. They became placid, almost as if anesthetized.
I frequently saw pigs, each in its own basket, being pulled to market in a
cart or wagon. I also saw baskets containing chickens and pigs strapped
onto the back of bicycles or cyclo for their ride to market.

***

Vietnam never seemed to sleep. No matter what time I left my room to drive to my office, there was abundant activity in the streets of Da Nang. On the morning of 22 October, I left my room at about 0430 hours, and there were kids everywhere. They were playing in all available sheltered places, anywhere they could get out of the rain. It was rather discomfiting to see so many children playing at such an early hour. A combination of the driving rain, the darkness, the children's lack of clothing—many of them were completely nude—and the indecipherable games they were playing gave me a rather uneasy feeling.

The war raged on. When I got to my office at about 0450 hours, hoping to complete several required reports before the Saturday morning staff meeting, I got word that an ARVN battalion had been shot up pretty badly during the night. About fifty-five to sixty casualties were being prepared for evacuation to Duy Tan Hospital and would arrive later that morning. I felt the need to drive to Duy Tan and see if I could be of assistance in preparing for the arrival of the casualties. It was imperative that they marshal as much ground transportation as possible to meet the aircraft when it landed at the Da Nang Air Base, as the ARVN were under strict orders to minimize the off-load and ground time for the aircraft. My reports for the Saigon bureaucracy had to be set aside for yet another day.

I worked with the staff at Duy Tan until about 0830 hours then returned to I Corps HQ for the morning staff meeting. General Walt came into the meeting wearing a poncho for protection from the pounding rain. He also wore a sour disposition. Based on his comments, I perceived that his relationship with General Westmoreland was worsening by the day. He railed on about the strategy of attrition that was being "pushed down his throat." I couldn't help but agree with him. Based on everything I read, coupled with what was said by the ARVN officers and influential Vietnamese civilians I had talked to, I simply could not envision the North Vietnamese leadership being willing to capitulate because of heavy losses of men and equipment. The VC and NVA seemed resolved to stay in the fight for the long haul. I was also well aware that the collective psyche of the American public was such that high casualty rates and lack of discernable progress would rapidly turn the American people against the war.

***

I always had great difficulty reconciling the Vietnamese matter-of-fact approach to death. In trying to understand the dynamic of what was going on in their minds, all I could conclude was that they had lived with the specter and nearness of death for so long, they were conditioned to accept it as a normal and frequent happening. On the way back to my office after lunch on 22 October, I saw an example of what I'm describing. I was stopped at an intersection to allow an ARVN convoy to pass. The wait was perhaps five minutes in length. I watched a man, absolutely drenched by the lashing rains, walk to an area where caskets were sold under a canvas awning. He picked out a small red casket, about three feet long, paid for it, placed it on his shoulder, and walked away. He walked about 100 feet when he spotted two people I assumed to be friends. He sat the casket down, and the three people huddled under a canvas awning, smoking cigarettes and chatting amiably, frequently smiling and laughing as if nothing untoward had happened.

Image 12. Vietnamese man transporting empty casket on his bicycle

Photo courtesy of the author

Although I of course did not know who the small casket was for, I assumed it was for one of his children who had died during the night. It all seemed so matter-of-fact and emotionless. I couldn't even imagine myself in similar circumstances. I'd be overcome by grief if I had to carry a coffin to my home for one of my children. But in Vietnam during the war, death was very commonplace. I estimated that one of every twenty adults on the streets of Da Nang was wearing a swatch of black cloth somewhere on his or her clothing, a symbol of mourning. And yet life went on, seemingly in near-normal fashion.

On Sunday morning, 23 October, I was surprised when three Vietnamese families attended Mass in our MACV all-faiths chapel. It seemed so good to see families worshipping together. All the little kids were barefooted, and I couldn't help but notice that several of them had open sores on their heads. The scabies problem was a very real one. Many little children, girls and boys alike, especially children of the poor, had their heads shaved to get some relief from the ever-present itch mites and head lice.

Several of the children entered the chapel wearing conical straw hats, commonly called coolie hats by the Americans, to ward off the rain. Laborers and many of the poor also wore them, usually to protect themselves from the sun. I was very surprised when one of the children held his hat up toward the overhead lights. A design or picture was woven into the straw. Some types of straw apparently admitted light, whereas others did not. The Vietnamese craftsmen had woven into the hats pictures or geometric designs that could only be seen if the hat were held up to the light. I found the pictures and designs to be quite artistic.

Monday morning, 24 October, it was not raining. I even saw small patches of blue in the sky as I awaited a helicopter ride to Tam Ky. I knew the Vietnamese, especially the poor, were extremely grateful for the brief respite from being drenched.

The visit to Tam Ky was rather depressing. The Quang Tin Province Hospital located there was not one of the better Vietnamese public hospitals. It had many problems. Bubonic plague had not subsided as had been expected. There were eleven new cases reported on the day of my visit. They had fifty-three cases of plague on their wards. The wards were all in tents adjacent to the hospital. The permanent part of the hospital was currently beyond capacity. I did what I could to insure that the MILPHAP team had the supplies and equipment they needed. What they really needed, to battle the plague, was better rodent control, but that was easier said than done. I knew the Vietnamese public health officials were doing their best to educate the people about the link between rodents, fleas, and plague and effective methods of flea and rodent control.

***

A very distinctive thing about Vietnam was the vast array of smells that one experienced, very different than those to which I was accustomed. Many were completely foreign to Westerners. There were smells that were so pungent that they made your eyes tear up and others so acrid that you wanted to wretch. Yet others were so overwhelmingly sweet that they almost made one nauseous, like putting your head in a plastic bag full of camellia petals. While at the province hospital in Tam Ky, I was acutely aware of the many different smells I was experiencing. In the plague tents, it was the smell of pus and death; on the burn ward, it was the smell of burned flesh and muslin dressings; in the maternity ward, it was the smell of lactose and woman; in the emergency room, it was the smell of ethyl alcohol and human body odor; in the kitchen, it was the smell of cooked rice coupled with the fishy odor of nuoc mam; on the medical ward, it was the smell of too many human mouths full of frequently decaying and usually unbrushed teeth and too many unwashed bodies lying in too close proximity to each other.

I felt so very sorry for the poor who had to rely on the province hospitals for all their medical support. The hospital staffs did the very best they could, and the MILPHAP teams were of tremendous assistance, doing truly heroic work, but the sheer numbers of people requiring medical care were frequently overwhelming and the facilities themselves quite inadequate. The war compounded this misery.

***

The dull pounding of artillery in the distance awakened me at about 0300 hours on 25 October. It appeared as though the guns were really pummeling an area about two or three miles, maybe even less, from Da Nang. It started about 0300 hours and was still going on at 0700. I couldn't help but wonder what they had targeted. I always hoped it was not an occupied village or hamlet.

Although it had rained most of the night, the morning sky seemed to indicate that we would see the sun for at least a part of the day. I was hoping that would be the case. The poor desperately needed some sunshine. Many thousands of homes in Da Nang were partially under water. It made for rather miserable living conditions when a mother had to wade through knee deep water to get to a crying baby whose bed was temporarily on top of a table to keep it out of the water. This I witnessed in several humble homes near the Han River.

Change did not come easily in the Vietnamese society. While I admired greatly the respect most Vietnamese showed their elders, it was somewhat disconcerting and disheartening to witness how the elders frequently impeded progress by their intransigence. It seemed that before any innovative idea or approach could be adopted it had to be presented to the elders for approval. Many of the elders were exceedingly tradition bound and of the mind set that "if it was good enough for us, it should be good enough for you." As an example, on my way to work there was a large pond where a man, perhaps in his early thirties, washed jeeps for the Americans on a fee for service basis. While not washing jeeps, he frequently fished in the pond. His family members probably relied on the fish he caught for at least a part of their daily sustenance. How did he fish? With a length of fishing line wrapped around his left hand. He would throw the baited hook as far as he could into the water and, when he felt the tug of a fish, jerk the line to set the hook and then started rapidly wrapping the line around his left hand. About 90 percent of the time the fish was gone before he got it to shore.

The U.S. Marines, whose jeeps he washed, told me they had observed his inefficient fishing methods and, because they liked him, decided to buy him an inexpensive rod and reel. The marines showed him how to cast and retrieve his bait. He tried it and seemed to quickly get the knack of how to use it. He caught several fish in a short period of time and seemed delighted over his success.

He then took the new rod and reel home to show to his parents. The next day when he came back to the pond, the rod and reel were with him. But when the jeeps were washed and he started fishing, he went back to the old, ineffective method of wrapping the line around his hand. The marines tried to determine why he wasn't using the rod and reel. In pidgin English, while shaking his head from side to side he said, "Cha toi no like," which translated to "My father doesn't like it." So, even though the young man liked the rod and reel, and seemingly was having great success with it, he would not use it because his father preferred that he employ the old method of fishing.

On the night of 26 October, I had duty as the staff duty officer. The phone rang incessantly, not allowing any sleep. The night was complicated by the fact that we had two American district advisors hit by small arms fire. Both required surgery but were expected to recover as their wounds were not life threatening. As the staff duty officer, I was required to prepare and submit to Saigon what was called a "crown report." Such a report was prepared each time an American serviceman or woman was seriously injured or killed. The report was transmitted by telephone to Saigon. Saigon officials then reviewed it for completeness and wired it to the United States to be used for notification of next of kin. It was an important report. Nobody wanted to transmit inaccurate or incomplete information to the next of kin.

On 27 October, as I was relieved of SDO responsibilities at 0700 hours, the sun was shining once again. At least temporarily, the monsoon seemed to have lost its punch. Then I looked to the west and saw dark, ominous clouds forming over the mountains. Before I got to my room to take a shower, it was raining once again.

After my shower, I had to hurry off to a Medical Coordinating Committee meeting, a session that brought together medical representatives from the USAID Hospital in Da Nang, the U.S. Navy, the U.S. Air Force, the VNAF, and the ARVN. I served as secretary of the committee.

As I was returning to my office after the meeting, I witnessed something very interesting. As background, the illiteracy rate, especially among Da Nang's older people, appeared to be very high. It seemed that a high percentage of the senior population, especially the poor, could neither read nor write. As I was driving through the city, I came upon a street in Da Nang where scribes had established their businesses. What was a scribe? A scribe was a person who typed letters and filled out forms and documents on a fee for service basis.

Lining both sides of a beautiful tree-lined street, for quite some distance, were the scribes' places of business. All of the scribes appeared to be men. Each person approved to go into business as a scribe was allotted a small plot of ground immediately adjacent to the street. I'm not sure if they paid for the ground or if it was simply assigned to them by virtue of their serving the community as a scribe. Each scribe then set up some type of crude shelter from the elements, typically only an overhead canvas on a wooden frame, and placed a typewriter on a small folding table about the size of a card table. The scribe had a chair to sit on while he typed and another chair on which his customer sat. A person who wanted a letter written, a document prepared, or a form filled out approached a scribe of his or her choosing and negotiated a price. Once a price was agreed upon, the person sat down and either dictated a letter or provided information to be used in filling out a form or preparing a document. The scribe typed away as the customer spoke, sometimes stopping to seek more definitive information. Most of the scribes seemed to be the one-finger, hunt-and-peck sorts of typists. I was told that when the workday was over, each scribe gathered all of his equipment—typewriter, table, bond paper, chairs and canvas—placed it in a cart or wagon, and pulled it home for safekeeping.

***

I taught school Thursday evening, 27 October, then went home for a few hours of much needed sleep. I was very tired since I had had no opportunity to sleep Wednesday night while serving as SDO. I set the alarm for 2330 hours and woke promptly at that time. It was raining ferociously hard, a thunderstorm, which was unusual in Da Nang and even more unusual during the monsoon season. Rarely was there lightning followed by thunder.

I dressed and drove to the hotel where Captain Dave Stephens was billeted. He was a fellow officer and friend who wanted to call his wife in California. Together we drove through the pounding rain to the MARS station set up in a CONEX container at the far end of the runway at Da Nang Air Base. We arrived ahead of the scheduled time and waited for roll call. When it was over, we waited again. Promptly at 0130 hours they started placing calls. All emergency calls were placed first, those reporting such things as sickness, accidents, and hospitalizations. When those calls were taken care of, the station manager started placing the routine, non-emergency calls. While waiting for our calls to be placed, we all sat on folding chairs in an old leaking GP medium tent. It was better than standing in the monsoon rains, but not much. One at a time, those on the priority list to place a call were admitted into the soundproof, air-conditioned CONEX container to make their call. About half were disappointed because the person they were trying to reach was not at home. I waited my turn, all the while hoping that my wife would be home to receive the call.

Finally, at 0220 hours on Friday morning, I was admitted to the modified CONEX container. At first, the radio operator in California who placed the phone call to my wife in San Antonio had difficulty getting a San Antonio connection, but all of a sudden I heard my wife's voice as the MARS operator in California was giving her instructions regarding how to conduct the call. It was all I could do to restrain myself from interrupting. She sounded ever so wonderful. Soon, I was talking with her, my life's partner. I was completely thrilled by the three-minute conversation. I wished we had had more time to talk, but the three-minute limit was strictly adhered to so as to allow the placement of as many calls as possible each night. A technician was sitting next to me as I spoke to make sure that sensitive or classified information was not being transmitted. He told me he was certain the NVA monitored all MARS calls. The MARS technician also had to flip a lever whenever we switched from my wife talking to me talking. He warned me about the time remaining by holding up one finger at the one-minute point and then ten fingers at the ten-second point. At the exact three-minute mark, the call was ended. It thrilled me greatly to hear my wife's voice for the first time in almost four months. During the drive back to my room, I became aware of just how tired I was. I had gotten less than four hours sleep during the past thirty-six hours and was exhausted.

On Friday, 28 October, someone pounding on my door at about 0330 to tell me I had a phone call awakened me. I shuffled down to the phone, only to find that I had to go to the Air Base to oversee off-loading and movement of forty-two ARVN patients to Duy Tan Hospital. They were coming from Nguyen Tri Phuong Station Hospital in Hue aboard a USAF C-130 aircraft and were being moved to open up critically needed beds in Hue should all hell break loose in Quang Tri Province. Despite the early wake-up call, I had managed to get five hours of sound sleep, so I was feeling much better.

***

I had by this time been in Da Nang less than four months, but during that time, my maid, Bá Vy, had washed her way through two sets of my field uniforms. John Bullard had warned me when I arrived in Saigon that "the bathroom floor and a brush are very hard on clothing." In my instance, the maid did not use the bathroom floor, but instead the rough cement sidewalk surrounding the well in the hotel courtyard. My bathroom, which I shared with others, was not big enough to spread out a pair of jockey shorts, to say nothing of a field uniform. As Bá Vy brushed away at the soaped-up clothes, frequently slapping them against the concrete to insure that every stain or particle of dirt was removed, she hummed a Vietnamese song. One couldn't help but like her.

***

We followed with great interest the Manila Conference that was concluded near the end of October.[9] As I read the accounts of that high-level meeting, attended by President Lyndon Johnson and seven other heads of state, I didn't feel as though it brought the world any closer to peace. From our side of the world, in Vietnam, it did not appear to have accomplished very much. I was disappointed, because I had become more and more convinced that diplomacy was our best hope to resolve the differences that battles could not.

When I arrived at the office on Saturday morning, 29 October, I opened the door and there was a big, fat rat sitting on top of Captain Stephen's desk, chewing on a long yellow tablet. Specialist Behner had set three baited traps in the office, but the rat seemed to prefer Captain Stephen's tablet to the peanut butter bait that Behner was using. Behner had caught four rats and a mouse in our office up to that time and was gunning for more. As I was chasing the rat around the office, using a ruler as a weapon, the phone rang. I was being summoned upstairs yet again by Colonel Hamblen to try to explain why ARVN soldiers in certain battalions were experiencing such high rates of malaria. As I walked to his office, I pondered what I could tell the good man that I hadn't already told him on multiple occasions.

He kept me in the hot seat for about fifteen minutes, making life very uncomfortable with a barrage of questions and a few accusations. He was of the opinion that significant numbers of ARVN soldiers were purposely exposing themselves to mosquito bites in order to contract the disease and thereby escape the war. The facts of the matter were, I told him, that some ARVN battalion commanders took malaria prevention seriously and others did not. The ones who took it seriously insured that their soldiers used mosquito repellents, kept their sleeves rolled down when in the field, slept under bed netting, and took their weekly chloroquine-primaquine tablets. Those commanders who did not take it seriously simply blew off the preventive measures as unimportant and never checked to see their soldiers followed them. The good commanders had controls in place to insure that proven malaria prevention measures were being followed; the poor ones did not. I told him that General Lam should use the number of malaria cases in each battalion to determine which commanders were deficient in the area of malaria control and then to rack their asses demanding improvement.

He said, "Why don't you tell him that?"

I responded, "Sir, I'll do it if you give me the opportunity."

He said, "You'd infuriate most of the ARVN battalion commanders in I Corps."

I said, "So be it, sir. If that is what it takes, so be it."

When I left Colonel Hamblen's office, after having been chewed on for what seemed like a long time, I went directly to the Saturday morning staff meeting. The primary topic of discussion centered on how quiet the tactical situation had been for the past couple of weeks. It was reported that this was true not only in I Corps, but also throughout the entire Republic of Vietnam. For the past couple of weeks, the weather had been good. The G-2 and G-3 both presented their belief that the tactical situation would change for the worse just as soon as the monsoon returned. It was also reported that during one five-day period earlier in the month, Da Nang had received twenty-seven inches of rain. A briefer also told us that when the monsoon was at its peak, we could expect up to fourteen inches of rain in a twenty-four hour period. I couldn't help but reflect upon the fact that the five-day total of twenty-seven inches approximated the amount of rain San Antonio had received in the entire previous year.

***

Since it was a beautiful Saturday afternoon, I headed for China Beach and a touch football game using combat rules. I was hoping that Roger Staubach, the ex-Naval Academy All American who was then assigned in Da Nang, might be on the beach and interested in a game. I fantasized about going down field, on the beach, for one of his long passes. With his arm and my speed, I thought, we'd be an unbeatable combination against the marine enlisted men, our usual opponents. So much for fantasy, as I never got to meet Roger Staubach.

Sunday morning, 30 October, was another sparkling day in Da Nang. The sun was shining brightly after an all-night light rain. It really was a beautiful day. God was in his Heaven, and all was right with the world, at least temporarily. I had been to Mass, followed by breakfast at the Officers' Club, and was in my office to check the mail on Sunday afternoon when the phone rang.

I was being summoned to the command suite yet again, atypical for a Sunday afternoon. This time Colonel Hamblen, Colonel Beeson, and the G-3 advisor wanted to discuss the pros and cons of General Lam ordering an ARVN medical unit be positioned permanently at the Dong Ha airstrip. To me this was a clear indication that things were again heating up in Quang Tri Province.

By Monday, 31 October, the monsoon rains were back, but not with the intensity of the past. During the afternoon, I was able to fly to Hoi An. A major battle had been fought near the city recently, and they asked that I try to get there for the intelligence wrap-up. There were medical implications, so they thought I should be there. Apparently, some type of NVA medical treatment facility had inadvertently been hit and, upon examination of the resulting casualties, they noted that three of the NVA medics were female. To some, it appeared as if the NVA were hurting to the degree that they now had to employ females as front-line medics.

I had also been asked to inspect some drugs that had been found in an attempt to determine what types of diseases were giving the enemy concern at that time. Knowing virtually nothing about pharmacology, I explained that the best I could do was take samples of the pharmaceuticals to ARVN and U.S. Navy pharmacists and physicians and ask them to analyze the drugs and give me an opinion as to what diseases the enemy was attempting to prevent or treat.

When I got back to my office, I was informed that there had been an ARVN convoy ambushed on Highway 1 in the Hai Van Pass, resulting in seven seriously wounded ARVN soldiers. In keeping with established procedure, an advisor from our team was with the convoy, and he had called in the report of the ambush. Helicopters were dispatched to evacuate the casualties. All were taken to Duy Tan Hospital. One soldier died while in flight to the hospital.

CHAPTER 5

NOVEMBER 1966

When I looked out of the only window in my hotel room, I viewed a new building being constructed. One of the exterior walls of the building was less than thirty feet from my window. I had watched the progress of the building during the almost four months I had been in Da Nang. When completed, the building was supposed to be among the largest in the city. It was to be the headquarters for the United States Agency for International Development, an organization with which I frequently worked. Vietnamese civilians were hired to guard the construction site around the clock. At any given time, there were four or five men walking the perimeter of the building with slung rifles.

Several of the guards had moved their families to the construction site. Two or three of them had even built small lean-to habitats next to an exterior wall of the new building in which to house their families. Constructed primarily of tin and corrugated paper, the sides of these structures were open, so I could look right into their homes. They were only about eight feet by eight feet in size, but all daily living tasks were conducted within. I watched the families who occupied these structures do their cooking on small gas or sterno burners, eat their meals, wash their bodies, suckle and bathe their babies, and wash their dishes and clothing, all in that tiny space. When nature called, they simply walked to the other side of the building to relieve themselves.

Women seemed to do much of the manual labor, not only at this construction site but also throughout the country. This may have been because such a high percentage of the young males, those between eighteen and thirty-five, had been conscripted into the military. Women seemed to carry all the bricks at construction sites. They manually mixed all the cement. They plowed the fields in rural areas behind an oftentimes-surly water buffalo. They butchered the hogs and chickens. They planted the fields and harvested the crops. The few men I saw doing these types of things were well beyond middle age.

***

As October turned into November, I began to realize that I rather admired the ARVN enlisted soldiers, almost all of whom were conscripted from peasant-class lives. I never heard them complain. They seemed to enjoy being around Americans. They were very small in stature, probably averaging about five-feet-one-inch tall. It was unusual to see an enlisted soldier over five feet four inches. Their strength and endurance always amazed me, as did their uncomplaining attitudes. They had very lithe, wiry bodies, and it seemed they could work for long periods of time before tiring. I frequently observed them in staging areas just before they were to be airlifted into battle. There was a lot of nervous apprehension, bordering on fear. Their American-manufactured helmets were typically too large, appearing to roll around on their small heads. Practically all of them seemed to be puffing on a cigarette to relieve the tension as they waited. Some joked with their buddies, but most were content to lie on their backs with their eyes closed and their heads on the tops of their helmets while puffing on a cigarette. They all seemed to be in a reflective mood as the upcoming battle loomed closer.

Image 13. ARVN soldiers in staging area after being alerted for airlift into battle

Photo courtesy of the author

On Wednesday, 2 November, I thought I was going to have to spend the night in Dong Ha or somewhere in the Lang Vei-Khe Sanh area. It had been a disappointing and frustrating day. I tried to fly to the Lang Vei-Khe Sanh area to take one last look, assuring myself that the ARVN medical personnel had done all they could, in regard to preparation, before that area was essentially cut off by the monsoon. The weather in Da Nang was quite good on that day, plenty of ceiling to fly safely. Our helicopter took off as scheduled, proceeded over to the Special Forces pad on the other side of the Han River to marry up with an accompanying helicopter, and then headed north. The pilots stopped in Hue to top off their fuel, then flew to Quang Tri and headed west. Soon, we were flying over the wilds of the Ba Long River Valley toward the Laotian border. Below us, the growth rose to heights of 150-200 feet, the so-called triple canopy jungle. One canopy of thick, heavy foliage reached the seventy-five foot level, another the 125-foot level, and the third between 150 and 200 feet above the floor of the jungle. I had not been on the ground in such a jungle, but was told that on the floor of a triple-canopy jungle, it was quite dark, even in mid-day, in fact so dark as to make photography with normal speed film not possible. Not enough sunlight penetrated the three canopies to allow a picture to be taken unless you had very fast film.

The pilots of the two helicopters headed up this lonely valley at maximum altitude. Since we had seven passengers aboard, 4,500 feet was the absolute maximum at which the pilots could fly safely. Even this height seemed to be taxing the helicopter. We started running into bad weather about twenty miles into the valley, and soon the weather became even more problematic. Eventually, we had no alternative other than getting out of there. The pilots turned around and hastily made our retreat. After refueling at Dong Ha, we flew to Quang Tri, where I accomplished some needed coordination with the MILPHAP team at the Quang Tri Province Hospital and then had lunch. At about 1400 hours, the two pilots jointly decided to give it another try since it was an important mission, especially for the Special Forces soldiers aboard. Again, we headed down the Ba Long River valley. This time the pilots decided to chance it at lower altitudes. The plan was to try to get under the storm clouds. The pilots didn't like this kind of flying, and neither did the passengers. We all knew that the NVA had .50 caliber weapons on the hillsides on both sides of the valley. Floating down the river valley at ninety knots at an altitude of 1800 feet, with the mountains rising to 3400 feet on both sides of us, we felt rather vulnerable.

It appeared for awhile that we were going to make it. We got to within ten miles of Khe Sanh when very suddenly the weather became unbelievably bad. There was zero visibility, and the winds and rains were buffeting the helicopter around quite severely. The pilots of the two ships were concerned about flying into each other. Soon, the inevitable decision came—again we had to get out of there and fast. The pilots turned the choppers around, but soon it was apparent that the weather had closed in behind us. The weather heading for Quang Tri seemed as bad as the weather had been when we were heading toward Khe Sanh. The pilots looked for an opening and, very fortunately, found it. There was a patch of blue sky toward the north. We were already very close to the DMZ, so the pilots didn't have too much room to maneuver, but nevertheless they both headed north. In order to skirt the storm, they had to dip into the DMZ for a few miles. I know we had to be very close to the North Vietnamese border, but eventually we got around the storm and headed for the airstrip at Dong Ha. All of us, especially the pilots, were relieved when we finally landed.

After refueling, we headed back to Da Nang and arrived without further incident. I came to the realization that I probably was not going to get to Lang Vei and Khe Sanh during the duration of the monsoon. I couldn't help but wonder how those outposts would be re-supplied.

***

Lying on my desk when I arrived at my office on 4 November were four letters from my wife. The mail had been very erratic of late. The letters brought the unwelcome and disconcerting news that our fragile child was once again ill with a sore throat, an ear infection, and a bad cold. My wife had done the right thing by getting him to a pediatrician as soon as he started running a fever above 100 degrees. We just couldn't take a chance, fearing that a cold or infection could turn into pneumonia.

There is an old axiom in the army that says, "When you think you've done everything, there's just one more thing to do." I always left the office knowing that there was just one more thing to do. I had never before been in a position where there was more to do and it was harder to get things done than in Vietnam. Many of the ARVN officers and non-commissioned officers I worked with seemed to have little sense of urgency. There seemed to be a mañana mentality—don't sweat it, it will still be there in the morning. I worried that perhaps this lackadaisical approach was due to some fault or deficiency on my part. Many other advisors, however, reported similar experiences. I thought about addressing the problem with Major Tu and Captain Phat, even though they themselves had not adopted this mentality. I thought of confronting them together concerning the attitudes of some of their subordinates. I realized fully that I, personally, had no authority. I couldn't order that anything be done, but it got very frustrating when I would make a recommendation that was seemingly accepted for adoption and then rarely implemented. Sometimes I got discouraged over my inability to get things moving.

Friday, 4 November, was absolutely sparkling and beautiful. The monsoon was nowhere to be seen, although it was predicted to pick up again the following week. Fortunately, the staff of the ARVN medical depot had done a good job of resupplying ARVN medical units and remote outposts throughout the I Corps area. Many of the remote areas operated with only one or two enlisted medics, and some of the more remote sites, like Khe Sanh, Lang Vei and Duc Pho, were always vulnerable to attack. I knew that if attacked, they were pretty much on their own regarding medical support. The weather would, in all likelihood, preclude ARVN from rushing to their assistance.

***

Brigadier General Joe Blumberg visited Duy Tan Hospital during the early afternoon of 4 November. He commanded the Armed Forces Institute of Pathology in Washington, D.C. He brought three full colonels and a lieutenant colonel with him. Captain Phat gave them an excellent tour of the hospital, concentrating particularly on the pathology section. This visit, by a well published scientist and general officer, boosted the morale of the physicians in the hospital appreciably. Prior to his departure, General Blumberg spoke to an assembly of the hospital staff, lavishing praise on the facility and calling it "the crown jewel of Vietnamese military medicine." When I took General Blumberg and his party to the airport for their flight back to Washington, he told me that he had meant every word of what he said.

Later that afternoon, LTC Mabra and I went to Duy Tan Hospital for a brief review of the hospital's ongoing construction program. Among the topics discussed was the newly authorized morgue, yet to be started. Surprisingly, Colonel Mabra revealed that he had trained as a mortician before entering the army. He indicated that he would like to see the morgue operation. Captain Phat graciously gave him a short tour of the entire facility. As we were about to leave the morgue, an old man approached, bowed deeply, and told Captain Phat that he was there to pick up the body of his son. Captain Phat examined the papers the man presented to him, shouted an order, and within minutes the red casket containing his son's remains was placed on the man's red wagon, and the man departed, pulling the casket home for burial. It was a poignant moment that I think of often.

On Saturday morning, 5 November, there was a discernable change in the weather. It had rained hard during the night, and the temperature had plummeted. On the way to my office, I couldn't help but think that this was the time of year when a large percentage of the civil population would suffer, especially the poor and the refugee population. I saw many children inadequately dressed for the fifty-eight degree weather. Some very small children, including toddlers, had on woolen caps and woolen sweaters but no pants or shoes, totally bare on the bottom. Some of the girls wore little dresses, but no panties or pants. On that cool morning, their little bottoms looked blue from cold.

During the 5 November I Corps Saturday morning staff meeting, General Walt, whom I admired greatly, seemed highly agitated. It seemed to me that he was under an inordinate amount of pressure to take the fight to the enemy and conduct a war of attrition, killing and wounding as many VC and NVA soldiers as possible and destroying their supplies and equipment. As a strong proponent of pacification, he believed that the only way the war could be won was by pacifying and protecting the people and by denying the enemy access to the villages which provided vitally needed foodstuffs and places to conceal supplies, equipment and ammunition. In his efforts to pacify and protect the people, he had initiated the Combined Action Program, where squads of U.S. Marines were integrated into platoons of Vietnamese Popular Forces, government-sponsored village militia, letting them work together to gain the trust of the people.[1] I could only conclude that he and General Westmoreland, the overall commander of American forces, were on a collision course. General Walt believed fervently that only through pacification could the war be won. General Westmoreland seemed to have a totally different strategy in mind. He believed that only through punishing the Viet Cong and the NVA, by killing or wounding as many as possible and denying them supplies by bombing their supply lines, could the war be won. He was pushing General Walt to go after the enemy more aggressively.

Although I felt reasonably certain that General Westmoreland's proposed strategy would prevail, since he was the overall commander, I was not at all certain his approach would succeed. It seemed to me, as a non-combatant, that the NVA and the VC were in the war for the long haul and realized full well that the costs in human life and fortune would be great. While we had the advantage of superior technology, the enemy had the advantage of being able to blend in with the population, making it virtually impossible to ascertain, with certainty, who the enemy was. I got the impression that General Westmoreland was under great pressure from the White House to bring the war to a conclusion as quickly as possible, hence the strategy of attrition. Would it work? I had my doubts, based on myriad conversations with South Vietnamese officers, non-commissioned officers, and prominent community leaders, and limited contact with VC and NVA prisoners of war.

**

For the first time since I had been in Da Nang, we had three U.S. Army advisors in the hospital with malaria. That was cause for concern on the part of our advisory team commander. I envisioned myself getting called on the carpet during a staff meeting and being asked, "Why is this happening?" What could I tell him? That the afflicted advisors were probably not taking their weekly chloroquine-primaquine tablets; that they were probably not using mosquito repellent; that they were probably not using mosquito netting over their beds, hammocks or sleeping bags? If I responded in this manner it would sound as if I was "ratting" on my fellow advisors who were hospitalized. Fortunately for me, the topic did not come up at the Saturday staff meeting.

On Sunday, 6 November, I was the SDO. I was sitting in the command suite typing a letter to my wife when Colonel Hamblen and another man entered the large room. Colonel Hamblen introduced me to the man and explained that he was an agricultural advisor working for USAID. During our subsequent conversation, he revealed that he was working in a mountainous region in the western part of the country and that he had great empathy for the Montagnards. He noted that they especially liked pork, and yet when he looked around their hamlets and villages, all he saw were runty little pigs that weighed no more than forty to fifty pounds. He requested that "Chester White" hogs be transported from the United States to the region of Vietnam in which he was working. Chester White hogs become huge as they mature. A full-grown hog could weigh several hundred pounds. Eventually, the hogs arrived and seemed to thrive, but for the Montagnards they were not practical. Why? Because once a hog was slaughtered the people had no way to keep the meat that was not immediately consumed from decaying, whereas when a small forty- or fifty-pound hog was slaughtered, it fed the entire hamlet for a day or two, and there were no leftovers. In contrast, much of the meat from a big three- or four-hundred-pound animal spoiled before it could be consumed. Such were the vagaries of life in the mountainous parts of South Vietnam. Big was not necessarily better.

On Monday, 7 November, two physicians from Duy Tan Hospital and I worked with a senior ARVN officer and several Da Nang city officials on a project to repair and renovate a road running to the hospital. We were reviewing the plans to make certain that ambulances would have easy access to the emergency room entrance after the road was completed. We had several areas of concern and were suggesting a series of minor modifications to the plans.

We had about fifteen minutes of work remaining to complete the review. Suddenly the senior officer got up and announced that it was 1200 hours and that we would resume our meeting at 1500 hours. I more or less blew my top, openly and strongly expressing my displeasure at his taking a three-hour lunch and siesta break when we were so close to concluding our work. I told him that I had other plans for the afternoon and suggested we complete our business first and then go to lunch. I said, "Sir, this is ludicrous. Why can't you delay your lunch break for fifteen or twenty minutes and let us conclude the review? We've all got other important things to do this afternoon."

He looked me in the eye, smiled, and said, "Major, I'm thirty-nine years old. I was awarded my first medal for valor at age seventeen as an enlisted man. Since that time twenty-two years have elapsed. I've been at war much of those twenty-two years. If I jumped every time an American advisor asked me to jump, I'd be an old man in a hurry. Calm down, would you? Tomorrow's another day. Ask yourself, and answer honestly, would you have all of this zeal and energy if you were in my place. I'm very tired of war. I owe it to myself to relax from time to time. I owe it to my family. You advisors come and go. You have one year in which to make your mark, and then you're gone. And a new advisor comes to us, usually with different ideas about how we should go about our business. The new advisor, too, must show some achievements during his year of duty in our country or he'll go home with no medals and a bad performance report. Please, Major Van Straten, look at it not only from your perspective but from mine as well. The war will still be with us at 1500 hours. I'm on my way to lunch. My wife is expecting me." And with that he stood and was off.

His remarks rocked me back on my heels. His perspective was one that hadn't even entered my consciousness. My entire mindset was directed at the urgency of war in which things couldn't wait; they had to be done right now, or there would be dire consequences. I began to wonder who had the right mindset, the American officer who served in Vietnam for one year or the Vietnamese officer who had been at war for a long, long time? The ARVN officer's remarks caused me to modify not only my thinking but, to a degree, my approach. I knew I had to back off. Pushing the ARVN officers and non-commissioned officers hard was not getting the results I had hoped for.

On that same day, Monday, 7 November, I was invited to attend an awards and decorations ceremony at Duy Tan Hospital. Major Tu called and asked that I be there at 1630 hours, thirty minutes before General Lam was scheduled to present the awards. I thought he wanted my assistance regarding how to set up the ceremony. The lawn outside the hospital was to be the site of the event. A temporary platform had been erected, flags were flying, the band was decked out in its finest uniforms, an honor guard was ready to greet the general, and much of the hospital staff was standing in formation at parade rest. I was shocked to learn that I was to be decorated for my actions at Dong Ha after the Vietnamese Airborne Task Force had been decimated there. General Lam awarded me the Vietnamese Cross of Gallantry with Silver Star. I couldn't understand a single word of the citation as it was being read in Vietnamese, but Major Tu explained later that it concerned the mass casualty situation at Dong Ha on 5-6 October. I remember hoping that Captain Bob Helton's actions on that grim October day were also being recognized. In my mind, his actions had been far more noteworthy and commendable than mine.

Later on that same day, I drove over to the leprosarium located part way up Marble Mountain. Several U.S. Marines escorted me to the site. I was delivering clothing that had been donated by charitable organizations in the United States. What these men and women endured was beyond description. Isolated from family and friends, they had little to look forward to as their fingers and toes were slowly but surely being eaten away by the disease. And yet they smiled and expressed their gratitude for my visit and for the donation of warm clothing from America. It was humbling.

***

While reading the *Stars and Stripes* one day, I noted an article about the capture of a large VC supply cache. The article highlighted how many weapons, how much ammunition, how many tons of foodstuffs, and how many pieces of equipment were captured but also mentioned how much salt had been found. I wondered why there was such emphasis on salt. I asked Major Tu, who explained that salt was the Viet Cong's only means of preserving food. They had no refrigeration, and in order to preserve their meat and fish, they needed salt. Without salt, the chicken, pork, and fish, important sources of protein, would spoil in a very short period of time because of the stifling heat and humidity that prevailed for much of the year.

As of Tuesday, 8 November, the medical advisory effort at I Corps HQ consisted of Sergeant First Class August Davis and myself. Although authorized four non-commissioned officers in Da Nang, I was down to only one. At that time, we were desperately short of people. In addition to serving as my NCOIC, Sergeant Davis, an outstanding black soldier, also ran the advisory team's dispensary and advised an ARVN medical company, requiring that he be away from the office much of the time. I had assignment authority over forty-seven enlisted medic positions, primarily to meet the needs of the sub-sector advisory teams located throughout Quang Nam Province. On that morning, 8 November, only twenty-four of those forty-seven positions were filled. I couldn't help but wonder if perhaps it was time for President Johnson or Secretary McNamara to call up the Reserves or National Guard. I wasn't certain where the authority for a call-up resided, with the president or with the secretary.[2]

On Tuesday evening, 8 November, I was invited by Barry Ballow to join the Board of Directors of the Vietnam-American Association. I welcomed the invitation, thinking it would allow me to take a role in the formulation of policy for the center and perhaps meet Vietnamese educators from the community. I told Barry that I would accept the appointment, but that I needed to give up my teaching responsibilities at the end of the semester. I couldn't do justice to both.

***

On Wednesday morning, I saw an elderly priest standing in the Air America terminal on Da Nang Air Base. He looked totally perplexed and confused. I approached him and found that, surprisingly, he was reasonably conversant in English. He explained that he was trying to get a ride to Tam Ky, the site of his parish. I explained the procedures and helped him get a seat on the plane, for which he was most grateful. To show his gratitude, he reached into one of the baskets at his feet and withdrew a live chicken, smiled, and offered it to me. I didn't want to hurt his feelings, but what could I possibly do with a chicken? I explained that I was very grateful for his generosity, but that I did not have the means to prepare the chicken for eating. I asked that he give it to the poorest of his parishioners on my behalf and he promised to do so.

Early in the morning of 10 November, at about 0445 hours, as I drove from my hotel to the office, I noted that merchants were already out in force, setting up their wares to attract customers despite the very early hour. The three-wheeled pushcart restaurants were all aglow. Each had a candle burning inside the glassed-in bread storage space. Major Tu had told me that the candles provided light for the exchange of money and served to keep the loaves of French bread warm. Heat for the other food products offered for sale, the kettles full of rice and noodles, was provided by a gas fire that burned in the lower part of each small pushcart. The carts were laden with food, despite the early hour, and many of the cart owners, men and women alike, seemed to be enjoying their own breakfasts before the business day began. It seemed to me that a very high percentage of Vietnamese city-dwellers ate their breakfast meal at these little mobile restaurants. The U.S. Marines called them "Mobile Howard Johnsons."

Later that morning, Captain Phat called and asked if I would come to Duy Tan Hospital to help with a logistics problem. When I arrived, I noted that one of his staff members, a woman, was preparing invitations to be hand delivered to a group of American dignitaries later in the day. She asked me if I would look over the invitation for spelling errors. A South Korean troupe of singers and dancers was scheduled to entertain the patients in Duy Tan Hospital on Friday, 11 November, the very next day. Captain Phat thought it would be a morale boost for the patients if they were to be joined by a few of their American allies. After looking over the invitation and finding no errors, I gently suggested that the next time something like this came up she should try to get the invitations out a little earlier. I told her that with only one day's notice, it would be difficult for senior-level people to modify their schedules so as to accept the invitation. She thanked me for the suggestion and said she hadn't thought of it in that light before. She went on to say that in Vietnam invitations were typically extended at a time very close to the event, usually the day before. This was apparently yet another cultural difference.

Prior to arriving in Vietnam, I had been essentially unfamiliar with the hospital environment. I had seen virtually no trauma. During my ten years in the Army Medical Service Corps, I had never been assigned to a hospital of any type, field or fixed. As a lieutenant, I had served in Germany, initially as the Medical Platoon Leader, 1st Battalion, 13th Infantry Regiment, 8th Infantry Division then later as the Medical Detachment Commander, 68th Armor Battalion, 8th Infantry Division. My next assignment, as a captain, was as Chief of the Instructor Training Unit at the Medical Field Service School. This was followed by attendance at the Officer Advanced Course at Fort Sam Houston, then enrollment in Graduate School at the University of Texas at Austin, after which I was assigned to Vietnam.

Dr. John Giles introduced me to the hospital environment and U.S. Navy medicine as practiced at the U.S. Naval Support Activity Hospital in Da Nang. Doctors Tu and Phat contributed greatly to my understanding of Vietnamese military medicine and the ARVN hospital systems, just as U.S. military physicians Steve Barchet and John Driscoll, both commanders of MILPHAP teams in I Corps, patiently guided me through the way medicine was practiced in Vietnam's province hospitals.

Helpful as those experiences were, nothing prepared me emotionally for the casualties coming off the battlefields and out of the hamlets and villages of Vietnam. The memories of the wounded being off-loaded from helicopters and ground ambulances are so vivid, so powerful, and so painful that even now, forty-nine years later, it grieves me to think of some of them. I can see clearly, in my mind's eye, the faces of some of the severely wounded U.S. Marines, ARVN soldiers, and Vietnamese civilians, especially the children, as they were being taken into the casualty receiving areas for triage and treatment.

My son Michael, now a commander in the U.S. Naval Reserve, recently sent me a U.S. Navy publication entitled *Navy Medicine in Vietnam: Passage to Freedom to the Fall of Saigon.* The publication included a brief article by LCDR Marie Joan Brouillette, a Navy nurse assigned to the U.S. Naval Support Activity Hospital in Da Nang during the same period I was in Da Nang. Ms. Brouillette described one patient whom she remembered "above all the others." Although I can't be 100 percent sure that I saw this same patient, I am almost certain that I did. Ms. Brouillette wrote:

> I remember one patient above all the others. This much wounded Marine was the worst I had ever seen. His brains were coming out of his head. He had one leg blown off at the hip. The other was blown off mid-thigh. His belly was wide open.
>
> One arm was off at the shoulder joint and the other was off at the elbow. His eyeballs were lying on his cheek. His jaw was missing. And he kept saying, "I'm not dead! Please help me!" He was one of the ones we prepared very quickly to get him to the operating

room. Even up until the time he was put under anesthesia, he kept saying, "Please save me! Please save me!" We got him off the operating table but he didn't last very long afterwards. We were unable to save him.

That patient got to both the triage surgeon and myself. We both went back to our quarters and that was it. I just couldn't take anything for the next 18 hours. We had to build up our defenses again before we could go back. It's amazing, first of all, that someone prior to him didn't get through my defenses. To this day, it's still very emotional for me.

When I think back on Vietnam, that was the most rewarding year of my life, professionally. I think I made a difference with a lot of patients—and being able to speed up the process so we could save more. I didn't get emotionally involved with any of the patients. Each was a casualty we had to save. And that was it. I wasn't thinking of the person, his family, or anything else. You can't do that and remain sane.[3]

May the U.S. Marine described in that passage rest in peace, and may God bless Marie Joan Brouillette and all the health care providers, American and Vietnamese alike, who gave so much of themselves that others might have a chance to live.

Although the rains pounded I Corps for much of November and December and it turned quite cold, there was one group of entrepreneurs who prospered during the monsoon season—the coffin makers. One elderly man had a humble little shop that I passed frequently on my way to Duy Tan Hospital. He not only constructed and painted the coffins by himself, but sold them as well. It seemed that every time I passed his shop during the monsoon, there was some poor man, woman, or family standing at his canvas-covered business selecting a coffin for a loved one. There wasn't much to the selection process, because all of the coffins were essentially the same. About the only matter of concern was buying one the right length.

***

Image 14. LCDR Marie Joan Brouillette and medical colleague wheel a patient into an operating room at U.S. Navy Hospital, DaNang

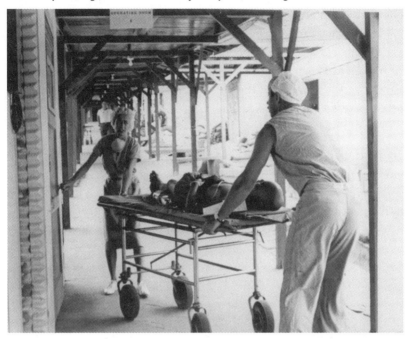

Photo courtesy of the U.S. Navy Bureau of Medicine and Surgery Archives

After dinner on Thursday, 17 November, I went up to the club's barroom to enjoy an after dinner drink. Excitement was running high, as it had just been announced that Saturday's big football game would be televised in Vietnam. The pundits in the United States were billing it as "The Game of the Century." The Fighting Irish of #1 Notre Dame were playing the Spartans of #2 Michigan State. The broadcast was to start at 0200 hours Sunday morning, and the club, which had the only television set we had access to, would be open to accommodate viewing of the game.

***

A little after midnight on Friday, 18 November, there was an insistent knocking at my door. When I answered, a written message labeled "urgent" was given to me by one of the ARVN hotel guards. The message said I was to call the SDO as quickly as possible. I shuffled out to the phone in the hallway only to find that it was not working. I dutifully got dressed and drove to an SP Station a short distance from my hotel to use their telephone. When I reached the duty officer, he told me that a phone call had been received from Captain Len Schumacher, the medical advisor to the surgeon of the ARVN 2nd Infantry Division, which was headquartered in Quang Ngai. Len wanted me to know that there was a serious outbreak of cholera in the province's POW compound.

I reached Captain Schumacher by phone at about 0500 hours that morning. He explained that he had been mistaken. It wasn't a POW compound but "some kind of a refugee camp." He went on to tell me that he had called me in the middle of the night only because he knew that the news of the cholera outbreak would get the attention of the commander of Advisory Team #1, Colonel Hamblen, sometime over the weekend. Captain Schumacher didn't want me to be caught unaware on Monday morning. He was protecting me from being blindsided by my commander.

I was naturally quite concerned about the outbreak, as I knew that cholera could sweep through a congested population quite rapidly, not because it was easily transmissible from one person to another, but because the resulting vomitus and diarrhea, if not handled properly, could easily infect food and water supplies. This would be especially true in a refugee camp where the water supply was probably problematic to begin with and the human waste disposal system likely inadequate. After the Saturday morning staff meeting, I met with Dr. Phat and together we marshaled the meager resources available to try to quell the outbreak. We had about 700 doses of injectable cholera vaccine and an air pressure gun available. I agreed to be the courier, along with a physician from Duy Tan, to deliver the vaccine and the air pressure gun.

The weather was very bad. We made three attempts to get to Quang Ngai, but all had to be aborted because of the weather. The fourth attempt, on Monday, 21 November, was successful. Upon arrival, we found several slightly embarrassed and apologetic Vietnamese public health physicians. They had over-played their case. They now stated that there were only four or five cases, and all were relatively mild. They also stated that it was not a refugee camp where the cases occurred, but instead a political reeducation center for known or suspected VC sympathizers.

Since we had come so far for what turned out to be not a true emergency, we decided to nevertheless go with the Quang Ngai Province public health officials and three American enlisted medics to the site of the outbreak to see what could be learned.

The public health officials took us there by jeep. The camp was about four or five miles from Quang Ngai City. I was uneasy during the ride because we had no security other than the rifles carried by the enlisted medics and me. We were traveling through an area covered by tall elephant grass and palm trees on both sides of the road, ideal conditions for an ambush.

Our convoy of three jeeps suddenly broke out of the high grass into a small clearing that contained several buildings inside a barbed wire-enclosed compound. Sitting on the ground inside the compound was a large group of people identified as "VC suspects and VC sympathizers." The camp, although not a prison per se, was guarded by the Republic of Vietnam National Police.

Image 15. Viet Cong suspects or sympathizers at political re-education camp

Photo courtesy of the author

The detainees, including a few with their entire families, were brought into the encampment and provided a place to live, adequate food and drink, and six weeks to six months of political reeducation. They were then allowed to return to their home villages and hamlets. We were told the camp contained a total of 428 people: men, women, and a few children. As expected, food preparation, waste disposal, and water systems were all primitive. The public health officials decided to vaccinate the entire population, which didn't take very long thanks to the speed of the air gun.

While walking among the detainees, I was very cautious, protecting my rifle from possible seizure and at the ready if needed. An armed guard escorted us through the encampment. Other guards stood on the perimeter, watching very carefully. Practically all detainees were dressed in black pajama-style clothing, which was characteristic of both the VC and all peasant-class people. When they saw the air pressure vaccination gun, they all seemed leery. The men were instructed to take off their shirts in preparation for the injections, and the woman automatically did the same thing. We encountered no problems during the process of vaccinating the detainees.

Image 16. Political detainees being vaccinated against cholera using air gun

Photo courtesy of the author

Since the monsoon rains curtailed my travels during much of November and December, I went on several nearby MEDCAP operations. I sent my wife several pictures of me lecturing, through an interpreter, a large group of people in a small coastal village not too far from Da Nang. Before the people could see a physician or a medic concerning their medical problem, we required that they listen to a twenty-minute lecture on the proper disposal of human waste. I would say a sentence or two, and the interpreter would then try to capture the essence of my statement and repeat it in the Vietnamese language. How effective these lectures were I do not know, but I suspect only minimally so because we were attempting to change deeply ingrained behaviors in a very brief period of time. In a few of the hamlets that I worked in during my year in Vietnam, it seemed to be common practice for the people to urinate or defecate wherever they happened to be when nature called. Typically, the adults were somewhat discreet when doing so, but the children were not. Most villages and hamlets seemed to have a large open area set aside for defecation, but urination could occur almost anywhere. These practices, typical in the small hamlets and villages, were not as common in the cities.

While participating in one specific MEDCAP operation, I couldn't help but notice a little boy, about five years old, standing in the foreground during my lecture. He wrung his hands incessantly during the entire lecture, very unusual behavior for a five-year-old. I watched him for quite some time. Even after the lesson was over, the hand wringing continued. Although I was not qualified to make such a judgment, I thought the little boy suffered from severe mental illness. I believed he was gravely ill, but what could we do? Nothing but pray that he eventually got professional help, which was highly unlikely in a war-ridden developing nation. As far as I could determine, there were virtually no provisions for helping the mentally ill in the Republic of Vietnam. I saw a small number of raving, maniacal people literally locked behind bars, usually in the padded cubicles of province hospitals. This shielded the general public from their abusive ranting. Some of the mentally ill screamed and hollered and ripped off their clothing and scratched themselves until they bled, while others lay on the floor in a fetal position, holding their hands over their eyes as if trying to shut out the external world. Still others just rocked back and forth in an almost hypnotic rhythm. I empathized greatly with the mentally ill.

Image 17. Little boy who wrung his hands incessantly standing behind group of children

Photo courtesy of the author

One night in mid-to-late November, I was rudely awakened by a tremendous blast at approximately 0200 hours. The VC had blown a big generator just 150 yards from the house in which General Walt lived. We all concluded that if Victor Charlie, as the VC were sometimes called, could get that close to the commander's house, it demonstrated, quite conclusively, that he could strike almost anywhere and at any time.

Shortly after breakfast on 23 November, I inspected the kitchen in the MACV Officers' Club. I didn't like that duty because the kitchen staff, all Vietnamese civilians, strove so hard to keep it clean, yet I frequently found serious deficiencies. They seemed to personalize all my findings. They were not at all careful about cutting boards and greasy serving plates and serving utensils. On several occasions, I saw them cutting up raw chicken on a cutting board and five minutes later use the same cutting board, before washing it, to cut up lettuce, cucumbers, and tomatoes for salad. Could there be any wonder why many of us who ate there had frequent bouts of diarrhea?

During the late afternoon of 23 November, my interpreter and I were on our way to the Navy Hospital for an important meeting with Dr. Giles. As Sergeant Thong was driving down a long uninhabited stretch of the unpaved road in East Da Nang, we saw a strange sight. Walking toward us was a young man carrying a woman in a most unusual way. It was as if she were standing up, facing forward in the same direction he was walking. He had his arms around her waist. He would lift her, walk eight or ten steps, then set her down on her feet while he took a brief rest. Then, he would lift her again and walk another eight or ten steps, repeating the process. I stopped and asked my interpreter to find out what was going on. After a brief conversation, Sgt. Thong told me that the woman being carried was gravely ill and that her son was trying to carry her to the provincial hospital in Da Nang, which was still three to four miles away. He was carrying her in that manner so that he could set her down on her feet, rest for a few seconds, and then resume the long journey to the hospital. The woman was comparatively large, at least as big as her son, and if he laid her on the ground while he rested, he could not pick her up again. She seemed to be in considerable pain, and the manner in which she was being carried added to her discomfort, but what was her poor son to do? I wanted so badly to give them a ride to the hospital, but if I did so, I would miss my important appointment with Dr. Giles. We looked for the couple after we left the hospital but did not find them.

I was continually surprised at how different the Vietnamese customs, culture and traditions were from ours. We had a young woman working in our Officers' Club who was very fond of a certain young Vietnamese man. I was told that they had been seeing each other for almost a year and intended to marry. But the young man, while professing his love for the girl, had a brief but torrid affair with another young woman. During their brief affair, she became pregnant and eventually delivered a healthy baby. The young man claimed to have no affection for the new mother, but readily acknowledged that he was the father of her child. He felt no obligation to help either the young woman or the child.

Girl number one, the one who worked as a waitress in our club, still professed her love for the young man and still wanted to marry him. In late October, the young man was conscripted into the Vietnamese Army. He was ordered to Saigon to attend some type of military school. Before departing, he vowed to marry the girl who worked in our club, upon satisfying his military obligation. She pined away for a few weeks in Da Nang, missing him dreadfully. She then decided that she wanted some part of him near her until his return. So what did she do? She approached the young woman who gave birth to his child and asked her if she would give the baby to her. Girl number two seemingly had no real love for the baby, so she was willing to negotiate a deal. She apparently looked upon the set of circumstances she was presented with as an opportunity to get something she wanted. She offered to swap the baby for a Sony radio. Girl number one agreed, and the deal was consummated. Both girls were happy about the deal. Whether or not they ever found it necessary to legalize this transaction I do not know.

Thursday, 24 November, was Thanksgiving Day. Although separated from my family by an ocean and over 8,000 miles, I had much to be thankful for. Instead of feeling sorry for myself, I was resolved to count my many blessings and be thankful. I went to Mass and received Communion in the early morning hours, then enjoyed a bountiful Thanksgiving Day meal at the Officers' Club at 1500 hours. Other than those special events, it was a work day as usual.

On that same Thanksgiving Day, I called the MACV Surgeon's Office in Saigon to complain about enlisted medic staffing levels. I was told that at present the MACV advisory teams, throughout the entire country, were at 61 percent of authorized strength for personnel trained in military occupational specialties 91B and 91C. Top priority was being given to filling the USARV units, the U.S. units involved in direct combat, as opposed to those serving in an advisory capacity. That made sense from an ethical point of view, but I couldn't help but ask why any of the slots had to go empty. I was told that the training base in the United States simply couldn't keep up. Practically all draftees were leaving the army at the end of their obligatory period of service, and new medics couldn't be trained fast enough to replace all those departing. Supply couldn't keep up with demand; it was as simple as that. At the end of the conversation, I was told, "You've got to stop your whining, Major, and suck it up." It wasn't a very satisfying Thanksgiving Day conversation. I was then faced with the unenviable task of having to explain to the commanders of several sub-sector advisory teams why they had to get by without medical support, even though they were vulnerable to attack at any time.

***

Martha Raye, the entertainer, was in Da Nang in late November. About 30 percent of the marines and sailors in Da Nang were being given time away from duty to see her show. Everyone I talked to said that she was really a good sport and that she put on a very humorous and entertaining show. While I did not get to see her performance, I did get to meet her in the barroom of our Officers' Club. I was surprised to see that she was wearing a U.S. Army field uniform with the insignia of rank of a lieutenant colonel pinned on the lapel. I was later informed that she was an Army Nurse Corps officer in the U.S. Army Reserve.[4]

On 25 November, I took a little boy with the most disfiguring harelip that I had ever seen to the U.S. Navy Hospital for evaluation. I felt so sorry for the little guy. I first saw the child getting on a school bus at the French school. I immediately stopped my jeep, in the middle of the street, in order to catch the driver of the bus before he departed on his delivery route. The driver spoke no English whatsoever. I had to get him to understand I was offering help for the little boy. I wrote my name and phone number on a slip of paper and then went down the aisle of the bus until I found the child. I gently took him by the hand and walked up to the front of the bus. I pointed at the boy's deformed upper lip and then at the medical caduceus on my uniform hoping that he would recognize

it as being symbolic of medicine. I then gave the driver the slip of paper
with my name and phone number on it, pointed at the boy, and said,
"Give to mama, give to mama," hoping the bus driver would understand.
Miracle of miracles, he did. Two days later, I got a phone call from an
English-speaking person concerning the boy. We arranged a meeting
with the boy and his parents that very afternoon, and on 25 November,
I took the boy and his mother to see Dr. Giles.

After evaluation and a physical exam, Dr. Giles agreed to operate on
the little boy. He said the child had what is called a "double harelip." It
was the first one that I had seen. The two indentations in his upper lip
were so deep that one actually intruded deeply into the left nostril of his
nose. Dr. Giles told the mother that the boy would look quite normal after
the double harelip was corrected. The operation was to be approached
in two stages. One of the indentations was to be corrected early the very
next day and then allowed to heal for about ten days before the other side
was done. The hospital was overcrowded with wounded marines at the
time, so the mother was not allowed to stay with the boy at the hospital.
He started to cry when his mother was saying goodbye, so we hung
around the hospital a little longer. When we left, he was playing with
another little boy who had had his harelip corrected a day or two before.

After his first surgery, the boy spent two days in the hospital and then
Sergeant Thong and I returned him to his home. A week later, we brought
the boy and his mother back for the second surgery. I could tell that it
was very frightening for the child. The hospital was still very crowded
and the boy was suddenly alone in a hospital where virtually no one
spoke his language. Because of the space crunch at the moment, he was
assigned a bed in an open ward along with many U.S. Marines. Dr. Giles
told me later that within an hour or two, the marines had him "loosened
up and comfortable." They seemed to dote on the child. Having the little
boy on the ward was probably therapeutic for the recovering marines.

Image 18. Little boy with double harelip prior to surgery

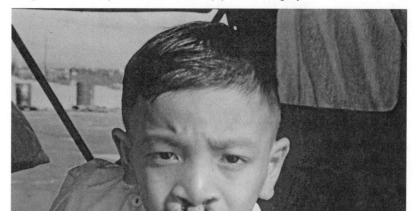

Photo courtesy of the author

On that same day, 25 November, I visited the ARVN Convalescent Center. I tried to stop by once each week in an attempt to cheer up the patients as well as the staff. They seemed to enjoy the banter, the hair tousling, the hand shaking, and the laughter, even though we couldn't really understand what the other was saying. As I approached one poor double amputee, I noticed all sorts of pin-up girls on the wall over his bed, some even taped to the frame of his bed. I smiled at him, pointed at his collection and said, "Number 1."

He laughed and then walked to the wall and took one of the pictures down and gave it to me. He insisted I take it. I was surprised to see that on the back side of the picture was a piece of Vietnamese sheet music. I had Sergeant Thong translate the words of the song into English. I then sent it to my children in the hopes that one of their music teachers would play it for them on the piano while they sang the words. It didn't work, however. The English words didn't seem to fit the melody.

***

The Saturday morning staff meeting on 26 November was frustrating, to say the least. We heard discouraging reports of poor farmers who raised their crops and their animals only to have them plundered by the VC. The poor were caught squarely in the middle, and they had virtually no voice in the matter. The war ground on. There had been very few large-scale operations for several weeks. The U.S. leadership didn't know how to interpret this. The VC and the NVA seemingly did not want to get involved in any large-scale operation. They were willing to engage in frustrating little brush-fire skirmishes and hit and run operations, which were difficult to predict or prevent because there was typically no troop buildup preceding the event. General Walt was frustrated and didn't quite know how to read the signs. Were the VC and NVA regrouping for one big push at the height of the monsoon in January, or had they been punished so badly that they couldn't afford more losses without risking the total disintegration of their forces? It was difficult to determine what was going on. The ARVN intelligence analysts were perplexed. The actions of the enemy were difficult to predict, obscured by many conflicting factors. General Walt had exerted considerable pressure on the intelligence officers to figure out what was going on. The meeting ended on a rather sour note with a frustrated senior American commander and a demoralized ARVN staff.

During the staff meeting, we were also informed that we were on the fringes of a tropical storm that was nearing typhoon proportions. It was blowing very hard and the winds were bringing in heavy sheets of rain, rain that seemed to drive right through you. I had great empathy for the Vietnamese children, as well as for the troops in the field. I knew first-hand that many of the babies and small children of the poor were suffering greatly. I saw them every day on my way to work. Many had runny noses, diarrhea, and pus-afflicted eyes. The public health challenge of trying to fulfill the basic survival needs of the poor was daunting under the best of conditions. But when it rained incessantly, the temperature plummeted, and there was a demoralizing war going on, it became almost impossible to meet the survival needs of the poor. This was especially true of the displaced refugee families who flocked to the cities for protection from the war. I had nightmares about some of the suffering children I saw during MEDCAP visits to remote hamlets and refugee settlements.

Image 19. U.S. Navy corpsman treats child, malnourished as a result of tape-worms

Photo courtesy of the U.S. Navy Bureau of Medicine and Surgery Archives

After this demoralizing staff meeting, Colonel Beeson, our deputy commander, asked that I accompany him to his office. He told me that he wanted me to represent the MACV Advisory Team at a breakfast meeting at III MAF HQ, the largest U.S. combat element in I Corps, to discuss the possibility of a German hospital ship being moved from the Saigon harbor to Da Nang's harbor. The ship's medical staff would work exclusively with wounded Vietnamese civilians. Colonel Beeson had intended to go to the meeting himself, but his schedule became complicated because of the visit of a flag rank officer. He thought I was the logical person to attend the meeting. I told him that I would gladly represent the advisory team at the meeting, as the Vietnamese needed all the help they could possibly get in order to take care of the mounting number of civilian casualties generated by the war in I Corps.

Later that morning, I had to go to the USAID Hospital for a meeting with the American physician who headed the USAID team. On the way to the hospital, passing through the crowded streets of Da Nang, I witnessed two very contrasting funerals. The first had about fifty paid mourners. Grieving could be bought for a price in Vietnam. The casket was on the back of a two-and-a-half-ton Vietnamese Army truck, what the military called a "deuce and a half." Large burning candles flanked both sides of the casket, and the mourners each carried a burning candle as well. As the funeral procession wound its way through the streets of Da Nang, the paid mourners were chanting something, probably one of the ancient and sorrowful dirges of Buddhism.

The other funeral was that of a much poorer person. The characteristic red casket was suspended on two ropes with poles through loops tied into the ends of the ropes. The four pallbearers each had one end of the two poles on their shoulder, carrying the casket in this manner. Following the casket were a grieving man and three children. Although I couldn't be certain, I assumed the deceased was the spouse of the man and the mother of the three children. They were making the sad trip to their loved one's grave, bereaved and pretty much alone.

On Monday, 28 November, Captain Phat and I escorted Jim Lucas, a Scripps Howard reporter, through Duy Tan Hospital. Mr. Lucas's story concerning the hospital was to be published in a week or ten days and, according to him, would reach about twenty-five million readers. Scripps Howard was one of the larger news agencies in the United States. Duy Tan had recently been selected as "functionally and operationally the best Vietnamese military hospital in South Vietnam." It was a real honor for the young commander, Captain Phat. I was pleased for him and for the entire hospital staff. They needed a little recognition.

On that same day, we learned that the commander of our advisory team, Colonel Hamblen, has been extended in his position for an additional six months. He didn't seem upset when he told us this news, so we concluded that he had probably sought the extension. He also told us that he would be given one month of "home leave" in the United States before the start of his extension.

That evening, 28 November, I was invited to a cocktail party, if you could call a gathering of men wearing grubby field uniforms a cocktail party. There were about fifty invited guests. The party was held in a Vietnamese home that had been rented by the Department of Defense to house the members of the Criminal Investigation Division in Da Nang. Mr. Horgan, a CID agent whom I had met at the bar in our Officers' Club, invited me to the event. The home was a very gracious French-style villa. I wondered why the owners of the home had decided to rent it to the American government. It was filled with art and beautiful Asian-style lacquered furniture. I spent about thirty minutes just wandering around the home looking at the art. There were some beautiful mahogany carvings, lots of brass work, and probably forty to fifty drawings and paintings. I thought one piece of art was exceptional. It was done not with oils or watercolors but with crayons. It was a very large picture, perhaps thirty-six by forty-eight inches, of a young mother with a suckling baby. I found it to be very beautiful.

It was always a little intimidating to go to a party such as that described above. Outside the doors of the home were stationed at least fifteen armed guards, two or three of whom carried sub-machine guns and grenades.

There was even one guard on the roof of the home. I was told he was positioned there to guard against a satchel of explosives being dropped down the chimney. To me, it looked almost ludicrous to see fifty men in boots and field uniforms tromping around that beautiful home. Such were the incongruities of war.

Later that night, for the third time, the VC attempted to blow the main bridge over the Han River in Da Nang. The bridge was in such bad shape that the U.S. Marines had to put in a pontoon float bridge right alongside the old bridge to carry the military traffic. But the monsoon rains swelled the river to the point where the float-bridge was in danger of being swept away, so it had to be dismantled before it was destroyed by the fast-moving water. The city was then limping along with the inadequate old bridge. It carried all traffic, military and civilian. The VC knew full well that destroying that bridge would put a serious crimp in both ARVN and U.S. mobility. A new permanent bridge was under construction, but wouldn't be ready for another three or four months.

For the last half of November, I had to have my jeep pushed every time I wanted to start it. Both batteries were dead. There were no jeep batteries to be had in Da Nang, and mine needed two very badly, since it had a 24-volt system requiring two batteries. Pushing the jeep to start it was getting to be a pain in the neck and also a bit dangerous. I didn't like being out at night, teaching for example, with a jeep that would not start unless it was pushed. I hoped batteries would soon arrive, as I was not the only one who needed a couple.

On 29 November I met a man by the name of Martin Rusk. He came into my office in the late afternoon and said he wanted to ask a favor of me. We talked for about thirty minutes without his getting around to asking the favor. By then, it was dinnertime, so I invited him to our Officers' Club. We had a nice relaxing dinner then went up to the bar for a snifter of brandy and more talk. I was not sure then, nor am I now, how much of his story was factual. But I gave him the benefit of the doubt, since I had no way of refuting what he told me, and I didn't want to call him a liar. He said he was a writer and that he had written many articles that were published in reputable journals.

Rusk told me that he was about to embark on writing a book on the Vietnam War, looking at it from the perspective of both North and South. He said he had already gathered most of his source material and had started writing that portion of the book which presented the South's position regarding the war. In order to gain firsthand information about the North's position, he intended to live with the VC and NVA for a prolonged period of time. He claimed that he had "arranged to be captured or abducted by the VC sometime in late January or early February" of 1967, just a couple of months from the time of our meeting. Somehow it all seemed too preposterous to be true. He said that his abduction would occur during the celebration of Tet, the Asian New Year.

I was conflicted as to whether I should report this conversation to the commander of our Advisory Team. I thought he might laugh me out of his office if I did so. On the other hand, it seemed almost traitorous to have oneself purposely captured by the enemy in order to gather material for a book. I had an idea that his preplanned capture, if it came about, would not play well in the United States. I just didn't know if I should believe the man or not, but I kept asking myself why he would make up such a story. I had to admit that he made it all sound very plausible. Since I can find no indication that Mr. Rusk ever published the book he claimed to have started writing, I simply do not know the truth regarding the project or his planned capture.

When we were about to conclude our lengthy barroom conversation, Rusk suddenly remembered why he had wanted to talk to me in the first place. It wasn't to tell me his cockamamie story about the book and his planned capture but to inform me of a young man in Da Nang who desperately needed the services of a good surgeon. Rusk had heard, via the grapevine, that I had a working arrangement with several surgeons at the U.S. Navy Hospital and was hopeful that I could arrange to have a certain young man seen. He said the boy had some type of horrendous growth covering the side of his face and extending down onto his neck.

Mr. Rusk gave me a slip of paper with a Da Nang address, 97 Doc Lap Street, written on it. He explained that this was the address of a small bakery shop. He asked if I might personally go there and, in his words,"try to get a glimpse of the boy who lives in the shadows behind the curtain because of a physical deformity."

At 0830 hours the next morning, the last day of November, Sergeant Thong and I drove to the bakery shop. I wasn't supposed to go into a shop without getting prior approval because the city was still officially off limits, but I decided that in this instance the policy had to be ignored. I parked my jeep right out front of the bakery so we could keep an eye on it. I also locked a chain through the steering wheel and around the steering column so no one could steal it. This was standard practice for all Americans who were fortunate enough to have a jeep.

Upon entering the bakery, we were greeted by a very pleasant Vietnamese lady about forty-five years old. Working with her was an older lady, perhaps seventy years old. They were both surprised to have an American officer, accompanied by a Vietnamese sergeant, enter the shop. Assuredly, it was not an everyday occurrence. Through my interpreter, in very reasoned language and with as calm a demeanor as I could muster, I explained to the younger woman the reason for our visit. She responded by saying, in essence, that she was unaware of any young man who had a growth on the side of his face, that Mr. Rusk must be mistaken, and that perhaps we had the wrong address.

Just as she was saying this, I caught a fleeting glimpse of a young man in another room of the shop as he walked behind a beaded curtain. Though he looked normal, something told me that he was indeed the boy Martin Rusk had told me about. Seconds later, the boy passed by the curtain again, this time moving in the opposite direction and revealing the other side of his face. I couldn't believe what I was seeing. There was some kind of a growth that had almost encapsulated his right ear, and the further it went down the side of his head and onto his neck, the larger and more grotesque it became. It was gray and red in color and looked very much like the waddle on a turkey. Martin Rusk was right. It was a horribly disfiguring growth.

I decided to push ahead. I told Sergeant Thong to tell the lady exactly what I was saying. Then, speaking slowly and using short sentences and simple phraseology, I said something like this: "Madame, you seem like a good person. I saw the young man pass by that curtain. Do you want him to live like that all of his life, to live without friends, to live in the shadows? Maybe he can be helped. I can't promise, but maybe he can be helped. Please let me talk with him."

Suddenly, she put her hands to her face and the tears began to flow. She led us through the beaded curtain into the back room of the bakery. There at a table sat twenty-year-old Nguyen Van Khoi with the grotesque growth on his head. And standing beside him was his mother, the woman with whom we had been talking. I had never seen anything even similar to this growth. Khoi revealed to us that he was very lonely, spending most of his waking hours in the back room of that bakery. If you saw only the left side of his face and head, you would say that he was a very handsome young man. He told us that he had seven years of schooling and was interested in Western literature. He had spent the past five years essentially as a social recluse. He said his mother was his only friend and most others stayed away from him.

His father was dead and his mother, Madame Nguyen Thi Hein, worked in the bakery shop to sustain herself and her son. Khoi also worked in the bakery, but only in the back room because he didn't want to be seen by customers.

Khoi told us that several years ago someone promised that the growth would go away if he would apply a specially formulated ointment for three or four weeks. Khoi said "the man took all of his mother's money in payment for the ointment and then disappeared without doing any good."

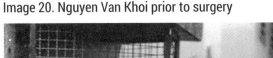

Image 20. Nguyen Van Khoi prior to surgery

Photo courtesy of the author

The very next day, Sergeant Thong and I took Khoi to the Navy Hospital for an evaluation. Dr. Giles was astounded by what he saw. With Khoi's permission, he took a series of photographs of the abnormality. He also called in at least seven or eight other doctors to take a look and give their opinions regarding the feasibility of surgical removal of the growth. Soon, word spread around the hospital and other doctors and nurses poked their heads into the examining room to take a look. All were respectful of Khoi's dignity, and all agreed that they had seen nothing even remotely similar to Khoi's growth during their medical practices. They had heard and read about such growths, but had never seen one. Dr. Giles diagnosed the growth as some type of a nevus, a medical term that I had not heard before. Pathology results showed that it was not malignant. After a careful review of the laboratory results, Dr. Giles decided that he could operate, that it would be done in three stages, and that the pre-op physical exam should be done immediately.

He said that all he needed to proceed with the surgery was the written consent of Khoi's mother. There were definite risks associated with the surgery, and he wanted to explain them to Khoi and his mother. In view of the fact that Dr. Giles wanted to go ahead with the first surgical procedure that very day because his schedule was open, I went back across the bridge over the Han River to try to bring Khoi's mother to the hospital. I thought she would be elated with the news that the growth was operable. I was wrong. After we had met with her the day before, and she had seemingly agreed to have the growth evaluated and possibly removed from her son's head, she had changed her mind. I was crestfallen, and so was Sergeant Thong. She did, however, agree to come with us to the hospital, as the morning rush in the bakery shop was over. As she entered the ward, Khoi ran to her with tears in his eyes, embraced her, and obviously pleaded with her to give permission for the surgeons to proceed. She turned to Dr. Giles, smiled, and nodded her consent to proceed. It was an emotional moment for all of us.

I hoped and prayed that all would go well during the surgery. Khoi seemed to be a fine young man who deserved a chance at a normal life. That afternoon, Dr. Giles and another surgeon worked on removal of that portion of the nevus encapsulating Khoi's ear. It was a very difficult and time-consuming procedure. The growth looked to me like convoluted tissue, something like brain tissue. The various tentacles of the growth were interwoven, making it difficult to sort out points of origin. Dr. Giles told my interpreter to tell Khoi that after the growth was removed, he would need a series of skin grafts. The skin would come from the other side of Khoi's neck. Three or four weeks from the date of the first surgery, Khoi returned for the second stage, and eventually the third. It was a long, drawn-out process, but it changed Khoi from, in his own words, "a lonely person with not much hope" to one who had a chance to live a happy and productive life.

CHAPTER 6

DECEMBER 1966

On Thursday evening, 1 December, I was sitting in the Officers' Club dining room enjoying a second or third cup of coffee with friends when a man approached our table and introduced himself as David Burrington of NBC News. He told me he wanted to do a human interest story on the repair of children's harelips that could be televised in the United States sometime during the Christmas season. He had been given my name as a point of contact. Specifically he was hoping to get some footage of a child, boy or girl, with a harelip prior to repair, during surgery, and a couple of weeks after the repair had been completed. I told him I'd be pleased to work with him but that I could make no promises because I did not know if Dr. Giles would allow television cameras in his operating suite. I said I would discuss the matter with Dr. Giles. We agreed to meet again a few days later.

I talked to Doctor Giles the next day and he agreed, providing the camera would be positioned in a place of his choosing and that Mr. Burrington and his cameraman would stay behind the camera. I relayed that information to Burrington when next I saw him. He agreed to the terms Dr. Giles had established. I also told him that I would notify him just as soon as I had a child scheduled for harelip surgery.

Two days later, a note from David Burrington was left on my desk during my absence. It informed me that NBC had ordered him to go to Dong Ha as quickly as possible. The harelip story had to be put on hold. From the note, I concluded that Mr. Burrington was a very thoughtful and humble man. I had no idea why he was ordered to Dong Ha. As far as I knew things were quiet throughout Quang Tri Province at that moment. All I could conclude was that NBC News was privy to information I did not have.

Shortly after Mr. Burrington left for Dong Ha, I found the perfect subject. He was a six-year-old boy, five according to the Western way of computing age, by the name of Ho Thien. Ho was just a delightful little guy, uninhibited and full of fun. At his early age he did not seem overly aware of his abnormality. He appeared to have two good friends and played with them very actively, like a normal five-year-old child, but most of the other children seemed disinclined to play with him. Sergeant Thong and I first saw him on the playground at Thanh Tam School (Sacred Heart School), which was not far from my hotel.

We sought out Ho's mother. She was ecstatic about the possibility of getting the harelip corrected. Two or three days went by, and I still hadn't heard from Mr. Burrington. Dr. Giles called to tell me that his schedule was still pretty much open and that he would welcome a surgical case or two. I decided that if I didn't hear from David Burrington soon, I'd have to go ahead and schedule the surgery for Ho Thien. Somehow, it didn't seem ethical to delay operating on the little boy in order to accommodate NBC News. I started thinking of the "what ifs." What if something were to happen to Dr. Giles and his services were no longer available? What if the Navy Hospital suddenly became extremely busy and stayed that way for a prolonged period of time? What if Ho Thien's mother changed her mind as a result of the delay? The "what ifs" weighed on my mind.

I called Dr. Giles and told him of my concerns. He agreed with all of them, so we went ahead and scheduled Ho Thien for his pre-op physical exam. He passed it with flying colors and, in hopes that Burrington would soon be back, we scheduled the surgery for two days hence. Miracle of miracles, David Burrington called that very evening to tell me that he was back in Da Nang and eager to get on with the filming. He told me that the first filming he wanted to do was in Ho's kindergarten classroom, so I scurried around to get permission from the principal of Sacred Heart School and Ho's teacher. I also informed Ho's mother of the plan.

Two days later, Burrington filmed the first part of Ho Thien's story. Ho and his classmates were shown coming out of morning Mass. Ho was one of 126 kindergarten students marching off to their respective classrooms. Then Burrington and his cameraman did some filming in the classroom itself. The nuns, all dressed in white habits, were bustling around the room, typical of a kindergarten classroom. Footage was also taken of the children singing songs, learning to count, learning the names of the various parts of their bodies, and so on.

Image 21. Ho Thien in kindergarten classroom prior to surgery

Photo courtesy of the author

Sergeant Thong and I then transported Ho and his mother to the Navy Hospital. David Burrington filmed our arrival and my carrying Ho into one of the hospital's many Quonset buildings. Ho's mother and Sergeant Thong were walking alongside. The next footage was of Dr. Giles performing the surgery. Burrington and the cameraman quietly left the surgical suite after about five minutes of filming. The surgery went well and Dr. Giles was confident the results would be good.

Ten days later, Burrington and his cameraman filmed the little boy going back into his classroom for the first time following the corrective surgery. By that time the sutures had been removed and the swelling was starting to recede. The healing process was well underway. Ho's classmates stood around him, admiring the change as the little boy smiled. One little girl reached up and gently touched Ho's repaired lip.

Image 22. Ho Thien ten days after surgery

Photo courtesy of the author

Burrington was hopeful the film could be made into an NBC Special Report, but unfortunately the camera work was not very good, so thoughts of a thirty-minute special had to be abandoned. But a roughly three-minute segment was shown on the *Huntley-Brinkley Report* on the evening of 20 December and repeated the next morning on NBC's *Today Show*.

***

I've always been a morning person. I very much enjoyed the early morning hours in Da Nang. On the morning of Friday, 2 December, it was pitch dark, and there was no moon. There were very few street lights in Da Nang, except in the primary business district in the very center of the city. About the only lights I saw on my way to work, other than the headlights of my jeep and other passing vehicles, were those in the Buddhist altars or shrines, the gas lanterns in all the shops and small dwelling places along the road, and the bread-warming candles burning in the mobile restaurants.

Thousands of people, especially workers, were already on the streets. Many of them worked for RMK-BRJ, the large American construction conglomerate that seemed to get practically all the defense construction contracts awarded. The amount of defense-related construction in the country staggered my imagination, and RMK-BMJ seemed to hire people from all over the world. This hodge-podge of humanity created some communication and social problems, but somehow the required work seemed to get done.

I Corps was quiet on 2 December, as it had been during late November. Nobody knew quite how to interpret the lack of contact with the VC or NVA. There was speculation that the relative calm was because of the weather. For the past week or two, the monsoon hadn't been as ferocious as it had been earlier. The enemy liked bad weather. He knew that weather impaired our mobility and diminished our technological advantages.

I decided to take advantage of the break in the weather and fly to Quang Ngai. The new commander of the ARVN 2nd Medical Company was under fire, and consideration was being given to relieving him of command. The

Vietnamese made frequent command changes, too frequent in my mind. I was reluctant to offer criticism of a new commander for fear he would immediately be relieved of command. It seemed that whenever I pointed out the shortcomings of one of their commanders, instead of taking corrective action, they immediately replaced him. That was not good. I was resolved to somehow get them to understand that new commanders often make mistakes, and only if they failed to learn from their mistakes should they be replaced. It was difficult getting some of their mid-level leaders thinking along those lines. Fortunately the I Corps Surgeon, Dr. Tu, understood fully, but as a staff officer he had no command authority.

The mail delivery on 3 December brought me a package from my good wife and children. It contained, of all things, a Christmas tree—a small collapsible tree, about three feet tall, with all the lights and ornaments already on it. I was the envy of my fellow advisors. No one else in our hotel had a Christmas tree. I placed it on my seldom-used hotel room desk, where it brightened my drab room considerably. Many officers stopped by to see it.

During the morning of 3 December, Esther Clark, a staff writer for the *Phoenix Gazette*, interviewed me for an article she was writing about the exemplary work U.S. Navy physicians, nurses, and technicians were doing to help the poorest of Vietnam's poor. She told me that, while some of her stories got wider circulation than just her own paper, she didn't know if other publications would pick this one up. I was delighted to spend an hour with her, as I felt the American people should be aware of the humanitarian work the staff of the U.S. Naval Support Activity Hospital in Da Nang was doing. Ms. Clark was later the recipient of a prestigious USMC award for her reporting while in Vietnam. The award was named in honor of Dickey Chapelle, a female reporter who was killed by a VC booby trap while on patrol with a USMC company in I Corps.[1]

Later that same morning, Jim Lucas, the Scripps Howard reporter, dropped into my office to ask a few questions about my relationship with Duy Tan and the U.S. Navy hospital.[2] During our conversation, he told me that he had been trying for several weeks to get an interview with Madame Nam, a very wealthy Da Nang resident. He described her as supposedly one of the wealthiest women in all of Asia. I told him that I had never heard of Madame Nam.

Just by chance, during lunch on that same day, I mentioned this conversation to Captain Bob Williams, the officer in charge of procuring rental real estate for the MACV Advisory Team in Da Nang. Bob responded by saying, "I know her. I'll see what I can do." He then told me that he had negotiated the rent for over a million dollars' worth of property from Madame Nam, adding that he had tremendous faith in Madame Nam's integrity as a landlord and businesswoman. He described her as aboveboard in all her dealings, highly ethical, and highly intelligent.

About three hours later, Captain Williams called and said, "Well, it's all set up. You, me and Jim Lucas are to have dinner with Madame Nam tomorrow evening." I hadn't expected such an immediate response and wondered if I could even reach Lucas on such short notice. I called the press center. Fortunately he was there. Although he had other plans for the next evening, he cancelled them because of the rare opportunity to spend an evening with Madame Nam. The appointed time for the three of us to arrive at her home was 1900 hours.

Bob Williams picked me up at about 1830 hours, and, in the rain and cold, we drove to the press center and got Jim Lucas. We arrived at the Nam residence promptly at 1900 hours and were greeted by a smiling woman about fifty years old, dressed in a very plain white blouse and black silk pajama-like pants, the typical Vietnamese household garb. I assumed the woman to be a servant. I was wrong. It was none other than Madame Nam. Her home, though quite small, was beautifully furnished. She had all sorts of lacquered furniture with mother of pearl and ivory inlays, very characteristic of Southeast Asia. It was easy to determine her religious affiliation. From the little sitting room off the living room where we were enjoying a glass of good wine before dinner, I counted eleven objects of Christian art. There were several Christian crosses with the corpus of Christ hanging on the cross, a number of painted and ceramic Madonnas, several oil paintings by European artists depicting both the birth and death of Christ, and a large portrait of the late Pope John XXIII. Madame Nam had a very effervescent, outgoing personality and talked openly and proudly about her Christian faith.

Soon, other people started to arrive. Whereas we had thought we were going to be with Madame Nam by ourselves, it turned out that there were eleven invited guests. Jim seemed disappointed. The three of us were the only Americans. Dinner parties appeared to be frequent events for Madame Nam. Although she was the hostess, she was totally relaxed and very casual. Never before had I seen a woman so completely at ease and yet so completely in charge. Although I felt certain that servants had prepared the six-course meal, she served it all herself. It was a gourmet delight, and she explained each dish as we sampled it.

As the evening moved on, it became more and more obvious that we were talking to a very exceptional person. A few of her guests did not speak English, so she moved back and forth between Vietnamese, English, and sometimes French, making sure that everyone was included in the conversation. The surroundings, although rich and elegant, were not extravagant. Her home was very welcoming and tastefully decorated.

After the two-hour meal ended, the guests started to depart, but Madame Nam invited the three of us, the Americans, to stay. We moved out of the dining room back into the small sitting room where we had been earlier. Madame Nam then offered brandy and, after serving those who wanted it, she smiled and said, "Mr. Lucas, you may ask me any questions that you wish as long as they do not involve politics. I refuse to discuss politics." Thus the ground rules were set for Jim Lucas to begin the interview.

I'll try to summarize some of the things that Lucas, through his skillful questioning, learned about Madame Nam and her family. Prior to the Communist takeover in 1954, the Nam family apparently owned somewhere between 35 and 50 percent of all the commercial real estate in the city of Dong Hoi, a coastal city in North Vietnam. I had never heard of the city before listening to Madame Nam. When the Communists took over North Vietnam, all members of the Nam family, except one, decided to leave Dong Hoi. Madame Nam's sister decided to remain in Dong Hoi and take charge of the family's real estate holdings. Within two months, everything was taken away. Madame Nam said, "Today the sister in Dong Hoi is penniless and in poor health but not allowed to leave." Madame Nam said that recent secretive correspondence revealed that her sister was living the life of a destitute pauper. There was seemingly nothing that Madame Nam could do to improve her sister's situation.

Madame Nam moved to Da Nang in 1954 and, since that time, had accumulated her vast wealth. It was obvious that she was a very savvy businesswoman. What she used as seed money to get started in Da Nang, I do not know. In addition to vast property holdings in Da Nang, she was also in the construction business. Just recently, her firm had built a new Officers' Club for the U.S. Navy in Da Nang. Although I hadn't been in the club, Bob Williams told me that it was strikingly attractive. According to him, everyone liked to do business with Madame Nam because of her integrity and sincerity.

Jim Lucas dug out of Madame Nam the fact that she was currently providing total support for two Vietnamese orphanages. She did not divulge this to him on her own, but Lucas had knowledge of this generous act and brought it up. She reluctantly admitted that Jim's information was accurate. According to Lucas, she was giving millions of dollars away each year. Again, she reluctantly admitted that she kept virtually no monetary reserve. She said, "My property holdings are my reserve." In short, Jim was able to determine that she gave practically all her earnings to an array of charitable causes.

We also learned that Madame Nam had been a "good friend" of Pope John XXIII, who died in 1963, and that she had had personal audiences with all the last four popes, including the serving pope at that time, Paul

VI. She traveled to Rome about once each year. She told us that, while she was Catholic, she considered herself "a missionary for all of Christianity."

One of her sisters was a Carmelite Nun living in France. Her parents were both deceased. She described herself as "completely happy." She said she was "totally at peace with her God and the world around her." She also said, "I love both God and humanity." When Lucas asked her why she gave so much to charity, she laughed and said, "Well, there's that camel and the eye of a needle." We did not find out whether she had ever been married. That was not discussed.

The evening was a most memorable experience. I cherish the memory of that remarkable woman. Madame Nam was living testimony to the fact that wealth doesn't necessarily spoil or corrupt. Afterward Jim Lucas thanked Bob Williams profusely for setting up the invitation. Strangely, I can now find no reference to Madame Nam online. It's as if she never existed.

***

Sunday morning, 4 December, dawned cold and raining. During the night I had to get up and put another blanket on the bed in order to be comfortable. All I could think of, as I shivered in my room, were the babies of the poor. The day before, I had seen several young mothers button their tiny babies inside their sweaters or coats next to their breasts in order to keep the babies warm.

On Monday morning, 5 December, it was not raining but still was quite cold. About mid-day, I had to drive over to the Navy Hospital. On the way, I couldn't help but notice the cold toddlers and small children. To get to the hospital, I had to pass through one particularly poor area, a refugee settlement not too far from the bridge over the Han River. Temperatures were in the low fifties, and there was a brisk wind that seemed to cut right through one. Playing alongside the road were several little refugee children, ranging perhaps from two to five years old, without a stitch of clothing on their bodies. They were blue from cold. They just kept running. Their running seemed almost a reflex action to ward off the cold. Later that day, I drove out to the Marine Civil Affairs Unit and picked up a large amount of children's clothing. I carried clothing in my briefcase and, whenever I saw a nude child, tried to find the mother to give her some warm clothing for her children. I had found that if clothing was distributed in bulk, such as to a hamlet or refugee community, the poorest of the poor never seemed to get their fair share.

When I returned to my hotel room on the evening of 7 December, Pearl Harbor Day, after a hard day's work followed by dinner at the Officers' Club, I was greeted by no electricity and no running water. It was hard to even take a sponge bath using water poured into the sink from a five-gallon can when it was pitch dark in the bathroom. And it was especially hard when you were as dirty as I was. Bathing out of a small sink by candlelight, in a very cold, diminutive bathroom, was not my idea of fun. But I wasn't complaining, as I knew only too well that there were thousands, hundreds of thousands, of young soldiers and marines who would consider my surroundings luxurious.

For want of something better to do, in the complete absence of any light for reading, I got in my jeep to drive to the Officers' Club and wile away a couple of hours at the bar. While driving along the Han River, I saw an old lady trip and fall into a pile of rubble at a construction site. She couldn't seem to get up, but nobody stopped to help her. I couldn't pass her by, even though I knew it was a bit dangerous to stop and give assistance when there were few people around, and it was in a relatively isolated area. I eventually got her out of the scrap heap and onto her feet, but she seemed unstable. I didn't know what to do with her. We couldn't communicate at all. Finally, in desperation, I hailed a pedicab, shoved some piastres at the driver, loaded the poor woman onto the seat and hoped the driver could find out where she lived and take her home.

I proceeded to the Officers' Club and spent about two hours at the bar drinking a beer or two while playing a dice game. Then calamity struck. When I walked to the parking lot, I noted that my jeep was missing. The security chain had been cut and the vehicle was gone. Only the padlock and cut chain could be found. The MP who responded to my report of a stolen vehicle said that my fellow Americans probably stole it. He explained that there had been several vehicles stolen in Da Nang in recent weeks, and in all cases where the perpetrator had been apprehended, it turned out to be an American soldier who had committed the crime. He went on to explain that jeep parts were in such short supply, troops who lived in the boonies resorted to thievery in order to keep their jeeps running. They would steal a jeep, cannibalize the parts they needed, or thought they would need in the near future, and then abandon the inoperable vehicle somewhere on the edge of the city. I hoped my jeep would quickly be found and that it would be operable. Without it, I simply couldn't do my job. I dreaded having to tell my boss the next morning.

Being without a jeep, I was relegated to walking. The distance from my room to my office was approximately two miles, but at 0500 hours, it seemed much longer. On 9 December, while walking to work, I couldn't help but notice how many Buddhist altars and small shrines there were in front of people's homes and businesses. I previously had been told by Sergeant Thong that the altars were considered to be so sacred that no one, for any reason, could move or destroy one of them. I couldn't help but think that this would be a definite deterrent to economic development and community revitalization. All buildings, roads and infrastructure projects had to be planned so as not to interfere with one of the altars or shrines. Almost every prominent Buddhist family had an altar or small shrine situated near their home or place of business. The shrines all seemed to have a night light that cast shadows on the ground and nearby foliage. I was most aware of the unusual, somewhat disconcerting, shadows as I walked the two miles to my office on that early Friday morning.

Friday, 9 December, turned out to be a very sad day for MACV Advisory Team #1. Four advisors were seriously wounded. All required hospitalization, and three needed surgery. Fortunately all were expected to live and eventually recover from their wounds. All were evacuated, first to Japan and then to the United States. It saddened all of us deeply. There was a pall hanging over the headquarters. I didn't personally know any of the four. All of them served on sub-sector advisory teams. It always confounded me how an incident such as this impacted individual advisory team members in such diverse ways. Some advisors became blustery and angry, others cursed and swore and threatened revenge, while still others seemed to quietly retreat into their own protective shells.

Also on 9 December, Captain Phat, the capable commander of Duy Tan General Hospital, was promoted to major. I was most pleased that his talents and dedication were being recognized. An equivalent command in the United States Army, that of a 1,000-bed general hospital, would have called for an officer serving in the rank of full colonel or brigadier general.

On Saturday morning, 10 December, Vietnamese public health authorities reported that there were forty-eight new cases of bubonic plague in east Da Nang. If left untreated, about half to two-thirds of those infected would die within four or five days. It was an extremely deadly disease. The cases were concentrated among the residents of three hamlets, all of which provided housing for Buddhist refugees. I was told by an ARVN physician that Buddhist beliefs, practices, and traditions impeded progress in controlling and preventing these types of plague outbreaks. Yersinia pestis, then known as Pasteurella pestis, is the bacterium that causes bubonic plague. The bacterium is transmitted from a flea to a human. Usually the flea inhabits the body of a rat. The rat serves as the host. Therefore, according to the ARVN physician, two things were of great importance when trying to prevent or control an outbreak of plague. The rats and the fleas had to be exterminated simultaneously. If the rats were exterminated and no attention was paid to the fleas, the fleas simply moved to another warm-bodied host, usually a human, and transmitted the dreaded disease. The Vietnamese public health authorities did reasonably well in their attempts to control the fleas. They would simply go in and thoroughly dust a hamlet or village with insecticides, destroying most of the fleas. But if the rat was not controlled simultaneously, the few remaining fleas inhabiting the rats' bodies sometimes moved to human hosts, thereby infecting them with the disease.

I was told that in the predominately Christian hamlets and villages, the public health officials had reasonable success in controlling both the flea and rat populations. To control the rats, they simply initiated programs whereby the people brought dead rats to a central point and exchanged the carcasses for things their families needed for daily living—soap, salt, rice, etc. Thousands of dead rats were turned in under this exchange program, which was similar to many state and locality programs initiated in the United States in the 1920s and 1930s. But in the Buddhist hamlets and villages, these incentive programs didn't work as well. Why? I was told it was because of Buddhist beliefs regarding reincarnation, that people, upon dying, may be reincarnated as another human or as an animal, to include rodents. Therefore, some believed that when they killed a rat, there was a chance they were destroying the life of one of their reincarnated ancestors. That belief, I was told, proved very difficult for public health officials to overcome. I was not able to determine the veracity of this information.

On Monday morning, 12 December, it was not raining. The day before had also been quite nice. There was hope that the monsoon was tapering off. During the height of the monsoon, combat units, American as well as South Vietnamese, were living in far more dangerous conditions. Surveillance equipment was not nearly as effective in bad weather and the elusive enemy could get within a couple hundred yards of defensive positions before being detected.

As of 12 December, I still had no jeep. I relied upon catching rides with others, when they were going my way, but I really needed reliable transportation to do my job. Jeeps were in such short supply that my chances of getting one anytime soon seemed remote. It had been a week since my assigned vehicle had been stolen.

When I returned to my room that evening, I noted that my maid, Bá Vy, had left a Christmas card and gift for me in my room. The gift was a lacquered vase. I wished she hadn't expended the money to purchase a gift, as I was certain her growing family was in desperate straits. Obviously, I had to accept it in the spirit in which it was given—with a grateful heart. She was grateful for the job, and I was equally grateful for her laundry and cleaning services. I was resolved to find for her a gift that would make her life and the lives of her ten children and her husband a little easier.

On Tuesday morning, 13 December, I experienced a significant setback. My NCOIC, Master Sergeant August Davis, a fine soldier, was supposed to open the MACV dispensary for sick call at 0600 hours, as he did all mornings. When he didn't show up, which was uncharacteristic of him, I borrowed a jeep and rushed to his room. I found him lying unconscious on the floor. I immediately summoned an ambulance, and he was rushed to the Navy Hospital, where it was determined that he was in a diabetic coma, a very serious condition. The attending physician told me that had he remained undetected in his room for another two to three hours, he probably would have died. He also told me that he would have to be medically evacuated to Japan and then to the United States just as soon as they could get him stabilized. I really hated to see him go, as he was an exceptionally loyal and capable non-commissioned officer. I was authorized five NCOs in Da Nang, and, as of Sergeant Davis's departure, I had none, not even a medic to run the dispensary.

On 14 December all MACV advisors in the HQ were asked to attend an early morning briefing. We were informed that there had been a flurry of incidents throughout I Corps. The G-2 and G-3 didn't know how to interpret the heightened activity on the part of the enemy. The incidents had started the previous Friday and had intensified in number and strength since then. The VC and NVA had been concentrating their efforts on disrupting our lines of communication and transportation. The big question seemed to be whether these were stand-alone actions or tied into some much larger planned action still to come. In short, were these incidents a prelude to a large attack? Many of the intelligence analysts seemed to be reaching that conclusion.

On 15 December, my boss, LTC Mabra, departed for a five-day meeting in Saigon. Before departing, he appointed me as the acting G-4 advisor and specifically ordered that I not leave Da Nang during his absence "unless there was an extreme emergency." He graciously threw me the keys to his jeep and told me to use it during his absence.

Later that same day, I got an early Christmas gift. Totally unexpected, I received a call from the Da Nang Air Base. The person calling said, "Sir, I'm SFC Richard Simmons and I've been assigned to your office. I'm wondering if someone could come pick me up?" My new NCOIC had arrived just one day after Sergeant Davis was hospitalized. I looked upon his arrival as being almost providential.

Colonel Hamblen stopped in my office just before dinnertime that same day to tell me that he was going home on thirty days leave. He was to depart the very next morning, weather permitting. He also told me that when he returned, he wanted to sit down with me and "have a long talk." I couldn't help but wonder what that was all about, but since he said it in a pleasant manner I wasn't overly concerned.

On 16 December, I drove to the Navy Hospital and said goodbye to Master Sergeant Davis. He was scheduled to depart Vietnam early the next morning on a medevac flight to Japan. He vowed to return, but I knew in my heart that I was probably seeing him for the last time. He was a good and decent man and a fine soldier.

Christmas was rapidly approaching, but it was difficult to get into the spirit of the season. On the morning of 17 December, however, it actually looked a little like Christmas. During the night, it had cooled down into the low sixties, whereas the day before it had been in the low nineties. The result was ground fog. Heavy fog in Da Nang, for some inexplicable reason, was not very common. That morning, all the grass and tropical foliage had a coat of white dew. As I drove to work in Colonel Mabra's jeep, I couldn't help but feel a little more in the spirit of Christmas.

I noted that there was a red glow over the mountains. "Red sky in the morning, sailor take warning. Red sky at night, sailor's delight," came to mind. It was tranquil and beautiful. I vowed that someday, long after this struggle was over, I would come back with my loving wife to show her the natural beauty of this country.

By Sunday, 18 December, there were more signs of Christmas starting to appear. Several offices in I Corps HQ were decorated with wreaths, tinsel and greenery, and all the wards at the U.S. Navy Hospital had small decorated trees on display for the enjoyment of patients and hospital staff. The Officers' Club was nicely decorated, and Christmas music was being piped into the dining room and bar. Also, the Christians of Da Nang were starting to decorate the exterior of their cathedral. It was a beautiful day, in the mid-eighties, and the sun was shining brightly. Unfortunately, I was the SDO and so unable to get out and enjoy all that.

The SDO activities were rather routine until about 1600 hours, when I received a call from the MACV Surgeon's Office informing me of two things: one, I was to receive two additional NCOs to be assigned to my office, which delighted me, and two, I had to attend an ARVN medical convention coupled with an ARVN Officer Basic Course graduation exercise in Saigon commencing on 27 December, which bothered me greatly. I wondered why a medical convention would be scheduled during wartime. As I was sitting there trying to decide how I could best adjust my schedule to accommodate the Saigon meeting, my routine day suddenly turned interesting.

Two U.S. Marine Corps jeeps came screeching into the I Corps compound at about 1645. Each contained an enlisted Marine driver, and one jeep had a Marine guard as well. The guard had his rifle trained on the passengers in the rear seat of the first jeep, three men in black pajama-like attire. All three were blindfolded, and their wrists were tied. They had been captured in an on-going operation in Dien Ban District, just outside of Da Nang. All three had been armed when captured and were said to have inflicted casualties on the Marines. Clearly these captives had to be imprisoned.

The second jeep, however, contained a man and a woman, both probably twenty to twenty-five years old, and a baby about a year old. The man was blindfolded and gagged, and his wrists were bound and tied with a rope to a U-bolt welded to the floorboard of the back seat. The woman was not bound, tied, or gagged, but she was crying hysterically. At first, I didn't even notice the baby, who was lying on the lap of the mother and covered with a straw mat. The baby was dressed in her Sunday best, a pink dress and a new pair of blue thongs on her tiny feet. A bullet or piece of shrapnel had nicked the upper part of the baby's arm. The wound was not serious. Bleeding was minimal, and there was no bone damage.

The marines explained that the prisoners had been captured in Dien Ban District and that they had been ordered by their commander to take the captives to Hoa Vang, the adjoining district, and turn them over to the district chief for processing and imprisonment. Dien Ban District HQ was still being contested, so they could not take the captives there. Upon arriving at Hoa Vang, they were told, through an interpreter, that the district chief would not accept the captives because they had not been captured in his district. This seemed to be typical Vietnamese reasoning at district level. They were very territorial in their thinking.

The marines then brought the captives to I Corps Headquarters for want of something better to do with them. And I, being the SDO, along with the ARVN SDO, had the task of deciding what to do with them.

There was no question about the occupants of the first jeep. All three had to be taken to the POW camp on the other side of the Han River and imprisoned. But the occupants of the second jeep bothered me. I requested an interpreter from upstairs and had her read their accompanying interrogation tags to me. The man was said to be a member of an organization that was considered to be pro-VC. The woman was the daughter of a man who was believed to be an active member of the

VC. Because of this fragile evidence both were classified as Viet Cong suspects. I hated that kind of reasoning. If your father was thought to be a member of the Viet Cong, you too, almost by default, were considered either a VC or a sympathizer.

If I had had my way, we would have taken the man, the woman, and the baby back to their home village and released them. But my way did not prevail. The ARVN SDO and I ended up by calling in the ARVN G-2 and the American G-2 advisor, LTC Lufton, to advise us regarding what to do with the captives. They ordered that all were to be imprisoned overnight and that on Monday morning the fate of the man and woman would be determined after thorough interrogation. I told Colonel Lufton that it was my opinion that if the man and the woman were not Viet Cong sympathizers when all of this started, they assuredly would be after spending a night incarcerated in the POW camp.

I had to admit, however, that I could readily appreciate the viewpoint of the marines who had captured the detainees. Their story was that, while sweeping through a small village in Dien Ban District, they took heavy fire. Two U.S. Marines were killed and three badly wounded. I could understand that; when your buddy next to you is gunned down, you would be unwilling to take a chance with anyone. Nothing was black and white. There were so many shades of gray in the war. It had become a very frustrating conflict.

While Colonel Lufton and his Vietnamese counterpart were deciding on the disposition of the prisoners, I dressed the wound on the baby's arm, hoping it would not become infected. The woman smiled her gratitude before being taken off to the POW camp.

The Viet Cong had been exerting themselves throughout the five provinces that comprised I Corps for the past eight to ten days. They had some noteworthy and surprising successes. Some of their ambushes and brushfire attacks had hurt us badly. No one seemed to know exactly what was happening. Conjecture was that perhaps the enemy wanted to show his strength prior to the proposed Christmas and New Year's ceasefire or temporary truce. That way, if talks aimed at a more prolonged truce were to be initiated, they would be in a better bargaining position. This was a very strange war, indeed. To the best of my knowledge, we, the United States and the ARVN, had lost very few major battles, and yet the VC and NVA seemed able to strike back, with strength, at a time and place of their choosing. We were victorious in practically all the major battles, but they hurt us badly in many of the firefights and skirmishes.

In the early morning of Monday, 19 December, the night sky was alive with flares. I could see them as I drove to the office in my borrowed jeep. Flares were used to light up areas that were deemed vulnerable to attack. The flares actually provided enough light to see an attacking or infiltrating force for quite some distance. If flares were constantly kept in the sky over vulnerable areas or prime targets, the chances of an actual attack were minimized. An ignited flare floated to earth on a parachute, and its rate of descent was so slow, it took seven or eight minutes for the flare to hit the ground. The flares were shot high into the sky by mortars or dropped from airplanes referred to as flare ships.

LTC Mabra got back from Hong Kong on 20 December and reclaimed his jeep, so I was again without transportation. I spent much of the day orienting the newly assigned NCOs. I told them of the desperate situation we were in regarding staffing as a prelude to telling them that it might become necessary to assign one or both of them to sub-sector advisory teams. I couldn't allow the sub-sector advisory teams in more dangerous situations to go without medical support.

On Thursday morning, 22 December, I had to again walk the lonely two miles from my billet to my office. As I neared I Corps HQ, I was feeling rather melancholy and a bit sorry for myself, being so far away from home during this the most joyous time of the year. Suddenly, I noticed something very different about the entrance gate to the HQ. Erected alongside the guarded gate was a metal scaffolding, and attached to it was an illuminated Star of Bethlehem. It cheered me greatly. Suddenly, the self-pity that I was feeling disappeared. I found out later that the star was purchased and erected by the ARVN officers and soldiers assigned to the I Corps HQ. It was most thoughtful of them, especially since so few were Christian. Practically all were Buddhist. It was a kind gesture on their part which I think of often.

The signs and symbols of Christmas elsewhere were growing more visible by the hour. I noted that a platform, on top of which was a wooden altar, had been constructed in front of the cathedral. The Archbishop of the Da Nang Diocese was to celebrate a high Mass outside the cathedral on Christmas Eve. A light blue spire reaching up to the heavens, placed against a red silk banner, served as a backdrop for altar. It looked very impressive in an Asian sort of way.

It was announced that Billy Graham would preach at the U.S. Marine Amphitheater in Da Nang on Christmas Day. The amphitheater was built into the side of a hill on the edge of Da Nang. I was hoping to go to the service, as I had great respect for the man. Cardinal Spellman was scheduled to celebrate Mass in that same amphitheater the day after Christmas.[3] I knew I would not be able to attend that service because I would be on my way to Saigon to attend the meeting called by the MACV Surgeon. Also, the Bob Hope show was scheduled for 28 December, again in that same hillside amphitheater, during my absence from Da Nang.[4]

On 22 December, I received a phone call from the MACV Surgeon's Office passing on the most welcome news that Advisory Team #1 would be receiving a large influx of medics during the next two weeks. The scheduled assignments would bring the medical section almost up to its authorized strength. Within two weeks we would have on board thirty-seven of the forty-three medics we were authorized. Needless to say, I was elated.

On that same day, I received news of major medical personnel changes in I Corps. Recently promoted and multi-talented Major Phat, who commanded Duy Tan General Hospital, was to be reassigned to the ARVN Airborne Division stationed near Saigon. This assignment change was at his request. He had long wanted to get back to an airborne division. Major

Tu, the serving I Corps Surgeon, whom I respected greatly and worked with very well, would take command of Duy Tan General Hospital and Captain Nhan, who was the I Corps Preventive Medicine Officer, would temporarily be assigned as the I Corps Surgeon and become my primary counterpart. The changes were to be effective on 1 February.

Friday, 23 December, was a very memorable day. I was invited by General Lam, the ARVN commander of I Corps, to join him aboard the USS *Repose*,[5] where he and Madame Lam were to present Christmas gifts to each of the U.S. Marines, ARVN soldiers and POWs hospitalized aboard the ship. I was to help coordinate the event. The ship was floating in the South China Sea about twelve miles offshore. I flew out to the ship by helicopter, along with Major Dien, an ARVN Civil Affairs Section representative, an ARVN photographer, and three pretty young women, all members of the ARVN Women's Army Corps who worked in the Social Services Section of I Corps HQ. The young women were to help General and Mrs. Lam present gifts to every wounded serviceman or woman on board, regardless of religion, gender, race, rank, or nationality. Five seriously wounded Viet Cong soldiers were also aboard the ship. They, too, were to receive a gift from General or Mrs. Lam. Christmas knew no bounds on that day, nor should it ever.

The helicopter that we flew on preceded General and Mrs. Lam's by about forty-five minutes. Upon arrival, I was greeted by the skipper of the ship, Captain Gossom; the commander of the hospital, Captain Nadbath, (there are two separate commands on a hospital ship); and the chief nurse, Commander Yasevicitch. After a brief tour of the ship, we positioned the gifts in each of the hospital wards for ease of distribution. During the tour that preceded the gift giving, I was most impressed with the sophistication of the equipment onboard and the comprehensiveness of the medical services the ship provided. After positioning the gifts in the wards, we were invited to Captain Gossom's cabin for coffee. We were in his cabin for no more than two minutes when the first of the three young women got seasick from the constant rocking of the ship, then the second, and then the third, followed by the photographer and then Major Dien. All were put to bed, so I was the only member of the advanced party left standing.

At 1015 hours, General and Madame Lam, along with the I Corps Chief of Staff and his spouse, Colonel and Madame Nghia, and Colonel Beeson, the Acting Commander of MACV Advisory Team #1, arrived on board. Captains Gossom and Nadbath, along with Commander Yasevicitch, saluted smartly, welcomed them aboard, and made the necessary introductions. I quickly explained to the arriving group what had happened to Major Dien, the three enlisted women, and the photographer, but assured them that everything was ready to proceed with the distribution of the gifts. The gifts were then distributed, taking about ninety minutes.

The visit was a huge success, greatly cheering the patients aboard the ship. Over 350 gifts were presented, each with a spoken thank you from General Lam or his wife. Every patient received either a very attractive ebony cigarette box (cigarettes being much in use at that time) or an ebony jewelry box with mother-of-pearl inlay. Each gift was individually wrapped in Asian-style Christmas gift wrap, and on each gift was taped a printed card that read, "From the most grateful people of the Republic of Vietnam."

Before entering the guarded ward where the five VC patients were recovering, General Lam removed the printed cards attached to their gifts. I was with the party when they entered that ward and it seemed to stun the VC patients to be in the presence of a senior leader of their avowed enemy. The prisoners accepted their gifts without comment, but with quizzical looks on their faces.

I found the chief nurse, Commander Yasevicitch, to be a delightful person. She remarked that she came from a family of eleven children. She called Bessemer, Michigan, her home. She told me that she was fifty-three years old and would soon retire to "hopefully spend a couple of years with mom and dad before they die." Both her parents were in their eighties at that time.

For me, the time aboard the USS *Repose* was a very memorable Christmas experience. Every ward on the ship was gaily decorated, to include the POW ward. The vessel had twenty-eight women aboard, twenty-five nurses and three Red Cross "donut dollies." I attributed the festive look of the ship to the presence of those women.

Each member of the ship's crew and the hospital staff were also given a gift by General or Madame Lam. Just before boarding the helicopter for the return flight to Da Nang, General Lam reached into the box of remaining gifts, picked up one, and handed it to his wife while whispering something in her ear. She smiled, came over to me, bowed, and presented me with one of the gifts and sincere thanks for helping coordinate the event.

Image 23. The U.S.S. *Sanctuary*, the sister ship of the U.S.S. *Repose*, afloat in the South China Sea

Photo courtesy of the U.S. Navy Bureau of Medicine and Surgery Archives

On 24 December, the Christmas-New Year's truce went into effect. Whether or not it would be honored by the VC and NVA remained to be seen, but I felt confident that MACV Advisory Team #1 would adhere to all its many stipulations unless forced by enemy actions to do otherwise.

The day before Christmas was eventful, to say the least. It started by my receiving a most welcome call from Colonel Beeson telling me there was a jeep awaiting me in the motor pool. I couldn't believe my good fortune. The vehicle had seen far better days, but I was nevertheless most grateful.

The Saturday morning staff meeting on 24 December focused on what members of Advisory Team #1 had already perceived. The war in I Corps had not been going well for the past couple of weeks. As a result of my having perused all consolidated casualty reports, I knew that the enemy had inflicted more casualties than he had taken in recent days. It was also revealed, during the staff meeting, that the VC and NVA had captured almost five times as many weapons and pieces of signal equipment as had been captured by combined U.S. and ARVN forces. The enemy's tactics were working. How we were going to counter his successes was the primary focus of that unsettling staff meeting.

One of the bold headlines above an article that appeared in the 24 December edition of *Stars and Stripes* was "Christmas and You Cry a Little." And I almost did shed a tear when, that very day, I opened a box of children's clothing that my wife had sent to distribute to the poor. I recognized most of the items of clothing as having been previously worn by my own children. I decided to distribute the clothing that very afternoon to several families in a tragically poor hamlet in east Da Nang. It was a cold, rainy day, so it would be an opportune time to pass the clothing along to the needy.

Image 24. Refugee children on China Beach in East DaNang

Photo courtesy of the author

The monsoon, meanwhile, was back in full fury. Since mid-afternoon of the day before, it had rained over eleven inches. That was a lot of rain, even for the tropics, and it was still raining. I was grateful that General and Mrs. Lam's visit to the patients aboard the *Repose* the day before had not been negatively impacted.

Christmas Eve was unquestionably the loneliest time of my year-long separation from family. I was lonely almost to the point of depression. What was I going to do? Where would I spend the evening? It had been announced that there would not be Christmas Eve church services because of the ongoing threat of terrorism. I couldn't envision spending the evening all by myself in my room, even though my wife had done her best to brighten it with a Christmas tree and ornaments made by our children. Since the city of Da Nang was off limits, I had no alternative but to do what almost every other officer assigned to MACV Advisory Team #1 did—go to the Officers' Club for a few drinks followed by dinner with friends.

When I arrived at the club, the mood was reasonably festive. The barroom was crowded and Christmas carols filled the air. There was a lot of friendly banter, good cheer, and camaraderie. Snacks were provided at the bar and everyone seemed to be partaking freely in the food and drink and the spirit of the moment. Peace on earth, goodwill toward men was the prevailing sentiment. The war was temporarily set aside.

After about ninety minutes at the bar, three friends and I decided it was time for dinner. We went downstairs to the dining room and enjoyed a very nice meal. The Vietnamese chef had added special things to the menu for the occasion and we all savored the tasty and nicely served dinner.

But soon the dinner ended, and then what was I to do? Going back to the loneliness of my room on Christmas Eve sounded dismal, so along with the others I headed back to the bar. The mood had changed, now becoming melancholy. There were more "Bah, humbugs" than there were Merry Christmases. The Christmas carols seemed to add to the loneliness. "I'll be Home for Christmas." Bah, humbug! "Chestnuts Roasting on an Open Fire." Who cares?

Meanwhile, the mixed drinks and the beer continued to flow. Soon the heads and shoulders of those sitting at the bar began to sag, signaling the loneliness of the moment. A few tried to play horse, usually a spirited dice game, but even that seemed dispirited and out of place. The clacking of the dice, as they were rolled onto the bar, and Bing Crosby crooning "White Christmas," were about the only sounds in the barroom. Conversation diminished. The spirit of the holiday was being held captive by the loneliness caused by separation from family and friends on Christmas Eve.

Soon my fellow officers started drifting away, returning to the loneliness of their rooms. I soon followed. I drove back to my hotel, arriving at about 2230, and immediately got ready for bed. Sometime after 2330 hours, a pounding on my door awakened me from a deep, alcohol-induced sleep. Groggily, I went to the door and was told to go to I Corps HQ immediately. There had been a plane crash, and maybe I could help.

I quickly got into a field uniform and threw on my field jacket and poncho. It was still raining very hard and had turned quite cold. I drove to I Corps HQ and, upon arrival, was told that a U.S. Flying Tiger cargo plane, trying to land at the Da Nang Air Base, had crashed into a small village. A driver was standing ready to take me to the crash site. When we arrived, on that tragic Christmas night, the recovery operation was well underway.

The plane had crashed into the small village of Binh Thai in Hoa Vang District, about a mile south of the Da Nang Air Base. It had skidded through the village for about 400 yards. The fuselage and wings of the plane had demolished all the homes in its path. The crew members of the plane all died on impact, and the devastation in the village was unbelievable. I recognized one of the Vietnamese medical officials at the site. He spoke passable English. He and I moved through the destroyed village, doing what we could to insure that the American and Vietnamese medical responders were working in a somewhat coordinated manner. Most of the responders were American servicemen. There seemed to be scores of U.S. Marines digging through the rubble, attempting to locate injured survivors and get them transported to Da Nang hospitals as quickly as possible. The marines also had the sad task of extracting the bodies of the dead. Many children were among the injured and dead. Several were decapitated or dismembered, and many were seriously burned. It was heart-rending for all of us who were trying to help out at the site of the disaster.[6]

The villagers seemed to be predominantly Christian. It appeared that many of the families had been celebrating Christmas Eve in their humble homes when the crash occurred. About 100 persons were reported to have died, and many homes were destroyed.

Those of us trying to provide assistance made one grave error. Despite the protestation of the Vietnamese families of the victims, we insisted on evacuating the dead to an established morgue in Da Nang, several miles away from the village. Initially, a temporary morgue had been established in the destroyed village itself by simply roping off an area and trying to shield it from the sight of onlookers, but as the number of corpses grew, a decision was made to take the corpses to established morgues in Da Nang. This proved to be culturally insensitive, as the Vietnamese looked upon a morgue very unfavorably. They much preferred retaining the bodies of deceased loved ones in their own village, performing their own preparation of the remains for burial, and following their own burial customs. Later, we regretted this decision, but at the time, it seemed proper. We attributed the protestation of the victim's families to the anguish of the moment. We were wrong. Eventually an American military directive was published addressing this lesson learned. After conferring with many of my Vietnamese friends and colleagues, I provided input for the writing of this directive.

I returned to my room at about 1100 hours on Christmas morning, very dirty and very tired and too late to attend church services. I cannot say how many times during the past forty-nine years my thoughts have gone back to the people of that small village and the tragedy that occurred there on Christmas Eve 1966.[7]

***

I received a number of Christmas gifts from my Vietnamese friends, but the most touching and appreciated gift of all came late in the afternoon of Christmas day. I was in my room, about to change clothes to go to the Officers' Club to enjoy a Christmas meal. One of the two guards from the sandbagged emplacement in front of our hotel came to my room and told me, in pidgin English, that two Vietnamese men wanted to see me. I walked out onto the balcony and looked down. There were Sergeant Thong, my good and faithful interpreter and driver, and Khoi, the young man who had had the growths on his ear, neck, and side of his face removed by Dr. Giles. I signaled to the gate guard to admit them to the hotel.

They came up to my room, where Mr. Khoi presented me one of the most touching thank you letters I have ever received. After I read it and thanked him for his kind words, he gave me the first of two gifts: a large ebony plaque with mother-of-pearl inlay portraying a Vietnamese coastal fishing village. He had hand-lettered on the top edge of the plaque, "To: Maj. Straten" and on the bottom edge "From: Mr. Khoi." He also gave me two fish, sculpted out of marble quarried from Marble Mountain. I greatly regretted that he had probably spent a week's wages on the two gifts, but could not refuse a gift given from a generous and thankful heart. All I could do was graciously accept the gifts.

And then my good and loyal interpreter, Sergeant Thong, presented his gift. The Vietnamese artisans have a process whereby the fleshy part of a turtle's body is removed, leaving only the head, legs and shell. Those parts are then heavily lacquered, thereby preserving them. I was given the gift of a turtle. I assured him that I treasured the gift. Sergeant Thong also wrote a very touching note thanking me for "teaching me many important lesson" and for "being good Christian husband."

Before going to dinner, I transported Mr. Khoi to the Navy Hospital, where he presented a gift to Dr. Giles. We found Dr. Giles on one of the wards and, while we were talking, who should walk in the door but Chris Noel, a Hollywood starlet. As one might imagine, she created quite a stir among the young Marine patients. She was wearing a mini skirt, the first one I had ever seen. She had a kind and encouraging word for every single Marine she encountered in the hospital. Without question, the patients were cheered by her visit. The ward was still buzzing long after her departure.

Shortly after that young woman took the hospital by storm, Billy Graham also visited. We had already departed the hospital before he arrived, but Dr. Giles told me later that the Reverend Graham was most humble and sincere in his approach and very well received by the young marines. To follow a movie actress when trying to bring the message of Christmas to a bunch of virile eighteen- to twenty-two-year-old men was a difficult task. It took a Dr. Billy Graham to do it successfully.

Upon leaving the hospital, Sergeant Thong, Mr. Khoi and I sought out some of the little urchins in east Da Nang who needed clothing to ward off the cold. I gave their mothers the clothing that my wife had so thoughtfully sent. I had not had an opportunity to distribute the items the day before, as originally planned. After transporting Sergeant Thong and Mr. Khoi back across the Han River, I drove to the Officers' Club for Christmas dinner.

After dinner, while sitting in the solitude of my room, I opened the many gifts that my wife, children, and parents had sent. It was a Christmas that I would never forget. I had much to be thankful for but couldn't get the poor people of that devastated village out of my consciousness.

***

The next morning, at 0900 hours, I was on my way to Saigon in the belly of a C-130 cargo plane. Upon arrival, I noted that Saigon seemed much cleaner than it had been when I arrived almost six months earlier. The garbage collectors' strike had obviously been settled, as there were no more mounds of rotting garbage with rats scurrying all over them. The city was still teeming with people, though, congested and displaying the full spectrum of humanity, from the lowliest of beggars to the most beautiful of women. Saigon had a flavor of its own. The "Paris of the Orient" tag so often applied to it seemed an apt description, but I was still glad I was stationed in Da Nang and not Saigon.

The next day, 27 December, our meeting agenda mandated that we attend an outdoor three-hour graduation ceremony conducted under a blazing Saigon sun. Seventy-three newly commissioned Vietnamese physicians were graduated from the Basic Officer Course. All were bedecked in dress white uniforms, in sharp contrast to the advisors, who were sitting there as spectators in our khaki uniforms. This was only the second time since my arrival I had worn a Class A uniform.

That afternoon, we had a short meeting of medical advisors who were assigned throughout the country. The session was productive. Several helpful suggestions were presented and discussed. It amazed me that the experiences of the American medical advisors, stationed in different parts of the same country, were so diverse. There seemed to be relatively little commonality.

While in Saigon, I talked extensively with Majors John Davis, Bill Leach, and Bill McLeod, three very capable career officers whom I had gotten to know quite well during the Officer Advanced Course at Fort Sam Houston. All three were serving as corps-level senior medical advisors. During our lengthy conversations, one of them, I'm not sure which, said something that took my breath away. I asked that the statement be repeated and, sadly, I had heard correctly the first time. Major Kent Gandy, a MEDEVAC pilot and very good friend of mine, had been killed in a helicopter accident on 13 August. I had not heard of his death and was shocked and deeply saddened.

That evening, we attended an outdoor dinner held near the ARVN Surgeon General's office to honor the seventy-three ARVN physician graduates. There were about 500 persons in attendance, mostly ARVN military officers, but also a few civilian members of government. Only twenty-five of the attendees were American. The whole affair seemed a bit incongruous to me. The country was involved in a war, fighting for its very survival, and yet almost half of the physicians in its military medical system were involved in a medical convention and a graduation exercise. I didn't understand the logic. One other thing bothered me as I sat there enjoying my meal. Wouldn't this outdoor gathering make a prime target for the VC? But then again, I thought, there is a Christmas-New Year's truce in effect. Perhaps that was why the ARVN decided to schedule the convention and graduation exercise at that particular time, knowing in advance that there would likely be a truce.

At the conclusion of the outdoor meal, and a couple of brief speeches, the American medical advisors were transported back to our assigned hotel in a military bus. As we strode through the spacious hotel lobby in our khaki uniforms, which clearly identified us as American military officers, we noticed that there were twenty to twenty-five young women, each dressed in the traditional ao dai, in the lobby. The pajama-style, loose-fitting, silk pants they wore were predominately black, but the silk tunic-like tops were in bright assorted colors. All the young women appeared to be between the ages of eighteen and twenty-five. As I walked through the lobby, I remember thinking that perhaps the young women were celebrating the engagement of one of their members, or possibly participating in something like a pre-nuptial shower for a bride to be.

Upon entering my room, I immediately undressed, put on my pajamas, and then went into the bathroom to wash my face and hands and brush my teeth. Just as I was finishing these tasks, there was a knock on the door, and a woman on the other side said, "Thieu ta?" Recognizing this as my military rank spoken in the Vietnamese language, I thought that a person from the front desk was at the door to give me a message of a phone call, so I responded, "Yes."

The conversation continued through the closed door.

"You want girl to sleep with you, Thieu ta?"

"No, thank you."

"Me nice clean girl. Doctor say so."

"I believe you, but please go away."

"You no like girls?"

"Yes, I like girls, but please go away. I'm a married man with a family."

"But your wife not here."

"How well I know. I miss her very much."

"She long way away. She never know if you sleep with me."

"Please go away."

"Nobody know. I tell nobody."

"But I'll know."

"You no like girls?"

"Yes, I like girls, but I'm a married man."

"Maybe you want young boy. I get you young boy."

"No, I don't want a young boy."

"I nice clean girl. I come from good family."

"I'm sure you do, but please go away."

"I teach you new things about sex."

"Now look, please go away, or I will call the hotel manager and complain."

With that, the young woman left my door and disappeared. I then knew, unequivocally, what all the pretty girls in the lobby were doing. And it appeared as though the hotel management was complicit. Someone had to have informed the young woman of my military rank. I feel certain that the other advisors experienced similar conversations.

The convention continued the next day. The program of events had been structured for a physician audience, which we advisors were not. The two most useful sessions were those where the corps and division-level medical advisors got together separately to discuss lessons learned and different approaches to bringing about behavioral and organizational change.

That evening Major Charlie Christ, a good friend of mine who was among the very first males to be commissioned in the U.S. Army Nurse Corps, took those of us who were interested to a very good Chinese restaurant. A bevy of singers, mostly pretty young women, sang softly in the background as we ate. Everyone in attendance seemed to enjoy the event. I needed a relaxing evening, and I'm sure the others did too. I was having a tough time getting over the Christmas Eve plane crash. I felt so empty and helpless during the search for survivors. The grief of the parents who lost children was palpable and weighed heavily on my mind.

While in Saigon, I couldn't help but notice that, during the evening hours, thousands of people gathered at public TV sets located throughout the city. During the daytime hours, the sets remained locked in a wooden box sitting atop six- to eight-foot poles. The evening broadcasts were apparently for the dissemination of public service announcements and propaganda. But the government propaganda was seemingly being presented in a subtle, fairly persuasive manner. I couldn't resist the temptation to join the crowds and view the presentation for awhile. Although I couldn't understand a word of the audio, it was easy to ascertain the basic message from the video.

The next day, the convention ended at about 1500 hours. I lucked out and got manifested on a flight scheduled to depart Tan Son Nhut Airport at 1845 hours that same evening. Charlie Christ gave me a ride to the airport, so I made the flight in plenty of time. Unless you've been in a major air terminal in a combat zone, you can't appreciate the environment. Soldiers, marines, sailors, and airmen were sleeping all over the floor, many with rifles cradled in their arms. There was the heavy odor of human sweat. Web gear, back packs, and other pieces of equipment were lying all over. Men with unwashed and unshaven faces and a few women, but not many, were in abundance. Everyone was hoping that his or her plane would depart on time.

An hour after takeoff, we were forced down by weather into Phan Rang Air Base. I didn't have a clue where Phan Rang was, but assumed it was somewhere in the II Corps area. It was a very rough flight. My eardrums really took a beating during the rapid descent.

Flying in Vietnam was quite different than anything I had ever experienced. There were no conventional passenger seats. Instead, there were four long rows of passenger seating made of nylon netting, similar to a bench constructed of pliable, lawn chair-like material. Almost all of the passengers were armed, carrying either a holstered sidearm or a rifle cradled between their legs.

I had an ABC reporter and his camerawoman seated to my right. They had all of the usual gear that news reporters carry. On my left, I had an ARVN private. Sticking out the top of his backpack were the heads of two chickens. Both were alive and occasionally squawking.

We were on the ground in Phan Rang for only about twenty minutes. But shortly after takeoff, we were forced down again, this time into Cam Ranh Bay. The weather was very rough. When we finally landed at Da Nang it was almost midnight, about 2345 hours.

When I got back to my room, well after midnight, everything smelled musty. I even had to clean the mildew off the leather case of a new manicure set my children had sent me for Christmas. Because of the humidity, it took only a matter of a few days before all leather objects started to mildew or mold. Books, for some reason, also took a beating. I tried to protect mine by placing them in a cardboard box with a light bulb hanging from an extension cord inside, but even that was only partially successful because the power was off so frequently, sometimes for two or three days at a time.

The next morning, 31 December, the last day of the year, we were informed that the Christmas-New Year's truce seemed to be holding up quite well, not only in I Corps but throughout the entire country. There was even talk of the possibility that the truce could be extended and that serious peace talks might soon commence. There was cause for optimism.

That evening, I was invited to a party in Captain Woodruff's room to ring in the New Year. He was scheduled to go home in two days, so it was also more or less a goodbye party. The champagne, Ba Moui Ba, and Carling's Black Label flowed freely for several hours, but the party broke up well before midnight. The 2300 hours curfew remained in effect for Da Nang and no one wanted to take a chance at being caught in violation, especially after consuming more alcohol than we should have. I was back in my own lonely bed by the time the New Year arrived.

It had rained unceasingly since I returned from Saigon. The monsoon season in Da Nang was not a myth; it was reality. In a couple of respects, though, living conditions during the monsoon were better. It was much cooler, and the otherwise omnipresent dust was gone. I couldn't forget, however, that for the poor, the monsoon was very harsh and disheartening. Their babies died at an alarmingly high rate. They suffered greatly when the winds blew, the rains fell, and the temperatures dropped.

CHAPTER 7

JANUARY 1967

For New Year's Day, our acting commander, Colonel John Beeson, decided on minimum staffing. The temporary truce was holding up quite well, and he decided that everyone needed a break. One of the newly assigned medical NCOs was providing the necessary coverage for our office. I spent the day in the office typing letters to family and friends and reflecting upon the events of the past six months, many of which I would remember for the rest of my life.

On Monday, 2 January, I arrived at the office very early, intending to take care of all the administrative reporting requirements that had accumulated during my absence. Lying prominently in the center of my desk was a note from my boss that read, "Jim, pack a bag Monday night. You're going to Bangkok Tuesday morning." It was signed "Fred Mabra." I thought it was a joke until LTC Mabra arrived at the office. As he entered, he smiled broadly and asked, "Did you get my note?" I told him that I had and asked what was going on. He then queried, "You did want to go to Bangkok, didn't you?" I responded by telling him that, yes, Bangkok was my first choice for R&R. I then added that there were no slots available until February.

He explained that a slot had opened up during my absence and that he had filled it with my name, feeling certain that that was where I wanted to go. He told me that he had tried to get to Bangkok halfway through his one-year tour of duty, the logical time for an R&R, but for various reasons, it had kept getting shoved back farther and farther, and he didn't get to take his authorized R&R until his time in Vietnam was almost over. He wanted me to go now, about halfway through my tour, so the same thing that happened to him wouldn't happen to me. He went on to say, "Things are quiet right now, and since I'll be going home in just a few more days now is the perfect time for you to get away, while I'm still here to cover for you."

Captain Dave Stephens, the Assistant G-4 advisor, called later that morning to remind me that he would be away from I Corps HQ for two weeks. He was to join a sub-sector advisory team to learn all he could about a new program that showed promise. The sub-sector advisory team was involved in the trial implementation of a Revolutionary Development program that was scheduled for implementation throughout all of I Corps during the next several months.[1] It was a nasty day, weather-wise, a miserable day for Captain Stephens to be traveling in an open jeep. But since the truce was still in effect, Colonel Beeson wanted him to get out to the sub-sector while the usually dangerous roads were ostensibly safe.

On Tuesday, 3 January, my R&R flight to Bangkok was scheduled for 1000 hours. Fortunately, the tactical situation was still stable. Before departing my office, I briefed the two newly assigned NCOs on potential problem areas. Both seemed to have their feet on the ground and expressed confidence that they could hold down the office for the next five days. I also met with Doctors Tu and Phat and reassured them that they could rely on the two NCOs should they run into communication problems with the U.S. Air Force if it became necessary to transfer patients from one hospital to another. But I didn't anticipate inter-hospital transfers being necessary, unless the tactical situation changed significantly during my brief absence.

While aboard the Pan American flight to Bangkok, which was packed with young, enlisted marines and a few officers, I had my very first glass of milk since leaving the United States. What a delight! The meal served aboard the flight was good, but the cold milk seemed to be the highlight for everyone aboard. We flew over a part of South Vietnam and then across Laos before entering Thailand's air space. The Bangkok airport was located a good distance from the city. Upon arrival, we were loaded aboard several buses to transport us from the airport to the center of the city.

My first impressions of Bangkok were very positive. As we rode the bus to the R&R Center, I noted that the central part of the city was very clean and ultra modern. A friendly demeanor and an attitude of service seemed ingrained in the people with whom I interacted. Since tourism was a key component of the Thai economy, this did not surprise me.

During our check-in at the R&R Center, we were told that only 220 American servicemen and women were allowed to visit Bangkok on R&R at any given time. A city of 3,000,000 could absorb a mere 220 very easily. We would not be conspicuous. During our orientation, we were encouraged to pair up. The U.S. Air Force briefer told us that it was much safer if two or more Americans were together. We were, he said, far less likely to be taken advantage of while making purchases or paying taxi fares.

After the brief orientation at the R&R Center, we were taken to our assigned hotels. Mine was the Hotel Grace, the most modern and sophisticated hotel in which I had ever stayed. My room was luxurious, with two full-sized beds, a sitting room, a very large bathroom with a Jacuzzi bathtub and a glassed-in shower and three sinks, all with bronze fixtures. All the furniture in the room was made of teak or mahogany. My balcony overlooked the bustling city of Bangkok. It cost me the grand sum of six dollars per day. What a bargain!

Later that afternoon, after a long shower and a short nap on clean white sheets, I ignored the advice given at the R&R Center and took a long, leisurely stroll around Bangkok all by myself, walking perhaps six or seven miles. I wanted to get a feel for the people and the sights, sounds and smells of the city. That evening, I joined up with two Marine Corps officers, and we went on a nightclub tour, along with about thirty English-speaking tourists, primarily Australians. The tour included dinner. During the meal in a very nice restaurant, we were entertained by an Italian combo.

Then came the highlight of the night club tour. We were taken to a Thai teakwood theater. The place was actually a combination restaurant and theater. The people who chose to eat there were all seated on large pillows placed on the floor. All were required to remove their shoes before entering the dining area. We arrived just in time for the performance of the traditional Siamese dancers. All were women. They were sensual, exotic, and beautiful. The very slow and rhythmic movement of their bodies, especially their hands and arms, to the music of xylophones and drums was unusual and entertaining, especially for those of us who had never experienced anything similar. All of the dancers were garbed in silk with high, Siamese-style bejeweled headdresses.

After the Thai theater, we were taken to the Café de Paris, another splashy nightclub. The show was international in scope. There was a Philippine chorus line, an Australian brother-sister singing act, an English clarinet soloist, a Thai production of *An American in Paris*, and several other acts. We greatly enjoyed the show but, at the conclusion, were ready to return to our hotel after a long and interesting day.

The days in Bangkok moved along swiftly, too swiftly. Captain Oliver and Major Fleming, my newfound Marine Corps buddies, and I did a variety of things, all entertaining and instructive. One day we toured several fascinating Buddhist temples, each quite different in decor and the manner in which it functioned. The sorcerers were in abundance, each willing to forecast the future, using various means, for a small fee.

One evening, we went to see Thai boxing. In this form of boxing, anything goes. Although I didn't especially enjoy seeing one human being inflict pain on another, it was interesting. In this form of boxing, the boxers can use their heads, knees, elbows, feet or any other body parts to inflict damage on a foe.

One night, at the suggestion of a Thai shopkeeper, we attended a carnival. The Thai Red Cross sponsored the carnival, so our money went to a good cause. There were hundreds of games of skill and chance, eating places, special exhibits, displays, and a plethora of differing types of entertainment. We found the carnival to be festive, colorful, tastefully done, and highly entertaining. We attended the opening night of the ten-day carnival. The Thai King and Queen presided over the opening ceremony. Prior to the ceremony, there was a dinner to honor the royal family in a covered pavilion on the carnival grounds. About 400 guests attended. The meal was served by what appeared to be hundreds of men wearing white jackets, knee-length black pants, and white knee-length stockings. We stood on the outside to enjoy the pageantry and get a glimpse of the King and Queen.

One morning, we toured Bangkok's floating market by boat. It was unique and, for me, fascinating. I couldn't help but wonder how it got started. The people, mostly women, used boats to do their daily shopping. They paddled from one small business to another in their wooden boats, buying the necessities of life. You could purchase virtually anything in the floating market that you could buy in a supermarket.

While still in Da Nang, I had been told by officers who had been to Bangkok that you could hire a taxi for an entire day, with an English-speaking driver, for two cartons of American cigarettes. I bought four cartons at the PX, the first cigarettes I had ever purchased in my life, and brought them along. The advice proved accurate. Captain Oliver, Major Fleming, and I enjoyed the services of a taxi for two days, and it cost us only my cigarettes, plus a generous tip for the driver at the end of our stay.

One day, we had the driver take us up country in order to get a feel for Thai life outside the city. At one point, we stopped to take a picture of some rice harvesters when an old toothless lady insisted that I put on her straw hat and have my picture taken. The resulting photograph was good for a few laughs. At another point, we stopped to watch a young boy shimmy up a very tall coconut palm tree in order to harvest the fruit. He wore no safety belt. It looked very dangerous. The tree was at least eighty or ninety feet tall, but the boy reached the top without difficulty, smiling all the way up and all the way down. He insisted on giving us a coconut, which he cracked open for us to enjoy. It was obvious by his eyes that he was hoping for a generous tip, which we gave him. Just before returning to Bangkok, we stopped to see a demonstration of the abilities of an elephant. I was stunned to see a young woman lie on her back on a hard surface and have the huge elephant gently place one of its front feet on her face.

Late one afternoon, we had the driver take us through the poorest sections of Bangkok. Some of its neighborhoods were depressingly poor, similar to Vietnam, but there was still a spark of human dignity, despite the grinding poverty. Bangkok had an estimated three million plus people at that time. We were told that many of the rural poor had in recent years moved to the city as a result of not being able to find work in the countryside. Most had no marketable skills, making their lives in the city most difficult.

And of course, we shopped for our wives and families. My wife, mother, mother-in-law, and five sisters had each sent me a list of things to purchase for them. Princess rings, birthstone rings, and silk cloth were the "in" things at that time.

On Sunday morning, 8 January, I returned to Da Nang. Specialist Behner met me at the airport and, as we drove through the city to my office, I couldn't help but think that Da Nang looked pretty unimpressive after the bright lights and modernity of Bangkok. But in a sense it was good to be back in Da Nang. I was beginning to like the city and its people.

Upon reaching my office, I found lying on my desk a note from LTC Mabra wishing me well. His departure from Da Nang had been moved up a couple of days, and he was gone. I regretted the fact that I had not had the opportunity to properly say goodbye and wish him well. He was a good and honest man, a fine army officer. I learned much from him about logistics, and I treasured his friendship.

Also lying on my desk were five letters from my wife, one of which informed me that our youngest son, Michael, was once again battling illness, a virus causing diarrhea and a high fever. All I could do was hope and pray that his lungs were getting stronger and less infection-prone, but until they became resilient and mature, my wife had to be very careful. I knew that any illness could easily lead to more significant problems because of his fragility. Before going to my hotel room, I sat down and typed a letter to my wife, expressing my concerns while at the same time trying to reassure her that she had done the right thing by getting the infant to the doctor as quickly as possible.

After attending a Sunday evening Mass, I went to the Officers' Club for dinner. After dinner, I drifted up to the bar for a snifter of brandy. All of a sudden, somebody clamped his hand on my shoulder and said, "Look who's here, stranger. I'm your new boss." There stood Major John Hennigan, an infantry officer whom I had gotten to know at Fort Sam Houston. He explained that, since leaving Fort Sam, he had been reoriented into the logistics career field and was soon to be promoted to lieutenant colonel. It was good to see him. I was totally surprised when he said he was to be my new boss. When I left on R&R, I was of the opinion that LTC Mabra's replacement was to be a Corps of Engineers logistician. I found out later that the officer had been retained in his previous unit while an investigation over some missing property was being conducted. I was delighted that John Hennigan would instead be leading our office staff.

It was still raining on Monday morning, 10 January. Specialist Behner told me that it had rained most of the time during my five-day absence. The monsoon was back.

During the process of getting reoriented to the tactical situation throughout I Corps, I was amazed over how much things had changed in such a brief period. Areas that were of little concern when I departed had suddenly become hot spots. I thought back to the comments of Dr. Giles about the ebb and flow of war.

Major Hennigan hit the ground running. He was a very capable officer and seemed to keep things in proper perspective. If everything was labeled a crisis, a manner in which some seemed to operate, then when a true crisis came along, the response was usually inadequate or inappropriate. John Hennigan seemed to bring balance to the table. He realized that he would be making some decisions based on incomplete data. Complete data were rarely available and, when decisions were deferred while the staff tried to develop answers to sometimes insignificant questions, it was frustrating and counterproductive. John Hennigan also had a good sense of humor and could laugh at himself. I was most fortunate to have had two good bosses in a row. Hennigan seemed to have zillions of questions about the tactical situation, the ARVN units we advised, and how our office operated. That was typical of those taking over jobs involving broad responsibilities. Since Hennigan's assistant G-4 advisor, Captain Dave Stephens, was away for two weeks, he asked me to stick pretty close to the office while he was getting his feet on the ground.

I was the SDO on Monday, 10 January, a night fraught with worry and concern. I came on duty at 1800 hours. The G-1 advisor briefed me on all on-going actions and areas of concern that might need attention during the night. He also explained that the standing operating procedure for obtaining the evening meal had changed. Whereas in the past one simply sent the duty driver to the Officers' Club to pick up a couple of sandwiches, a bowl of soup, and a cold drink, the new procedure allowed the SDO to actually go to the club and eat his evening meal while the Staff Duty NCO covered the headquarters. Upon the return of the SDO, the NCO was then allowed to go and eat his meal. I decided that, since the restriction about leaving the HQ had been rescinded, I would go to the club, enjoy a nice hot meal, then return to the HQ for the night's duty.

I wish I hadn't made that decision, as it turned out badly. It was raining cats and dogs when I left the HQ. As I was exiting the main gate to the I Corps compound, which was guarded, I was approached by an ARVN officer and asked if I would give a young woman and her eight- or nine-year-old daughter a lift downtown, a distance of about a mile and a half. Since it was raining very hard, I couldn't refuse. The mother and daughter got into my jeep. They both sat in the front passenger seat, the little girl in the middle. We had driven only a short distance when we came to a very busy intersection clogged with commercial vehicles and the private cars of affluent people going home from work. Two military convoys were waiting to move through the busy intersection, further complicating matters. The weather was horrible, rain just lashing down, and it was cold.

Immediately in front of me was a three-quarter-ton ARVN truck, not a part of either of the two convoys. It was driven by an ARVN enlisted man. He stopped at the stop sign preceding the intersection and so did I. He noted a break in the traffic and rapidly moved into the intersection. Seeing no traffic to my left or right, I followed him, not wanting to get bogged down when the two convoys moved into the intersection.

Suddenly, the driver in front of me stopped abruptly. For no apparent reason, he just slammed on his brakes. I couldn't react in time and plowed into the rear end of his vehicle. I immediately looked at the little girl and her mother. Both had hit the windshield, but not hard enough to shatter it. The safety glass probably kept the windshield from shattering. I immediately noticed that neither mother nor daughter was cut, but both were holding their foreheads. The little girl was crying. Her mother was trying to calm her. Both were conscious and seemed alert. I assured myself that neither was bleeding. I then looked up and saw that the driver of the other vehicle was about to leave the scene of the accident. I got out of my jeep, ran to the driver's side door, and hammered on the window with my fist in an attempt to stop him. He noted that I was an officer and then reluctantly stopped and got out of his jeep. An English-speaking ARVN officer in charge of one of the two convoys came up and told me that he would notify the Shore Patrol, the U.S. Navy equivalent of the Army's MPs.

I found out later that the truck I collided with was half full of bagged cement, which had been stolen from a U.S. construction site. Apparently, that was the reason the driver was attempting to leave the intersection so rapidly. He was attempting to flee the scene so the stolen goods would not be detected. By this time, there was a group of onlookers, all sporting umbrellas or rain gear to shield themselves from the driving rain. I was soaking wet. I was looking over the damage to my jeep—both headlights were smashed—when I noticed that the mother and daughter had gotten out of the jeep. I was somewhat relieved to see that both were standing and that their arms and legs appeared unbroken. I again visually examined them. Both appeared to be okay, other than growing lumps on their foreheads. Both were very wet and scared. I couldn't find a single soul in the intersection who could act as an interpreter, so I couldn't talk to either one of them. Soon, the SPs arrived. They explained that, since my passengers may have suffered injuries, a special accident investigation team had to be summoned. I explained to the SP that I was the SDO at I Corps and asked that they please notify my HQ that I would be late to assume my duties. I gave them the phone number for our HQ. They made a call on their radio and then assured me that my HQ would be notified. We waited and waited for the accident investigation team to arrive. Over an hour had already passed. The mother and daughter stood by patiently, under a tarp that the SP had provided. Unexpectedly, they crossed the street to converse with friends. By this time, the crowd of onlookers had grown considerably. Suddenly, the mother and daughter simply disappeared into the crowd. They were gone. I wanted so badly to have them examined by a doctor, but they were nowhere to be found.

Finally, after waiting over two hours, the accident investigation team arrived on the scene. It was still raining hard, and I was soaked to my skin and very cold. I told them precisely what had happened and expressed my concerns about the mother and daughter as they filled out the required report.

I felt reasonably confident that the mother and her daughter would be all right, but I wanted to be absolutely certain. I knew they would, in all likelihood, have very black eyes and big lumps on their foreheads in the morning. I regretted the fact that I had not simply sent the duty driver to the club to get me a sandwich and a bowl of soup as I had in the past. But the accident had happened and there was nothing I could do about it. I returned to the I Corps entrance gate, hoping the guard could identify the mother and daughter, but he could not. Nor could he remember the name of the officer who asked if I would give them a ride. Although I hadn't eaten, I wasn't hungry. I spent a long night worrying about the mother and child.

***

The weather had now turned bitter cold. As a person who grew up in Wisconsin, I never dreamt I'd be describing temperatures in the low fifties as bitter cold, but this cold seemed to go right through you. The winds and rains were key factors in making it feel so miserably cold, but constantly having soaked boots and wet clothing also contributed to the chilled feeling. On 12 January, it reportedly had snowed on the North Vietnamese-Chinese border, a rarity, I was told. The high temperature in Da Nang on that day was only in the low fifties, and the rains continued. Despite the cold, I saw semi-nude little children, with only tee shirts or sweaters on top and nothing on bottom, scurrying around the refugee camps trying to stay warm. That morning, Major Tu told me a cold weather record had been established during the past couple of days. I felt badly because there wasn't much I could do to help the shivering children. Most had snotty noses and virulent diarrhea. I felt so helpless.

On 13 January, it never got above fifty degrees. An NCO told me that in An Lo, a village just a few miles from Da Nang, the U.S. Marines were covering little, semi-naked babies with cardboard from C-ration boxes in an attempt to keep them warm. Radio Hanoi again reported that it had snowed on the North Vietnam-Chinese border. The rain temporarily stopped, but the wind and the cold seem to penetrate everything. Our office had no source of heat. All the Americans in the headquarters seemed to be wearing a GI issue olive drab sweater, a field jacket, and black leather gloves with woolen inserts to keep warm.

I still hadn't been able to locate the mother and child who were in the accident with me. I could only assume they were all right. The only after-effect I felt was some pain in the sternum. My chest had hit the steering wheel at the time of collision, probably bruising the sternum.

During the afternoon of 13 January, I had to go to the Navy Hospital to check on several ARVN patients who had been intermingled with Marine casualties upon being evacuated from the field of battle. Since my jeep was in the motor pool having its headlights replaced, I asked a friend to give me a lift to the hospital. To get to the hospital from my office required that we cross the bridge over the Han River, drive a short distance and then take a ninety-degree right turn and proceed straight ahead for about two miles. Along this two-mile stretch, after passing through a densely populated, extremely poor refugee hamlet near the bridge, there was nothing but windblown sand flats along the Han River. It was barren and deserted.

As we drove up this lonely stretch of road, I noticed a family walking alongside the road toward the Navy Hospital. There was a man carrying a small rectangular wooden box, and a woman with a three- or four-year-old boy holding onto her right hand and a girl of perhaps eighteen months cradled in her other arm. I wondered what they were doing walking along this deserted stretch of road.

As we passed them, I realized precisely what was going on. The wooden box the man cradled in his arms was a casket. They were going to bury their dead baby in the sand flats along the Han River.

I asked my friend to stop the jeep, turn around, and drive back to the family. He did so and, as we neared the family, he stopped the jeep, and I gestured for them to get into the back seat. Because it was very cold and wet, they did so willingly. We proceeded down the road for about a mile when the man tapped me on the shoulder, signaling to stop the jeep. We had arrived at the burial site. I looked into the sand dunes and noted simple burial grounds that many others had used to bury their dead. We watched as the grieving family trudged off into the sand along the Han River to find an appropriate final resting place for their child.

***

On Sunday morning, 15 January, the rain and cold showed no signs of abating. The skies looked as if it could rain forever. My Vietnamese colleagues told me that shortly after Tet, the celebration of the Chinese New Year on 8 February, the rains would stop. I hoped they were correct.

On 15 January, Major Hennigan, my new boss, was involved in an accident very similar to the one I had experienced a few days earlier. He was a passenger in Sergeant Tipton's jeep when it ran into the back of a truck. As had happened to my passengers, Hennigan hit the windshield with his forehead. Although the windshield shattered into a thousand pieces, the only marks on him were a couple of minor abrasions, a lump on his head, and two slightly blackened eyes. This gave me some confidence that my passengers, the mother and daughter, were probably not seriously injured. I felt better about it.

Despite it being Sunday, I didn't leave the office until 1630 hours. The weather was so miserable, I didn't bother going to dinner. I just pulled off my wet clothing, toweled the cold moisture from my body, put on my pajamas, brushed my teeth, crawled into bed, and pulled the sheet and blanket over my head in an attempt to get warm. I had an inflamed throat, resulting in chills and fever. One minute I was too hot, the next too cold. To make matters worse, someone had taken my raincoat from the Officers' Club on Saturday evening, so I had been wet most of the day. Maybe a fellow officer had picked it up by mistake, as they all looked alike, but the fact was it was gone and I got drenched.

***

I sat in my cold office on Monday morning, 16 January, trying to figure out what was going on in Quang Tri Province. The disposition of forces from Lang Vei to Khe Sanh to Dong Ha was perplexing. Why there was such a buildup of U.S. and ARVN forces in that remote area of the country, I did not understand. To me, it was inexplicable. It was almost as if we were trying to draw the VC and NVA into a fight. Khe Sanh and Lang Vei were so isolated and so difficult to reach for much of the year because of weather, as to give me pause over such a tactic. If indeed my conclusion that we were attempting to draw the enemy into a fight was correct, I couldn't help but wonder how we would resupply and, if necessary, reinforce those lonely outposts if the enemy took the bait and a major battle ensued. I wasn't comfortable with what I perceived to be our tactic or our overall strategy.

At noon, I was feeling so bad that I decided to go to my hotel room and take a brief nap. My throat was raw, and the chills and fever were making me miserable. Bá Vy, my maid, was in the hotel lobby as I entered. Through hand gestures, she told me that she was pregnant with her tenth child. She was also very sick with a high fever. I tried to communicate to her that she should go home, but she simply wouldn't even consider doing so. She kept pointing at my damp clothing hanging in the hotel entryway, along with the damp clothing of several other officers. There was no chance that my field uniforms would dry. Poor Bá Vy was feeling bad about it, wringing her hands in despair.

I felt certain that her large family was probably miserable and discouraged from the rain and cold. The poor led desperate lives at this time of the year. I couldn't even imagine my faithful maid giving birth to a new baby under these conditions. And we, as generous and caring as we were, could seemingly do little to alleviate the misery and suffering of the poor while at the same time trying to defeat an elusive and savvy enemy who measured time differently than we did.

We thought in terms of months and perhaps a few years at most to accomplish our goal of winning the war, whereas the enemy didn't seem to care if it took decades to defeat us. I never doubted that our Communist enemy was in it for the long haul. Never before had I felt so totally helpless and alone. I stood there in that frigid entryway of my hotel, chills and fever wracking my body, with a pregnant, sick, and discouraged Bá Vy worrying about my clothing. She was a good and decent woman who needed more help than I could possibly give.

Later on Monday, after I returned to work, still feeling miserable, I was delighted to learn that the Green Bay Packers had beaten the Kansas City Chiefs for the professional football championship. The next day *Stars and Stripes* reported that this was the first time the NFL winner had played the AFL winner to determine the overall champion. The article referred to the game as the "Super Bowl." It was new terminology for me. I wondered what had brought that term about and whether or not it would stick. The article further stated that the game had been played in the Los Angeles Coliseum to a final score of 35-10. I couldn't help but smile when I recalled the days when I was a student at St. Norbert College and scores of students would climb over the fence of old city stadium in East Green Bay to watch a Sunday afternoon Packers game without purchasing a ticket. The authorities always seemed to look the other way and allow it to happen. There seemed to be a special bond between the Green Bay Packer's organization and St. Norbert College.

The weather on Tuesday, 17 January, remained nasty. It was cold, windy, and raining. That evening, I experienced yet another event that bothers me still. In many respects it was very similar to the accident that I had had on 10 January, just a week prior. I had been at the Navy Hospital that evening and was returning to the office in my jeep. It was dark and raining as I was about to cross the bridge over the Han River. As I approached the bridge, I noted a young woman shuffling along the side of the road with a don ganh over her shoulder while carrying a baby in one arm and trying to hold onto a toddler with the other. She was straining under the weight of the two buckets hanging from the don ganh. It was obvious that she was going to have great difficulty crossing the narrow and busy bridge with her two children.

I had an empty jeep, and despite having been repeatedly warned about picking up strangers, I decided I just couldn't pass her by. I stopped the jeep and gestured for her to get in. She shyly approached my jeep. She bent down in order to place the two buckets hanging from the don ganh on the ground. I reached for the handle of one of the buckets to put it in the jeep. *Oh, no,* I thought, *night soil!* Both buckets were sloshing full of human waste to be used as fertilizer for a garden. But what could I do? I had committed myself to help. I gingerly lifted the buckets and placed them on the floorboard in the back of the jeep. She then got in the front passenger seat with her baby, and I placed the toddler on the back seat with his legs between the two buckets. By this time, it was pitch dark and the rain was coming down in sheets.

As I approached the bridge, the visibility was horrible. The bridge was congested with vehicles and people. Traffic was moving very slowly. An American SP was trying to push it along. Suddenly, and without warning, the two-and-a-half-ton U.S. Marine Corps vehicle in front of me stopped abruptly. I couldn't stop in time and plowed into its rear end. The woman, attempting to protect the baby in her arms, flew forward and hit the windshield hard, shattering the glass. She had a small laceration on her forehead and was bleeding from her nose. Fortunately, the baby in her arms appeared uninjured, as did the toddler riding in the back seat. It was so dark that I couldn't really assess the extent of the woman's injuries. The Marine driver of the truck in front of me then came back to my jeep with a flashlight. We agreed that, as soon as we cleared the bridge, we would pull over to assess the damage and exchange names, units, and phone numbers. We did so, and after we looked over the damage, which was minimal, we got in the cab of his truck for the exchange of information. I was gone for no more than two or three minutes. When I returned, the woman and her children, along with the two buckets and the don ganh, were gone. I simply could not find them. Where they had disappeared to, I do not know. I think about that incident often and hope and pray that the woman was not seriously injured.

***

On 18 January, Radio Hanoi reported that it had snowed in much of North Vietnam the previous night and that many children, mostly babies, had died of exposure. It was a very cold winter, especially for the tropics. On the way to dinner that evening, I saw many little street urchins clutching their hands and arms to their chests with their shoulders hunched up and their teeth chattering from the cold. It tore me up emotionally, but what could I do about it? I felt so completely helpless that it hurt.

By that time, my sore throat had progressed into a miserable cold. I went to the dispensary and replenished my supply of APCs. There was no cure for a cold other than toughing it out. My throat felt somewhat better, probably due to the warm salt water gargles I had been subjecting myself to at every opportunity.

At noon on Thursday, 19 January, I decided to go to lunch at the Officers' Club, something I rarely did. En route back to my office after lunch, I witnessed what, according to Major Diem, was probably the largest Buddhist funeral ever held in the city of Da Nang. There were approximately 1,000 paid mourners, stretching for about two city blocks. All were wailing and chanting. The coffin, on an elaborate red and white bier, was borne by ten men. Although I was tempted, out of respect for the grieving family, I did not take any photographs. Hundreds of mourners were carrying silk banners with written inscriptions. In Vietnam, rather than sending flowers, people prepared banners with laudatory statements about the deceased printed on them. The banners were of white silk with black lettering. They were some ten feet high and a foot and a half wide. Each was suspended on a bamboo pole and carried by a mourner. About twenty little girls, wearing white ao dais, followed the casket. Each time the pallbearers placed the casket on the street to take a brief rest, the girls knelt down. They looked very cold on that frigid day. Fortunately it was not raining. At one point the procession stopped and a woman, I presume the grieving widow, climbed onto the bier, then she and the remains of her husband were carried together down the street for a short distance. Later, I watched the same procession coming from the cemetery after the burial. The widow was being helped along, almost carried, by two women.

In Buddhist cemeteries, the individual gravesites were not rectangular but round. Affluent families each seemed to have their own private cemetery. I found their burial customs fascinating.

***

The clerk typist in the command suite called on Thursday, 19 January. When I answered, he said, "Sir, Colonel Hamblen wants to see you at 1330 hours today if your schedule permits."

I said, "I didn't know he was back from his stateside leave."

He said, "Yes, sir, he's been back since Tuesday. Does 1330 hours work for you?"

I said, "He's the commander. I'll make it work." Then I asked, "Do you have any idea what he wants to talk about?"

He responded, "No, sir, I don't. He just told me to put you on the schedule without telling me why."

I closed the conversation by saying, "Okay. I'll be there."

I immediately started juggling my schedule to accommodate the meeting, all the while wondering what he wanted to talk about.

When I arrived in the command suite a little before 1330 hours, the door to the colonel's office was closed. The G-1 advisor, who was in an adjacent office, invited me to take a seat and told me that Colonel Hamblen was on a lengthy phone call but would be with me in a minute. I asked the G-1 advisor if he had any idea what the commander wanted to talk about. He responded by saying, "Jim, I do, but I'm not at liberty to tell you about it." The plot thickened, and I was becoming a little bit apprehensive.

Several minutes later, the door to Colonel Hamblen's office opened, and he invited me to come in. Before I could render a salute and report properly, as called for by military protocol, he said, "Jim, sit down please. You'll recall that before I went on stateside leave, I told you that I wanted to talk with you when I returned."

I responded, "Yes, sir, I remember the conversation. You came down to my office to tell me, which I thought was unusual."

He then said, "That's right. But before I tell you what I've got in mind, would you like a cup of coffee?"

I said, "No, sir, I'm trying to cut down on the coffee. I drink too much of it."

He then said, "Ya know, you're doing a hell of a job. I keep getting good reports about your work."

I said, "Thank you, sir. I appreciate your kind words."

He said, "I'm not being kind, I'm being factual." He went on to say, "Before this assignment I didn't realize the power of medicine in wartime, especially in a war like this where we're trying to win the hearts and minds of the people."

I said, "I appreciate what you're saying. I know the people, especially the poor in the hamlets and villages, seem grateful for the meager support we're able to give them."

He then got up, walked around behind his desk, and said, "Look, I'll not beat around the bush. I've extended my tour for an additional six months because I believe in what we're doing. I think we've got a good chance to succeed, and I want you to be a part of my team."

Not quite understanding what he meant, I said, "Sir, I am a part of your team, unless you know something that I don't know. From time to time I hear that I'm going to be moved to Saigon, but I'm hoping that doesn't happen. I think I can do more good in Da Nang than in Saigon. I'm confident I'll be on your team until July when I go home."

He said, "Four more months is not enough time. Advisory Team #1 needs you at this critical juncture of the war. I'm asking you to voluntarily extend for six additional months."

I was stunned. Eventually I blurted out, "Sir, I can't do that. I've got to think of my poor wife struggling to keep it all together with six children, all aged ten and under, one of whom is very fragile with a congenital lung disorder. I just can't do that."

He then asked, "You do know, do you not, that a thirty-day stateside leave to be with your family is a part of the package?"

I again said, "Yes, I do, sir, but I just can't do that."

The conversation ended with him telling me that he had the authority, under MACV regulations, to extend me for six months involuntarily, but he was reluctant to use that authority. We parted with him telling me to think it over and let him know my decision no later than the first of February. I was dispirited as I left his office.

***

The war in I Corps had been very cruel for the past couple of weeks. There were fewer and fewer large-scale operations being fought, but, at the same time, mining of roads, sniping, boobytrapping, terrorizing people in the hamlets and villages, stealing foodstuffs, and the killing of animals had increased markedly. During the past three weeks, the combined U.S. and ARVN forces in I Corps had taken more casualties than they had inflicted. It was a demoralizing struggle. And to compound matters for the ARVN, it seemed as if the civilian population was constantly battling serious outbreaks of one disease after another. The ARVN medical resources in I Corps were not great, but in order to provide even a modicum of support to the civil population military physicians were openly encouraged to moonlight. It seemed as if most of the ARVN physicians I knew had an evening practice to treat civilians.

***

On the morning of Friday, 20 January, we got the sad news that three advisors had been seriously wounded the night before when the VC had attempted to overrun a district headquarters. The advisors were all members of a sub-sector advisory team. One was seriously injured and not expected to live. I wasn't well acquainted with any of the three, although I had met all of them during MEDCAP interventions in villages in their district. Advisors working at the district level were far more vulnerable than any other advisors. I felt they were even more vulnerable than those assigned to advise a rifle company or an infantry battalion. All members of the district advisory teams were vulnerable, but the medic was the most vulnerable of all. I cannot overstate how difficult it was for me to brief a newly arrived enlisted medic, prior to his being assigned to a sub-sector advisory team, when the medic he was replacing had been killed in action. Inevitably, the new medic would ask me, "Sir, if I might ask, what happened to the soldier I'm replacing?"

***

That morning, 20 January, I was off to Hoi An, about twenty to twenty-five miles south of Da Nang. Owing to security concerns, I joined a convoy of three jeeps driving down there. Hoi An was an old and historic city, one I always enjoyed visiting. The purpose of my visit was to spend time with SFC Palevo, the senior MACV medic in the province. He had big responsibilities for an E-6. He was a dedicated and talented man, but administration was not one of his strengths. He needed to be shown how to prepare some of the many required reports. The MACV Surgeon's Office had kicked a couple of his reports back to him because they couldn't reconcile the numbers he had reported. He called me for help. I tried to assist over the telephone, but my explanation was too complex for him to comprehend. I had no recourse other than to go to him or have him come to me. While in Hoi An, I also spent time with the MILPHAP team at the province hospital. They had continuing problems with the calibration and maintenance of certain items of medical equipment. Their maintenance support, which was supposed to come from the U.S. Naval Support Activity, was spotty at best.

On 21 January, I attended a rather troubling Saturday morning staff meeting which focused on the irrefutable fact that the war was not going well. We weren't losing any major battles, but losses from hit and run and terrorist activities were mounting. We were fighting a ruthless enemy who seemingly cared less about human life than did we. He was terrorizing the people in the countryside, and we didn't have the manpower to protect them. The enemy could simply blend in with the people who, for the most part, were too frightened to divulge his presence among them. The poor peasant-class people were caught between two conflicting ideologies, neither of which they understood. Their allegiance was dependent upon who was in control of their village or hamlet at the moment. It seemed to me that it swung dramatically from day to day.

After the staff meeting, I received a phone call from the MACV Surgeon's Office informing me that, once again, I was being summoned to Saigon. A meeting of corps-level medical advisors, plus those who advised the commanders of medical supply depots, was scheduled for 26 January. I told the caller that I hadn't even been reimbursed for my last TDY trip to Saigon to attend the medical convention, and here they were calling me for yet another mandatory meeting.

At noon on that Saturday, I was feeling miserable, so I went to my room. My chest cold was hanging on, causing me to cough incessantly. My rib cage was hurting from the coughing. Also troubling me was the distinct possibility that I would be involuntarily extended. I knew in my heart that this would be a devastating blow to my wife, who was laboring so hard to keep it all together while I was away. I never left my room on that cold Saturday. I munched on a few remaining Christmas cookies that my wife had sent and drank a coke. That was my dinner.

I just didn't have the get-up-and-go to go out into the continuing rain and cold. I went to bed early.

Sunday, 22 January, I was again the SDO. On my way to I Corps HQ I noticed that the streets were lined with small movable shrines and altars. It must have been some sort of Buddhist feast day. Burning incense and joss sticks were in abundance. Food offerings were on all the altars. Small groups of people were squatting or standing around many of the altars. The people squatted down by spreading their legs quite wide and then going into a sitting-down motion until their butts almost, but not quite, touched the ground. It seemed they could remain in that squatting position for hours at a time. It was an unusual sight in the early morning, but it made the drive to work interesting.

The rain was still coming down, a good day to pull duty. With nothing better to do on that relatively quiet Sunday, I wrote a lengthy letter to my wife telling her more about Vietnamese customs and traditions and then settled in with a good book while hoping that the tactical situation would remain calm.

***

On Monday, 23 January, I attended a special briefing concerning the changing role of the advisors assigned to MACV Advisory Team #1. Plans for fiscal year 1967-1968 called for the ARVN to be primarily involved in what was labeled "Revolutionary Development." Free World Forces (American, South Korean, Australian, New Zealand, Thailand and Philippine) would fight the VC and NVA hard core units in the field while the ARVN were to be engaged in civic action programs and reconstructing the war-torn country. Since the program would not be implemented until fiscal year 1967-1968, I would not be directly involved. My job would be to help prepare ARVN medical units to take on their new responsibilities in the fall of the year, a few months after my June departure.

It was an eerie sort of morning on Tuesday, 24 January. The VC had been steadily increasing their level of activity in and around Da Nang. Consequently, defensive positions were being strengthened. Many of the manned defensive positions surrounding Da Nang were without electricity; hence, fires were built to provide some light with which to see an approaching enemy. On my way to the office on that morning, I could see the glow of dozens of bonfires on the periphery of the city.

On 24 January, an engineer from the MACV Surgeon's Office, Captain Jim Peacock, and I, along with Major Phat and several other officers from the hospital, took a comprehensive look at Duy Tan General Hospital from a sanitary engineering perspective. Although there were problems, especially in the area of medical waste disposal, Captain Peacock expressed his feeling that Duy Tan was the best of the ARVN hospitals he had inspected. This provided a morale boost for Major Phat and his entire hospital staff.

The next day, Wednesday, 25 January, Captain Peacock and I were scheduled to fly to Tam Ky. The weather, though improved from the day before, was still marginal. After an hour's delay, the pilot of the Otter aircraft got clearance to take off. The flight itself was uneventful, but the landing in Tam Ky was downright scary because of sniper fire over the north end of the runway. We spent a productive day with the MILPHAP team and with an ARVN medical unit. As the day went on, however, we could tell that the weather was going to make our return flight problematic. It was closing in on us. We didn't really know to what degree it had closed in until we were airborne, when it became necessary for the pilot to fly at very low altitudes for much of the way back to Da Nang. The pilot used Highway 1 as a guide and just followed it all the way. Fortunately, Vietnam didn't have many towers, high electricity lines, or tall buildings to worry about. The few obstacles there were seemed to be well known by the pilot. As he flew at these very low levels he always seemed to be dodging around something or bouncing over something, turning sharply, elevating or descending rapidly and so forth, all the way back to Da Nang. There was very little straight-line flight. Some of the passengers were quite anxious, and a couple got airsick. My feelings were that you just had to have faith in the skills and good sense of the pilot. He was trained to fly a plane, we were not.

***

My flight to Saigon was scheduled to depart at 1310 hours on Thursday, 26 January. That gave me the entire morning to finish up some administrative reports. The I Corps Surgeon, Major Tu, was in Manila presenting a professional paper at a medical conference. Since I now had two very capable NCOs to hold down the fort while I was away, I could breathe a little easier. I had spent over two hours with them the prior evening, over a beer and a bowl of pretzels, bringing them up to speed about ongoing events and necessary actions.

Captain John McLean, advisor to the ARVN Medical Supply Depot in Da Nang, and I attended the one-day meeting on Friday, 27 January. The meeting, though brief and rapid-fire, was helpful. It served to highlight some deficiencies that needed to be addressed if the ARVN's limited medical resources were going to be used as effectively and efficiently as possible. The MACV Surgeon's staff did a good job in putting together the agenda of "lessons learned."

When we departed Saigon early Friday evening, the weather was very good, but we were warned, upon check-in for the flight, that it would be very rough over the Central Highlands. We were also told that the monsoon rains continued to slash away at Da Nang and all of I Corps. We were advised that we might not get into Da Nang that night. We were flying on a C-130, a very noisy and uncomfortable cargo aircraft, but one that had a good record of reliability and safety.

We actually got back to Da Nang from Saigon without incident. Surprisingly, we were able to fly straight through. Shortly after getting off the plane, I was informed of the fire aboard Apollo I and the death of our three American astronauts. Although the accident had happened the previous day, because of time zone differences, we did not receive the sad news until the next day.

From the air base, I went straight to my office to see if I had any mail. There was one letter from my wife informing me that our infant son was battling yet another bad cold. In my mind, this sealed the decision regarding what I was going to tell Colonel Hamblen on 1 February. I simply could not agree to an extension. Family had to come first.

The next day, Saturday, was a beautiful day in Da Nang. The sun was shining brightly and temperatures got into the low eighties that afternoon. What a pleasant and unexpected change! The "mua mua," the Vietnamese words for monsoon, was seemingly over.

By Sunday, 29 January, I was feeling much better. After Mass, I went to the Officers' Club for breakfast and met a group of officers hoping to get into a volleyball game that afternoon. The weather remained near perfect —sunshine, low humidity, and about eighty degrees. Volleyball sounded good to me. We agreed to a 1400 hour start, giving me time to get to my office and write a couple of letters. I felt as though I needed some really rigorous exercise, and the kind of volleyball we played provided just that. We played by "Jungle Rules." Rule number one: there are no rules. During the game that afternoon, Captain Bob Williams dislocated his shoulder, and one of the NCOs took an elbow in the chops that required six stitches in his lower lip. It was not a game for the faint of heart, but it was rigorous exercise and fun.

Tet was, by this time, almost upon us, and it promised to be a great celebration for the Vietnamese. I was continually surprised that events of this nature would be celebrated with such intensity during time of war. We were informed that Tet celebrations would run from 8 February through 13 February and that 40 percent of ARVN soldiers would be given leave in order to join their families for the festivities. Everyone seemed tradition-bound to try to get to their home city, village, or hamlet for the Tet celebration. It was a huge family-oriented celebration. There was to be a mass migration of people, all trying to get home. It was kind of Christmas, Easter, Thanksgiving, and Halloween all rolled into one. We were also informed that we could, conceivably, be restricted to the

I Corps compound, or to our rooms, during the celebration, depending on circumstances. The intelligence analysts were expecting an upsurge in VC activity during that time. Also, the Buddhist activists were once again exerting themselves in and around Da Nang. They felt maligned, under-represented, and under-appreciated by their government leaders, most of whom were Christian. I personally didn't know enough about the situation to determine the legitimacy of their complaints, but I suspected they were valid.

By the end of January, as the weather improved, high-altitude bombing resumed. The number of B-52 strikes seemed to increase markedly. From my perspective, that of a medic, the high-altitude bombings were a mixed bag. Whether or not they were an effective means of waging this particular kind of warfare remained unanswered. Without question, they denied the enemy crucial lines of supply and disrupted his command and control, but at what cost? It seemed to me that within days, new supply lines were established and command and control reestablished. Admittedly, I knew little about the subject. What I did know, with absolute certainty, was that high-altitude bombing created havoc in the lives of the people in the countryside. The peasants knew precisely which nation was responsible for raining terror upon them, and it seemed to diminish their trust in the United States. They also condemned their own government for authorizing the bombing.

CHAPTER 8

FEBRUARY 1967

As February arrived, plague again broke out in I Corps, this time in Hue. The outbreak caused a great deal more concern on the part of public health officials than usual. First indications were that they were dealing not only with bubonic plague, but with pneumonic plague as well. I knew very little about the pneumonic strain except that it was infinitely more deadly because it could be transmitted directly from person to person. It didn't require a flea as carrier.

On 1 February, I experienced something that was poignant and unusual. Captain Carlos De Los Santos, a liaison visitor from the MACV Surgeon's Office, and I were at Duy Tan Hospital. As we were being escorted around the large 1,000-bed hospital and the adjoining grounds, we eventually got to the morgue, which was separated from the main buildings of the hospital. Outside the morgue, before the Buddhist and Christian altars, were eleven flag-draped coffins. Inside the morgue were four or five corpses being prepared for burial. All were the bodies of young seventeen- to twenty-five-year-old ARVN soldiers.

In one corner of the preparation room, there were three people: a woman and two fairly young men, one wearing the uniform of an ARVN second lieutenant. They were kneeling on the floor before a pile of obviously human bones. Some bones were carefully positioned on a Republic of Vietnam flag, while others lay alongside the flag. The three people were looking at an anatomical drawing showing all the bones of the human body. The skull and jawbone had been isolated and positioned on the flag, as were the vertebrae and long bones of the legs and arms, as well as the rib cage. The feet and hand bones were partially in place, but there was still a pile of bones waiting to be placed, among them the shoulder bones, the scapula, the hip bones, some finger bones, and others.

Suddenly, the ARVN lieutenant stood, approached Carlos and me, and asked in broken English, "Please, sirs, you are doctors?" I told him that we were not. He then went on to explain what they were doing. If I understood correctly, his brother had been killed in a VNAF plane crash about nine months earlier. His remains, the bones on and near the flag, had recently been found. His mother, brother, and he were attempting to put the skeleton of his deceased brother back together for placement in a coffin prior to burial. I couldn't help but be touched, and I know Captain De Los Santos was as well.

***

At 1630 hours on 1 February, I had an appointment to see Colonel Hamblen. I walked into his office, saluted smartly, and said, "Sir, Major Van Straten with my decision concerning extension of tour for an additional six months."

He returned the salute, looked me in the eye, and asked, "Well, what is it?"

I said, "Sir, after careful thought and reflection, and also praying on it, I simply can't do it."

He said, "I understand. The ball's now in my court. I'll have to decide whether or not I'm going to request that you be involuntarily extended. I'll let you know on Monday." And with that the meeting was over. I saluted smartly and was excused. I didn't feel good about the abruptness of the encounter.

The pre-Tet celebrations had been going on for a day or two, and I found them disconcerting. For the life of me, I couldn't differentiate between the explosions of certain types of firecrackers and the crack of a rifle. I'd flinch every time I heard one go off, especially while driving my jeep when all sounds were somewhat muffled and distorted. I later found out that many others experienced this same uneasiness.

Tet also gave public health officials concern, for a totally different reason. I attended a meeting on 2 February where the primary topic of discussion was the mass migration of people and the high likelihood that it might cause diseases that were prevalent in one area of the country to be transmitted to people living in many different areas. The public health officials knew that it was difficult to contain an outbreak of any disease when the people, all potential carriers, were moving around the countryside freely. The annual migration also placed hordes of people on buses, the most common form of mass transportation, in close proximity to other people who might already be infected with a disease. Those with mild cases of communicable diseases didn't want to stay home and miss all the family fun.

***

The weather had again turned foul. It was windy and a cold, with slashing rain coming in from the mountains. I had been trying to get to Hue for the past two days, but was so far unsuccessful.

On Saturday, 4 February, we all sensed the excitement that was in the air. Tet celebrations were growing in number and intensity. The whole country seemed alive with new energy and excitement. Unfortunately, based on information I received at the I Corps staff meeting that very morning, it appeared that some Vietnamese peasants and their families would go hungry during the celebration. There was a significant shortage of rice, one of their dietary staples, in the entire country. Some blamed it on the weather, while others contended that the shortage came about because of our defoliation program. I didn't know wherein lay the truth —maybe it was a little bit of both. It seemed to me that a major part of the problem was graft, mismanagement, and corruption. The U.S. Marines had been asked to help transport 160,000 pounds of bagged rice into four different needy but remote districts where the people were apparently in dire need of food. The Marines, of course, obliged and did everything possible to get the rice delivered before Tet. But it was rather discouraging because, although records indicated that Vietnamese civil authorities in some of the districts had already been given sufficient rice to feed the people, the rice had disappeared. They simply could not satisfactorily explain to U.S. authorities where it went. Was it given to, or extorted by, the Viet Cong? That was a distinct possibility, as there were myriad VC sympathizers in I Corps.

It was rather discouraging, too, because the movement of that much rice by air would, in all likelihood, put some American pilots' lives at risk. When American helicopter pilots had to make repeated trips into the same LZ in contested areas, they ran a high risk of being killed while landing, while on the ground, or when taking off. Unless the pilots had a secure LZ with troops on the ground, or had the luxury of an accompanying gunship, they were vulnerable. One hundred sixty thousand pounds, eighty tons, was a lot of rice to transport just before Tet. It chewed up a lot of the U.S. Marine lift capability to move that much rice on short notice.

***

At noon on that Saturday, I attended a luncheon held at the 10th Medical Company in Da Nang. I think it was a kind of pre-Tet celebration, but I'm not certain of that. The invitation was in Vietnamese, and I didn't have time to get it fully translated. I ate sumptuously of the very tasty foods, many typically loaded with trouble for us Americans—lettuce, tomato and cucumber salads, pastries, seafood dishes, etc. The Vietnamese seemed to have built up immunity to many of the bugs that seemed to plague us Americans. I paid the price that evening.

***

Members of our advisory team couldn't escape the customs and traditions of Tet. Our Vietnamese colleagues took great joy in acquainting us with them. One involved the use of small red envelopes, known as "Tet envelopes." A ten or twenty piastre bill was placed within each of several envelopes which were then given to the children encountered during the day. I gave Dr. Tu an envelope for each of his six children as a goodwill gesture, even though I had never met the children. Tips to favorite waitresses in the Officers' Club or to the barber were also given in the Tet envelopes at that time of the year. The tradition was somewhat like our custom of tipping the boy who delivers the newspaper or the person who delivers the mail at Christmas-time.

***

Commencing at noon on Sunday, 5 February, I had to make brief appearances at two different pre-Tet celebrations. Every ARVN medical unit commander felt he had to host such an event. If the commander didn't sponsor one, his soldiers complained, and morale suffered. As the senior medical advisor I was invited to all of them. If I didn't attend, the unit commander felt slighted, and the advisor-advisee relationship was weakened. I decided to suck it up and try to attend as many of them as I possibly could.

That evening, I attended General and Madame Lam's big pre-Tet party. I had to wear a suit, only the fourth time my suit had been removed from its hanger in seven months. I had had to carry that suit all the way from San Antonio to Da Nang to wear it only a few times, but as a field grade advisor, it was mandated that I bring one. I knew my suit smelled musty. There was little I could do about it other than airing it out.

All this celebration, right in the middle of a war, was something I did not expect. I was conflicted by the celebrations. On the one hand, it seemed as if they didn't take the war seriously, didn't devote their full energies to winning it. On the other hand, when you looked at it from their perspective, it took on a different meaning and was more understandable. They had been at war for a long time. While the war ground on, they tried to maintain the customs and traditions of their culture and wanted to bring about some semblance of normal family life. Without an occasional opportunity to celebrate their culture, life in their war-torn country might have been even more unbearable. I just wished they wouldn't celebrate so often.

***

Every workday morning, when I drove in to my office, the streets were alive with workers trying to get to their jobs on time. Most rode the little, always over-crowded buses. While waiting for a bus, many of them tried to hitchhike a ride. I had a penchant for picking up hitchhikers, probably because I did so much hitchhiking as a kid. We were given a number of stiff warnings against picking up hitchhikers, but I largely ignored them if the person seeking a ride looked kindly. However, on Monday morning, 6 February, an ARVN officer apparently picked up a hitchhiking worker in the pre-dawn hours, only to be found, after the sun rose, lying in a ditch alongside the road after having been savagely beaten and knifed in the abdomen. His private vehicle was stolen. From that time on, I hesitated to pick up hitchhikers during the hours of darkness.

On Monday morning, 6 February, I was expecting Colonel Hamblen's call. It came early, at 0715 hours. It wasn't what I had hoped for. He told me that he needed me on his team and that what I was doing was "mission essential" work. Therefore, he was going to submit a request that I be involuntarily extended for six additional months. With that disquieting information, I saluted smartly and left his office.

Later that day, I went to the G-1 advisor's office and studied the MACV regulation that authorized involuntary extensions. I noted that there was a provision whereby the officer being recommended for involuntary extension could put forth a written request for reconsideration, citing any extenuating circumstances that mitigated against the extension. I decided to exercise that option. That evening, I stayed in the office until 2000 composing and typing my request for reconsideration. The request had to be forwarded to MACV HQ through command channels, so the next morning I dutifully gave it to my boss. He gave my request a positive endorsement and then took it to Colonel Hamblen's office for his action prior to its being forwarded to MACV HQ in Saigon for final decision.

I also wrote a letter to a personal friend in San Antonio, LTC Arthur Criswell, explaining to him what was happening and asking that he say nothing to my wife until my request for reconsideration was acted upon. If my request for reconsideration was denied, I wanted him, along with his wife, ElDora, to go to our home and explain to my wife what had happened. I didn't want her to find out about an involuntary extension in a letter from me. I was fearful she might suffer a breakdown.

At noon on that same day, Tuesday, 7 February, I was invited to a huge Tet celebration at Duy Tan Hospital. I gave an impromptu speech that was greeted with wild applause. I didn't know if the speech was that good or if the people in attendance just appreciated one of their American advisors' presenting an impromptu speech. Major Phat, who was supposed to have relinquished command on 1 February, was still in Da Nang and in command of Duy Tan. His orders had been changed, extending him in Da Nang until 18 February. After my speech, he presented me with a memento, a ceramic team of miniature horses pulling a wagon. In the wagon was a miniature barrel of whiskey, and hanging alongside the wagon were six small shot glasses. I appreciated Major Phat's gesture.

Ground transportation arteries and conveyances were busier than ever the day before Tet. Everyone seemed to be going somewhere, or buying something, in order to get ready for the New Year. The hustle and bustle, so conspicuous by its absence at Christmas-time, now seemed to characterize all of South Vietnam. Forty percent of all ARVN soldiers and VNAF airmen were allowed to go home for the Tet celebration. The problem was getting them to their ancestral cities and villages. The small buses, about the only means of getting from one city to another, were packed like sardine cans. In order to accommodate as many ARVN and VNAF personnel as possible, ten to fifteen soldiers or airmen were allowed to ride on top of the buses. It was rather amusing to see one of the small buses chugging down the road. They were probably manufactured to accommodate twenty to twenty-five people, but in actuality, many of them carried close to fifty.

Road mines had to be of great concern to the people riding those buses. It was a terrifying thing to see one of the buses hit a mine. I never saw the actual explosion of a mine under a bus, but I did see the horrific aftermath of such an explosion from a helicopter. The pilot swooped down to about 300 feet above the road and we could see the carnage. It looked as if the bus was an over-ripe watermelon that had been hit with an ax. But, instead of spewing out seeds and juices, it spewed out the mutilated bodies and blood of people.

It seemed as though I had been at some type of Tet party, luncheon, or dinner for half of my waking hours in the few days leading up to Tet. But, as my commander had told me, "That's your job, to learn as much as you possibly can about the Vietnamese people and their customs and traditions so that you can motivate them, as best you can, to act in their own best interests." I had heard that little lecture on several occasions when I had mildly objected to his giving me yet another invitation that he wanted me to accept on his behalf.

***

The Medical Section of the G-4 Office, the NCOs and I, were able to obtain about 700 children's gift items—dolls, trucks, airplanes, stuffed animals, etc.—from the U.S. Marine Civic Action Team. We gave all of them to Duy Tan Hospital, where they were distributed to the children in attendance at the hospital's Tet party for patients, their families, and the hospital staff. After the party, I was assured by Captain Phat that every child in attendance got at least one gift. They tried to give the children gender and age appropriate gifts but weren't totally successful. I almost cried midway through the party when a little girl came forward to receive her gift. She was perhaps four and all alone. She was wearing a soiled dress at least four sizes too big. It actually dragged on the floor.

She was very dirty and kept scratching the many itches she had. Her hair, I'm certain, was laden with head lice or mites. Her eyes were swollen, which was very characteristic of scabies. She was a mess. All she wanted was a cookie, and I made sure she got several, along with a nice little doll. It bothered me to see innocent children in this pathetic state. Although I'm not certain, I think she was an orphan.

***

Firecrackers were typically used to signal the start of a Tet party. At Duy Tan's party a string of perhaps a thousand firecrackers was ignited to start the merriment. It was deafening inside the hospital auditorium. Later, near the end of the celebration, one of the ARVN soldiers took two smaller strings, one in each hand, and had another soldier light the firecracker at the very end of each string. At the very last second, just as the individual explosions were nearing his hands, he flung the remainder of the string aside. I couldn't understand why there weren't more accidents. Even small children, five or six years old, played with firecrackers.

After the Tet party at Duy Tan, Major Phat invited me and several others to his bachelor apartment for a drink. I was very surprised to see that he had a Tet tree in his living room, not totally unlike our tradition of a Christmas tree. It was a small tree, barren of leaves or buds. He explained that the tree would start budding in about a week. Captain Phat said it would get a flower-like bud that was very beautiful. It was kept in a large vase of water until it started to bud, and then transferred into soil. The many Tet greeting cards that Captain Phat received from family and friends were all hung on the branches of the Tet tree, along with a few festive lights. It really was quite attractive. Also, every one of Major Phat's subordinates, those who reported directly to him, came to visit him at some time during the Tet holiday period. Each of them brought their entire family with them and presented Captain Phat with a small gift of gratitude. The families seemed to come unannounced. Three families showed up while we were enjoying a snifter of very good brandy. This was not unlike the tradition in the U.S. military where many commanders host a New Year's Day reception for their subordinates.

Tet was also a time of the year to visit the graves of deceased family members. Entire families were clustered in cemeteries throughout the city. All seemed to be wearing their very best clothing. The children gathered obediently around their parents (or parent, as so many families seemed to be missing at least one parent). This was also the time of year when the vast economic differences among families stood out. The rich were well dressed as they stood around their ancestors' gravesites, while the poor were usually in their everyday work clothes, standing alongside the graves of loved ones.

The day of Tet finally arrived, as did Ash Wednesday, both occurring on the same day, 8 February. "Remember man that thou art dust, and to dust thou shall return" was softly intoned as the ashes of Lent were placed on my forehead. The weather on that day was magnificent. I was pleased for the sake of the Vietnamese families who had invested so heavily in making the day enjoyable and memorable for their families.

We were restricted to our hotel effective twelve noon on the day of Tet. That evening several of my colleagues and I watched the celebration on Doc Lap Street from our third floor balcony. The celebration started in earnest at about 2030 hours, shortly after it got dark. Two hours later, by 2230 hours, it was unbelievable. The exploding firecrackers and fireworks were deafening, and the sky was filled with exploding fireworks of all types. No one seemed to light just a single firecracker. They always lit strings of them. Some strings, eight to ten feet long, were strung between trees, light poles or other objects before being lit. The wick was lit at one end and the children screamed gleefully as the explosions moved along the entire string.

Every family, even those who were poor, seemed to have expended a considerable amount of money on fireworks. We were told that there was religious symbolism involved in the firecrackers. If I understood correctly, the belief seemed to be that the explosions drove away evil spirits, thereby preventing them from invading the lives of the people who comprised the family.

The next morning, after Tet had ended, the streets and entryways of many of the stores and other places of business were covered with the confetti of exploded firecrackers. As I drove to my office that morning, the smells of cordite, incense, and burning joss sticks hung heavily in the air. I suspected that Tet was celebrated more enthusiastically by the Buddhists than by Christians, but I wasn't certain of that. Still, I thought that since Da Nang was a predominately Buddhist city, I may have witnessed a more exuberant celebration than those that had taken place in cities where the predominant religion was Christian.

The members of our advisory team seemed pleased to see the seven-day celebration come to an end. The intensity and all-encompassing nature of the celebration had surprised all of us. The lengthy period of celebration was religious as well as civil. It was a time when many, perhaps most, spent all the money they had been able to save during the preceding year. It was also a period during which the Vietnamese tried to pay off all their just debts so as to be able to face the New Year with a clear conscience. Tuesday was the last day of the Year of the Horse. Wednesday began the Year of the Goat.

***

MACV advisors were back at their desks on Thursday, 9 February, but there weren't many ARVN officers around to advise. The ARVN offices in the I Corps compound were essentially deserted and would remain so until the following Monday. I couldn't help but wonder why the VC and NVA hadn't looked at the Tet holiday as an opportune time to strike. Things had been very quiet during the entire seven-day period of celebration. All I could conjecture was that the VC and NVA were celebrating Tet with the same intensity as their adversary.

On Friday, 10 February, I flew to Hue. The plan was to stop there briefly to pick up Captain Bob Helton then continue to Quang Tri. We never got to Quang Tri. The weather was perfect when I left Da Nang, but worsened as the helicopter got into the Hai Van Pass and became almost impossible as we approached Hue. I had to spend Friday night there, then, on Saturday, I couldn't get back to Da Nang until early afternoon. I had missed the Saturday morning I Corps staff meeting and, unfortunately for me, General Walt had asked a couple of medically-related questions that Major Hennigan, my boss, was unable to answer. Captain Stephens, the Assistant G-4 advisor, was in the office when I got back from Hue and told me that Major Hennigan was "not at all pleased," even "pissed," that I hadn't been there to answer the general's questions. He also told me that Major Hennigan wanted to talk to me first thing Monday morning. I knew I'd be called on the carpet.

That Saturday afternoon, about twenty of us went to China Beach and engaged in our version of the Super Bowl, a football game for those over the age of thirty. Many of those taking part had formerly played in college, but the intervening years, diminished skills, and expanding waistlines made the game what Major Dick Austin, an MP advisor, labeled "The Battle of the Pissants." But it was fun, and that's what physical recreation was all about—having fun and getting the heart to beat faster for a prolonged period of time. The only downside to the game was that when I got back to my hotel, there was, for the fourth consecutive day, no electricity and no running water. A sponge bath, using water from my five-gallon can of drinking and tooth-brushing water, was the best I could do for my sweaty and dirty body.

On Sunday, 12 February, we still had no water or electricity in our hotel. Also, for the past five days the maids had been on their Tet holiday. The hotel was a mess. The laundry was piled high, and the whole place stank from infrequent flushing of the toilets, as nobody wanted to use his drinking and tooth-brushing water to flush the johns. No one was in a very jolly mood.

Late that afternoon, it started to rain hard as I was driving to Da Nang Air Base to pick up two more visitors from Saigon, Major Charlie Christ and SFC Sullivan. I got them settled in their guest quarters, then spent the afternoon trying to revise the itinerary that I had developed for their visit. It seemed doubtful that we would be able to fly to Tam Ky and Quang Ngai the next day as originally planned.

The next morning, Monday, 13 February, I arrived at the office very early. It was still raining, so I knew I was going to have to implement Plan B, which was to simply show Major Christ and Sergeant Sullivan the construction project at Duy Tan and the ARVN Convalescent Center. I purposely scheduled my NCOIC, SFC Simmons, to take them to breakfast, as I wanted to be in the office when Major Hennigan arrived.

Right on schedule, at about 0700 hours, Major Hennigan walked in the door. I arose from my desk and said, "John, I'm sorry about the problem you had with General Walt's questions during Saturday's staff meeting."

He grumpily replied, "Forget about it. You can't control the weather. If I had paid more attention maybe I would have understood all that gobbledygook you told me about plague and malaria and would have been able to answer his questions." That was the end of the issue.

The next day, Valentine's Day 1967, was a day I would long remember. Major Christ, SFC Sullivan, and I flew to Hue at 0800 hours. The weather was marginal. After spending a productive morning with Bob Helton at Nguyen Tri Phuong Station Hospital and the 1st Medical Company, we went to Bob's room to review our observations and decide on an advisory course of action prior to eating lunch. When we entered his room, at approximately 1130 hours, the weather was still marginal but probably flyable. When we exited to go to lunch at about 1245 hours, the weather was downright hellish. We wanted badly to get back to Da Nang. I was scheduled as SDO that night and doubted that I could line up a replacement on short notice, especially by telephone. Charlie Christ and SFC Sullivan were also eager to get back because of their scheduled flight to Quang Tri the next morning. Captain John McLean, advisor to the ARVN Medical Supply Depot, was going to accompany them to Quang Tri, as I had other things scheduled for the day.

After eating a rather hurried lunch, we went out to the military airstrip to see if our flight aboard a scheduled courier would be departing. We were booked to go in an Otter aircraft at 1430 hours, but were told that the chances of that light aircraft flying were not good. So we were scouting around the airstrip for a flight of opportunity. Nothing seemed to be flying. Suddenly we saw an L-19 observation aircraft trying to land. It crashed into a ditch just short of the runway. The winds were swirling and the rain was pelting down at the time. A strong gust of wind seemed to force the small plane into the ditch as it was decelerating in order to land. Miraculously, the pilot crawled out of the wreckage and walked away from the badly damaged plane uninjured.

The time for our scheduled flight on the Otter aircraft, 1430 hours, came and went, and soon it was 1700 hours. We were almost resigned to spending the night in Hue when SFC Sullivan noticed two air crews walking out to two helicopters sitting on the edge of the runway. We ran over to the operations center and found out that one of the aircraft was going to Da Nang. We were able to get ourselves manifested on the flight as "mission essential" passengers. The aircraft going to Da Nang was an aging H-34. We climbed aboard and were seated and buckled in for the flight.

About five minutes later seventeen or eighteen people, all Vietnamese, left the operations center and walked out to the helicopter. There was one child, three attractive, giggling, young women, five or six other Vietnamese civilians, and seven or eight ARVN soldiers. They all squeezed onto the helicopter. Soon the pilot, co-pilot, and crew started their pre-flight routine. The crew chief made a rapid count of the people on board then talked to the pilot. The crew chief then shouted something in Vietnamese. Apparently, it had been determined that four people had to get off. The crew chief seemed to be the decision-maker as to which four. It appeared to us as though the three young women were girlfriends of the pilot and crew. They were allowed to remain aboard, as was the child with them. A father and son were kicked off, as were two pleading

ARVN enlisted men. Both enlisted men showed their military orders to the crew chief and begged him to allow them to remain on the flight. I suspect they were trying to return to their units after spending the Tet holiday with their families.

The two young men strenuously resisted getting off the helicopter. They clung tenaciously to the door. The crew chief grabbed a metal wrench and threatened to hit their hands. He then stepped on their fingers as they gripped the base of the door as the huge helicopter was rising from the ground. At that moment, I could fully understand what had happened in the Aschau Valley. I remembered seeing those horrifying pictures of Vietnamese civilians clinging to the struts of helicopters and being shot and killed when the helicopters could not take off because of their weight. While our Valentine's Day incident didn't come close to that, it did result in the crew chief's threatening the enlisted men with bodily harm.

Finally, the helicopter was airborne. The weather was very bad, with a ceiling of about 200 feet. We had to get out to the South China Sea as quickly as possible, since when flying that low, the hulking helicopter was a big target for ground fire. In order to get out to the sea fast, the pilot opened it up to full throttle and flew just a little above tree-top level, even clipping the tops of a couple of trees as we swept over them. But he got us out to the sea safely. We then had the long trek down the coastline back to Da Nang, where we arrived safely, and I assumed my duties as SDO at I Corps HQ right on time.

The SDO activities were fairly routine until early in the morning of 15 February. At that time, all the phones in the HQ started ringing at once. The ARVN 2nd Infantry Division compound in Quang Ngai was under mortar and ground attack. The duty NCO and I couldn't keep up with the telephone traffic, scribbling notes to ourselves during each call to remind us of things that had to be done, follow-up actions that had to be taken, and people who needed to be notified. One of the MACV medics, SFC Melvin Bender, was among the casualties. He caught a chunk of shrapnel in the shoulder. The night was the perfect time for an enemy attack. It was cold and windy and rained all night. Based on my having observed the guards in front of the hotel where I lived, I knew that ARVN guards had a tendency to be less than vigilant in such weather. Practically all of the guards had been conscripted into the army and were planning to get out as quickly as possible. During bad weather, they hunkered down in their fortified positions, trying to stay dry and warm. They were definitely less alert and vigilant. I couldn't help but think that the guards in Quang Ngai had probably reacted that same way.

***

During a discussion with Major Hennigan at the Officers' Club that evening, I learned that General Walt, the U.S. Marine Commander, had been in Da Nang for twenty-five months. During that time, he had seen his wife twice and his children only once. I was not sure when he saw them, but I assumed it was when he was summoned to Hawaii to confer with General Krulak. Mrs. Walt probably flew to Hawaii to see him. Major Hennigan also told me that General Westmoreland was about to start his fourth year in command. I came to realize the huge sacrifice that the families of high-ranking military officers made and the pressure that they were under.

***

Officers assigned to MACV Advisory Team #1 enjoyed a unique and stimulating experience when they got their hair cut in the barbershop located in the Officers' Club. Although I have no way of verifying this information, I was told that shortly after an old home in Da Nang was rented and turned into the MACV Officers' Club, a little man on a bicycle wheeled up to the front door. He smiled broadly and passed a printed note to the club manager. The note stated that he was an experienced barber and that he would like to set up shop in the Officers' Club and work on a fee for service basis. The club manager showed the note to the commander of Advisory Team #1, who was intrigued by the idea of the team having its own barber. The little man was brought in for an interview by the club officer, and then his name was sent through a background check for security purposes. Terms of hire were then negotiated and he was hired. Advisory Team #1 now had its own barber.

The question of where to locate the barbershop within the confines of the small club then had to be addressed. As one entered the club, he had to pass through a small vestibule where officers placed their weapons and rain gear before entering the dining room or bar. On the left side of the vestibule was a door leading to the dining room and kitchen. Straight ahead of the entry door was a flight of perhaps ten steps which led to a very small space on the second level of the club. On the left of this small space there was another flight of five or six steps leading to the barroom of the club. The only conceivable place for the barber to set up shop was in the small space at the top of the stairs on the second level.

The barber proved to be a delightful man. He had a welcoming smile for everyone who passed his shop on the way to the barroom. I cannot, with certainty, recall the barber's name, but for sake of this memoir, I'll call him Nha. Nha eventually got to know all the advisors by their names and ranks. He befriended all and was a respected member of the MACV family.

When you entered his little shop, which he kept exceptionally clean, he whipped out the apron with a flourish, seated you in the chair, pinned on the apron, and started to cut your hair, first with electric clippers and then with scissors. He chattered all the while he was cutting, sometimes in pidgin English, but mostly in Vietnamese. He invariably hummed or even sang a bar or two of a Vietnamese song. When he was finished with the cutting and trimming of the hair on your head, he carefully trimmed the hairs from your ears and nostrils. Then he took his straight razor in hand, again with great flourish, and gave it several good swipes across a leather strap attached to a cabinet to make certain it was ultra-sharp. He took his shaving cup in hand, added a little hot water to the cake of soap therein and, using the shaving brush, whipped the soap into a thick lather. Need it or not, you were going to get a shave. After completing the shaving of your face he lathered up and shaved the back of your neck with great precision, never once drawing blood.

He then had you lean forward in the barber chair, so that your head was over the sink, while he washed your hair. He had no electric dryer, so a freshly laundered towel was used to dry each patron's hair. You were then asked to select which ointment you wanted him to apply to your hair from an assortment of four or five. After the ointment was applied and your hair was combed, the apron was removed and the fun began.

Nha stood on a small platform so that he was at the proper level to execute the next step in the process. Unknown at the time of his hire, Nha was an exceptionally skilled, well-trained masseur. It was sheer, hedonistic pleasure to have him massage your head, neck, shoulders and spine—all for the meager cost of a haircut. We experienced everything from karate chops to the shoulders and along the spine to electric vibrators along the neck and shoulders to deep massage of the shoulders and neck. It was one of the highlights of Da Nang to get one of Nha's massages.

When he was finished with the massage, Nha again combed your hair, then insisted that you inspect his work with a small hand-held mirror. When you nodded and smiled your approval, Nha gave the signal that the process was over and you could get out of the barber chair.

Although I can't recall his exact fee, I believe it was either twenty-five or thirty-five cents. This included the haircut, shampoo, and massage. Most officers seemed to give him $1.00, a very generous but much deserved tip.

During my year in Da Nang, our commander, Colonel Arch Hamblen, assigned me the additional duty of doing a monthly sanitary inspection of the MACV Officers' Club, to include Nha's barbershop. Nha took these inspections very seriously, unlike the kitchen staff, and was always prepared. After my second inspection of his shop, which resulted in no demerits, Nha looked at me intently and asked, "You give me something to put on wall?" It was obvious that he wanted some public declaration that his shop was clean and well run. I designed a certificate and had it printed by the I Corps print shop. I then had our advisory team commander sign it, as did I. When I left Da Nang in late June 1967, the certificate was still proudly hanging on the wall of Nha's shop. To this day I've never met a more conscientious businessman than Nha.

***

A fairly large-scale operation was initiated in Quang Ngai province on 16 or 17 February. We were told that it might turn into the largest single operation of the war, but after getting his nose bloodied, the enemy decided that discretion was the better part of valor and withdrew rather than fight. Quang Ngai was a hotbed of communist activity. Prior to 1954, it was the countrywide HQ for the Viet Minh, the forerunner to the Viet Cong.

Marines from the Republic of Korea had a significant victory on the opening day of the battle. By actual body count, they killed 243 VC while losing only nineteen of their marines. Although this battle was being hailed as a resounding victory, it became more and more apparent to me that the war was rapidly evolving into a war of attrition. I couldn't see how we could possibly win such a war. It seemed to me that to expect the present leadership of North Vietnam, Ho Chi Minh and his generals, to be pressured to the negotiating table by the deaths of large numbers of men and the loss of military supplies and equipment was being unrealistic. We had repeatedly seen the VC and NVA limp off the battlefield seemingly defeated, but they always seemed to have the ability to reconstitute their units and be back in the fight in a relatively short period of time.

As of 18 February 1967, I had a new primary counterpart. Captain Nhan was now the I Corps Surgeon and Major Tu the Commander of Duy Tan Hospital. I was very sorry to see Major Phat depart Duy Tan Hospital for his new assignment near Saigon. He and I had a very professional relationship, and I always found him to be trustworthy, forthright and honest. The change of command ceremony at Duy Tan was held during the afternoon of 18 February, and that evening's dinner to honor the outgoing and incoming commanders was catered by perhaps the best restaurant in the city, the New China World.

***

The battle in Quang Ngai Province heated up again on 18-19 February. All ARVN hospitals in I Corps were full beyond capacity, and something had to be done to alleviate the pressure. The ARVN hospital commanders, working with the I Corps Surgeon, had done about all they could to spread the workload among the various hospitals and other treatment facilities. ARVN policy was to keep patients as close to their home of record as possible. This allowed hospital commanders to tap into families to help with patient care, bathing, shaving, feeding, etc. But sometimes that procedure was simply not feasible. This was one of those times. The ARVN was forced to move patients a considerable distance from their homes.

On 19 February, a friend gave me the January 27, 1967 edition of *Life* magazine and pointed out a controversial article written by Robert Sherrod entitled "A Monstrous War."[1] Sherrod, a respected war correspondent, had recently been in our HQ, although I had not met him. I found his article to be thought-provoking, factual, and seemingly credible. My feelings essentially coincided with his. As much as I abhorred Communism as an ideology and wanted to see Ho Chi Min defeated in his quest to take over the Republic of Vietnam, I thought Sherrod was probably correct in his conclusion that the United States was locked into a war it probably would not win.

The United States, it seemed to me, didn't have the national will to see the war continue on into the indefinite future, whereas our enemy's will was quite different. We saw the time line of the war in terms of a year or two, three at most, whereas, the North Vietnamese saw it in terms of many years or decades and, if necessary, beyond. I knew that President Johnson had some tough decisions regarding the conduct and duration of the war, and I didn't think he would be willing to buck the downward trend-line of national support for the war. I believed the

American people's support, at that time, early in 1967, was still reasonably strong, but starting to waver. When U.S. casualty counts went up, as they inevitably would if we were to fight a war of attrition, I knew in my heart that the American people's support for the war would go down.

***

On Monday, 20 February, I was forced into action as an EMT, something I had not been trained for, except in a very rudimentary way. I was sitting at my desk late Monday afternoon, helping Major Hennigan prepare a briefing to be presented to three general officers the next morning. When we finished the job, he left the office to go to dinner, and I stayed behind to type a letter to my wife. About ten minutes later, Major Hennigan rushed back into the office and told me to hurry out and get into his jeep. There was urgency in his voice and concern in his eyes, so I responded quickly. He drove a short distance to the site where an American construction worker, driving an open jeep, had attempted to pass an old Vietnamese truck on a very rough road near our compound.

The front wheel of the construction worker's jeep had hit a deep chuckhole, and the driver was thrown from the vehicle and landed hard on the back of his head. Upon our arrival, it was clear that the injury was life-threatening. In addition to his caved-in skull, blood was coming out of one of his ears and his mouth. He was unconscious, totally unresponsive, and in respiratory distress. All I could think of were the ABCs of emergency care—check for an Airway, stop the Bleeding, and Control for shock. I didn't have an airway device with me, so, in order to keep his tongue from blocking his trachea, I gently pushed an empty ammunition clip into the back of his throat. It seemed to allow him to get some air into his lungs.

I put a compress bandage on the back of his head to try to stop the bleeding, but was afraid to apply any pressure because of the caved-in skull, concerned about further damaging his brain. The compress bandage was only partially successful in stanching the flow of blood, but it helped. I elevated his feet to get blood to his brain and hopefully prevent him from going into shock or respiratory arrest. I was shaking all the while I worked on him. As an MSC officer, I was trained primarily as a medical administrator, not an emergency medical technician.

The next morning, I called the Navy hospital to check on the status of the man. While he was still living, the doctors assessed his chances of full recovery at about 40 percent. I found that his name was Robert Lockwood. Although I told Major Hennigan not to do so, he insisted on writing a letter commending me for my actions. After the incident, I questioned the adequacy of my actions, especially my having elevated the man's legs to get blood to his brain and thereby prevent shock. By so doing, I probably intensified the bleeding. Mr. Lockwood eventually recovered sufficiently to be evacuated to the United States.

***

I learned of the death of Bernard Fall, the news corespondent and historian, on the evening of 21 February, the day he was killed, while eating dinner. It hit me hard, for I had met Mr. Fall on two occasions: once in Hue and once in Da Nang. He was killed in Thua Thien Province, while accompanying a company of U.S. Marines during Operation Chinook II, when the jeep he was riding in hit a mine. As a sidebar, I recently read General Colin Powell's autobiography, *My American Journey,* and was struck by what he had to say about Bernard Fall's insightful book, *Street Without Joy.* General Powell pointed out that Fall felt strongly that the leadership of the United States had almost no understanding of what we had gotten ourselves into in Southeast Asia. He wrote, "I cannot help thinking that if President Kennedy or President Johnson had spent a quiet weekend at Camp David reading that perceptive book, they would have returned to the White House Monday morning and immediately started to figure out a way to extricate ourselves from the quicksand of Vietnam."[2]

***

By 21 February, all ARVN hospitalization units in the southern part of I Corps were full well beyond their listed capacities. The I Corps

Surgeon and the Commander of Duy Tan Hospital had freed up quite a number of beds by moving patients into the Convalescent Center in Da Nang a little faster than usual and by discharging others earlier than the attending physicians would have liked. The physicians were aware of the fact that these actions would probably take their toll on recovery times and outcomes, but they had no feasible alternative.

After a considerable number of hospital beds were emptied at Duy Tan Hospital, the problem became getting aircraft, VNAF or USAF, to move patients from Quang Ngai and Quang Tin Provinces to Da Nang. All transport aircraft were committed to moving supplies, munitions, POL products, and fresh troops necessary to fight the war. I argued strenuously, but my powers of persuasion hadn't produced a single aircraft as of the morning of 21 February. Captain Nhan and I had figuratively dragged wounded and dead bodies across the runways of Da Nang Air Base to get an aircraft, but to no avail. We had to keep trying, as the need was acute. I felt rather inept and helpless when dealing with both the VNAF and the USAF, as I knew relatively little about how either one of them operated, but I had to learn fast. Still I couldn't seem to find the right strings to pull. My boss, Major Hennigan, was trying to help too, but we both seemed somewhat powerless when it came to working with a service other than our own. We had very little leverage. This was especially true when working with the VNAF.

At the peak of my frustrations over my inability to obtain a VNAF aircraft to move patients, I typed a letter to my wife. The initial part of that letter read as follows:

22 February 1967

My Dear Pat,

"It is not good for the Christian health

To hustle the Asian brown;

For the Christian riles and the Asian smiles,

And he weareth the Christian down.

At the end of the fight is a tombstone white,

And the epitaph drear: A fool lies here,

Who tried to hustle the East."

Rudyard Kipling

Poet Laureate of Great Britain

Since my days at St. Norbert College I've always appreciated the work of Rudyard Kipling. Reading Robert Sherrod's article the other night, which I subsequently sent to you, reminded me of Kipling's prophetic words. I regret having to say this, but I think Kipling's words are pretty much on target when it comes to this war. I'm very skeptical about our chances for outright victory. A negotiated truce of some type is probably the best we're going to do as a nation. My feeling is that as this war drags on and becomes ever more costly, insofar as the expenditure of human lives, both ours and our allies, the president will be willing to grab at almost any straw that allows us to disengage with our honor as a nation intact. I know there are several others in our advisory group who feel as I do. Obviously we'll soldier on, doing everything we possibly can to defeat a very savvy and vicious enemy, but it's difficult to be optimistic about the final outcome. How do you defeat an enemy that you can't even recognize from a man or woman on a city street or a farmer in the field, an enemy who can blend in with the people so perfectly and so easily as to make detection almost impossible? I often wonder how many members of the I Corps HQ staff might covertly be VC or VC sympathizers. I feel confident there are some, but how many and who they are remains an enigma.

The most poignant line in Kipling's poem for me is: 'For the Christian riles, while the Asian smiles, he weareth the Christian down.' Pat, never having been in Asia you can't possibly comprehend the truth contained in that line. Things that bother American advisors deeply don't seem of great concern to many of the Vietnamese officers. For example, this past weekend the ARVN had 283 patients jammed into a facility designed for 200 and more battlefields casualties were expected. The I Corps Surgeon wired an emergency request to VNAF HQ in Saigon for air transport to move some of the patients from Quang Ngai Province to Da Nang. Subsequently we found out that the request laid on the desk of the officer who had approval authority from 0900 hours on Saturday until 1530 hours on Monday. Three follow-up telegrams were ignored. To me this seemed almost criminal, so I riled, but to them it seemed almost routine, so they smiled. It is maddening for me and my fellow advisors. Fortunately for me, none of my Vietnamese counterparts have acted in this manner. They have been timely in their decision making and have not deferred until tomorrow decisions that should be made today.

***

On 23 February I received a letter from my oldest of five sisters, Joan (Van Straten) Laffey. Included with her letter was an article written by Martha Gellhorn, who had briefly been married to Ernest Hemingway, entitled "Suffer the Little Children."[3] It highlighted USAID's ineffectiveness in getting U.S. medical aid and assistance to the points where it was most needed. The article was published in a January 1967 issue of *The Ladies Home Journal.* My experiences in the province hospitals led me to concur with the basic thrust of the article. Civilian casualties resulting from the war far outnumbered the military casualties. While in Vietnam, I never saw hard data comparing military and civilian casualty rates, but I would not have been surprised if the ratio was 2:1 or possibly even as high as 3:1.

Most of my fellow MACV advisors in Da Nang didn't have an appreciation for the huge numbers of women and children who were being killed and injured. They saw very few civilian casualties. But I saw the broken and bleeding bodies of not only the women and children, but also the elderly, almost daily in the province hospitals and district clinics. The only segment of the Vietnamese population that I rarely saw in the province hospitals was young men. For the most part, all able-bodied young men were in the military.

Image 25. Wounded child sitting on stretcher awaiting treatment.

Photo courtesy of U. S. Navy Bureau of Medicine and Surgery Archives

The words of LTC Darvin Patrick, executive officer in the MACV Surgeon's Office, came back to me every time I went into one of the province hospitals. He had admonished me, during my in-processing in Saigon, to "look after the MILPHAP teams." At the time he offered that guidance, I didn't even know what a MILPHAP team was. But he was right on target, as the MILPHAP teams were a crucial part of the very fragile civilian healthcare system. Although the provincial hospitals were doing heroic work, the casualty flow into those hospitals must have given the hospital staff the impression they were drinking out of a fire hose. It had to have been discouraging for them, but the doctors, nurses, technicians, and administrative support staffs never seemed to show it.

**

Friday morning, 24 February, two packages were delivered to my office. The first was a huge box of children's clothing sent by a woman living in New Jersey. An accompanying letter said that one elderly American lady had sewn all the items of clothing and asked that they be distributed "to Vietnam's poorest." Later that day, I wrote a short letter of thanks to the woman who sent the package and asked that she give it to the kind lady who did the sewing.

The second package was from my sister, Donna (Van Straten) Remmert. She sent three single-piece, stretch, pajamas that her son, David, had outgrown. I gave them to Bá Vy, my maid. She giggled and giggled as she tried to put them onto her squirming toddler. Later she borrowed my scissors and cut a vertical slit in the rear of each pair of pajamas.

**

At the I Corps staff meeting on Saturday morning, February 25, a wrap-up of the operation in Quang Ngai Province was presented. The joint operation had resulted in more than 800 confirmed VC dead. It seemed inevitable that body count would be the focus of the future. The policymakers had apparently decided to fight a war of attrition. I knew this apparent decision would not be well received by General Walt, and I couldn't help but wonder how long he would remain in command of U.S. forces in I Corps. While the operation in Quang Ngai Province was hailed as a major victory, it had come at a heavy cost. The ARVN hospitals were filled to bursting with the broken bodies of young soldiers.

After the staff meeting, I attended the bi-annual meeting of the Officers' Mess Association, during which I was elected to the Board of Directors. Technically, the MACV Officers' Club was an Officers' Open Mess because we paid only mess hall rates for our meals. While I didn't need yet another additional duty, like it or not, I was elected to serve on the board.

John Hennigan was also elected. I told him that "if we don't get decent food, it's our own damned fault, since we control the board." He laughed.

***

Earlier, I described the tragedy that occurred on Christmas Eve 1966 when a Flying Tiger cargo plane heading for Da Nang Air Base in horrible weather came down short of the runway and plowed right into a small Vietnamese village. That village was essentially destroyed and more than 100 people lost their lives.

Shortly after this tragic event, III MAF HQ formed a working group to study the U.S. response to the disaster to see what could have been done better. I was asked to serve as an ex-officio member of that working group by virtue of my having been there. I couldn't meet with the group very often, but I did manage to provide some input.

One of the lessons learned, pertaining to our decision to take the bodies of the deceased to an established morgue in Da Nang, illustrates very graphically the differences that existed between our culture and that of the Vietnamese. The Americans managing the disaster, including me, didn't understand the survivors' resistance to this decision and attributed it to the emotions surrounding loss of a family member or friend.

This turned out not to be the case. There was much more to the resistance than that. The working group definitively determined why there had been such resistance. The findings of the group were published in III MAF ICCI 3050.1, dated 26 February 1967, which set forth instructions for managing future disasters. Paragraph 2 presented background information, referring directly to the Christmas Eve crash and one other disaster. But the part of the document that I found fascinating was an attachment entitled "Vietnamese Customs Applicable to Emergency Situations." Vietnamese community leaders wrote this portion of the document. While the language is stilted, the intent is clear. Here are a couple of excerpts from the attachment. I've changed nothing. The punctuation, grammatical inconsistencies, word choice, quotation marks and capitalization are exactly as published. Paragraphs I and II of the attachment read as follows:

Vietnamese point of view concerning the deaths caused by war accidents.

I. "This is a 'sudden accidental death', the most unhappy death of all. The death on the battlefield is a glorious one. But when a person dies while he is at home or is walking in a rear area due to a stray bullet or bomb, due to a plane crash or an automobile accident, his death causes to his relatives a deep sorrow and shame."

II. "As a result, if those who cause this death don't act skillfully and tactfully, with due respect to the local people's customs so as to appease public opinion, and especially to console the victims' families, they will face the villagers' anger and psychological reaction.

III. Typical problems related to the recent plane crash (Quang Nam Province)

1. "According to the civilized custom of Western countries, it is advisable to ASSEMBLE THE BODIES AT THE MORGUE OF THE HOSPITAL. But according to Vietnamese custom, the people are reluctant to send their relatives' bodies to the morgue. They think that the 'MORGUE IS THE DIRTIEST PLACE: A DEATH WITH THE BODY AT THE MORGUE IS AN UNGLORIOUS AND MOST UNLUCKY DEATH'."

2. "If the victim's bodies were left at the crash-site, their relatives would be able to recognize them based on the location where the bodies were found.

3. "If we take unilateral actions, in a hasty and unskillful manner, we may easily provide an opportunity to VC for making distorted propaganda among the people."[4]

It was easy for war planners to err when they made assumptions, especially about customs, traditions, and other aspects of culture. The U.S. military has always demanded that when a staff study to address a problem area is prepared, all assumptions have to be clearly identified and defended. The assumption in this matter was that the Vietnamese would react to a morgue as we do. It was an erroneous assumption and we learned from the experience.

***

On 27 February I arose to the realization that it was my son Steven's third birthday. I couldn't help but wonder if he would recognize me when I got home. How I missed him.

On that same day, 27 February, the war took an ominous turn. The Da Nang Air Base was subjected to an attack by long-range rockets. The attack did significant damage to a number of aircraft and destroyed several military buildings. It came from rocket-launching positions located as far away as seven or eight miles. It was later determined that Soviet-made 140-millimeter rockets, with great range and bursting power, had inflicted the damage. The rockets were fired from multiple launching positions. This weapons system added a totally new dimension to the war. The enemy could now strike from long range with seemingly great accuracy. About 200 homes in the village of Ap Do, which was near the air base, were also destroyed, many of them by fires resulting from the shelling. This was, we were told by General Walt, the heaviest and most powerful ground weapon used by the VC thus far during the war. Forty-seven people were killed, twelve Americans among them, and more than 100 were wounded. The experts determined that conventional mortars were also used in the pre-dawn attack, but the long-range Russian-made 140-millimeter rockets did most of the damage and were responsible for the casualties.[5]

The next day, Tuesday, 28 February, I had a very interesting experience. I was asked by Colonel Hamblen to spend an hour explaining my role as I Corps' senior medical advisor and the humanitarian programs I was involved in to Charles B. MacDonald, Deputy Chief Historian of the United States Army.[6] I enjoyed Mr. MacDonald's questions. They were very insightful and gave me a new appreciation for how an historian approaches his work. Mr. MacDonald was trying to determine the best approach for writing a definitive history of the U.S. Army's involvement in Vietnam.

As February came to a close thousands of people in the I Corps area were being relocated to get them out of dangerous areas, to include known enemy infiltration routes and avenues of approach. Some villages were in the process of being abandoned while new ones were being established. What a strange war it had become. Peasant-class people, all depressingly poor, were being asked to abandon their ancestral homes and villages in order to protect themselves from the ravages of war. How could we possibly explain what was happening to an uneducated, peasant-class person whose whole life was wrapped up in a little piece of land, his village, his family, and his God? On that last day of February, I sent my wife a newspaper clipping containing a picture that seemed to characterize what was going on. Peasants were shown trying to move a huge statue of the Blessed Virgin from their previous village, a dangerous area, into a newly established village. In their attempts to move the statue, it seemed the people were trying desperately to cling to anything of permanency that would give meaning to their lives.

CHAPTER 9

MARCH 1967

On the morning of 2 March, Sergeant Quan, an ARVN NCO whom I sometimes used as an interpreter when Sergeant Thong wasn't available, came to me and said that he had a very sick baby. I asked him what the doctor had to say about the baby. He explained that he wasn't married. and therefore a doctor within the ARVN medical system could not see his illegitimate child. He went on to explain that he was Buddhist and that his girlfriend, the mother of his child, was Christian. Neither his parents nor her parents would consent to an inter-faith marriage, so he and his girlfriend simply lived together. I was able to get the baby, only eleven days old, seen by an ARVN physician as an exception to policy. When the doctor saw the baby girl, she was near death. The Sergeant expected a miracle of medicine. The miracle didn't happen. The baby died late that very afternoon. The next day, Sergeant Quan told me that he would now separate from his girlfriend. He said he and his girlfriend both felt as if they had failed their parents.

On 3 March there was a heart-rending bombing of Lang Vei, a village near Khe Sanh. Preliminary estimates were that at least 150 civilians were killed and about 170 injured. Nobody seemed to know precisely what had happened, but it appeared that one of our own planes may have accidentally dropped the bombs that caused so much carnage and human suffering.

I spent part of that day helping coordinate medical support and humanitarian aid for the survivors of the bombing. Because of bad weather, it proved difficult to get anything into Lang Vei. We all felt rather heartsick and helpless. Attempts to evacuate the most severely injured were made even more difficult by bad weather. Later in the day we learned it had been determined a U.S. Air Force F-4 Phantom jet aircraft had mistakenly dropped the bombs. How it happened was yet to be determined. I felt so heartsick, not only for the victims and their families, but also for the pilot who dropped the bombs in error. He would have to live with that sad memory for the rest of his life.

By the next day, 4 March, the casualty estimates for the Lang Vei tragedy had been revised downward. It appeared that the loss of life would not exceed eighty-five persons. Earlier estimates, as with most estimates when death was involved, appeared to have been grossly inaccurate. American soldiers, I had learned from experience, tended to overestimate the number killed and underestimate the number wounded. Eighty-five, nevertheless, was a depressingly large number to have died as a result of an accident. The victims were almost all Montagnards.

On that same day, Da Nang was the scene of a very large and boisterous semi-political rally. Ostensibly, the rally was pro-government and anti-VC. It mattered not to me what the source of their anger was. I was determined to stay away. Over 20,000 angry men and women, primarily young people, gathered on that day to protest the VC rocket attack on Da Nang and to voice their objections to the coalition government the VC were attempting to form in France at that time. I gave a wide berth to the rally as I traveled through the city. I felt that it wouldn't take much to change the tenor from an anti-VC demonstration into an anti-war demonstration, and from there, it was only a short leap to its becoming an anti-American demonstration. Dr. Tu and I were supposed to escort a large contingent of American physicians, all civilians, through Duy

Tan Hospital that morning, but the visit was canceled because of the rally. Senior ARVN officers at I Corps HQ had decided that discretion was the better part of valor and we were asked to cancel the visit and stay away from the rally.

Life went on in Da Nang. The dynamics of the city were so different from any of the American or European cities in which I had lived. The bridge between the "haves" and the "have nots" was depressingly wide. The rich, a very small minority, had life-styles very similar to ours. They seemed to take good care of their bodies, keeping them clean, well groomed, and well clothed. They ate well-prepared, tasty, nutritious foods. They lived in comfortable homes. The people in the city were either rich or poor, there didn't seem to be much of a middle class. And if you were poor, you were depressingly poor, so poor that you didn't have the wherewithal to properly care for yourself and your family. The poor lacked the basics necessary for good hygiene and nutrition. They aged rapidly. They seemed to live a more or less hand-to-mouth existence.

On the same day as the rally, Saturday, Sergeant Thong and I were scheduled to transport a young mother and her year-old baby to the Navy Hospital for an evaluation. A few days prior to the rally Sergeant Thong and I had been driving near a refugee settlement, thought by many to be occupied by a sizable number of VC. The settlement was fairly close to the Navy BX on the outskirts of Da Nang. As we approached the settlement, we noted a young woman walking alongside the road carrying her baby on her hip, which was typical in Vietnam. The baby, a little girl, appeared to be about a year old. As we passed the mother and child, I noted that one of the baby's legs was jutting out at an unusual angle.

I stopped the jeep, backed up, and asked Sergeant Thong to find out what had happened to the baby's leg. She told Sergeant Thong that the baby was born that way, which was doubtful, but I let it go. I told Sergeant Thong to tell the woman that maybe the American doctors could fix her baby's leg, and that if she consented, we would take her and the baby to the American hospital for the doctors to evaluate the child's leg. The mother didn't understand the translation of the word "evaluate," so I told Sergeant Thong to use the Vietnamese words for "examine and possibly fix." These words, she understood. She smiled, bowed, and held her hands together, her way of saying thank you. She seemingly gave her consent for an evaluation. I then had Sergeant Thong ask her where she lived. She pointed at the refugee settlement and gave Sergeant Thong a general idea of where her home was located in the maze of small houses. We obtained her name and told her that we would be back on Saturday, 4 March, at 1530 hours to transport her and the baby to the hospital to have the American doctors evaluate the baby's leg. I took a chance that a Navy doctor would be available at the time I had proposed.

Upon returning to my office, I called Dr. Giles, who put me in touch with an orthopedic surgeon. I explained the situation to him, and he agreed to see the child at the time I had proposed, 1615 hours on Saturday.

When we arrived back at the refugee settlement on that Saturday afternoon, I parked the jeep on the road and told Sergeant Thong to go into the settlement and find the mother and child. He had only a general idea of where they lived, but he knew the family's name. Shortly after he left, I sensed that something was wrong. The village was almost eerily quiet. Usually when you parked near a village or hamlet, the children flocked to the jeep. But no children came running to my jeep looking for a handout of candy, which they typically did. Their mothers, most of whom seemed interested in why you were there, usually followed the children. Today was different. Nobody came running to the jeep. I was isolated and alone. All I saw were dark, unfriendly eyes peering at me from behind the partially opened doorways and windows of humble homes. I sat there with my rifle alongside me as my only protection. I felt vulnerable and was also concerned about Sergeant Thong, who was somewhere in the maze of the settlement.

Ten minutes went by. Where was Sergeant Thong? After about twenty-five minutes, I was becoming very concerned and apprehensive. Where was he? Should I abandon my jeep and go into the seemingly hostile refugee settlement to try to find him? Should I shout his name and hope for a reply? Should I flag down a passing American vehicle and ask for help? Surely I couldn't leave Sergeant Thong in that settlement alone.

As I was weighing the alternatives, Sergeant Thong suddenly appeared from behind me, startling me because I hadn't seen or heard him coming. He quickly explained that it had taken him about fifteen minutes to find the right home. He said that, although the young woman still wanted to take the baby to the Navy Hospital for evaluation, her husband and father would not allow it unless they had a chance to "talk with the American officer."

I was tempted to tell Sergeant Thong to get in the jeep and drive away, but I kept seeing the face of the young mother when she gave her consent. We simply had to try.

I told Sergeant Thong to return to the home and ask them to please come to my jeep where I would try to answer any questions they might have. Sergeant Thong did as I requested. He soon returned, all alone. He explained that the young woman's father was ill and too weak to come to my jeep. He asked that I come to him.

Did I dare abandon my jeep and walk into that seemingly hostile settlement? I couldn't leave Sergeant Thong to guard the jeep. I needed him to interpret the conversation. What was I to do?

I had just about firmly made up my mind that we could not risk going into that troublesome settlement without protection, when the young mother came rushing up to the jeep carrying her baby. She looked down at the baby's malformed leg and then pleaded with her eyes for me to come and talk to her father and husband. Reluctantly, I got out of my jeep, locked the chain through the steering wheel and around the steering column, and, along with Sergeant Thong, followed her into the settlement. We could sense many dark eyes peering at us from behind partially closed doors and shuttered windows. There were still no children playing outside their homes, as I would have expected on a pleasant Saturday afternoon. As we moved through the settlement, it suddenly dawned on me that I should not be carrying my rifle in front of me, which could be perceived as a threatening position, so I slung it over my shoulder with the muzzle pointed down, the least threatening position I could think of.

We walked about two hundred yards before reaching the young woman's home. As we entered, I noted the sparse furnishings, a series of bamboo sleeping mats, a table with three chairs, and a crude bench. There were several cooking pots and a few cups, bowls, glasses, and dishes. The baby's grandfather was lying on a bamboo mat raised off the dirt floor with a wooden pallet. The woman's young husband was seated on the bench and looked sullen. The older man started asking questions, looking only at Sergeant Thong, never directly at me even when I was responding. After about ten minutes of questions and answers, he rendered his decision. No, he would not give his consent for his granddaughter to be seen by the American doctors. It was unequivocal. The young woman's husband nodded his head in approval of the decision. The young woman pleaded, but to no avail. The grandfather would talk no more. The matter was closed. As we left the home, the young mother was silently weeping. We returned to my office and called to cancel the orthopedic evaluation. Although I was disappointed, I had to set the incident aside and move on.

**

When my boss, Major Hennigan, was in a jovial mood, he referred to me as his "personal physician." He would occasionally come bouncing into the office with a sheaf of papers in his hand and a twinkle in his eye and shout, "Where's my personal physician?" He did just that on Monday, 6 March, then went on to tell me that the I Corps G-4 had just informed him that two C-130s would fly an inter-hospital transfer mission the next day, one bringing patients from Hue to Da Nang and the other bringing patients from Quang Ngai to Da Nang. This was indeed good news, as Captain Nhan, the new I Corps Surgeon, had submitted the air movement request on 18 February, sixteen days prior. I immediately called Captain Nhan. He had already received the good news and was in the process of alerting the commanders of the units involved in the transfer of the patients.

Also on that day, 6 March, four weeks had elapsed since I had submitted my request that I not be involuntarily extended for an additional six months. Having heard nothing, I went up to the G-1 advisor's office and asked the enlisted man who handled personnel requests if anything had been received from MACV HQ regarding my request. He told me that nothing had been received and promised that he would let me know just as soon as something arrived. I went back to my office and wrote a short letter to my friend in San Antonio, LTC Criswell, giving him a status report and telling him not to address the matter with my wife until he heard from me.

In the late afternoon of Tuesday, 7 March, word swept through the HQ that another rocket attack on Da Nang was imminent. An observer aircraft, an 0-1, which patrolled the skies over and around Da Nang all day long, had spotted the VC or NVA setting up a rocket launcher a few miles from Da Nang Air Base. It appeared as if everything was being readied for another attack. But the expected attack never came. We speculated that the U.S. Air Force had been able to scramble a couple of jets in time to neutralize the site before the rockets were launched.

On 8 March, I received a very thoughtful note from a very capable and beautiful Vietnamese nurse. She had studied at the University of Colorado for two years. Her spoken English was exceptionally good. About three months prior to receiving her note, I had had the pleasure of escorting her through the Navy Hospital at the request of General Lam, the I Corps commander. She was most appreciative of the opportunity to see a sophisticated combat hospital.

Five or six weeks prior to receiving her note, I had received a package from the United States containing six complimentary copies of the *Merck Manual*, an excellent medical reference book put out by the Merck Pharmaceutical Company. I gave copies to Major Phat, Major Tu, and Captains Helton and Schumacher, keeping one for myself. I had one left over so, on the occasion of Tet, I sent that copy to this nurse via her brother, an ARVN officer who worked in our HQ. She was, at that time, serving as a faculty member in the Vietnamese medical school located in Hue. She was most appreciative of my giving her the manual and expressed her feelings in the note. The language of most Vietnamese professionals, when writing a thank you note, was so flowery that it was easy to mistake it for the language of romance. Such was assuredly not the case in this instance. I sent the note to my wife as an example of the Vietnamese manner of expression, explaining very carefully to her the cultural differences.

Also on 8 March, I found a very recent issue of an American magazine in the Air America Terminal at the Da Nang Air Base that contained an article summarizing the 27 February rocket attack on Da Nang. I was greatly surprised by the article's accuracy and completeness, as well as by the fact that it had reached Da Nang so quickly. The article, surprisingly, contained information that we, the MACV advisors, did not have. It reported that the rockets were manufactured in Russia in 1962 and that fifty-one rounds actually hit the Da Nang Air Base, damaging eleven aircraft. It stated that the range of the rockets added a totally new dimension to the war. It also reported that it had been determined that most were fired from different firing positions located a distance of 8,000 to 9,000 yards from their targets and that the rockets were fired in salvos of six to eight rounds. It further stated that each round weighed about ninety pounds and that its bursting radius was quite large. Finally, it reported that one Vietnamese village near the Air Base was essentially destroyed and that the U.S. Marines lost twenty-four men. Some of this information was new to all of us on the advisory team. It gave me a new appreciation for the ability of the press to ferret out information.

It was still quite cold in I Corps on 8 March. But the weatherman promised a warming trend starting the very next day. We were all hoping the forecast was correct. The monsoon had been brutal.

On 9 March, I received a thought-provoking letter from my father. In it he raised many questions about the war. His recent letters had given me the impression that the American people's support for the war was waning.[1] I was certain that our young enlisted soldiers and marines were receiving similar vibes. I was starting to hear comments such as, "If the American people don't care, why should I put my life on the line?" These comments troubled me.

I spent the morning of Thursday, 9 March, in Tam Ky working with the MILPHAP team at the province hospital. Dr. John Driscoll, the commander of the team, had met my flight at the crude airport outside of Tam Ky. That airport consisted solely of the runway. There were no buildings whatsoever. In the summer, when it was fiery hot, people would stand alongside the strip, in temperatures approaching 110 degrees, waiting and sometimes pleading for a ride to wherever they had to go. I personally saw, on two occasions, ARVN soldiers brandish their weapons at Air America pilots in order to get on an already over-crowded airplane. Transportation was a huge problem in a developing nation, and war served only to exacerbate the problem.

Dr. Driscoll and his team were seeking my support in getting some additional equipment for the province hospital. They were losing a high percentage of the babies born prematurely. The doctors believed that many lives could be saved if they had better equipment. They pleaded for anything available, even hand-me-downs, from American hospitals that were upgrading. I respected Dr. Driscoll greatly and told him I would personally raise the issue with the MACV Surgeon, which I did during a phone call when I returned to Da Nang. No physician that I knew adhered to the Hippocratic Oath more rigorously than did Dr. John Driscoll.

The MILPHAP team members were truly a dedicated group of men. Their actions, in my opinion, were just as heroic as the riflemen out on patrol. When I arrived in Da Nang, I had expected that the younger physicians on the MILPHAP teams would have an attitude problem. For the most part they were physicians who had been drafted right after completing their internships or, in a few instances, residencies. Instead of moving into a civilian practice, they had been drafted into the service of their country. But their attitudes, with only one exception, were superb. I heard no bitching or grumbling whatsoever, except from one doctor who claimed to have lost a prestigious residency at Johns Hopkins because he had been drafted.

In early March, it seemed to me, Quang Tri Province was about to explode. The ARVN and the U.S. had committed so much manpower to that province that I was convinced something was about to happen. I flew up there on 10 March, along with an ARVN physician, to take one last look at the readiness of the ARVN medical units available to support combat. It appeared to me that the ARVN had done a good job in resupplying and, in some instances, reequipping the units. We observed two classes being taught to upgrade the skills of recently assigned medics, which was reassuring, as the ARVN had a tendency to give continuing education a fairly low priority.

While in Quang Tri I had an opportunity to sit in on the interrogation of a captured VC combat medic. One thing became very apparent. The VC had essentially no means of moving patients off the battlefield except on the backs of other soldiers or by litter bearers. They had no motorized vehicles whatsoever dedicated to moving patients. Occasionally they used a bicycle, pedicab or water buffalo, but all these means were pretty crude and improvisational in nature. It also became very clear that enteric diseases and malaria were significant problems for them, eating into available manpower.

Saturday morning, 11 March, was a sad day for all members of MACV Advisory Team #1. We received the news that Second Lieutenant Roger Rabey, our recently assigned supply officer, had been killed when a C-47 on which he was a passenger crashed the night before somewhere between Cam Ranh Bay and Saigon. Later that same morning we were informed that the Phu Thu sub-sector, in Thua Thien Province, had been overrun and Major Richard Heydt, Sp-4 James Hutton and the advisory team medic, Sp-4 Hayward Spencer, were all killed in action. Sp-4 Spencer had been in my office about ten days prior to being killed. VC mortars had started raining down on them at 0210 hours. They radioed that they were under attack and needed help. That was their last transmission. When the relief column got to Phu Thu, they found the three dead advisors and about fifty dead ARVN soldiers. Major Heydt, whom I had not met, arrived just two weeks prior to being killed in action. This served as yet another reminder of just how vulnerable the sub-sector advisory teams were.

I was the SDO on Saturday, 11 March, and my relief, because of an emergency, didn't show up until 1030 hours on Sunday. I, therefore, had to attend Mass late in the afternoon instead of attending in the morning as planned. A rather diminutive Vietnamese priest routinely celebrated that afternoon Mass because Father O'Neill, our Catholic chaplain, traveled to several remote outposts each Sunday afternoon to hear confessions and celebrate Mass and was, therefore, not available. The Vietnamese priest couldn't possibly have weighed more than eighty pounds. He was eager, but struggled with his English. Even though he butchered the language, everybody seemed to like and respect him.

Later that evening, after a very sad and trying day, my fellow inmates —what we called those of us who lived in our hotel—and I enjoyed a very tasty charcoal-grilled steak. One of the officers had scrounged about fifteen T-bone steaks, some baking potatoes, and a pound of butter, so we ate royally. And the beer flowed freely, too. About the only kind we could buy at that time was Carling's Black Label, which wasn't bad. A couple of the officers had known those men who had died when Phu Thu District was overrun, so we had a kind of private wake service. Though somber, the evening was much appreciated. We all needed a little relaxation.

***

Major Hennigan continued to generate a lot of activity around our office. He was an exceptional officer, among the best I had worked with during my almost eleven years in the army. One evening, I was plugging away at a report, and he was on a series of logistically related phone calls, at a time when we normally would have been at dinner or enjoying a beer at the bar. He suddenly looked at me and, in a very serious tone of voice, said, "Van Straten, if there's anything I can't stand it's an officer who drinks during working hours, or works during drinking hours. Let's go have a beer." So we did.

Shortly after I arrived at work on Monday, 13 March, I was informed that the MACV compound in Hoi An was under attack. Plans were being finalized to get an ARVN relief unit in there as quickly as possible. The relief unit would obviously require medical support. I called the I Corps Surgeon. He was on top of it, awaiting more information about the size and composition of the relief force before deciding how to medically support it.

I was also informed that the Hieu Nhon sub-sector had been overrun during the night. That was the second sub-sector overrun in just three nights. My very good friend, Captain Thomas Sauble, was killed in action at Hieu Nhon, and all four members of his team were wounded. One was the team medic, Sp-4 Wright. It appeared the VC was doing everything possible to disrupt initiation of the Revolutionary Development Program throughout I Corps. At the previous Saturday's staff meeting, General Walt had predicted that these types of attacks, on district HQ and sub-sector advisory teams, would happen. His words were prophetic.

I was very saddened by the thought that somewhere in the United States, probably that very afternoon, a casualty assistance officer and a chaplain would have to knock on Mrs. Sauble's door and tell her that her husband would not be coming home, that he had been killed in action. And she, in turn, would have to tell her children. The task of serving as a casualty assistance officer carried with it grave responsibilities and a lot of sadness.

***

The orientation of newly assigned soldiers was a duty that the NCOIC, SFC Simmons, and I took very seriously. We shared the belief that lives could be saved by proper orientation.

As mentioned earlier in this memoir, I found it particularly difficult to orient enlisted medics who were being assigned to a position in which the previous incumbent had been killed in action or incurred life-altering wounds. Inevitably, the medic being oriented would ask a question related to his predecessor, such as, "Will I have any overlap with the person I'm replacing?" Or, "What happened to the man I'm replacing?"

One day, sometime in March or April, SFC Simmons and I were orienting a new medic being assigned to a sub-sector advisory team. These five-man, sub-sector advisory teams were instrumental to the success of the pacification program. The team usually lived near district HQ and typically the only security they had was provided by the team itself and soldiers from the local community, the Regional Forces or Popular Forces. These citizen soldiers were somewhat equivalent to our Reserves or National Guard, though not nearly as well trained or equipped.

SFC Simmons and I had thoroughly briefed the newly assigned medic on his duties as a part of the five-man sub-sector advisory team. We made certain he understood his chain of command, how he was to be resupplied, how he could communicate with us when necessary and myriad other topics. We stressed the fact that, while he worked directly for the commander of the district advisory team, we were his backup in case he ran into medically-related problems. We hammered away on how important medicine was in winning over the hearts and minds of the Vietnamese people, telling him that there would be many medical conditions among the people in his district that he could safely and effectively treat. We also told him that experience had taught us that the children would be very open about approaching him, usually looking for a handout of candy, and that if he could establish good rapport with the children, their mothers would soon be seeking his help in curing their children's ailments.

To this point, the orientation had gone exceptionally well. I was pleased, and so was SFC Simmons. Then came the inevitable topic of his predecessor. Before I could even broach the issue, the man asked, "Sir, if

I might ask. Who will I be replacing, and will he be there when I arrive to help me get my feet on the ground?"

Sadly, the man he was to replace had been killed in action. Adding to the difficulty of answering his question was the fact that the medic who preceded the one killed in action had been seriously wounded and had to be evacuated to the United States. As a result of these facts, and wanting to phrase my response appropriately, I hesitated before answering the question.

I sensed that my hesitancy in responding had been interpreted by the soldier as evasive. I found it very difficult to give him a complete and honest answer without causing him so much concern that he might overreact and become hyper-cautious to the point of endangering himself.

When it was time for the man to get to the helipad for his flight to the sub-sector he was being assigned to, SFC Simmons volunteered to transport him, along with his duffel bag full of military and civilian clothing, a backpack, his web gear, his rifle, and his medical aid bag.

When Simmons returned to the office, he walked up to my desk and said, "Sir, with all due respect, you didn't handle his question about the man he was replacing very well. You shouldn't be answering those kinds of questions. You're doing NCO work. That's my job to tell him what happened to those who preceded him."

I accepted SFC Simmons' constructive criticism. From that point on, prior to the orientation process starting, SFC Simmons would invite new assignees to share a cup of coffee in a corner of our small office while I continued to work at my desk. While enjoying coffee he would openly and honestly address the subject of the soldiers' predecessors. He would then give the soldier an opportunity to ask any questions he desired. After this had been accomplished, SFC Simmons would introduce the man to me and the formal orientation process would begin. This new procedure worked far better. For me it was a lesson learned.

***

About a month prior to my going to Bangkok on R&R in early January, I had sent carbon copies of a letter to my mother, mother-in-law, and each of my five sisters asking if they would like me to purchase a piece of jewelry for them while in Bangkok. Bangkok was known for its high quality, inexpensive jewelry. Princess rings were in vogue at that time and could be purchased for twenty-five dollars each. I told the women that if they were interested in my buying rings for them, they should immediately send me their ring sizes and a postal money order in the amount of twenty-five dollars. I specifically cautioned them not to send a personal check, as it would be very difficult to cash in Da Nang. We had no banking service whatsoever.

Several of my sisters and my mother ordered rings. Each sent me her ring size and a twenty-five-dollar postal money order, except my sister Donna. She responded by sending her ring size and a personal check, despite my having specified a postal money order.

During the late afternoon of 13 March, Specialist Behner, the clerk typist in our office, came to my desk and said in a rather hushed tone, "Sir, Colonel Hamblen called and said you should get your ass up to his office immediately." What was going on? Why the strong language? As I hurried up to our commander's office, I mentally reviewed my actions during the past few days. I could think of nothing that I had done that was controversial. As I approached the colonel's office the adjutant looked at me and said, "He's really pissed. Go on in and make sure you report properly."

I knocked on the door and in a very loud, gruff voice Colonel Hamblen said, "Come in." As I entered his office, I noted the very stern look on his face, and sitting on either side of his desk were his Deputy Commander, Colonel John Beeson, and my immediate boss, Major John Hennigan. Both looked equally stern, almost like the members of a court martial prior to trial. I couldn't help but wonder what was happening, what had I done?

I walked within two paces of the commander's desk, clicked my heels together, smartly saluted and said, "Sir, Major Van Straten reporting as requested."

Colonel Hamblen then asked, "Major, what in the hell's going on?"

I responded, "Sir, I'm not following you. I don't know what you're talking about."

He then asked, "Are you aware that an officer is supposed to set the example for all of the men he has the privilege of supervising?"

I responded, "Yes, sir. I always try to set a good example."

He then asked a series of questions: "Have you ever had to counsel a soldier about keeping his financial house in order? Have you ever had to counsel someone about living beyond his or her means? Have you ever had to counsel a subordinate about cashing bad checks?"

He paused and I replied, "Sir, in response to all three of your questions the answer is yes, I have had to counsel individuals concerning such problems."

"Well, then, why in the hell don't you take your own counsel to heart?" he exploded. I was then severely lectured about financial responsibility and the need for an officer to set a good example. Colonel Hamblen went on and on with his tirade. I was very concerned, but had no idea what he was talking about.

Suddenly my immediate boss, Major Hennigan, jumped into the conversation and said, "Sir, I think this is Major Van Straten's first offense. He's otherwise been a highly responsible officer. I recommend that you not be overly harsh with the punishment you assess." Punishment, I thought, what was I being punished for? Colonel Hamblen then opened his center desk drawer, reached in and handed me my sister Donna's check, which I had cashed at the Officers' Club after giving the manager my absolute assurance that it was good. Stamped on the front in bold letters were the words: CHECK RETURNED—ACCOUNT CLOSED.

Oh, no, I thought, *how could that be?*

Colonel Hamblen then asked, "Is that your signature on the back of the check?"

I turned the check over, looked at it, and responded, "Yes, sir, it is." Suddenly it dawned on me what had probably happened. At the time my sister wrote the check, she and her husband were preparing to move from Chicago to Houston. My brother-in-law, a lawyer, had been employed by the American Bar Association in Chicago and had accepted a new position in Houston with the Exxon Oil Corporation. I could only assume that their Chicago bank account had been closed just prior to their moving and that my sister had underestimated the time it took for her check to reach me and for me to present the check for payment in Da Nang.

Before I could offer up this probable explanation, Colonel Hamblen stood up, smiled broadly, and said: "Van Straten, you've been had. This sting has been our feeble attempt at combat humor. I want you to know that you're doing a helluva job. Now get your butt out of my office and get back to work."

Hennigan and Beeson laughed raucously. Naturally, I was relieved when they started to laugh. I realized that I had bought into their sting, hook, line, and sinker. I explained what probably caused the check to be returned. They howled with laughter over the irony of a bad check being written on the joint account of an attorney who had worked for the American Bar Association.

On the way back to our office, John Hennigan admitted that he was the culprit who set up the sting. He explained that Colonel Hamblen had given him the returned check and told him to give it back to me, along with instructions to give the club officer twenty-five bucks and then rip up the check. Hennigan, with his mirthful Irish spirit, decided that a little fun was in order first, so he proposed an alternate plan to Colonels Hamblen and Beeson. They bought into it.

I've thought about this sting operation on many occasions in the past forty-nine years and still laugh about it and marvel over how skillfully they pulled it off. That very evening I took the returned check to the club officer, Captain Doric, and gave him twenty-five dollars and an apology. I told him that I'd extract my "pound of flesh" from my beloved sister when I got home. He, too, laughed about the incident, as did many others when the story got around the HQ. It helped to relieve the stress after a couple of very rough weeks.

***

On 14 March, I received a letter from my father, who is now deceased, that for some reason compelled me to answer immediately. In the intervening years, I have often wished I had set the letter aside for a day or two before responding. My hasty and somewhat sharp response, I'm certain, caused my father considerable angst.

In reading his letter, it became apparent that the war had become a matter of great concern for him. The rocket attack on Da Nang, widely reported by the U.S. media, brought the war much closer to his family. In his letter, he stated that he thought we were embroiled in the war because God was punishing us for the evil that existed in the world. In my reply, I told him that I totally disagreed with him, that this was not "God's War" but "man's war." I went on, writing, "To deny that it is man's war is to deny the very existence of free will. Our elected leaders made the decision that it was in our national interest to go to war. God didn't make the decision, our president did." I also wrote that, "There's no doubt in my mind that war grieves God infinitely more than it grieves man." In his letter, my father had written that, "War is the shame of civilization." I responded by writing that, "I believe there are more shameful and worse things than war, enslavement and lack of freedom being but two examples." I also wrote that "war is shameful only if man has not fully exploited all avenues available to settle differences before resorting to war" and that "I looked upon war as a failure of diplomacy and reason." From that point on, my father's weekly letters were apolitical in nature, usually focusing on family and friends and things going on in the small Wisconsin village where he lived and I had grown up.

***

During the night of 14 March, all was quiet until shortly after 0200 hours, when all hell broke loose. The VC again struck Da Nang Air Base. They hit it quite hard, but not as hard as the previous attack. About twenty 140mm rocket rounds made direct hits on the air base. The base was only a half-mile from my hotel, so I was awakened by sounds of the exploding rockets.

That afternoon, Dr. Tu and I hosted a small group of U.S. Navy surgeons at Duy Tan Hospital. I had been lobbying for several months to initiate a program whereby navy surgeons would come to Duy Tan and operate with their Vietnamese colleagues. I knew such a program would upgrade the skills of the ARVN surgeons assigned to Duy Tan. During this first meeting, Dr. Tu and I showed the American surgeons the facility and then had a preliminary discussion exploring the feasibility of navy surgeons spending a few hours each week operating with their ARVN colleagues there. I knew this would be a tremendous boost for the Vietnamese surgeons, not only in the acquisition of skills, but also in improving morale.

***

I spent the entire day and night of 16 March in Tam Ky, working in the morning with an ARVN medical unit and during the afternoon with the MILPHAP team in the Quang Tin Province Hospital. I completed my work with the ARVN medical unit at about 1130 hours, and then went over to the province hospital. Dr. John Driscoll and several members of the MILPHAP team were about to go to lunch with a Dr. Thuy in what was described as "the best restaurant in Tam Ky." Dr. Thuy turned out to be one of the more westernized Vietnamese physicians I became acquainted with while in Vietnam. He invited me to come along as his guest. Tam Ky, it appeared to me, was the poorest city in all of the five provinces that comprised I Corps. It was also among the dirtiest.

The restaurant mirrored the city's filth. Hungry flies were present in abundance, feasting on the garbage on the floor. It seemed as though food by-products that could not be consumed were simply dumped on the floor by some of the customers. Everything from chicken bones to tea leaves to pork chop bones to left-over salad greens to cigarette butts to chunks of fat off the edges of meat to chicken skin were deposited on, and ground into, the floor. The flies loved it. Some of the patrons of the restaurant seemed to look upon it as a sign of superiority if they disdainfully cast their waste on the floor. The wait staff tried to clean it up, but to no avail. It was a losing battle. We were served some of the most godawful food I had ever eaten. After the introductory soup, which was the best part of the meal, we had some sort of a blood sausage. As you bit into the meat, it seemed to ooze blood, some coagulated and some red. The small bowl of steamed rice placed before me was dotted with flies, and the flies were very insistent that they get their fair share of the food, following your fork as you tried to put rice into your mouth. It was a real struggle to get a bite of fly-less food. I was surprised that I didn't have raging diarrhea the next day. As advisors, we were told to always sample the food, despite its unattractiveness, or we would risk offending our host.

While eating, Dr. Thuy told John Driscoll and me something that disturbed us greatly. We were discussing wives and marriage and the differences between their society and ours. I brought up my observation that many Vietnamese wives appeared to be very subservient to their husbands in regard to almost all matters. Dr. Thuy agreed that many wives were indeed looked upon in just that manner, as being subservient. He went on to state that most Vietnamese men looked upon their wives as being "intellectually inferior," and because of this, many husbands did not take their spouses to social gatherings. Instead, they would rather be seen with a young, pretty woman to whom they were not bound by marriage. The wife stayed at home with the children while the husband escorted a pretty, usually younger, woman. He quickly asserted that, while he did not subscribe to this social conduct, many did and that it was not looked upon with disfavor in most segments of their society.

Dr. Driscoll then described to Dr. Thuy the relationship he enjoyed with his wife, who was a pediatrician. By virtue of being board-certified, she had credentials her husband lacked. His residency had been deferred due to his being drafted into the army. Dr. Thuy asked Dr. Driscoll if the fact that she was board-certified and he was not impacted their relationship. Dr. Driscoll quickly explained that it did not, that they looked upon each other as co-equals in their marital relationship. He added that his wife's number one goal in life was to be a good wife and mother and that medicine was secondary to her and would always remain so. Dr. Thuy seemed perplexed by this.

Dr. Thuy went on to say that in his culture, men actually feared their wives becoming their intellectual equals. Consequently, many beat them regularly to keep them in line. Dr. Driscoll and I expressed our shock, disdain, and some doubt as to the truthfulness of his statement. He then told us something that really shocked us. He said that it was his conservative estimate that 90 percent of the poorer peasant-class Vietnamese men beat their wives routinely, almost daily. He also estimated that 50 percent of middle-class wives were beaten and that 15 to 20 percent of upper-class wives also suffered physical abuse at the hands of their husbands. Whether or not this was valid information, I do not know. But it shocked us to hear these disturbing estimates coming from a respected Vietnamese physician. That was a side of Vietnamese society that had hitherto not been exposed to either Dr. Driscoll or me. Although we questioned the validity of the information, it was nevertheless disturbing. If true, John Driscoll and I concluded, it presented yet another hurdle to Vietnam's becoming a respected nation on the world scene.

***

While I was in the province hospital later that afternoon, the wife of the province chief, a lovely woman, and about twelve other female spouses of city luminaries came to the Quang Tin Province Hospital to pass out gifts to those who were sick or wounded. Dr. Driscoll interpreted this as a very positive sign of civic pride and a new-found sense of civic responsibility. This was the first time, during the ten months that he had been in Tam Ky, that members of the city's elite had even visited the hospital, to say nothing of passing out gifts.

The things that Dr. Driscoll and his team had done to improve that province hospital amazed me. As the year progressed, I noted significant changes each time I was in the hospital. While the improvements to the hospital's physical plant and the equipment upgrades they were able to bring about were impressive, of greater significance was the spirit of hope for the future they were able to instill in the community. It was the little things that Dr. Driscoll and his team had been able to do that really counted. Foremost, they had been able to sell to the medical director several ideas for change, ideas that were almost revolutionary in Tam Ky at that time. As an example, they were able to sell the idea of separating the old people from the young. They established a pediatric ward where the children weren't being subjected to the realities of older people dying on a regular basis, maybe as many as two or three deaths per day. Now, there was hope among the children on the pediatric ward. Young mothers with hospitalized children conversed with each other as they went about meeting their children's basic needs, much as they do in open pediatric wards in the United States during visiting hours. Whereas that hospital used to be a dismal place, it had become a place of healing and hope.

There was one seventeen-year-old boy who had been brought into the hospital seven months earlier after not receiving solid foods for four months because he was constipated. At the time of admission, he was emaciated and near death. His parents said they had withheld solids because they "were afraid of blocking him up further." The constipation problem was cured and, while he was regaining weight and strength, Dr. Driscoll turned him into a hospital laborer. The hospital staff took his wasted body, sixty-one pounds upon admission, and built him into a fairly strong 103-pound young man.

Dr. Driscoll also hired seventy refugees to make bricks to be used in a new building that was under construction. Each laborer was given 100 piastres per day, about one dollar. The laborers now had a means of feeding their families, whereas in the past they did not. They had also been given the priceless gift of hope for the future.

The MILPHAP team had offered a deaf and dumb young man, who had suddenly showed up at the hospital, a paid position as a hospital guard. He protected the staff as they worked. He was the MILPHAP team's early warning system. He watched the area surrounding the hospital like a hawk and, at the first sign of danger, warned the staff.

Whether or not he saved anyone from bodily harm could not be ascertained, but on many occasions, he had properly warned them of impending trouble. The Americans nicknamed him Go-Go, because those were the only words he could say. Although mute, he had mastered the words Go-Go and knew precisely when to shout them. He was paid seventy piastres a day, the equivalent of about seventy cents U.S., but more important than the money was that he was given a sense of worth and hope for the future.

At the time of my visit, Dr. Driscoll was scheduled to go home in less than sixty days. He told me that his father had written to him every single day since his deployment. Dr. Driscoll felt bad that his schedule didn't allow him to write a return letter very often. He tried to write to his wife on a daily basis, as did many other Americans serving in Vietnam.

Tam Ky at night was a bit disconcerting. Prior to going to bed, I was shown the bunker I was to occupy in case of attack. I was instructed to place my helmet, flak jacket, rifle, ammunition cartridges, and all other articles that I would need if the compound were attacked in a convenient place next to my cot. Although artillery rumbled away all night and there was the occasional sound of small arms fire in the city, the compound was not attacked.

On the morning of 17 March, when I got back to my office after the return flight from Tam Ky to Da Nang, there was a sealed envelope lying in the center of my desk. On it, typed in capital letters, were the words: "MAJOR VAN STRATEN—EYES ONLY." Inside was a note from the clerk typist, who had promised to alert me when my rebuttal regarding involuntarily extension was returned from MACV HQ in Saigon. The note simply said: "Sir, your request has been approved. You will not be involuntarily extended." I breathed a huge sigh of relief.

On Saturday morning, 18 March, I awoke with a slight headache. I shouldn't have agreed to become an honorary Irishman the night before. But how can one resist when the Hennigans, the Tracys, and the Fitzpatricks all invite you for a drink at their respective St. Patrick's Day parties?

After the Saturday morning staff meeting, Colonel Hamblen asked that I accompany him to his office. I knew what the topic of conversation would be. We walked into his office, and he shut the door, then looked me in the eye and simply said, "You're off the hook. There'll be no extension of your tour."

I said, "Thank you, sir. I appreciate hearing the news from you."

He then said, "Don't thank me. I'm the one who requested that you be involuntarily extended, and I still think you're the right man for the job, especially with this new Revolutionary Development Program about to be implemented."

I said, "I appreciate your feelings, sir, but I've just got to get home."

He asked, "By the way, how's the baby doing?"

I responded, "Better, sir, but he's still pretty fragile. My wife is doing her very best to hold it all together."

He asked, "Any questions?"

I said, "Just one, sir. Have I shot myself in the foot insofar as a military career?"

He responded, "Look, I'm the one who requested you be extended. I did it because of the rapport you've been able to establish with the Vietnamese, both military and civilian. I'd be a duplicitous bastard if I now extracted my pound of flesh by giving you a bad efficiency report for your doing what you thought you had to do."

I said, "Thank you, sir. I feel strongly that my family has to come first."

He smiled and said, "Good for you."

I felt good about this encounter as I walked back to my office.

Sunday, 19 March, was Palm Sunday. At our Mass, palms were distributed as they are at Christian services all over the world on this special day. But the palm fronds passed out were very different from those used in the United States. Although not certain, I feel that those passed out in Da Nang were probably more authentic than the ones we receive in the United States. Those in Da Nang were large fronds, cut from the abundance of palm trees that grew in the city. I could easily visualize that type of foliage being thrown before the donkey upon which Christ rode into Jerusalem.

***

With only a little over two months to go before my time at war would be over, I had been attempting to get the name and address of the officer who would be replacing me. I had much information I wanted to pass on to him and was concerned that our combat tours might not overlap. I therefore felt a pressing need to communicate with him in writing. I had been making notes on many things I wanted to tell him about. Without some background, I knew he would flounder, probably making many of the same mistakes I had made initially. Because of my lack of knowledge of the Vietnamese culture and the uniqueness of the ARVN organizational structure, I had struggled during my first few months in Da Nang. I also definitely wanted to pass on a description of the programs the NCOs and I had initiated, along with a list of the many points of contact we had established throughout the city, especially at the Naval

Support Activity Hospital, III MAF HQ, NSA Da Nang, the Vietnamese public health system, Duy Tan Hospital, I Corps HQ, and the U.S. Air Force. Without this information I knew my replacement would struggle, as I had upon my arrival.

As I sat at my desk on that Sunday morning, I was also concerned about Captain Bob Helton, who so capably led our medical advisory efforts in the two critically important upper provinces of South Vietnam. He was scheduled to return to the United States about six weeks prior to my departure but still hadn't received his military orders. His wife and family had no idea where they would be living next. The orders situation was getting rather desperate at that time. We had several members of MACV Advisory Team #1 who were due to rotate the very next week and still didn't have a clue where they would be assigned next. They couldn't even ship their hold baggage without completing about a zillion forms authorizing the government to hold their goods in a warehouse until notified where it was to be shipped. This uncertainty was very hard on families. Many children had no idea where they would be attending school the following September. All they knew with near certainty was that, in all likelihood, it would not be the school they were currently attending. This ambiguity impacted military wives big-time. They were the true unsung heroes of the war. Without a supportive wife, a successful military career was almost impossible during the Vietnam era. It took a special kind of woman to adjust to the uncertainties of a military career.

***

On Monday morning, 20 March, I was sitting at my desk, drafting a letter to my as-yet-to-be-identified replacement, when Sp-4 Behner approached and said, "Sir, there is a Vietnamese man at the main gate who needs to see you." I wondered what that was all about, but went to the gate. There stood the elderly man I had taken to the navy ophthalmologist to have his eye socket stretched and scar tissue removed so his glass eye would fit. He had a big smile on his face as he pointed toward his glass eye. He bowed deeply and insisted on giving me a small statue of

Buddha as a gift of gratitude. The statue was made out of some type of soft stone, probably sandstone. He couldn't speak a word of English, but he bowed as he placed his gift into my hands.

***

That afternoon, Joseph Alsop spent three hours in our HQ. Colonel Hamblen asked me to give him a fifteen-minute briefing on my activities. Alsop wrote a syndicated column and also served as a staff writer for the *Washington Star.*[2] Alsop, who at first seemed a little pompous and ego-centered, proved to be a fascinating man. He was extremely knowledge-able about the war. It surprised me greatly that he had memorized the names and dispositions of all major enemy units known to be operating in I Corps. He was well acquainted with all recent operations throughout Vietnam. He knew infinitely more about the war than I did. Although I was pretty well wrapped up in only one part of the war, medical support, I thought I had a reasonable grasp of the big picture, but his knowledge was infinitely greater than mine. His breadth of knowledge astounded me. He was obviously a very intelligent man and capable journalist.

On Tuesday, 21 March, at the USAID Hospital in Da Nang, I witnessed something that touched me deeply. A man came rushing up to the main entrance carrying a little three- or four-year-old boy. The boy's right leg was just hanging on by a piece of muscle and ligament. The boy had picked up a grenade that had been rolled into the courtyard of his home. He probably thought the grenade was some type of ball or plaything. What a tragic way to find out differently. Sadly, the surgeons were unable to save the child's life.

The war ground on. As of 22 March, the ARVN hospitals in I Corps were way beyond their listed capacities, fuller than they had been at any time since my arrival. The I Corps Surgeon, Captain Nhan, told me that they had 641 more patients than available beds. Fortuitously, the ARVN soldiers were very small in size. Many of the hospital beds were occupied by two soldiers. Most of the casualties were the result of engagements near the DMZ or in Quang Ngai Province.

While at dinner at the Officers' Club on Good Friday, 24 March, I was informed that Dr. James Albertson and a group of his students from Wisconsin State University, located in Stevens Point, Wisconsin, had been killed in a plane crash in the Hai Van Pass.[3] I was told that the group was conducting a study under USAID sponsorship of South Vietnam's system of higher education. I couldn't help but wonder why USAID had commissioned a study of Vietnamese higher education during time of war. I felt sorrow for the families of Dr. Albertson and his students.

***

After eating dinner on Good Friday, I got in my jeep to drive the two miles back to my hotel. As I passed Sacred Heart Cathedral, I noted a large crowd gathering for what I assumed to be a Good Friday Passion Service. The cathedral was only two or three blocks from my hotel, so I pondered whether I should risk walking over there and joining the crowd of Good Friday worshippers. Americans in Da Nang were constantly being warned to avoid crowds, so it was with some sense of risk that I chose to go. I changed into civilian clothes so as to be less conspicuous, and then walked over to the cathedral.

The Passion Service was very moving and familiar. Although it was in a different language, I understood it, as the ritual and symbolism were essentially the same as in the United States. I was, however, feeling very vulnerable. I was about a head taller than most of the worshippers and, as a non-Asian, looked very different than all of the others at the outdoor service. I saw no other blue-eyed person in the crowd of worshippers. As my eyes swept around the assemblage, looking for any signs of trouble, I became very much aware that I was no longer on the fringes of the crowd but seemingly right in the middle. To attempt to leave the service would have been, in my opinion, far more conspicuous and hence more dangerous than to stay. I slouched down so as to be less obvious.

All of a sudden, someone tugged on my pant leg. I remember flinching, then looking down. There stood Ho Thien, the little boy whose harelip Dr. Giles had repaired at Christmas-time. He smiled up at me and then, quick as a flash, disappeared into the crowd. Moments later, he reappeared, this time holding his mother by her hand. She looked at me, smiled, put her hands up in a prayerful, Asian-type gesture, bowed her head toward her son's now near-normal face, and then moved back to her previous spot in the crowd.

I'll never forget the exuberance of Ho Thien and the gratitude his mother expressed to me on that Good Friday evening during outdoor services held on the plaza of the Da Nang Cathedral. It is one of my most vivid and poignant memories of Vietnam. I think of the incident frequently and usually end up whispering a silent prayer for Ho Thien and his mother. I have no idea what has happened to them in the intervening years. I also think of the good and charitable work of the now deceased Dr. John Henry Giles.

As I walked back to my room after that memorable service, I remembered that it was my oldest daughter's birthday. Leslie Marie would be eleven years old on that day. How I missed my wife and children.

***

Near the end of March 1967, I received the film footage of Ho Thien that had played on *NBC Nightly News* and *The Today Show* just before Christmas 1966. Upon returning home, I had no access to a projector that would play newsreel film, so the canister sat in a closet until 2012, when I took it to a video shop and had it converted into a DVD. By today's standards, the resulting video is a grainy, low quality, three-minute film clip. But I treasure it. The video shows little Ho Thien before the surgery, with the huge gap in his upper lip, sitting at his desk in a classroom at Sacred Heart School with his teacher, a nun wearing a white habit, bustling around the room. It then shows Sergeant Thong and me transporting the boy and his mother to the navy hospital in my jeep. We arrive at the hospital, and I then carry the little boy into a Quonset building, with his mother and Sergeant Thong walking alongside. The next scene is in the operating room, showing Dr. Giles doing the reparative surgery. The final scene shows the little boy back in his school environment with his kindergarten classmates staring admiringly at his repaired lip.

One of my San Antonio friends was kind enough to make several additional copies of the DVD, one of which was sent to Anne Giles, widow of Dr. John Henry Giles. I have since talked to Anne on two occasions, and she expressed her gratitude and that of the Giles' children for the copy of the NBC film clip of their deceased loved one. Although she was aware of her husband's work on behalf of Vietnam's children, she had no idea as to its scope or impact.

**

On the morning of Holy Saturday, 25 March, the fog was thicker than I had ever experienced it while in Vietnam. Although it didn't approximate the denseness of the fogs of Europe, it was plenty thick. This type of weather was ideal for the VC. They knew the terrain and the people, many of them having lived in the area, and they moved about quite freely, undetectable by our surveillance systems. It was a rather frightening drive to my office that morning. Bicyclists would suddenly appear in front of me as I slowly moved through the fog. Most of the bicycles were not equipped with lights and the riders, for the most part, were dressed in the black or white clothing worn by practically all laborers and farmers. I couldn't help but think how easy it would be for a bicyclist to drop a grenade into my slow-moving jeep, and then peddle away into the fog. I felt very vulnerable.

On 25 March, at the Saturday morning I Corps staff meeting, we were informed that certain geographic areas in and around Da Nang were being placed off limits to all American servicemen and women, to include an area near China Beach and another near Marble Mountain. There were growing problems with prostitution and marijuana, and also some evidence to support the conclusion that the VC had recruited and trained a group of attractive young woman to ply their trade among American servicemen. The authorities weren't quite certain whether the VC recruited and trained these young women, or if the young women were simply entrepreneurs who gathered intelligence-related information, using sex as the bait, to sell to the VC. Their modus operandi was to offer sex coupled with marijuana and then, in the afterglow, when the unsuspecting victim was feeling good about the sexual encounter and high on the weed, to pump him for information related to the war. Apparently, these young women had been quite effective at extracting sensitive information from some of our servicemen, so III MAF authorities placed certain areas off limits.

Later on that same day, Saturday, 25 March, an ARVN convoy of trucks was torn up pretty badly by a VC ambush. Eighty-two of the 121 trucks in the convoy were hit. Many of the eighty-two were declared a total loss. Only thirty-nine came through unscathed. It happened on Highway 1, just below Hoi An. The ambush was a classic example of good planning and execution on the part of the VC. Claymore mines halted the lead vehicles, and then a road mine was detonated from a remote location by a concealed person. The mine destroyed the lead vehicle and severed the road. Simultaneously the VC blew up the road immediately behind the last vehicle in the mile-long convoy, thereby entrapping the convoy. They then methodically cut the entire convoy to ribbons with mortars and small arms fire. Miraculously, only twenty ARVN soldiers were killed. There was an entire battalion on board the trucks. To make matters even worse, the VC ambushed the relief force that was sent to assist the convoy. In attacks of this nature, the advantage was all theirs. Despite our technological advantage, they could pick the place, the time, the duration, and the ferocity of many of the battles. Since the VC was not a uniformed force we couldn't differentiate friend from foe. One minute the U.S. Marines or ARVN would see a peasant farmer working in the rice paddies, and the next minute, the peasant farmer would be a VC rifleman. It was impossible to monitor and control every peasant. How could we make progress in such a war when we couldn't tell friend from foe? There were no front lines. The entire country was the front line.

***

When Easter Sunday arrived, I was on duty until noon. As I went about my SDO duties that morning I reflected on the fact that I Corps had had some very rough times of late. To me it was becoming more and more apparent that ARVN and the U.S. forces in I Corps simply didn't have sufficient manpower to do the job.

I went to Easter Mass late in the afternoon. There were several families in attendance, somewhat of a rarity. It caused me to think that Easter was another of those special days when fathers should be with their children and husbands with their wives. Because of that, I was missing my family even more than usual.

During the two or three weeks preceding Easter, it was somewhat disturbing for me to go to the navy hospital. The hospital was full almost to capacity and the severity of the battle wounds incurred by many of the young marines and navy corpsmen was disheartening. Although I didn't have firm data, it seemed to me that in I Corps the two most vulnerable categories of men in combat were the young lieutenants who led platoons into battle and the navy corpsmen who tried to save the lives of the wounded. The losses in these two categories must have been staggering. It was very sobering and sad for me to see the maimed bodies of America's youth. In fact, just a few days prior to Easter I had seen General Walt, exiting one of the navy hospital's many wards, brushing away the tears. Because of the hospital's heavy workload at this time, I had not been able to admit a single Vietnamese person for corrective surgery for several weeks. The surgeons and nurses, as well as their supporting technical staffs, were working exceedingly long hours and the strain was visible to all.

***

In early March, we had been informed that Ellsworth Bunker would be replacing Henry Cabot Lodge as U.S. Ambassador to South Vietnam. Shortly thereafter, we received notification that Mr. Lodge would be visiting I Corps HQ in Da Nang prior to the end of his tenure as ambassador. For some inexplicable reason, I did not include the date of the incident I'm about to describe in my almost daily letters to my wife. Although I'm uncertain as to the precise date, it was sometime in late March.

Ambassador Lodge arrived at Da Nang Air Base as scheduled and was taken by helicopter to the I Corps compound. After a short overview briefing in our conference room, he was escorted to a platform overlooking an area between two buildings that served as our parade ground. The members of MACV Advisory Team #1 and a platoon of ARVN officers and men were standing at attention, under threatening skies, as the ambassador ascended the steps to the platform.

While Ambassador Lodge was being introduced, it started to rain. As he began his farewell remarks, the winds picked up considerably, there was lightning and thunder, and the rains intensified. We stood there as the rain pummeled us. The ambassador hurriedly tried to conclude his remarks without being disrespectful of his hosts.

Suddenly I felt something hit my head. I remember thinking to myself, *What was that?* I glanced at the ground and noted quite a number of small fish, all seemingly between one and four inches long, thrashing around on the ground. It was literally raining fish from the sky. It was a phenomenon to which I had never previously been exposed or even heard about.

I have since learned that raining fish from the sky is not that uncommon. It occurs when a strong thunderstorm moves over water and mini-tornadoes and whirlwinds form. These strong whirlwinds pick up fish from the water and sometimes carry them inland. When the whirlwinds or mini-tornadoes hit land, the wind speeds diminish, and the fish fall from the sky like rain.

***

On 28 March, I was returning to Da Nang from Phu Bai as a passenger on a VNAF helicopter. The weather was beautiful. We were going through the Hai Van Pass, and I was enjoying the view. Suddenly, there was a flurry of activity in the front of the helicopter. The pilot yelled something to the crew chief, who was seated near me. He got up and leaned his head into the space between the pilot and co-pilot. They were talking about something in a very animated manner. The crew chief then came back where two other passengers and I were seated. Over the roar of the helicopter, he yelled something, not a word of which I understood. He made a point of reaching down and checking my seat belt to insure that I was buckled in and that I had pulled up the slack in the belt. Then, he closed the sliding door of the helicopter, sat down, and buckled himself in. In the meantime the pilot was on the radio talking to someone. I perceived that there was some type of mechanical difficulty.

Within a minute or two, we were in a fairly slow descent and soon were on the ground. We landed in high grass, not far off Route 1, which the pilot had been using as a navigational aid. In keeping with standard practice, I knew that the pilot was in command when we landed. He pointed each of his passengers in a specific direction and kept repeating something. Again, I couldn't understand, but I perceived that he was forming some type of a perimeter of defense and that I was to move in the direction he pointed. With my weapon at the ready, I moved out about 200 yards. I could still see the top of the rotor blade on the helicopter. I never felt threatened or in danger. I noted the faint smell of a chemical as soon as I started moving through the high grass but thought nothing of it. After about forty minutes of waiting and watching, in frightfully hot weather, I noted two helicopters approach, then hover over the downed helicopter. One landed shortly thereafter, while the other continued to hover. I then heard the sound of a whistle being blown and interpreted this as a signal that I should return to the downed helicopter. I did so and, immediately upon arrival, was pointed toward the helicopter that had just landed. The other passengers and I boarded that helicopter and flew to Da Nang.

During the flight to Da Nang, I noted that the skin on my hands, face, neck, and lower arms was tingling. My uniform was wet from perspiration, which seemed to further irritate the skin on my neck under the collar of my shirt. When I got back to my room, I stripped off my boots and perspiration-saturated clothing and took a long cold-water shower, soaping my body as well as the cold water allowed. No hot water was available.

I knew what Agent Orange and Operation Ranch Hand were because, on several occasions, I had flown on C-130s that were carrying barrels of the chemical defoliant and had talked to the crew chiefs about the contents.[4] I had no health concerns at that time as a result of my probable exposure. It was not until Admiral Zumwalt started writing about the dangers of Agent Orange that I reflected upon the incident I just described and became concerned. I scheduled an appointment to have myself screened by the Veterans' Administration. No problems were found. I now receive periodic informational updates from the VA, but thus far have experienced no side effects other than mild neuropathy in my feet, which may or may not be related to my exposure to the chemical. I feel most fortunate that there are no repercussions as a result of my probable exposure.

***

The 29 March edition of *Stars and Stripes* carried an Associated Press article that brought back Dr. Thuy's remarks about the prevalence of wife-beating in Vietnam. The headline over the article stated: "Ho Nags N. Viet Wife-Beaters." I was pleased to read that Ho Chi Minh had the courage to label wife-beating as "savage and against the law." The article quoted Ho Chi Minh as saying, "It is bad to beat one's wife. Why are you sometimes so intimate with your wives and why at other times do you beat them? If you have been beating your wives you must get rid of this bad practice because beating your wives is savage and against the law. If one citizen beats another he acts against the law. I have learned that those husbands who beat their wives side with one another to mutually cover up their acts."

If indeed wife-beating was as prevalent in South Vietnam as Dr. Thuy had estimated it was, I thought maybe it was time for South Vietnam's leaders to speak out too.

That same edition of *Stars and Stripes* carried a picture and article about the ambush of the ARVN convoy near Hoi An that had occurred on 25 March. That ambush was described locally as the VC's biggest single victory during the past six months. It was a tremendous loss for the ARVN. It seemed doubtful that the ARVN could move the necessary equipment, munitions, petrol and foodstuffs to sustain combat operations in I Corps unless given immediate help. The ambush was a classic in terms of good planning and execution. The attacking force, we were told, was almost 80 percent women. I have not been able to determine the validity of that report.

I spent the day of 29 March working at Phu Bai. In the early afternoon I went on a MEDCAP operation with SFC Morrison, the U.S. Army medic at the ARVN Dong Da National Training Center. Captain Glass, a military physician assigned to the 8th Radio Research Field Station went along with us. I can't recall the name of the village we were in, but Dr. Glass decided to spend part of his day working in the village maternity clinic. Many villages seemed to have a small maternity clinic where the women from the community and surrounding areas went to have their seemingly annual babies. Typically, the clinics were not run by a physician but by a midwife. Vietnam had schools of midwifery that did an exceptional job of preparing women for this vocation.

Image 26. Dedicated and proficient Vietnamese mid-wives

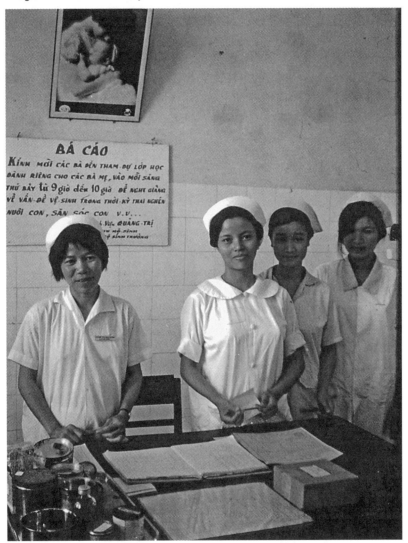

Photo courtesy of the author

While Dr. Glass was working in the maternity clinic, Sergeant Morrison was seeing anyone and everyone who showed up for treatment, friend or foe. Most of those treated were children, many having open sores or scabs oozing pus. When Dr. Glass finished his work in the maternity clinic he came to the room where Sergeant Morrison was working. As soon as he got there, he said, "Damn, there are lots of flies in here today. It isn't usually this bad. I wonder what's causing all the flies." He had been on several MEDCAP visits with Sergeant Morrison in this same village in the past. In order to find out why there were so many flies, he and I walked around to the back of the building to see if we could find a garbage or infectious waste disposal area that was attracting the flies. We noticed a five-gallon pail sitting alongside the building. The flies sitting on the pail or hovering over it were exceedingly thick. One swat with a fly swatter would have killed hundreds. He went up to the pail, shooed away the flies as best he could, and looked within. The pail was full of either stillborn babies or placentas. That's what was attracting the flies. Needless to say, Dr. Glass, through an interpreter, had a few strong words of admonition and advice for the midwife in charge.

***

During the night of 30 March, the high decibel sound coming from Da Nang Air Base was more intense than ususal. All I could speculate was that the weather over North Vietnam had cleared and the war planners had decided to hit certain sites with all they had available. The sound of twenty or thirty high performance jet aircraft taking off in rapid succession was more than I could sleep through, and I was usually a very sound sleeper. The way the crow flies, my room was probably about a half mile from the air base, but despite the distance, the noise was still deafening.

Captain Nhan and I spent most of Friday, 31 March, in Hoi An. We found the ARVN units there to be in better shape than anticipated. They had made improvements since I was last there, although they still had a ways to go before being fully combat ready. ARVN units had a tendency to let their guard down during periods of relative combat calm. Training was allowed to slip, as well as maintenance of vehicles and equipment. Captain Nhan had resolved to goad them into not letting that happen.

While in Hoi An, I had an interesting experience. Archbishop Peter Chi was in the city to dedicate a new church that had been constructed. Hoi An was in the Da Nang Diocese. A large crowd had assembled for the dedicatory ceremony. Just before the start of the ceremony, Archbishop Chi spotted me in the crowd and waved a wave of recognition as I was taking a photo of the event. It surprised the Vietnamese in attendance. Many looked at me, I'm certain wondering who I was and how I happened to know their archbishop. He was a very charismatic man. Some Vietnamese Christians told me that he might one day be elevated to cardinal, but such was not to be the case.

I also had the opportunity to spend time with LCDR Steve Barchet, the commander of the U.S. Navy MILPHAP team. We had a chance to review his latest equipment request. I assured him that, while I supported every item on the list, I was not the decision maker. That authority resided in the MACV Surgeon's Office in Saigon. LCDR Barchet would soon be rotating back to the United States. What a great job he had done. He had become a very good friend. I remember telling him that I thought he would go far in navy medicine. I was correct, as eventually he was promoted to admiral.

Chapter 10

April 1967

On 1 April, I sent a letter to my wife that I knew would not arrive until well after the date of full impact. It read as follows:

1 April 1967

Dear Pat,

I am so disgusted that I'm not even certain I can concentrate on writing this letter. I'm angry and frustrated. I've never understood the personnel policies of the army and now I'm even more confused. I would have thought that just after completing a combat tour and a year of family separation that I'd be given better treatment when it came to my next assignment. Pat, please get the family prepared to move yet again. We've been married almost 12-years and this will be the eleventh house that you've had to make into a home. I know that's asking a bit much, but I have no recourse. I hate having to tell you this, but we'll not be reassigned to Fort Sam Houston, as promised. Instead we'll be going to, of all places, Fort Barkley. If I had to select the ten worst army posts in the United States to which to be assigned, Barkley would be at the very top of the list. But what are we to do? We've invested almost eleven years in an army career, and it would be foolhardy, economically speaking, to bail out now. I think I'm going to sit down and type a letter to the chief of the Medical Service Corps, Brigadier General Bill Hamrick, and vent my spleen. I just can't see subjecting you and the children to the horrors of that post. I'm told that cockroaches, scorpions and rattlesnakes rule the post, intimidating all children and most of the wives. What did we do to deserve this?

I had so much to tell you in this letter, but I'm so upset that I just can't go on. I feel like the rug has been pulled out from under my feet and I'm crashing to the ground. Fort Barkley, the armpit of the army. Of all places to be assigned in the entire world that has to be among the very worst.

Now, Pat, if you haven't already figured it out, look above at the date. I wrote this letter on April Fool's Day, my dear. As far as I know we're still being assigned to Fort Sam Houston, a great post. And just so you know, as far as I know there is no Fort Barkley. You've been had.

Love you so,

Jim

***

On Sunday morning, 2 April, I was apparently in a reflective mood. In a letter to my wife, I wrote:

Strange as it may sound, I know that I'll miss Da Nang and its people when it's time to go home. I've had some very unique experiences during the nine months I've been here and, while the level of activity can best be described as frenetic, I must admit that it has been personally rewarding. I know this for certain: I've seen and done things that in my wildest dreams I never imagined I would see or do. Initially I was disappointed at being assigned to a MACV advisory role instead of to a USARV unit, but I'm coming to the realization that my contributions in this assignment are probably greater than they would have been had I been assigned to a non-advisory role with a U.S. hospital or medical battalion. I have also come to realize that, had I been assigned as the senior advisor to the commander of the ARVN Medical Service School in Saigon, or to a staff position in the MACV Surgeon's Office, my exposure to the culture and traditions of the people would not have been as great. It all seems to have worked out for the best.

That afternoon, Sunday, 2 April, I joined in an on-going football game on China Beach. The game resulted in my getting knocked out of the game with an injury. I took a hard hit in the rib cage and couldn't continue. It hurt like the devil and impaired my breathing. SFC Simmons was good enough to come to the dispensary late Sunday afternoon and tape up my rib cage. That made breathing less painful, but the tape made my chest so hot during the night, I had difficulty sleeping. I left the game right after halftime. Our team, consisting exclusively of MACV advisors, most of who had played in college, was leading a team drawn from enlisted marines 12-0, but I have no idea which team ended up winning the very rough game.

On Monday, 3 April, I had yet another visitor from Saigon who had chosen to grace us with his presence. I'm being facetious, of course, but the amount of "help" I was getting from the MACV Surgeon's Office seemed to me to be excessive. This time it was Major Frank Axtens, a logistician. He arrived Sunday evening and spent Monday and Tuesday with me, returning to Saigon Tuesday evening. Frank was a good guy, but he had a different modus operandi.

Upon arrival at Duy Tan Hospital, he said, "Show me your problem areas." Nobody was willing to admit to problems in their area of responsibility. It seemed to me that Major Axtens should instead have been sitting down with the senior logistician at the hospital and checking the key indicators of a quality operation, ferreting out problem areas to be addressed.

***

The weather over North Vietnam had finally cleared. I deduced this from the number of high performance aircraft screaming off the runways of Da Nang Air Base at all hours of the day and night. We were told the base had become the busiest in the world. I can't begin to describe how many times I was awakened by the almost deafening sound coming from the air base. The jets took off in rapid succession, perhaps one every ten to fifteen seconds. My friend Captain Duane Miller, whom I mentioned previously, flew the Grumman HU-16 Albatross, a high-winged plane ideal for rescue at sea. He told me that he hovered over the South China Sea for hours at a time when bombing raids were being conducted over North Vietnam. When a jet aircraft was hit by an antiaircraft weapon, or experienced mechanical failure, the pilot tried desperately to make it to the sea before ejecting. Captain Miller's job was to locate the downed pilot through a procedure known as radio triangulation and rescue him from the South China Sea.

Early in the morning of 4 April, I got a call from the MACV Surgeon's Office informing me that my replacement would, in all likelihood, be Major Richard Stoltz, whom I knew only by his reputation, which was very good. He was then on the faculty of the Medical Field Service School at Fort Sam Houston. Unfortunately, he was not scheduled to arrive in Vietnam until after my departure. I now had no recourse other than to send through the mails the packet of written materials I had prepared. While I knew it would not be nearly as effective as face-to-face orientation, it was the best I could do under the circumstances.

Late in the afternoon of Tuesday, 4 April, Major Axtens was in our office prior to returning to Saigon. I introduced him to Major Hennigan. Somebody had sent Hennigan a sign which he had prominently displayed over his desk. The sign declared in bold letters: "THE DIFFICULT WE DO IMMEDIATELY; THE IMPOSSIBLE MAY TAKE A BIT LONGER." He took great pleasure in pointing it out to Major Axtens. Hennigan grinned as he pointed at the sign and cockily said, "Just try us, Major Axtens."

***

During my year in Vietnam, I rarely had an aircraft dedicated solely to my mission. I always had to scrounge a ride—hitchhike, if you will.

I had good points of contact in flight operations at Da Nang Air Base, and they let me know of flights of opportunity that occasionally popped up on the schedule. The only times I had the clout to get an aircraft of my own were when I was escorting Colonel Eisner, the MACV Surgeon who also served as General Westmoreland's personal physician and, on a couple of occasions, when I was delivering vaccines produced at the Pasteur Institute in Saigon to cities throughout I Corps.

In early April, the MACV Officers' Club was in the process of upgrading its kitchen, which, until that time, had left much to be desired from a sanitation point of view. The deficiencies were always reflected in my monthly inspection reports. Our commander, Colonel Hamblen, apparently read every one of them. He called me into his office on 5 April and told me that he was going to arrange for me to go to Hong Kong to pick out two large refrigerators and a restaurant-style kitchen stove. I was to make the trip the next time there was an empty seat on one of the R&R flights that took off from the Da Nang Air Base on a weekly basis. I told him that I knew little about refrigeration units and stoves.

His response was, "Learn, dammit, learn. That's why I'm giving you this heads up, to give you some time to do your homework."

I quickly made an appointment to spend an hour or two with the steward in charge of the excellent kitchen at the U.S. Navy hospital.

On that same day, 5 April, I received yet another letter and package from a woman in New Jersey, whom I shall call Miss Engelhardt, not her real name. She frequently sent me large packages of children's clothing, and also wrote to me about twice monthly concerning the plight of Vietnam's children. She expected a response to every package and every letter, and I simply didn't have the time to satisfy her expectations. Initially, she had written a letter to our deputy commander, Colonel Beeson, telling him that she would be sending packages of clothing for the children. He sent her a polite note thanking her and telling her to send the packages to me in the future. This started the steady barrage of packages and letters. When I didn't respond to her letters or packages in what she perceived to be a timely manner, she wrote to Colonel Beeson, telling him that I was neglecting her. I informed her in a letter that, while I appreciated her thinking of the poor children of Vietnam, I was simply too busy to respond to all her packages and letters. That hadn't satisfied her. She kept writing to me right up to the time I left Vietnam.

Also on 5 April, Colonel Hamblen appointed me MACV's representative on a joint military-civilian working group to evaluate the feasibility of the German hospital ship, the *Helgoland*, being moved from Saigon to Da Nang. Of the four corps areas in the Republic of Vietnam, I Corps had far more civilian casualties than any other. Precisely why this was true, I do not know. The *Helgoland* was docked in Saigon harbor and admitted only civilian casualties of war. It had been sent to South Vietnam as an act of mercy by the German Red Cross. It had 140 beds, state-of-the-art medical equipment, highly trained professional and technical staffs, and excellent surgical capabilities. If it were to be moved to the Da Nang harbor it would be a godsend insofar as helping with the surgical backlog in the provincial hospitals of I Corps.

During the next two days, our working group met on two occasions with Baron Hermann von Richthofen, 2nd Secretary for Humanitarian Aid in the German Embassy. On one of those occasions, I was asked to describe for him the civilian casualty situation in I Corps as best I could. I used very graphic and descriptive language in doing so. I concentrated on making certain he understood that lives were being lost as a result of the surgical backlog in the provincial hospitals.

During our third meeting, which occurred ten days to two weeks later, Baron von Richthofen told us that he had been informed that there appeared to be "limiting factors, or problem areas" in bringing the ship into Da Nang harbor. The *Helgoland* drew fifteen to sixteen feet of water. Although the Da Nang harbor had been dredged to a depth of seventeen feet, he was told by an unidentified person that shifting sands and silt had reduced its actual depth in some places to around fifteen feet. The

Baron seemed dubious about the chances of getting the ship into Da Nang harbor without running her aground.

The *Helgoland*'s crew had recently received a good deal of bad publicity from the Saigon press. Allegedly, the ship's staff had had several raucous parties onboard the ship as it lay in the Saigon harbor. The Saigon press had described the parties as orgies involving both German and Vietnamese persons. I had no way of knowing if the stories were true, but what I knew for certain was that I Corps desperately needed the capabilities that the ship and its medical staff offered. The bad press explained, at least partially, why the Germans were somewhat interested in moving the ship away from Saigon.

The *Helgoland*'s modus operandi was to maintain strict neutrality and treat only non-combatants, whereas the U.S. Navy's hospital ship, the U.S.S. *Repose*, treated primarily military, but on occasion a few civilian, casualties. The overwhelming majority of its patients appeared to be U.S. Marines. The *Repose* continuously moved up and down the I Corps coastline, whereas the *Helgoland*, if the decision was made to move her, would be docked in Da Nang harbor. I Corps also received a second U.S. Navy hospital ship at about this time. The U.S.S. *Sanctuary* arrived in Da Nang on 10 April 1967. I never had the opportunity go aboard that ship, but I was told that it was very similar in design and function to the *Repose*.

In the next week or two, I learned more about ships, nautical matters, and port regulations than I had ever envisioned. Whether the *Helgoland* could safely get into Da Nang harbor was still a debatable point. Our working group couldn't seem to get anybody to absolutely commit one way or the other. The answers we were getting were as follows: "If everything goes right the ship should be able to get in without trouble," or "I think it will get in okay, but I can't be certain." Nobody seemed willing to state unequivocally that it could get in and out without difficulty. This uncertainty left the Germans hanging. No harbor authority seemed willing to make an unequivocal statement about access to the harbor.

The fear was that the hospital ship could be run aground and block entrance to the harbor.

***

There were no commercial laundry services available to members of MACV Advisory Team #1. While there were commercial laundries in the city of Da Nang, they were off limits to the members of our team. This reality necessitated that each advisor hire a maid to take care of his laundry and room cleaning needs or accomplish these tasks himself.

My maid, Bá Vy, was an absolute delight. She was a thirty-eight-year-old Buddhist woman who gave birth to her tenth child in mid-April 1967. Her husband was a laborer who made the equivalent of twenty-five U.S. dollars each month. Bá Vy—which translates into Mrs. Vy—was very happy when I hired her. The extra money made a big difference in her family's monthly income.

She worked for me three mornings each week, peddling up to my hotel on her bicycle, usually with at least one or two toddlers in tow. Invariably, she seemed happy, a big smile always on her face. I gave her a key to my hotel room, so in addition to doing my laundry, she tidied up the room, made the bed, hung my clothes after washing and ironing them, and cleaned the bathroom I shared with two others when it was her turn to do so.

In early April 1967, I received a package containing a layette. A letter from Mrs. Marie Buntjer, president of the Cicero-Maine Homemaker's Club, a group of women who lived near my home town of Black Creek, Wisconsin, requested that I give the layette to a poor woman who was about to give birth. Bá Vy immediately came to mind. She was due to deliver her baby at any time.

One day, while on my way to lunch at the Officers' Club, I stopped by my room, hoping to find Bá Vy. She was there, working at the well, along with one of her toddlers and three or four other maids. She was chattering away with the other women while doing the laundry. I went to my room, got the package containing the layette, and gave it to her. She absolutely beamed as I presented it to her, opening it immediately and examining each of the items and basking in the adulation of her colleagues, the other maids. When she got to the two dozen diapers and the package of safety pins she was perplexed, never having seen a diaper before. It was obvious that she had no idea what to do with a diaper. Being the father of six, I was well experienced in diapering babies. I decided to demonstrate my skills and thereby teach Bá Vy how to use diapers. I took one of the diapers, folded it into a proper triangle, and then picked up Bá Vy's bare-bottomed toddler. I gently placed her on her back on the smooth concrete pavement surrounding the well and skillfully put the diaper on, being ultra careful with the safety pins. Bá Vy and the other women laughed and laughed as the little girl toddled around the courtyard wearing this strange thing called a diaper. Bá Vy thanked me profusely for the layette and I departed for the Officers' Club and my lunch.

Several days later I had to stop by my room in mid-morning for something I had forgotten. What did I see? Bá Vy and all her maid colleagues were wearing a white diaper on their heads, some in turban style and others like a babushka. They all smiled at me, placed one hand on the diaper on their heads and bowed respectfully. I suspect the diapers, so lovingly given by the members of the Cicero-Maine Homemaker's Club, never graced the bottom of another child, but they were used and appreciated.

***

Image 27. Bá Vy receiving the layette donated by the Cicero Homemaker's Club

Photo courtesy of the author, from newspaper story

On the morning of Thursday, 6 April, someone from the I Corps operations center poked his head into my office and said that Quang Tri City was under heavy attack. He went on to say that PK-17, a hill mass northwest of Hue where an ARVN regimental HQ was located, had apparently been overrun. Additionally, the MACV compound in Quang Tri City was under a heavy mortar barrage at that very moment. Three separate attacks were happening simultaneously.

A later report stated that there were even more attacks in progress, and that it appeared likely that over 100 ARVN soldiers and U.S. Marines had been killed and over 200 wounded. The attacks were against a regimental HQ at PK-17,[1] an ARVN regimental HQ in Thua Thien Province north of Hue, Hai Lang sub-sector in Quang Tri Province, the La Vang airstrip, a regimental HQ in the village of La Vang, and the MACV compound in Quang Tri City. The multiple attacks were well planned and, according to all reports, expertly executed. Just as the ARVN or the U.S. Marines were reacting to one of the attacks another would occur.

On Friday morning, 7 April, I flew to Hue. I wanted to spend a few hours with Captain Bob Helton to assess continuing problems we were having with the movement of patients from one hospital to another in order to balance the workload. Inter-hospital transfers did not go smoothly. I was convinced there had to be a better way. It seemed that either the patients being transported from the hospitals to the airstrip by ground ambulance arrived at the designated airstrip too late, or the aircraft arrived late and the patients became dehydrated and died while lying in the back of an ambulance with an IV sticking in their arm, parked on the blazing hot tarmac in 100-degree weather. We had to find a better way. Communication between the ARVN and U.S. Air Force was breaking down, and ARVN patients were needlessly dying because of it. Both Bob Helton and I had offered recommendations to the ARVN to address the problem, but they didn't always accept our advice. It was frustrating.

Late that afternoon, Captain Helton told me there were 730 patients in Hue's Nguyen Tri Phuong Station Hospital. Its rated capacity was 400, so the hospital was rapidly approaching the point of being 100 percent over capacity. And more patients were coming off the fields of battle by the hour. Those patients who were near death were mercifully given a bed of their own to die in, but those expected to recover had to share a bed with someone else or lie on a thin straw mat placed on the floor.

I was acutely aware that the ARVN hesitated to move casualties too far away from their homes of record, but this was a life or death situation. I knew in my heart that patients were needlessly dying because of the over-crowding. My emotions were shot. On that day, I stood and watched two severely wounded patients in one small hospital bed quietly writhing in pain. Insufficient trained personnel were available to treat their wounds or address their pain. It made me feel helpless. I knew the other medical advisors joined me in my anguish.

Casualties were still coming in from the multiple sites that had been hit. We convinced the I Corps Surgeon and the commanders of Nguyen Tri Phuong and Duy Tan Hospitals that they should request an emergency inter-hospital transfer of as many patients as possible from I Corps to any facility with unfilled beds. We had grasped at every straw, exhausting our alternatives before putting forth the request for an emergency evacuation. I realized fully that we were getting involved in ARVN operational matters far more deeply than we should, but lives were at stake, so we charged on. We had kept the MACV Surgeon's Office in the communications loop and had convinced the MACV staff of the precarious situation in I Corps. We asked for their help in convincing the ARVN Surgeon General's Office in Saigon to intercede on I Corps' behalf. We had recommended that a C-130 be sent to Hue to move seventy or eighty patients as soon as possible. We also recommended that one or more surgical teams be sent to Hue to assist in reducing the surgical backlog. Although all of our recommendations were approved and acted upon by the I Corps Surgeon, they seemed to fall on deaf ears when they reached Saigon.

During April 1967, Nguyen Tri Phuong Station Hospital had only seven physicians on its entire staff. Only three of the seven were surgeons.

The surgical backlog was huge and growing. But no help came. Based on these conditions, Captain Helton and I convinced the I Corps Surgeon to request emergency help from the VNAF to move surgical patients to Da Nang, but no aircraft were available. We then jumped channels and went directly to the U.S. Air Force and begged for help. They responded to our pleading and made a CV-2 Caribou aircraft available to fly two inter-hospital transfer missions the very next day. The first was to arrive at the Hue Citadel airstrip at 0900 hours and depart at 0930. It would then fly to Da Nang, off-load its twenty seriously wounded patients, and return to Hue for the second load of twenty additional surgical patients.

That evening, I flew back to Da Nang to await the arrival of the first load of patients, scheduled for the next morning. Before I left Hue, I told Bob Helton that I would contact him when the first load arrived in Da Nang and again when the plane took off to return to Hue for the second load. The day turned out to be a day to top all frustrating days.

Early the next morning, Saturday, 8 April, Bob Helton called to tell me that the evening before, he had personally given the commander of Nguyen Tri Phuong Station Hospital definitive instructions about the tight time schedule of the aircraft and the type of patients that should be selected for movement. The hospital commander was told that this would be an excellent opportunity to both reduce his staff's workload and relieve the hospital's surgical backlog. Forty very seriously wounded surgical patients were to be moved to Duy Tan for surgery and follow up treatment. Captain Helton said the commander smiled and said he would do his best. Captain Helton called the hospital the next morning and was assured by the commander that everything was ready and that he fully understood what he was to do.

A few minutes before 0900 hours, the Caribou aircraft touched down at the Hue Citadel airport. Captain Helton was present at the airstrip to coordinate and oversee the loading operation, but not a single patient was available. Helton angrily jumped in his jeep to drive to the hospital to see what was wrong. He met the ambulances that were transporting the patients about halfway to the hospital. He turned around and returned to the airstrip. When the ambulances arrived, he found that not a single seriously wounded patient was among those selected to be moved to Da Nang. All were minimally wounded or well on the road to recovery. Little or no surgery was required to address their wounds. Captain Helton was steamed and told the ambulance drivers to take the patients back to the hospital and get some seriously wounded out to the airstrip as soon as possible. Finally, at 1205 hours, the aircraft was loaded with the right type of patients. Before taking off, the U.S. Air Force pilot fumed at Bob Helton and told him that he absolutely refused to return for a second load.

Before taking off from the Hue airport, the aircraft crew had to fend off about fifty members of the patients' families. Wives, some with children, mothers, and even a few fathers were insistent upon accompanying their wounded loved ones to Da Nang. The family members stormed toward the aircraft as the patients were being loaded aboard. Bob Helton told me that "it was mayhem." Family members' insistence on being with their wounded loved ones was one of the things we grappled with every day. It seemed almost impossible to design an effective and efficient system of inter-hospital transfer with this as a limiting factor. All ARVN soldiers and their families had an expectation that, if wounded, they would be hospitalized in a facility near their families.

In the meantime, the ambulances to be used to transport the patients from the Da Nang Air Base to Duy Tan Hospital were sitting on the tarmac in Da Nang, awaiting the arrival of the plane. Surgeons were standing by at Duy Tan Hospital to receive the wounded patients. It was a long three-and-a-half-hour wait before the first patient arrived.

As the ambulance drivers and medics were off-loading the patients from the aircraft when it reached Da Nang, the pilot told me he would not go back to Hue for the second load as we had been promised. He graphically outlined for me what had happened in Hue. To say he was angry is an understatement. I couldn't blame him. But the fact remained that the ARVN had a critical situation in Hue, so I had to try to get him to change his mind about returning. I once again had to figuratively drag the bodies of dead ARVN soldiers across the runway until he reluctantly agreed to return to Hue. I then ordered Captain McLean and Sergeants Simmons and Harker to go along with the aircraft to assist in loading the next twenty patients. When the plane started to taxi onto the runway, I hurried to the operations center to call Bob Helton. I told him that the plane would be returning to Hue for the second load and should be on the ground in thirty-five to forty minutes. He informed me that when he went back to Nguyen Tri Phoung Hospital to assist in the preparation of the second load there wasn't a single ARVN officer present. An NCO had to take the patient manifest to the Staff Duty Officer's quarters in order to get it signed by an ARVN officer as required by regulation. I couldn't even imagine a hospital with 700 patients without a single physician, and very few nurses, present for duty. All were enjoying a Saturday afternoon away from the hospital.[2]

The province hospitals at this time were in even worse shape. There were patients awaiting treatment all over, many lying on straw mats placed on the floors of the open veranda-style porches and narrow hallways characteristic of several of the province hospitals.

***

That same Saturday evening, 8 April, I learned that yet another of our advisors had been killed. We had about twenty Australian Army advisors incorporated into our advisory effort. Major Badcoe, a pleasant man whom I did not know well but occasionally chatted with at the Officers' Club, was killed just outside of Da Nang. That evening, I offered a few consoling words and a handshake to Major Buchan, the officer who headed the Aussie contingent. His reply was, "Yes, mate, it's a bloody shame. But you know, old man, those things happen. I do appreciate your kind words, though." Deep down, despite his rather matter of fact response, he was bleeding, as we all bled when we got news about the death of a respected brother-in-arms. However, if we allowed ourselves the luxury of prolonged grieving over every friend or acquaintance killed in action, we would lose our sanity.

***

At 0530 hours on Sunday morning, 9 April, a fairly dense fog covered the city and probably the countryside as well. Temperatures were predicted to reach 100 degrees, so the fog would burn off rapidly. But, until it did so, immediate air strikes, which were so vital in getting U.S. and ARVN units out of ambushes and other tough situations, were probably not possible. Fog definitely favored the enemy. Close air support became problematic.

On that Sunday morning, I sat at my desk trying to make an assessment of where things stood. The ARVN hospitals and other medical holding type units in I Corps were so crowded the hospital staffs didn't know where to put the next patient evacuated from any one of the many battlefields throughout I Corps. The U.S. Navy hospital in Da Nang, though nearly full, was infinitely less crowded because it had the capability to evacuate the seriously wounded, after stabilization, to the Philippines, Japan, Okinawa, or Hawaii. The ARVN hospitals didn't have that capability. All patients had to be retained in South Vietnam.

On Monday, 10 April, I was ordered to accompany an ARVN officer, Dr. Tuy, in making a sanitary inspection of the POW camp located not too far from Marble Mountain. I was somewhat surprised to find there were thirty-four women among the prisoners. As we moved throughout the camp, accompanied by two armed guards, I couldn't help but notice how fit the women looked, compared to the typical South Vietnamese peasant-class woman. All seemed cleaner than their South Vietnamese equivalents, none were chewing the abominable betel nut, and most had good complexions and nice figures. I wondered why this was the case. I asked Dr. Tuy if he had any insights, and, while he agreed with my observations, he couldn't explain the reason. Every time I got into that POW camp I was struck by the steely-eyed resolve of the prisoners. Clearly, the enemy was in it for the long haul. I saw no evidence that they were losing their determination.

***

Each Monday morning we had a semi-mandatory formation during which General Lam, the I Corps commander, gave a short speech to the HQ staff and a weekly news update was presented to the troops. Everything was presented in Vietnamese, and I feel certain it was propagandistic in nature, but the Vietnamese leadership seemed to think it was an important weekly event. Fortunately for us the entire ordeal took only about twenty minutes.

***

My good friend and colleague, Dr. Steve Barchet, commander of the Navy MILPHAP team in Hoi An, called on Monday morning, 10 April, to tell me he had finally received his orders. He was scheduled to leave in less than thirty days. In typical navy jargon he told me, "Soon you will be the oldest hand aboard." I couldn't help but think that this tour had been a unique experience for me, working with the navy, marines and air force. There were still no army units in I Corps, other than our advisory team and a few small specialized units. That was soon to change. There was more and more talk about an army division being moved into the I Corps Tactical Zone to take some of the pressure off the U.S. Marines. The marines were dangerously over-extended and the VC and NVA were exploiting that perceived weakness.

***

The weather over North Vietnam continued to be very bad, with heavy ground fog rising quite high. A USAF meteorologist had informed us that this was very atypical for this time of the year. The fog persisted. We all hoped it would change soon, as fog enabled the VC and NVA to move units as well as supplies and equipment pretty much undetected. General Walt had apparently groused about this at the Saturday morning staff meeting, which I was not able to attend because of the inter-hospital transfer of patients from Hue to Da Nang, in progress at the time of the meeting.

On 12 April, Major Hennigan and I had a lengthy discussion with Colonel Hamblen about a conference held recently on the island of Guam.[3] It had been a high-level conference attended by President Johnson and the South Vietnamese Prime Minister, Nguyen Cao Ky. According to Colonel Hamblen, one of the major topics discussed was the rising number of civilian casualties resulting from the war, especially in I Corps. Colonel Hamblen said that there was serious discussion about a recommendation that had been made to place three military hospitals in the upper part of South Vietnam, one at Qui Nhon (in the northern part of II Corps), one in Quang Ngai (southern I Corps) and one in Da Nang, with the mission of treating civilian casualties exclusively. The hospitals would initially be under canvas. Colonel Hamblen told us that if a decision were made to move forward with this recommendation, the G-4 Office would have to take the lead in helping to find appropriate locations and establishing the two hospitals recommended for I Corps. For me, this was good news, as I had been acutely aware of the rising number of civilian casualties. I told Colonel Hamblen that, in my opinion, the term "collateral damage" didn't do justice to the human misery embodied in the term. Why I Corps was generating far more civilian casualties than any other corps area, I frankly didn't know. But I did know that it bothered General Walt greatly and that he addressed the matter frequently, always in strong and compassionate terms.

I also told Colonel Hamblen that I thought I had unique insights into the problem because I saw the civilian carnage to a greater degree than any other member of our advisory team. I lived with the situation, seeing civilian casualties of war frequently, almost on a daily basis. I went on to tell him that my emotions were "sometimes at the breaking point" and that "I take to bed with me practically every night the sight of maimed children, some too scared to even cry, with their mothers hovering over them helpless to do anything to alleviate their fear and pain."

At the conclusion of our meeting, I informed Colonel Hamblen that three MACV advisors in Quang Ngai Province had been diagnosed with hepatitis. That caused him considerable concern, because hepatitis was known to be a disease that could ravage the body for years to come. He responded, "Van Straten, you always bring me such good news." What could I say?

13 April was one of those days. A decision had been made by Colonel Hamblen, a couple of days prior, that we should put together a team to be flown to Quang Tri to assess the damage to the MACV compound and try to figure out what had gone wrong during the attacks that had occurred during the past several days. I was designated as one of those to be flown to Quang Tri.

It was not the kind of trip I'd like to take too often. The pilot had to make four attempts to find a hole in the weather in order to get through the Hai Van Pass. Once the problem of penetrating the pass was overcome, the flying wasn't too bad. For the most part, the pilot stayed out over the South China Sea and away from the ground fog and turbulence. But eventually he had to turn inland. The pilot made a crack at Quang Tri without success. He couldn't seem to locate the city because the visibility was so bad. He then tried a different approach. Not being an aviator, I'm not exactly sure how it worked, but he got a radio fix on Dong Ha, a small city with an airstrip not too far from the DMZ, and then headed into the weather. After perhaps ten or fifteen minutes of zero visibility, he started a slow descent. At an elevation of about 200 feet, we broke out of the fog or clouds into clear weather. And there was Dong Ha. We landed uneventfully, discharged one advisor at Dong Ha, took off again, and followed Highway 1 south into Quang Tri. I don't think the pilot got above 150 feet elevation all the way to Quang Tri City. One of the officers on the flight told me that to get any higher would have been even more dangerous because of small arms fire. He said a rapidly moving target at very low altitudes is harder to hit than one a couple of hundred feet higher. After a short flight we landed at La Vang, a small village just outside Quang Tri. La Vang, too, had been hit hard in the recent attacks.

We journeyed into Quang Tri City by jeep and immediately went to the MACV compound. There was tension in the air. It was almost palpable. The compound had been hit by mortars three of the past four nights, and the advisors had reason to believe they would be hit again. Although I was not in a position to judge, by virtue of my background, it seemed to me that their defenses were minimal, and if I were them, I'd be very concerned about a frontal attack and being overrun. Everyone looked very tired. They had gotten little sleep in the past several days. Tempers flared on several occasions. The strain was showing. The nightly attacks had been going on since 5 April.

After gathering the information I needed to answer the twenty or twenty-five questions that I had prepared in advance to complete my section of the report, I asked to be taken to the Quang Tri Province Hospital. I wanted to talk to Dr. Pittard, a good friend, to get his assessment of the situation at the province hospital. Dr. Pittard was a U.S. Navy captain who, after retirement, had, at his own request, returned to active duty to lend his support during this war. He was an outstanding surgeon. His hometown was Anson, in the Texas Panhandle. He was a widower, and his family was grown, so he decided it was his duty to come back. He also looked very tired. It was easy to see why.

A medevac flight came in while I was there. A little girl, about six years old, was taken off the helicopter with a gaping hole in her belly and a piece of intestine hanging out. A little boy, perhaps eight or nine years old, God love him, died while in flight. He had suffered a bullet wound that entered above his right eye and exited below his right ear. A mother got off, unassisted, holding her severely wounded tiny baby in her right arm and clutching her belly with the other. It appeared she had gotten hit by shrapnel. She was very pale and appeared to be going into shock. An attendant tried to take her heavily bandaged baby, but she clung to the child. Another child had its nose almost ripped off by shrapnel. Dr. Pittard made a quick assessment, and then consulted with the Vietnamese physician in charge of the hospital. The Vietnamese physician then, in a very high and emotional voice, shouted instructions to the staff. Dr. Pittard excused himself and hurried off to one of the three operating suites within the hospital. He was another of those unsung heroes of the war.

Image 28. Mother with shrapnel in her belly clung to this severely wounded baby

Photo courtesy of the author

Just as I was preparing to leave the province hospital, an elderly man, perhaps seventy-five years old, came to the main entrance. A Vietnamese attendant who spoke English talked to the man and then told me that he had been hit in the shoulder three days earlier. The bullet smashed the bone where the shoulder is attached to the arm. The man had walked for three days to get help. He weighed no more than ninety or ninety-five pounds, his ribs stuck out all over, but he beamed when the staff treated him kindly and admitted him to the hospital. His wound looked angry, perhaps gangrenous. He was one of the many elderly Vietnamese men who allowed the hair growing out of a mole on their chins to grow forever. He had about four or five hairs, each at least six inches long, growing out of one chin mole.

As we flew back to Da Nang, I suddenly realized that it was my daughter Laurie's fifth birthday. She was the youngest of our four daughters. How I missed her and my family.

***

On 15 April, my maid came back to work after giving birth to her tenth child. She looked good and was in high spirits. The first thing she asked, through a series of gestures, smiles and giggles, was that I give her a copy of the photograph taken of her when I gave her the layette donated by the ladies of the Cicero Homemaker Club. I had forgotten about the photograph, but she hadn't. I found the picture and gave it to her. She seemed very happy to be back at work after a week's absence. I felt certain that she would be bringing the newborn and two or three of her littlest ones to work with her. I think she was trying to nurse two or three of them at that time. Baby formula was unavailable in Vietnam.

During the night of 15 April, I received word that the village of Mo Duc, south of Quang Ngai City, had been mortared quite hard. I quickly alerted the MILPHAP team that they should expect an influx of casualties.

On 15 April, I was notified that I was being summoned to Saigon for yet another meeting, this one to be held on 28 April. I immediately called to get permission to bring Captain Bob Helton along with me. He was scheduled to return home in late May, and I thought the MACV Surgeon's Office staff and the other corps-level advisors would benefit from hearing about his experiences and lessons learned.

The VC were very active, again, during the night of 15 April. I was the SDO, so I had to monitor all incoming reports of enemy activity. Hoi An, Hieu Nhon, Mai Linh, and Quang Tri were all hit during the night. The same pattern repeated itself. The VC would strike fast and hard, then retreat and blend into the indigenous population.

The next day, Sunday, 16 April, I was hoping for a bit of a break. Such was not to be the case. That morning, after spending the previous night as the SDO, I hurried back to my room, showered, shaved, and got into a fresh uniform before hurrying back to give an 0830 briefing to a group of senior advisors assigned throughout I Corps. The command element was once again shook up about high malaria rates among ARVN troops. Prevalence of the disease was seriously cutting into available manpower. A new malaria season was just beginning, and they wanted me to again tell the senior officers how to prevent soldiers from getting the dreaded disease. Additionally, I was asked to address the subject of how to prevent heat injury, a growing concern during the hot-dry season that we were in the middle of at that time. I was asked to present a brief rundown on the operational plan for the U.S.S. *Sanctuary*, the second hospital ship to be assigned in general support of the I Corps Tactical Zone. I was allotted twenty minutes to cover those three subjects.

I had about an hour off for lunch before returning to the HQ to brief Colonel Ulsaker, the newly assigned senior advisor to the ARVN 2nd Infantry Division headquartered in Quang Ngai. In addition, my in-box was full of reports to be completed. When I finished with all of this, there wasn't much left of my Sunday. I went to evening Mass and then had a relaxing dinner and a beer or two before going to bed. I was burned out. It had been a very rough couple of weeks and I needed sleep.

On 17 April, I sent my wife a photograph showing the damage that mortars had done to a sub-sector HQ. It showed very clearly the triangular shape of the HQ, a typical sub-sector arrangement for defense. Within the triangle lived the five American soldiers who comprised the sub-sector advisory team. These teams consisted of two officers, an operations and weapons sergeant, an enlisted medic, and an enlisted radioman. For their security, they depended heavily on the Vietnamese Regional Forces and Popular Forces. The picture that I sent showed the compound severely damaged as a result of a VC attack that took the lives of two American soldiers.

Image 29. Heavily damaged MACV sub-sector headquarters after VC mortar attack

Photo courtesy of the author

More details concerning the recent attacks on the city of Quang Tri became available on 17 April. Over 2,000 VC had roamed the streets at will. They had released over 250 prisoners from the province jail. Clearly, for a short period of time, the VC had control of Quang Tri City.

John Hennigan was promoted to lieutenant colonel on 17 April. I was so pleased for him. I told him that I'd now have to treat him with more respect. He laughed. General Walt, the senior American officer in I Corps, pinned on John's new silver leaves.

The day proved most interesting. The International Red Cross had two Swiss physicians, both volunteers, making an assessment of seriously wounded NVA soldiers in the POW Camp across the river near Marble Mountain. The physicians were charged to review the case of each of the seriously wounded prisoners. I received a call from the MACV Surgeon's

Office asking me to serve on an oversight board having to do with the repatriation of those prisoners who could never fight again by virtue of their wounds. I told the person who called that I was terribly busy and asked if I could be excused from this duty. They were insistent that I serve on the board. After clearing it with LTC Hennigan and Colonel Hamblen, I notified the MACV Surgeon's Office that I would do it. They in turn notified the International Red Cross that I would be the MACV representative on the oversight board.

It turned out to be a fascinating experience. One at a time, forty-five prisoners who had been severely wounded were brought into the small prison dispensary under armed guard. The two Swiss physicians rapidly reviewed the severity of their injuries then made a judgment call. If the prisoner was adjudged to have injuries so severe that he or she could never fight again, the prisoner was given a choice. He or she could be repatriated, returned to North Vietnam, or remain a prisoner of war. Thirty-eight prisoners were found to have injuries so severe that they could never again serve as soldiers. Many had an arm or a leg amputated, and one had both an arm and a leg missing. All thirty-eight were offered repatriation, but only two accepted. While I was shocked by the results, I was also elated. I interpreted this as a clear indication of the harshness of life in North Vietnam under Communism. But I started discussing it with a Colonel Allen, an MP representative on the oversight board, and he interpreted the results quite differently based on his experience during the Korean War. He said that prisoners in Korea, when given the same choice, almost universally decided to remain prisoners. Why? Colonel Allen stated that the reason was because the prisoners had a very strong feeling that "we came South to do a job, and by god we're not leaving until it's done." I didn't totally buy into that explanation, but what we saw and heard perplexed me greatly.

The next morning, 18 April, I was with the International Red Cross physicians again as they reviewed the cases of thirty-two prisoners who were then in Duy Tan Hospital as a result of wounds or disease.

The results paralleled those of the day before. Of the thirty-two POWs screened at Duy Tan Hospital, thirteen were eligible for repatriation to North Vietnam. Not one chose to go back. I couldn't understand it.

Both Swiss physicians, incidentally, were very fine men, volunteering their time to come to Vietnam for this assessment. One of them, Dr. Wepf, said if I ever got to Bern to look him up. He gave me his home and office addresses as well as a phone number. I told him that my wife and I had been to Switzerland one time while stationed in Europe but never to Bern. Both of the Swiss doctors were very impressed with the medical treatment the POWs were receiving at Duy Tan Hospital, but they were not at all pleased with the medical support available in the POW camp itself. The ARVN was responsible for running all POW camps in South Vietnam. The U.S. military was not involved.

On that same day, 18 April, I included in a letter to my wife a tag that was attached to a detainee at the time and point of his capture. After the detainee was processed and a record established, the field tag was removed and discarded. The tag identified the man who had worn it as a relatively old soldier. He had served as a hamlet guard. His name, according to the tag, was Pham Diet. He was born in 1917. That made him fifty years old at the time of capture. He was detained on 12 April 1967, only a week before I picked up the discarded tag.

Image 30. MACV Form 343 which was attached to all detained persons

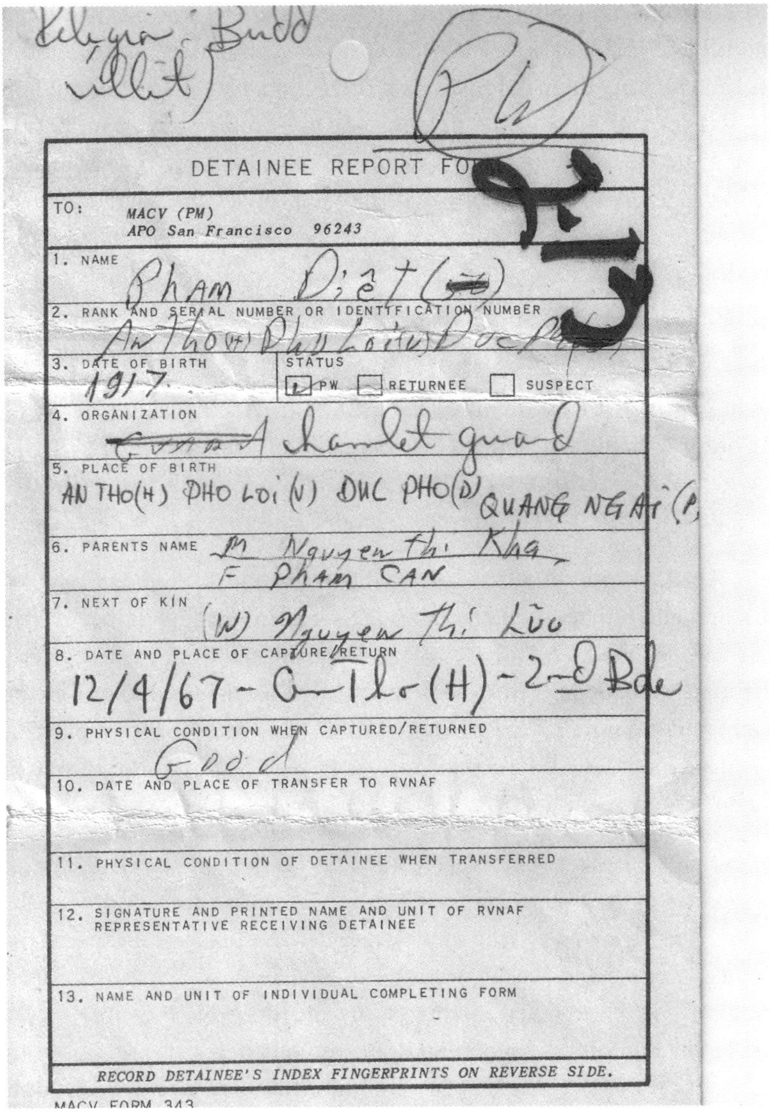

Photo courtesy of the author

There seemed to be a lull in the war at this time. I got a call from the U.S. Navy hospital telling me that the surgeons had time on their hands and if I had children with harelips or other deformities, now would be the time to bring them in for surgical correction. I had four children lined up, so I took all four to the hospital for pre-op physical examinations during the late afternoon of 19 April. I always kept my fingers crossed and whispered a silent prayer that the physical exams wouldn't reveal a problem that made surgery not possible. I had previously had three children rejected because of tuberculosis and one for a very bad heart murmur. One was found to be so undernourished that surgery would have been dangerous.

On 20 April, it was announced that the U.S. Army was now a part of the order of battle for I Corps. It was finally official. Task Force Oregon had become operational when the 196th Light Infantry Brigade landed at the Chu Lai airstrip. I Corps was no longer exclusively Marine territory.

21 April was my thirty-fourth birthday. I couldn't envision how any husband and father could feel more appreciated and loved than I did on that day. My wife and all six of our children had each made a special birthday card for me. All seven cards were unique and expressive of their own personalities. Even our infant son, twenty-two-month-old Michael, sent a card. His older sisters helped him prepare it, but his handprints were on it.

On that same day, I also received a very thoughtful letter from Master Sergeant August Davis, my former NCOIC. I was pleased to hear that he had been allowed to take a two-week leave from Walter Reed Army Medical Center and was spending the time in New Orleans with his family. He again thanked me for saving his life, which assuredly I had not done. I had simply found him in his room in a diabetic coma, but the doctors at the U.S. Navy hospital told him that had he not been found he would have died within another two or three hours. I did nothing heroic. I just happened to go looking for him at a fortuitous time. In a return letter, I wished him the very best. He was a good and decent man and a fine soldier.

On 22 April, I started working on a project that I think of frequently. It was among the most rewarding during my year in Vietnam. I worked with my ARVN counterparts to put together a preliminary plan to accommodate the hygienic and medical needs of a large refugee population. It had been determined that upwards of 20,000 people had to be moved from areas near the DMZ for their own safety and security. They were to be moved to an as-yet-to-be-established refugee settlement near Cam Lo in Quang Tri Province.

Refugee populations always need a considerable amount of medical support, far more than stable, well-settled communities. The civilian medical system in Quang Tri Province was already stretched to the breaking point, so I knew the support the province provided would have to be heavily supplemented with ARVN resources.

***

During the night of 22-23 April, military activity in southern I Corps was ferocious. When I arrived at my office the casualty reports were still coming in, but it was clear that we had lost a large number of U.S. Marines and the ARVN losses were even greater. I talked by telephone with Captain Len Schumacher, medical advisor to the ARVN 2nd Infantry Division. He was feeling pressure from his boss because so many ARVN wounded were not being promptly evacuated from the fields of battle and treated.

***

Captain Bob Helton finally received his orders on 24 April, just three weeks before he was scheduled to depart Vietnam on 16 May. He would be sorely missed. I could always rely on him for an accurate assessment of the situation and for solid recommendations regarding how to proceed. He never engaged in hyperbole, as some advisors and many ARVN officers tended to do. When he told me something, I could accept it as fact and move on from there. We worked well together.

***

On Monday, 24 April, we had an in-progress review of the construction project at Duy Tan Hospital. The project wasn't even close to completion, although it was supposed to have been completed by 31 March. But it dragged on. At the rate it was proceeding, I knew it wouldn't be finished by the time my tour of duty in Da Nang was over. The delay was caused by several change orders that had not been acted upon. They were caught up in the Saigon bureaucracy. The ARVN hierarchy in Da Nang didn't have the authority to approve even minor changes to the original plans. Everything had to be forwarded to Saigon. All changes, those brought about by a functional necessity or by the non-availability of certain types of construction materials in Da Nang, had to be approved in Saigon. At the time of the review, there was no asbestos roofing material available in Da Nang. There were all sorts of steel roofing materials and some aluminum. Both were suitable substitutes if a good insulating material was installed below the roof. The insulating materials were needed because both steel and aluminum absorbed heat and made for stifling hot hospital wards. With a good layer of insulation, both steel and aluminum roofs would work just fine.

On 1 February, the Duy Tan commander requested permission to switch from asbestos to a metal insulated roof. As of 24 April he was still awaiting a response from Saigon, despite follow up letters having been sent on 22 February, 8 March, 27 March, and 18 April. It was very demoralizing and irritating. In the meantime, Duy Tan's wards, which contained 1,358 patients on the date of the review, were depressingly crowded. All this aggravation seemed to those of us in Da Nang to be caused by an unknown bureaucratic office in Saigon. We couldn't even determine, with certainty, which office or individual had final approval authority. It was frustrating. The project was eating up far too much of Major Tu's and my time, and the biggest losers, as a result of the delay, were the patients.

***

Among the strongest and most poignant of all my memories of Vietnam is this incident: Sometime during the month of April—for some inexplicable reason I did not include the date in my letters to my wife—I was sitting in the Air America terminal at Da Nang Air Base waiting for a flight to Quang Tri. I couldn't help but notice a rather sad-looking American man. He was about fifty years old and in civilian clothing. All alone, he slowly and aimlessly paced back and forth across the small terminal. He seemed to want to be alone. I respected his privacy and chose not to bother him with conversation, even though I was curious about the circumstances of his being there.

Upon boarding the C-47 aircraft, we found ourselves in seats across the aisle from each other. Just a few minutes after takeoff, he leaned over and said, "Excuse me, major, but do you happen to know where Operation Hastings was fought?" I told him that I did and that I had been involved with an ARVN operation named Lam Son 289 that was fought in close proximity to, and supportive of, Operation Hastings. He handed me a map and asked if I would circle the area where Operation Hastings had been fought. After studying the area I had circled for a moment, he went on to tell me that his only son, eighteen years old, had been killed during Operation Hastings and that he "felt compelled to get over here to see where it was." I offered my condolences, and then he started talking about his son's death. It was as if the floodgates had opened. It seemed to me that this was probably one of the few times, possibly even the very first time, that he had really talked about it, so I let him go on uninterrupted, thinking it might be therapeutic for him.

He started by saying, "I didn't even know he was dead. I was in Chicago at a business meeting when Mary called the hotel where I was staying and left a message at the desk. When I received it that evening, I couldn't believe it. It said Michael had been killed in action. It wasn't real. A little piece of paper, hotel stationery, just couldn't take a son away." He then told me that he felt he had to get home to Mary as quickly as possible. He knew that she was alone and needed him badly. He said, "The boy didn't write much, but Mary and I understood. Maybe a letter a week, maybe not even that often—but that was fine with Mary and me. There was a letter maybe ten or twelve days before it happened. It didn't say much about where he was or what he was doing. He wrote a few lines about a fishing trip that he and I had taken just before he went to Vietnam, and about what we'd do when he got back. He was lonely, I guess. He was only eighteen years old, but even a boy of eighteen can be lonely, you know."

When I left the grieving man in Quang Tri City, he was trying to hire someone to take him out to the place where Operation Hastings had been fought. As we parted, I couldn't help but think, *Yes, a boy of eighteen can be lonely, and so can a man of fifty, not only lonely but heartbroken.*

And so it went as the war ground on. This man was the fourth or fifth American civilian I had encountered who was seeking solace or closure by visiting the site where a son had died. It surprised me somewhat that American civilians were allowed to visit Vietnam during wartime, but I found that there were no restrictions on foreigners traveling in the country. Travel was discouraged for American civilians, but not prohibited. A visa was required, but they were relatively easy to obtain.

***

On the morning of 25 April, I was summoned to brief Colonel Hamblen on the current status of the *Helgoland*, the German hospital ship that was being considered for movement from Saigon to Da Nang. The captain of the ship, Wilhelm Fehler, and Baron Hermann von Richthofen of the German Embassy in Saigon were to be in Da Nang the very next day. Colonel Hamblen needed up-to-date information before meeting with them. As the MACV project officer, it was my duty to have the latest information available. I was pleased that the matter was still alive and hopeful that a final decision would be made before I departed Da Nang in late June.

***

On 26 April, my boss, LTC Hennigan, was on convoy escort duty with an ARVN resupply convoy from Da Nang to Quang Tri. The next day he escorted the same convoy back to Da Nang. A convoy escort duty roster had been established with the names of all officers assigned to Advisory Team #1, except the commander, deputy commander, and chaplain. The convoy that Colonel Hennigan escorted had over 200 trucks in it, a very lucrative and inviting target for the VC or NVA. If the convoy ran into trouble, the escort officer had to provide interface with U.S. artillery and close air support, things the ARVN had difficulty doing.

***

I continued to work with my counterpart and other ARVN officers and non-commissioned officers to put together a workable plan to provide medical support for about 18,000 to 20,000 refugees being moved from areas near and in the DMZ to a safe haven. Consideration was being given to moving all the people currently living in the many villages and hamlets north of the Cam Lo River on up to the DMZ. I hadn't been briefed on the specific purpose of the planned move, but the project seemed to have a very high priority. On 26 April, we were awaiting a final decision as to whether those people who wished to remain in their villages, despite the risk, would be allowed to do so rather than being forced to move.

I was involved in many activities that in my wildest dreams, prior to deployment, I never thought I'd be doing. I found myself frequently flying by the seat of my pants. I often thought back to the Officer Advanced Course and the lessons imparted by Colonel Marlo Smith, a big, tall man with not a hair on his rather small, shiny head. Although he had a rather imperious manner, he was an excellent instructor. He was a sanitary engineer by profession, and he taught field and water sanitation. I was grateful for what he taught us. I frequently went back to his handout materials and my notes from his lectures. The printed materials were most helpful in the planning we were engaged in.

Also on 26 April, several members of the British Parliament were in Da Nang. I had been forewarned by Colonel Hamblen that I might be called upon to arrange a tour of Duy Tan Hospital for them. I was hoping the tour would come about, because I was rather proud of that hospital, but it did not.

The rumor mill at that time had it that General Westmoreland would be leaving Vietnam in the summer. General Creighton Abrams, an army general whom I knew nothing about, was already in country and working with General Westmoreland as his deputy commander. Everyone in the know seemed certain that General Abrams would soon be taking command. Although I had no information to support it, I felt that General Walt would also soon be departing.

During the afternoon of 27 April, I had a couple of very interesting meetings, one of which became somewhat confrontational. First, I went to a meeting attended by a bevy of Vietnamese civilian officials, Baron von Richthofen, and Captain Wilhelm Fehler. Also attending was the medical director of the *Helgoland*, whose Germanic name I was never able to catch. Some of the Vietnamese spoke English, although several did not. Much to my dismay, the meeting was conducted in French. I was seemingly the only participant who couldn't follow the conversation.

The meeting was called by, and under the control of, Da Nang-based government officials. It turned out that the major sticking point was Captain Fehler's and, to a lesser degree, Baron von Richthofen's continuing concern about the depth of Da Nang harbor. They couldn't seem to get their questions about the harbor depth answered to their satisfaction. In desperation, when they couldn't get the information they needed from the Vietnamese officials, they turned to me as if I were the authority on the Da Nang harbor. Suddenly, everyone was looking to me for answers, most of which I simply could not provide. After exhausting the limited amount of factual information I had, I looked at Captain Fehler and could tell that he was not at all satisfied, and rightfully so. The meeting was at a tipping point. Da Nang could lose the services of the ship unless reliable information could be provided in a hurry. I decided that the only recourse I had was to stretch the truth just a little. I told the group that I was aware of a U.S. Navy officer who had definitive information about the harbor depth and that if we could recess the meeting for sixty minutes, I felt certain that I could get the officer and bring him to the meeting to provide answers to the questions being raised.

Baron von Richthofen and Captain Fehler agreed, and I hurriedly took off to try to find the U.S. Naval Support Activity's operations officer whom I had relied on in the past to give me a quick course on harbors and port operations. Unfortunately, he was in the United States on business. His deputy, LCDR Albertson, agreed to come with me to the meeting. While he wasn't able to provide all the answers needed by the Germans, he had the good sense to tell them that he had a complete set of harbor charts and that he felt certain they would answer all of their questions. We then made an appointment for Fehler, Albertson, and myself to get together the next morning to look at the charts and, if necessary, take a tour of the harbor by boat. I thanked LCDR Albertson profusely. I felt that he may have saved the day.

I found Captain Fehler to be very intelligent, and his command of English was quite good. I enjoyed working with him. Baron von Richthofen, as one might surmise, was not into operational matters to the degree that Captain Fehler was, but he, too, was most impressive. As our meeting was about to end, I made an impassioned plea for the movement of the ship to Da Nang. The Vietnamese attendees were kind enough to strongly endorse my comments. My argument was based strictly on humanitarian needs and how grateful the Vietnamese people would be for the generosity and support of the German people during their hour of grave need. The three Germans listened intently, but did not comment. Captain Fehler's biggest concern seemed to be a "what if" concern. What if another ship was sunk in the main channel? Would there be enough room and sufficient depth for the *Helgoland* to get around the sunken ship and out of the harbor in case of an emergency? Captain Fehler didn't want to take that risk, and I couldn't blame him.

Image 31. From left to right are Captain Wilhelm Fehler, Baron Hermann von Richthofen, Major Van Straten, an unknown Da Nang governmental official and the German medical director of the *Helgoland.*

Photo courtesy of the author

Very late that afternoon, I had a heated, somewhat confrontational meeting on a different subject. Ironically, it too involved NSA officials, the same organization that earlier in the afternoon had come to my rescue.

I had the responsibility, which I took very seriously, to help the MILPHAP teams in I Corps in any way I could. The lack of reliable and timely logistical and maintenance support for these teams had troubled me deeply.

On 31 January 1967, a joint MACV/USAID directive had been published spelling out in considerable detail a structure whereby the Naval Support Activity, Da Nang, was to assume the logistical and maintenance support mission for all MILPHAP teams in I Corps, to include the USAID-sponsored team in Da Nang. And yet, in late April 1967, three months after publication of the MACV/USAID directive, support of the MILPHAP teams was mediocre at best.

I had pressed hard to try to get NSA to assume its assigned responsibilities, as spelled out in detail in the January directive, as rapidly as possible. They spun their wheels and hemmed and hawed to the point where I got angry. I wrote a nasty letter and got our commander, Colonel Hamblen, to sign it and send it to Admiral Paul Lacy, the commander of NSA, Da Nang. The letter decried the lack of support the MILPHAP teams were getting from the NSA. Admiral Lacy fumed when he received the letter. He cornered Colonel Hamblen at a dinner party one evening where he said that NSA, Da Nang, was proceeding dead ahead with the support of the MILPHAP and doing everything possible to assume its assigned responsibilities in a timely manner. He asked Hamblen for specific instances of NSA non-support.

The next morning, Colonel Hamblen came to his office angry. He summoned me and read me the riot act for "making him look foolish" by having him sign the letter. When he started implying that I had overreacted, I got angry. I told him that I probably had many faults as an officer, but overreaction wasn't one of them. I'm slow to anger, but I was very angry then. I went back to my office resolved to set the record straight.

I started gathering specific information about the non-support of the MILPHAP teams. There was much to gather. Again, I wrote a blistering letter to Admiral Lacy, with seven separate attachments outlining specific and documented instances of non-support. I was hoping that I could get Colonel Hamblen to sign it. Surprisingly, he did so without hesitation. He was still angry over being chastised by Admiral Lacy. The charges made in the original letter were now backed up with hard evidence. It was, in my opinion, compelling.

When Admiral Lacy received the letter, he turned it over to his staff for study and preparation of a response. His staff officers were shocked. They called me and demanded a meeting. We met at 1630 hours. They immediately went on the offensive. I decided that, since it was me against about seven NSA staff members, I had to be strong. I started by saying, "Point out one instance, if you can, gentlemen, where the letter Admiral Lacy received from my commander is inaccurate."

They looked at each other, and then finally acknowledged that they couldn't do so. They then tore into me about why I hadn't talked to them before the letter was sent. I recognized three or four of them as officers whom I had personally talked with on the telephone regarding problems with MILPHAP support.

I simply went around the room and asked, "Do you recall our conversation about the X-ray equipment at Hoi An that didn't work for four weeks? Do you recall our conversation about the extreme shortage of antibiotics at Tam Ky? Do you recall our discussion about the delay in getting vaccines to Quang Tri?" They didn't know how to answer. It was obvious that they were more than a little embarrassed.

It also turned out that Admiral Lacy's staff had not kept him informed. The admiral thought they were proceeding full speed ahead when in actuality they had done virtually nothing to improve support to the MILPHAP teams. It was also revealed during the meeting that the NSA, Da Nang, staff had actually sent a letter to the U.S. Commander of Naval Forces, Vietnam, asking that NSA, Da Nang, be relieved of the requirement to support MILPHAP. Admiral Lacy had not been informed of this action. The staff had purposely kept him in the dark, reasoning that it was an "inconsequential matter" and not worthy of bringing to the admiral's attention. The Commander of Naval Forces, Vietnam, had then forwarded the request to General Westmoreland's HQ for final decision. As of the day of our meeting, General Westmoreland's HQ had not responded to the request.

In retrospect it was almost humorous. Three navy captains and three navy commanders sat there trying to explain to a lowly army major what had happened. They told me, in essence, that they were sorry they hadn't kept Admiral Lacy informed, but they didn't think the action had been important enough to take to his level. I knew that Admiral Lacy would now have to eat some of Colonel Hamblen's crow. I purposely rubbed their noses in it for a little while, because I was still angry. Not to support MILPHAP, which I believed to be one of the most significant humanitarian programs in all of Vietnam insofar as winning the hearts and minds of the people was concerned, seemed to me unforgivable, almost despicable. Before departing from the meeting, I told them just that.

To calm things down, prior to my departure from the meeting, I said I would do what I could to relieve the tension between Admiral Lacy and Colonel Hamblen. As we parted, they were still concerned about the repercussions of their actions, and they should have been. They were wrong, and they knew it, but it was tough for them to openly admit it.

***

The meeting between Captain Fehler, LCDR Albertson, and myself on the morning of 28 April went well. Several NSA staff officers and NCOs joined us for the discussion. All of Captain Fehler's questions were answered to his satisfaction. The review of the harbor charts was most helpful. It was decided that a tour of the harbor was unnecessary as Captain Fehler had seen the harbor on a previous visit. Although I doubted that the *Helgoland* would be berthed in Da Nang before my departure, I felt reasonably certain that it would be coming. I had worked hard on the project, and it now seemed to be coming to fruition. The big beneficiaries would be the people in the rural villages and hamlets of I Corps, as very few city dwellers became casualties of the war.

That afternoon, Bob Helton arrived from Hue, and at 1730 hours, the two of us, along with Captain John Grier, an advisor to the ARVN Medical Depot, were on a C-130 headed for the Pearl of the Orient once again. Even its name, Saigon, sounded exotic to this midwestern boy. We arrived safely, although it was one of the roughest C-130 flights I had ever experienced. We ran into severe turbulence about halfway between Da Nang and Saigon, and the pilot had to battle the weather until we landed. Everyone was relieved when the ramp of the C-130 was lowered and we were disgorged onto the tarmac.

The all-day meeting on Saturday, 29 April, ended about 1800 hours. From my perspective, it was the most productive gathering of advisors that we had had during the year. It was good to have the division medical advisors with us, as they brought with them a different perspective. Their presence seemed to facilitate a more lively discussion. At that time, most of the medical advisors were well seasoned, having been in country for quite some time. That would soon change, as summer rotations were about to begin. It was wise of the MACV Surgeon's staff to schedule the meeting when they did. We could only hope that the lessons we had learned would be accurately transmitted to those who would follow.

***

Sunday morning, 30 April, was spent in the hustling, bustling city of Saigon. I attended Sunday Mass at the 17th Field Hospital's chapel and afterwards took a long walk. The city still did not appear to be heavily impacted by the war. Except for the presence of tens of thousands of men and women in uniform, and thousands of military vehicles on the streets, you wouldn't have known there was a war going on.

While walking to my hotel after Mass, I couldn't help but reflect on the fact that the next time I saw Saigon, I would probably be out-processing at the Koepler Hotel compound prior to going home. Just two more months to go. The past ten months had been fascinating and instructive. What would the next two bring? I knew I would miss Vietnam and its people. I had been most fortunate in having been assigned to the position I occupied. The exposure to the country, its people, and their culture, customs, and traditions had been unparalleled. I knew that many of my fellow advisors were more than a little envious of the opportunities I had been given in I Corps.

Saigon was Saigon. What more can I say? I didn't especially like the city, but I must admit that my negative feelings were probably heavily influenced by the Saigon I saw when I first arrived in Vietnam. At that time, it was a filthy, smelly, rat-infested place, the result of a prolonged garbage handlers' strike. It was much better this time, at least from an aesthetic point of view, but I could never get used to the large numbers of seemingly orphaned children sleeping in the doorways of business places. This time, I saw a young blind woman being led around by her hand by one of her children, a little girl of about four. The little girl would guide her mother, who was carrying a tiny baby, in the direction of large concentrations of people where the mother would beg for her family's daily sustenance. The world could sometimes be very cruel.

It would be good to get back to Da Nang. With a little luck I would not have to return to Saigon again before it was time to go home. There was some talk, however, of yet another meeting in early June. The powers that be felt that the meeting just concluded had been so successful that perhaps a follow-on meeting should be held. All the corps-level medical advisors were scheduled to leave the country within the next two months. Their institutional memory, the many lessons they had learned, would go with them. The personnel replacement system at that time wasn't sophisticated enough to provide a few days' overlap between the arriving officer and the one departing. In many respects, this was tragic. I would have willingly extended my tour of duty for a week or two in order to spend time with Major Dick Stoltz, my designated replacement. At the meeting in Saigon, we all decried this lack of overlap with our successors.

Chapter 11

May 1967

Our flight from Saigon to Da Nang was late in arriving. We landed a few minutes after midnight on Monday, 1 May. I decided to swing by my office to type a brief letter to my wife and pick up my mail. Lying conspicuously in the center of my desk was a note telling me that, since 1 May was the biggest holiday in the Communist world, Colonel Hamblen had ordered all advisors to stay off the streets as much as possible on that day. The note said the threat of terrorism was high. Colonel Hamblen would not have been pleased had he known that I was driving around the streets of Da Nang well after midnight. During the trip, I heard small arms fire—or fireworks, I'm not sure which—but encountered no difficulty in getting to my hotel.

After sleeping for a few hours, I arrived at the office about 0600 hours and started working my in-box. It was then I learned that the U.S. Army's 2nd Surgical Hospital was being relocated from An Khe, in II Corps, to Chu Lai, in southern I Corps. The move was to take place on 8 May, with the hospital placed in direct support of Task Force Oregon, the first U.S. Army combat unit in I Corps.

SP-4 Behner informed me that, while I was in Saigon, a sniper had severely wounded one of our mechanics, SP-4 Simpkins. A round caught him in the right shoulder. Ironically, he was supposed to leave for home the very next day. I didn't know Simpkins, but I felt empathy for his family, as they now had to await his return from Vietnam as a casualty of war.

On 2 May, the lengthy letter and packet of materials that I had sent to Major Stoltz was returned to me unopened. Major Stoltz had apparently left Fort Sam Houston quite some time ago. The packet had been forwarded to Fort Bragg, where he was supposedly attending a pre-deployment course of some kind, but it was unclaimed there too. The end result was that he would not receive the materials I had prepared for him until he arrived in Da Nang. That was far from ideal, but there was nothing I could do about it.

That afternoon, I had the pleasant task of presenting the patients in Duy Tan Hospital with a television set. An American physician had sent me $100 and asked that I buy something "to improve the lot of hospitalized ARVN soldiers." I could think of nothing that would give the patients more pleasure and boost their morale more than a television set.

On the morning of 3 May, one platoon from the ARVN 10th Medical Company departed Da Nang for Cam Lo. The area between the Cam Lo River and the DMZ had been the location of many bloody battles between the U.S. Marines and the VC and NVA during the previous year. A refugee center was to be established on the edge of this small city. Approximately 20,000 persons would be relocated from their homes in the small villages and hamlets that lie north of the Cam Lo River up to the DMZ. The area they vacated would then become a free fire zone where U.S. and ARVN forces could drop bombs or fire artillery and mortars on known or suspected enemy forces with impunity.[1] Prior to the closure of these villages, the enemy would fire his mortars and rockets, or attack our outposts, and then retreat into the sanctuary of these villages, knowing that we would not fire upon them. There were some people who lived within the DMZ who also wished to be relocated.

They, too, were to be moved to the Cam Lo settlement. Lieutenant Ha, a very capable and conscientious ARVN physician, headed the medical element of this relocation, which was named Operation Hickory. I wished him well prior to his departure for Cam Lo. He would have his work cut out for him. I promised him that I would assist in coordinating support for his efforts to the very best of my ability.

***

I was sitting at my desk during the morning of 4 May when a sergeant from the G-3 section poked his head in the door and said a Vietnamese bus had just hit a mine somewhere in the Hai Van Pass. I stopped what I was doing to see if I could get a fix on exactly where the tragedy had occurred. If it was closer to Hue than Da Nang, the casualties would probably be going to the Thua Thien Province Hospital. If it was closer to Da Nang, the casualties would in all likelihood be coming to the USAID Hospital in Da Nang. It seemed doubtful that either of those two hospitals had been alerted. I felt a responsibility to notify the appropriate hospital as quickly as possible. It was always heart-wrenching to see forty to fifty people maimed or killed by acts of terrorism. The last bus that had been blown up had cost the lives of nineteen, including five little children.

That evening, several of us were sitting on the third floor balcony of our hotel enjoying a beer when a little four- or five-year-old boy came to the guarded gate in front of the hotel. He peered up at those of us sitting on the balcony with big brown pleading eyes. He extended his hands above his head, palms up. He was hungry. All I had in my room were a couple of candy bars, a bag of peanuts, and a few cookies that my wife had recently sent. One of the other guys in the hotel gave him some homemade candy, and another gave him a stick of sausage. He seemed ever so thankful. It wasn't much of a diet, but it was better than going hungry. From that time on, he came to the hotel frequently. We asked the gate guards and maids where he lived, but nobody seemed to know. We were never able to determine whether he was an orphaned street urchin or had a home somewhere. From time to time we gave him food and clothing. Poor little guy. Life could be cruel.

On 5 May, I was at the USAID Hospital in Da Nang trying to see a physician about a reported shortage of rabies vaccine. He was in surgery and not available. I then was apprised of something that distressed me greatly. A teenage girl being treated by a Vietnamese staff physician for debilitating headaches was subjected to an ancient Chinese practice. The physician had determined that her headaches were linked to the onset of menstruation. When I saw her, she had very bad burns on her forehead. I was told that the practice involved heating the lid of a glass cup to a very high temperature and then placing the lid of the cup on the forehead of the patient. The resultant burn would cause a huge blister within minutes. The patient was then instructed to shatter the cup and use one of the shards of glass to cut open each of the several blisters on the forehead. The girl that I saw contended that her headache went away. It seemed to me that the pain from the burn and subsequent lancing of the blisters was probably so intense that it overrode the pain of the headache. These crude and difficult to understand practices occasionally occurred despite the fact that Western medicine had been introduced to Vietnam a couple of centuries earlier.

Seeing this concerned me greatly because two of the I Corps based MILPHAP teams were due to depart for home within the next ten days. The replacement teams weren't scheduled to arrive until the first part of June. This meant that there would be a two- or three-week period when the province hospitals at Hoi An and Tam Ky would be without American medical assistance. The Vietnamese health care providers had come to rely on American military help to such a degree that I feared what would happen during the projected lengthy absence of this support.

During the Saturday morning staff meeting held on 8 May, I learned that the U.S. Marines had taken alarmingly high numbers of casualties up north. The battle between marines and the NVA over Hill 881, near Khe Sanh, had taken a very heavy toll. I Corps had been, for the past several months, the most active of the four corps areas. It was believed that, of the nine known enemy divisions in South Vietnam, five were then operating in I Corps. Though geographically the smallest of the four corps areas, I Corps was, at the time, the most active. Because of the high concentration of enemy forces in I Corps, U.S. Marines and ARVN were in desperate need of help. During the battle over Hill 881, for example, the U.S. Marines had taken such a frightfully high number of casualties that the surgeons and nursing staff at the U.S. Navy hospital in Da Nang were stressed to keep up. They worked exceedingly long hours and some of the surgeons were looking like zombies after being on their feet in the operating rooms during an entire twelve-hour shift. It was a high stress environment. Tempers sometimes flared. Several of the surgeons seemed to be walking around in a half stupor. Assuredly, they couldn't do their best work under such conditions.[2]

***

Saturday evening, May 6, we said farewell to SP-4 Alfredo Chavez, one of the unsung heroes of the war. He would be leaving for Saigon and then home the next morning. We had a steak cookout to make him feel good about his many contributions to the advisory effort. He served as a very respected and capable refrigeration and generator repairman. Chavez traveled throughout I Corps keeping the equipment humming. He never complained. He just did his job, and did it well.

On Sunday, May 7, the casualties continued to pour into Da Nang from the north. We were beginning to get reports of just how ferocious the fighting for Hill 881 had been. Apparently, there was little room for maneuver and the battle became pretty much a frontal attack. It seemed to me that, unlike other wars, the occupation of real estate didn't mean a whole lot. We seemed to feel it important to occupy a certain hill today and then willingly give it up tomorrow. To me, it made no sense. Somehow I had it in the back of my mind that the fight over Hill 881 went back to General Westmoreland's insistence that General Walt take the fight to the enemy and drive up the enemy body count.

To expend 150 young American lives, and to wound another 500, in taking Hill 881 didn't make sense to me. But then again, what did I know about strategy or tactics for fighting and winning a war? I knew I'd better hold my tongue, but it was difficult for me to do so under the circumstances. I couldn't see us occupying the crest of Hill 881 for very long. The question in my mind was why we felt it was so important. What tactical advantage did the taking of the hill give us? Hopefully there was a logical and compelling answer.

***

Duy Tan General Hospital in Da Nang was bulging at the seams. Whereas the United States evacuated almost 30 percent of wounded U.S. servicemen to Japan, Okinawa, the Philippines, or Hawaii, the Vietnamese had to retain all of their wounded in Vietnam. Could there be any wonder why their hospitalization system was more crowded than ours? It seemed to me that the critics needed to give that significant difference some serious thought before passing judgment.

That Sunday afternoon, I spent about two hours on China Beach. As usual, there were about 10,000 young marines out there. This time, however, there was one woman. An Australian entertainer had enough courage—or stupidity—to go to the beach, knowing full well that she would be a minority of one. The number of virile eighteen- to twenty-year-old marines around her at any given time would have filled the ranks of a battalion, maybe even a regiment.

It was good to get a little sun, sand, and sea. China Beach surely had to be among the world's finest beaches. It far surpassed any beach I had ever been on in my lifetime. And on that Sunday afternoon, the waves were cracking, so surfers were having a great time. I was tempted to give it a try, but the boards were all constantly in use by young marines.

We had an unusual happening that evening. After getting back from China Beach and having dinner at the Officers' Club, a group of us were sitting on the third floor balcony of our hotel overlooking Doc Lap Street. Suddenly, a rifle shot rang out. It seemed very close, so we took cover in the hotel. After about fifteen minutes, we went back to the balcony because our rooms were sweltering hot. Major Jack Heinze walked to the railing on the balcony and happened to notice that the guard on duty, a U.S. Marine, was slumped over inside the sandbagged enclosure as if sleeping. We previously had had Vietnamese guards in front of our hotel, but about six weeks prior, the U.S. Marines had been assigned that duty. Sleeping while on guard duty is, as everyone knows, a very serious offense, punishable under the Uniform Code of Military Justice. Because of this, we tried to give the young Marine a break by awakening him. We yelled at him from the balcony and threw Tootsie Rolls at him to no avail. Then it struck us that maybe there was a connection between the rifle shot we had heard and the slumped-over Marine.

Three or four of us ran down the stairs and out the hotel door to the sandbagged guard station. As we approached the guard, we thought he was dead, but I detected a strong pulse, and we could see no evidence of trauma. We got him out of the bunker and laid him on the sidewalk. He was in a very deep coma. Nothing would rouse him. We called for an ambulance and notified the MPs immediately. When the ambulance arrived, a medic pulled out a flashlight and examined him carefully. There was no evidence of trauma. He wasn't wounded, just in a deep coma, so deep that nothing the navy corpsmen did could rouse him. They immediately transported him to the U.S. Navy hospital.

On Tuesday, 9 May, along with Captain Nhan, my counterpart, I reviewed patient census data for all ARVN hospitalization units in I Corps. The numbers were discouraging. As of that morning, there were 511 patients who theoretically did not have a bed. Collectively there were 511 fewer beds available than there were admitted patients, despite the fact that the physicians had been aggressively placing many patients on convalescent leave, well before it was medically prudent to do so. The physicians' hands were tied. They had to discharge some in order to make room for those coming off the battlefields. On the previous

Sunday, Duy Tan Hospital had admitted eighty-one wounded soldiers from Quang Nam Province alone.

It appeared to me as though the NVA and VC were trying to make a statement in the I Corps area. Wherever I went, especially in the rural areas, I saw growing evidence that terrorism and verbal intimidation of the people were having a major impact. Those in rural areas were less willing to talk to me, probably because they feared doing so. The people didn't know who to trust. Those who were brave enough to come forward with helpful information risked their families being terrorized and brutalized. Some were even reluctant to seek medical help during MEDCAP visits for fear that the VC or NVA would interpret this as their having adopted a pro-government stance regarding the war. It tore at my heart to see badly needed medical support rejected out of fear of reprisal.

***

The pressure on our office at this time was great. We were all tired and somewhat edgy and difficult to live with. There wasn't much levity in the office. We all sensed that President Johnson was desperately seeking a way out with our honor as a nation intact. Ho Chi Minh and his minions were clearly in it for the long haul, there could be no doubt. All one needed to do was go to the POW camp across the Han River and look into the eyes of the men and women who were imprisoned. The resolve of our enemy was great. The time horizon did not matter to Ho Chi Minh and his generals.

***

The Cam Lo resettlement project loomed larger every day. The exodus from the villages north of the Cam Lo River had begun. I was there on 10 May, and at that time, only a trickle of humanity was flowing out of those dangerous villages and hamlets, but soon it would become a torrent. A sociological phenomenon was occurring as the resettlement took place. Many of the small villages and hamlets that were being evacuated were inhabited by both Buddhists and Christians. Upon receiving notification that they were to be evacuated—a few forcibly, but most willingly—

the people were given a choice regarding which of two resettlement camps they desired to relocate to, either a refugee settlement on the outskirts of Quang Tri or the settlement near Cam Lo. Almost invariably, the Buddhists elected to go to Quang Tri, whereas the Christians chose Cam Lo. The ties of religion were apparently stronger than those of friendship and community.

At the time of my first visit to the Cam Lo resettlement project, about 100 families were occupying tents. All but two of those families were Christian. A Catholic priest by the name of Father Phan Van Co had apparently become the informal leader of the Cam Lo settlement. The refugees looked to him to provide interface with civilian government officials as well as with the ARVN and MACV. Father Co had fled North Vietnam with his parishioners at the start of the war. The current move to Cam Lo was the fourth that his group had made since leaving North Vietnam after the Communist takeover. He seemed capable and his attitude was positive.

Forty-two families had thus far been resettled on the edge of Quang Tri City. Every single family was Buddhist. Although I hadn't interfaced with that group, I had been told that a Buddhist bonze seemed to be the informal leader and that he, too, seemed to have the best interests of the people at heart.

When I left my home in San Antonio, I never thought I'd be involved in planning the movement and resettlement of refugee populations. Sometimes I decried the fact that the army had not prepared me better to deal with the situations that confronted me, but then I stopped to realize that that would have been impossible. War was too unpredictable. The diversity of problems that had confronted me, and I'm sure most other advisors, could not have been predicted. I felt certain that the other three senior medical advisors in country, Majors John Davis, Bill Leach and Bill McLeod, had also experienced things in their corps areas that they never would have envisioned before arriving in Vietnam.

Most of the villages being evacuated were located just above Gio Linh. This small city overlooked the famous Ben Hai River. My friend, Major Joe Perlow, commanded the MACV advisory team in the Gio Linh sub-sector.

Each relocated family was given a weekly stipend of rice, oil, and fish, the staples of their diet. The size of the stipend was dependent upon the number of people in the family. It had been promised by South Vietnamese government officials that the stipend would continue until the people became self-sustaining on the fertile plains of Cam Lo. In addition, each family would be given a 50x30-meter plot of land upon which to build a home and establish a family garden. The Vietnamese equivalent of seventy-five dollars U.S. would also be given to each family to help build and furnish their homes. Tin, cement, and limited quantities of wood would be made available by the government of South Vietnam to be used in the construction of their homes. Military trucks would be employed to transport the people from their former villages to the resettlement area. Tentatively, they had decided that, whenever possible, the families would be allowed to bring household furnishings, kitchenware, and clothing. Transportation would be somewhat limited, but ARVN officials had promised to do their best. Those families with animals posed a special problem. Many had pigs and chickens. A few owned cattle. Whether or not they would be able to bring the animals remained to be decided.

On 11 May, I returned to Cam Lo to work with the ever-expanding community of refugees. Soon the community would grow to over 18,000, primarily old men, women, and children. I say "old men" because I didn't see one able-bodied man between the ages of seventeen and forty in the settlement. The only young men were a few poor souls who were either mentally challenged or severely crippled. I knew it was going to be a long, hot summer for the inhabitants of that camp. I was hoping that Father Co and the other informal leaders who would inevitably rise out of the inhabitants of the settlement would be able to keep spirits high. If depression or apathy were to set in, I feared the consequences.

I spent part of the day working with an ARVN preventive medicine team that was focused on taking steps to prevent serious outbreaks of disease. A safe water supply was a must, as were means of disposing of human waste and garbage. Insect and rodent controls were also of great concern. There were literally hundreds of decisions that had to be made in order to minimize the risks of diseases spreading throughout the refugee settlement. Some wells had already been dug and others were in the process. I did not like the placement of one of the wells and voiced my objections quite strongly. It was in a location where it was likely to be contaminated just as soon as the monsoon rains started falling. Runoff would sweep human waste and garbage toward the open well. Eventually they abandoned the partially completed well and filled it in with earth. The overall sanitation plan, however, looked quite good. It seemed to me that the civilian public health officials and the ARVN preventive medicine team had made sound decisions.

At this time, there were still only about 100 families living in the settlement. It amazed me to see families with almost no resources and no source of income move into the resettlement area seemingly with confidence that it would all work out. I wondered how many American families would have the courage and the wherewithal to do it. Several families had already been assigned their small plot of land and started to level the surface to lay down a cement floor and begin constructing their homes. Children abounded throughout the settlement. For them, it was an adventure. I thought to myself that it would be wise of the parents to try and keep it that way, especially for the adolescents. I couldn't even imagine how teenagers from developed countries would react to that environment.

Image 32. Seven beautiful children in the Cam Lo refugee settlement

Photo courtesy of the author

Cam Lo was on the edge of the so-called hill country. There were several Montagnard villages in fairly close proximity. I liked the Montagnard people. They were a simple, largely uneducated people, but exceedingly loyal and friendly. For some reason, they had decided to back the government cause, and they especially liked to work with Americans. They sought opportunities to be supportive, especially in providing reliable information about enemy troop movements, storage of supplies, ammunition caches, and the like. It was very disarming, however, to enter one of their villages and see all the women walking around with their breasts exposed. Most wore nothing above their waists except beads around their necks, at least during the temperate months of the year. Although I'm not certain of its accuracy, I was told that young, unmarried, Montagnard women covered their breasts, but as soon as they married and had their first baby, their blouses came off. It may have had something to do with facilitating the nursing of their infants.

Image 33. Montagnard woman and child

Photo courtesy of the author

We had been briefed that the refugees would soon be arriving in large numbers. The current trickle would become a steady flow and perhaps a torrent. At that time, we still were not certain whether the refugees would be able to bring their possessions with them or be forced to leave them behind. Those that had arrived thus far had brought their meager belongings. The ARVN and civilian government officials were now talking in terms of allowing them to bring only those things they could physically carry. Later in the day, they were talking of allocating each family one small truck to transport all family members and their possessions.

Still unsettled was the question regarding animals. I had been arguing, as passionately as I knew how, to allow the refugees to bring both material possessions and animals. It seemed to me that if it were decided otherwise, they would be dealing with an angry, possibly rebellious throng of people, something they assuredly didn't need. The people's sense of loss was bound to be great as a result of leaving their home villages. Why exacerbate the feeling of loss by forcing them to abandon their life's possessions? I had also been pushing the point that the people must be allowed to bring all things that had religious significance or deep ancestral meaning, for example items handed down from generation to generation.

The VC had a compelling propaganda program going concerning the disposition of the bones of their ancestors. People who have been conditioned, throughout their entire lives, to worship their ancestors and try to maintain the integrity and continuity of the family by establishing individual family burial plots were open to the VC argument that by abandoning the bones of their deceased relatives they were desecrating the family. For the South Vietnam government and ARVN to even consider exhuming the bones of all ancestors of those being moved would be foolhardy, but they had to do something to counter the VC campaign to discredit the move. There were probably tens of thousands of gravesites that had meaning for the refugees.

Besides wells, latrines were being dug and quite a number of community cooking areas constructed. Cam Lo was a beehive of activity. Father Co was gone for the day when I visited, but two nuns, wearing full habit, were running the small dispensary they had already established. When I arrived, one of the nuns was delivering a baby. She looked up and smiled at me, and then looked down again just in time to welcome another little girl into the world. I couldn't help but wonder what the future held for that child.

As I boarded a helicopter for the flight back to Da Nang, I was hoping that government and ARVN authorities wouldn't start moving large numbers of people before the supporting infrastructure was ready. At that point in time, they had only enough tents to meet the needs of about 5,000 people, although more tents were supposedly on the way. Just prior to my departure, I was told that further delay of the movement of large numbers of people might not be possible because of increasing military pressure in and north of the village of Gio Linh.

***

On 12 May, I sent my wife a series of pictures that needed no explanation. They showed a U.S. Navy corpsman trying to save the life of a young Marine during the ferocious battle for Hill 881. A French female photographer had taken the pictures. The emotion and tragedy depicted in the images were almost palpable. The pictures alone told the story.

The level of intensity of the war in I Corps continued to build. The surgeons at the U.S. Navy hospital were frightfully busy. One of the nurses told me that the surgeons had been averaging fifteen to sixteen hour workdays for the past several days. God only knew how long that could go on before their judgment and skills were impaired.

***

I always appreciated the I Corps Saturday morning staff meetings. The one held on 13 May was no exception. General Walt attended and asked some very penetrating questions. For me, the meetings were always very instructive. In addition to highlighting the successes and failures of the past week, they provided insights into the days and weeks ahead. Although the briefers were frequently wrong in their predictions of enemy actions, I would say that, on balance, they were right far more than they were wrong. The prognostication gave me the opportunity to think my way through the medically-related issues that could arise if the predicted course of action became a reality. The meetings definitely facilitated advanced planning. General Walt presented his views of future enemy activities quite frequently. One thing I knew for certain about

General Walt was that he did not suffer fools gladly. He became very angry when he surmised that staff officers had not done their homework or when they provided him with incomplete or inaccurate information.

On 13 May, I was at the U.S. Navy hospital when three large Marine helicopters arrived bearing more casualties. It seemed as though the marines were being hit in a different part of I Corps each night. One night the action might be in Quang Tri Province, the next night Thua Thien or Quang Nam. It wasn't a single intense, prolonged battle that was producing the casualties but rather hit and run skirmishes all over I Corps. This seemed to reinforce my feeling that the enemy had the capability to hit us at any place and time of his choosing. This realization was not comforting.

Captain Bob Helton left Hue on that day, 13 May. He was such a fine officer. Because Quang Tri and Thua Thien Provinces had been so active in recent weeks, he barely had a chance to say goodbye. I would miss him greatly. His replacement wasn't due in country until 1 June. The lack of continuity in the assignment process was a distressing and continuing problem. It was widely believed that the personnel replacement system, especially for key positions, had to be modified so as to provide at least a few days overlap.

On Sunday, 14 May, I was sitting in my office in the late afternoon when Colonel Hamblen walked in and sat down in a steel folding chair alongside my desk. He wanted to talk about my departure. I told him that my replacement had been designated but, unfortunately, would not arrive prior to my departure. I explained that I had tried to communicate with Major Stoltz through the mail, but my packet of materials had been returned as "undeliverable." I expressed my concern that many of the seemingly worthwhile projects my NCOs and I had initiated would be discontinued or deemphasized because Major Stoltz wouldn't know what conditions had brought them about. Colonel Hamblen expressed his frustration and then asked that I prepare a letter for his signature to Brigadier General William Hamrick, Chief of the Medical Service Corps, urging him to expedite Major Stoltz's assignment so there would be a few days overlap with me. I immediately prepared the letter.

The mail on Monday, 15 May, brought to my desk two very tempting civilian job opportunities. I couldn't seriously consider either of them because I had a four-year obligation to the U.S. Army as a result of its sponsorship of my doctoral-level education. The opportunities presented, I had to admit, were attractive. I suspected that one or more of my good friends and fellow doctoral students at the University of Texas, Steve McMahon, Tom Hatfield, or Jan LeCroy, might have steered the opportunities my way.

I spent Tuesday, 16 May, in the cities of Duc Pho, Quang Ngai, and Chu Lai. The ARVN had encountered significant problems in dealing with the leaders of the U.S. Army's Task Force Oregon (TFO), so Colonel Hamblen dispatched LTC Hennigan and me, along with our ARVN counterparts, to see if we could come to some basic agreements. TFO was in the process of taking over many of the missions previously assigned to the U.S. Marines, who were withdrawing their units from Quang Tin and Quang Ngai provinces and moving them into the three northern-most provinces of I Corps—Quang Nam, Thua Thien, and Quang Tri. Unfortunately TFO officials had thus far refused to pick up two missions previously accomplished by the USMC units they were replacing. Specifically, they were refusing to take on the missions of evacuating ARVN casualties from the battlefields and of resupplying the remote and isolated outposts manned by the ARVN. The ARVN simply didn't have the helicopter assets to accomplish these two missions. Colonel Hennigan and I, along with our ARVN counterparts, had been sent to plead the case for continued support of the ARVN. TFO officials were contending that they, too, had an insufficient number of helicopters to take on these two missions.

Shortly after we arrived at the TFO Surgeon's Office, a group of visitors from the MACV Surgeon's Office in Saigon pulled up in two jeeps. I was pleasantly surprised to see among the group two old acquaintances from Fort Sam Houston, Colonel Dick Morgan, U.S. Army Veterinary Corps, and Colonel Jack Pollock, U.S. Army Dental Corps. We chatted about old times for about twenty minutes. Before they departed, they told the TFO Surgeon that they fully supported our request that the casualty evacuation mission be picked up by TFO. Colonel Pollack told them that if they failed to do so, many lives would be lost. The ARVN 2nd Infantry Division had only six or seven helicopters, not nearly enough to take on the mission of evacuating the wounded from the fields of battle. I appreciated Colonels Morgan and Pollock lending their support to our efforts to convince TFO officials that they had a moral responsibility to pick up these missions.

When we left Chu Lai to return to Da Nang, no firm decisions had been made, but at least we had sensitized top TFO officials regarding the consequences of their actions if they refused to pick up the two missions. We awaited their decision.

It was about 1645 hours when we landed at Da Nang and returned to our offices. As soon as I entered my office, all hell broke loose. There stood an angry and red-faced Colonel Hamblen. I had managed to provoke his ire once again. After ranting and raving at me for several minutes, in front of my immediate boss, LTC Hennigan, he cooled down a bit, and I was able to figure out what had caused the explosion. While I was in Quang Ngai and Chu Lai, several blood and urine tests were being run at the U.S. Navy hospital on General Lam, the Vietnamese commander of I Corps. I had arranged for these tests at the request of Colonel Hamblen. General Lam had been suffering from either gout or severe arthritis for many years. About three days prior, he had had an attack that put him in bed. It was so painful he couldn't walk. I was supposed to get the test results and, along with Colonel Hamblen, go to his home that very day and explain the results to him. I was also to give General Lam a report on the results of our meetings in Quang Ngai and Chu Lai.

Colonel Hamblen swore up and down that I had told him we'd be back from Chu Lai no later than 1600 hours. I was certain that I had told him that we would be departing Chu Lai no later than 1600 hours. Based on this misunderstanding, Colonel Hamblen had called General Lam and told him that he and I would come to his home at 1645 hours in order to give him the medical test results and to brief him on the results of the meeting with TFO officials in Quang Ngai and Chu Lai.

By this time, we were already fifteen minutes late for our meeting with General Lam, and I still hadn't even obtained the test results. I hastily got on the phone and, after a delay, reached the appropriate physician at the navy hospital. I jotted down the test results and then had to take a few minutes to make certain I understood what the results meant and to find out from the physician what I should tell General Lam. By the time Colonel Hamblen and I got in his staff car for the drive to General Lam's quarters, it was about 1730 hours, so we were already forty-five minutes late. We finally got to the general's home at about 1745 hours, an hour late. Colonel Hamblen and I were ushered into the general's bedroom, where I quickly and nervously explained the test results and gave him an overview of our meetings in Quang Ngai and Chu Lai. The general looked very tired. He told us that he hadn't gotten much sleep in the past three days because of the constant pain. He was normally a very robust man. On the way back to the office, Colonel Hamblen didn't say a word. There was icy silence. I felt duly chastised.

On 17 May, I was informed that the movement of refugee families to Cam Lo and Quang Tri was proceeding with due haste. An additional seventy-five to 100 families were to be relocated on that very day. The ARVN had to scrape the bottom of its transportation barrel to come up with enough trucks to support the mission, but it was proceeding. There was considerable urgency because the villages being vacated would, in all likelihood, become embattled areas within the next week or ten days. Sadly, something had caused a change in thinking among some of the people who were to be relocated. Whereas those in the first contingent had moved willingly, some now had to be forced. This made the exodus infinitely more difficult. I could only surmise that the VC propaganda had caused this change in attitude.

On that same day, 17 May, another ARVN convoy, this one bound for Quang Ngai, was ambushed. Fortunately it was stopped in a location where the drivers of the trucks were able to back off and turn the convoy around. VC mortars and small arms fire caused only minor damage. The convoy was not, however, able to get through to Quang Ngai.

That evening, at the Officers' Club, I talked to a reporter from *Life* magazine, patiently explaining to him the reasons for the relocation to Cam Lo. I told him that I could state unequivocally that it was the humanitarian thing to do. If combat in the villages being evacuated was inevitable, and it appeared to all that it was, the innocent civilians had to be moved out of harm's way. Later that very night, the Cam Lo settlement was mortared. Fortunately, the damage was minimal. We fully expected the VC to do everything in their power to stop or delay the moves. They wanted the villages and hamlets near the DMZ occupied so they could seek sanctuary there, knowing we would be reluctant to react for fear of causing more civilian casualties.

About two weeks prior to 18 May, we had been alerted that the U.S. Marines, supported by the ARVN, were going to kick off what was potentially one of the largest operations of the war to that point. We were told that this information was classified top secret and not to be discussed with anyone other than our fellow advisors and ARVN counterparts. When I arrived in the office on Thursday, 18 May, I was informed that the operation had begun. Friendly forces above Dong Ha had been pushing east toward the South China Sea. As of that morning, however, our forces had not made firm contact with enemy forces, although the intelligence analysts said there were at least two enemy regiments in that area. Those forces had been harassing our outposts at Gio Linh, Cam Lo, Con Thien, and Dong Ha for months.

On that same day, while I was at the navy hospital, I was informed that the marine guard we had found unconscious in front of our hotel had suffered a diabetic coma, as I had suspected. Fortunately, Major Jack Heinze had spotted him and we were able to get him transported to the hospital and treated quickly. I was somewhat surprised that diabetes was present among our young servicemen. I would have thought that pre-deployment physical examinations would have picked up practically all cases.

***

Ho Chi Minh's birthday was on 19 May, so we were again placed on alert. Apparently, it was the occasion for a major celebration in North Vietnam. The intelligence analysts said we should expect an uptick in terrorism on that day. They had picked up some information regarding threats made by the VC and NVA to carry out brazen attacks to honor Uncle Ho. It seemed to me that, more often than not, these threats didn't translate into action. I couldn't help thinking that soon the Chicken Little Syndrome would set in. If you yelled, "The sky is falling!" too often, and nothing happened, the soldiers would soon start to ignore the warning. The following week, on 23 May, the Vietnamese would celebrate Buddha's birthday. When Buddha walked the earth, he was supposedly opposed to fighting and killing, so I assumed we would not receive Chicken Little warnings of the probability of increased terrorism on that day.

On Saturday, 20 May, I received a most welcome phone call from the MACV Surgeon's Office in Saigon. As of the following Monday or Tuesday, depending on the availability of transportation, I Corps would have its full contingent of MILPHAP teams. Two teams, one army and one navy, had just arrived in Saigon, about ten days earlier than projected.

The expected major battle near Dong Ha, in Quang Tri Province, hadn't materialized as of the morning of 21 May. Contact with the enemy had been very limited. The intelligence analysts were still insisting that there were two NVA regimental-sized units operating in that region but, if they were there, so far they had chosen not to become engaged. It was a rather puzzling situation for the planners and the combat forces as well. Even though the enemy was very adept at blending in with the civil population, it seemed to the analysts that this would be difficult for regimental-sized units.

***

At about 0945 hours on 20 May, I was in Captain Nhan's office conferring with him about the tactical situation in Quang Tri Province when SP-4 Behner called and said that Colonel Hennigan wanted to see me immediately. I rushed back to the office, wondering what was going on. When I got there he said, "Grab your bag. You're going to Hong Kong to select some kitchen equipment at 1145 hours this morning." I couldn't believe it. I expressed concern about my being away when the tactical situation up north was so fluid and uncertain, but he told me that things were relatively quiet and that I should go. I asked SFC Simmons to come with me to my hotel room so I could brief him on some irons that I had in the fire while I packed my bag.

After packing, I hurried back to the office to finish a report that was due in the MACV Surgeon's Office during my absence. SFC Simmons then gave me a ride to the airport, and soon I was off to Hong Kong. I was aware that for the past several days there had been rather serious anti-war, and to a degree anti-American, rioting in Hong Kong. The U.S. State Department had been watching the situation very carefully and had expressed concern, but, so far, R&R flights were still being allowed. Hong Kong was an exceedingly popular tourist destination. There was great concern that American tourists, including those on R&R, could be denied access to the airport by the rioting mobs. Although I had never been to Hong Kong, and therefore had not seen it first hand, I knew the Hong Kong airport was built on a narrow piece of land jutting into the South China Sea. It would be relatively easy to cut it off and deny passengers access to or from the airport.

Upon our arrival at Hong Kong International Airport, we were given a copy of a memorandum explaining that Hong Kong Island had been placed off limits to all servicemen. The memorandum also stated that the R&R hotels on Hong Kong Island were, likewise, off limits, and that we would instead be staying at the International Hotel in Kowloon.

I checked into the hotel and went to my large and very nicely furnished room, where I immediately headed for the shower to remove the grit and grime of war. With the exception of my time in Bangkok, it was the first hot shower I had had since leaving the United States ten and a half months before. While in the shower, I decided to go to the hotel bar and enjoy a cold pint of Guinness Stout immediately upon finishing my shower and putting on civilian clothes.

The barroom was spectacular. The bar itself was very long and made of a continuous slab of marble. I chose a seat at one end, facing the full length of the long bar. The bartender was wearing a short, fitted-around-the-waist red jacket, a black bow tie and black trousers. He looked very distinguished and very British.

The bartender carefully drew the Guinness from the tap, making sure the head was just right then served it with a flourish. Just as he stepped away to serve another customer, I noticed a huge rat scurrying along the floor behind the bar. The rat suddenly jumped onto a box, then onto a refrigerated cabinet, and then onto the bar. It started running straight down the bar toward me. The creature tried to stop as it approached my end of the bar, but its momentum was too great and it slid right off the slippery marble bar and into my lap. *Welcome to Hong Kong, Jim,* I thought to myself. Suddenly, the International Hotel didn't seem nearly as luxurious as it had moments before. The embarrassed bartender came over and, after I assured him I had not been bitten by the rat, pointed at my frosty glass of Guinness and said, "This one's on the house, old chap."

In conversation, the bartender told me that the Communist-inspired riots had been increasing in frequency and intensity. Although I was on the Kowloon side of the metropolis, there were massive pictures of Chairman Mao prominently displayed. I witnessed several demonstrations showing support for "the cause." I understood why we had been ordered, in the strongest of terms, to stay away from the street demonstrations.[3]

Hong Kong and Kowloon had over four million people at that time. It was the most densely populated area in the world. Many of the people, perhaps the majority, were refugees who had fled mainland China. The people were physically much larger than I had anticipated. My initial impression was that they were also ambitious, polite, and most helpful.

The city wasn't as clean as Bangkok, but it was infinitely cleaner than Saigon. Kowloon's children seemed high-spirited, boisterous, noisy, and happy. Hong Kong was a city of skyscrapers, very visible from Kowloon. Whereas Bangkok's buildings were rarely over six or eight stories high, Hong Kong's reached up to the sky. Hong Kong was forced by its geography to go up if it wanted to expand. It had no room to spread out laterally, and refugees from mainland China kept coming to both Hong Kong and Kowloon.

I went for a short walk during the late afternoon. I explored the harbor area, full of small boats of all descriptions, many with families living aboard. I also explored the rail yards adjacent to the harbor. I tried to communicate with some of the people I met, but to no avail. I didn't find a single person who spoke English. I thought there would be many, since at that time Hong Kong was still a British colony. I would have walked further, but I first heard, and then saw, a demonstrating mob approaching. I quickly retreated. We were told that the mobs frequently jostled non-Asians while screaming obscenities at them. I didn't need that, so I left in a hurry.

That evening, I had a harrowing experience. I signed up for a night tour of the city of Kowloon. The tour participants were transported in a small eighteen-passenger bus. Our first stop was to be an open market. The streets the bus moved along were very narrow and congested. Swarms of people spilled off the sidewalks into the streets. I was fascinated by the diverse activities along the way. Some people were playing mahjong at street-side parlors, others were watching cockfights. There were fortune tellers, magicians, musicians, and myriad other activities going on. Suddenly, the street crowd turned surly. Precisely why this happened, I do not know. It may have been because they noted two young U.S. Marines walking along the sidewalk with Chinese girls. Or it could have been because they observed that all the passengers on the small bus were non-Asians. You could see the anger and hostility in their eyes. Soon their actions became more threatening. They started shouting what I assume were derisive comments or obscenities at us and at the young marines and their female companions on the sidewalk.

The driver of the bus was becoming very concerned while proceeding very slowly and cautiously so as not to hit anyone on the street. Then the shouts of the mob turned into pounding with their fists on the sides of our bus. One of the windows in the bus was shattered. Soon, the crowd started to tip our bus from side to side. A group of twenty or thirty angry men on one side of the bus pushed on the side of the bus until it was about to tip over. Then a group on the other side caught it just before it got to the point of no return and tipped it in the other direction. It was frightening. They then placed some merchandise from a nearby store, several suitcases and a large, box-type electric fan, directly in front of the bus and defiantly dared the driver to run over the merchandise. A teenage boy ran out to the bus with a can of gasoline and pretended to pour it on one of the rear tires while another boy lit a match. The driver of the bus started honking his horn repeatedly for long periods of time. Suddenly, three brave Kowloon policemen appeared on the scene, removed the merchandise from in front of the bus and ushered us through the crowd. The tour guide wisely decided not to go to the outdoor market. Instead, we proceeded immediately to a nightclub in a safer part of the city. After our harrowing experience, the nightclub show didn't seem nearly as glamorous as it otherwise might have. Nobody was in much of a nightclub mood.

**

The next morning, 22 May, I took a taxi to a warehouse full of kitchen appliances. Fortunately, the business establishment to which I had been referred was in Kowloon. Had it been in Hong Kong, I would not have been able to accomplish my mission. I followed the guidance I had received from the mess steward at the U.S. Navy hospital in Da Nang very closely when selecting the appliances. I picked out two large refrigerators and a gas stove with eight burners and two ovens. I did not have the authority to purchase the items. My role was to select the appliances, get model numbers, prices, and brochures describing the items and take them back to Da Nang.

That afternoon, I tried to do some shopping, but that too was interrupted by an angry mob. When I exited a store where I had purchased beaded sweaters for my wife and several of my sisters, I noted that my eyes were stinging, and there was an unusual odor in the air. I recognized it immediately as tear gas, having gone through gas chamber exercises on three or four different occasions. I decided I'd better hurry and get out of there. As I rapidly walked in the direction of my hotel, I couldn't help but notice that all of the merchants, on both sides of the very busy commercial street, were locking up their stores and removing items from the display windows. Suddenly, a mob surged around the corner of one of the small, narrow streets leading onto the main thoroughfare. The protesting people were moving in my direction very rapidly. I could have turned around and run, but decided that running might invite them to give chase, so I kept moving straight ahead, more or less hugging the storefronts along the street. Three members of the mob jostled me, pushing and shoving. One tore the pocket off my shirt and screamed at me, but soon left in order to keep up with the fast-moving mob. I hurried back to the safety of my hotel.

That afternoon, I booked a tour into what was referred to as the New Territories. They constituted that portion of the British Colony from Kowloon to the Chinese border. The drive to the border was scenic, but somewhat spoiled by the sight of abject poverty suffered by people in the area. As I stood on a hill mass overlooking the vastness of China, I couldn't help but wonder what the future would bring to that enigmatic country, the most populous nation on the face of mother earth. I felt just a little bit guilty over the fact that I probably had as much money in my pocket as the typical family in the New Territories made in a year. Their poverty was such a dehumanizing thing. The people, except the children, looked apathetic and spiritless, unlike the people in Kowloon. There was such a stark contrast between the luxury and wealth of Kowloon and Hong Kong and the poverty of the New Territories. It seemed almost surreal.

The next morning, 23 May, while sitting in the hotel dining room enjoying a third cup of coffee, I picked up the English version of a Hong Kong newspaper. One article caught my attention. It described the special life that had been lived by the American concert pianist, Philippa Schuyler. She was aboard a helicopter in Vietnam when it crashed into Da Nang Bay about ten miles north of the city. She had been working as a war correspondent for an American newspaper.[4] I had met this remarkable, multi-talented, black woman in Hue. She was a devout Catholic, and when Father O'Neill, our Catholic chaplain, celebrated Mass in Hue, she occasionally served as the organist. I was told that she was heavily involved in helping Vietnam's orphaned children, placing many in private schools in Da Nang. I was also told there were orphaned children with her aboard the helicopter when it crashed.

The rioting continued in the streets of Kowloon on 23 May, the day I was to depart. The mobs swirled past the front of my hotel, chanting in unison, in perfectly understandable English, "The East is Red. The East is Red. The East is Red." They screamed this phrase over and over, as if they wanted to imprint it on our very consciousness. I thought to myself, it well might be if non-Communist world leaders didn't come up with broad, imaginative programs that could lift the Asian masses out of their poverty.

As I packed my bag for the return to Da Nang, I reflected on the forty-eight hours I had spent in Kowloon. It seemed that many of the Chinese people I encountered were searching for a better, more meaningful life. Communism was not the answer. I had seen the effects of Communism on the peoples of Eastern Europe, and I knew in my heart that as the state was glorified and took on greater importance, the worth of the individual was devalued or diminished. I felt strongly that, without freedom, life lost its dignity. I also knew that true freedom was incompatible with Communist doctrine. Was our form of government perfect? Of course not, but it opened up a way of life that was infinitely richer for the human spirit than the boredom, apathy, and lack of creativity that Communism seemed to engender. All one had to do was look at Eastern Europe, at that very time, to see the downtrodden and dispirited people that Communism produced.

***

I got back to Da Nang in the early evening of Tuesday, 23 May. Lying on my desk were instructions regarding my departure from Vietnam. I was to out-process at the Koepler Hotel compound in Saigon at 0800 hours on Tuesday, 27 June. I then had to go to the MACV Surgeon's Office for a debriefing, commencing at 1400 hours. At 1700 hours. a bus would take me to Bien Hoa, where I would spend the night. The next morning, 28 June, at 0950 hours I would be departing on charter flight T-240 for the United States of America. I was scheduled to arrive at Travis Air Force Base in California at 1505 hours that same day. I was hoping there would then be an evening flight from San Francisco to San Antonio.

On 25 May, I received the discouraging news that my replacement, Major Richard Stoltz, would not arrive in country before my departure. Colonel Hamblen's request to Brigadier General Hamrick that he expedite Major Stoltz's arrival was denied. Major Stoltz would not arrive in Da Nang before 10 or 11 July at the earliest. I felt bad that I would not be able to provide the type of orientation he deserved.

On 26 May, it was officially announced that General Walt would soon be returning to the United States. His time in Vietnam was about to come to an end. This had been rumored for quite some time. On the morning the announcement was made, there was a very impressive outdoor ceremony in the I Corps compound, during which Premier Ky awarded General Walt the National Order Medal, Third Class. General Westmoreland was in attendance, as were about twenty other flag-rank officers. I couldn't help but notice the look of disdain on General Walt's face as Premier Ky pinned on his decoration. Clearly, General Walt did not like the man.

Things up north, in Quang Tri Province, continued to be relatively quiet. I wondered if the intelligence officers had been wrong in their assessment of enemy strength, or if the major fight they had predicted was yet to come

As Saturday, 27 May, dawned, I knew as I drove to my office that the day would be equally as hot as the past few days had been. The previous day, the temperature had risen to 108 degrees, and it was unbearably humid. I couldn't help but think of the poor refugees at Cam Lo, trying to survive under a tent or a tin roof that seemed to absorb heat and radiate it downward into their living space. Captain Nhan told me that thus far a small number had died of heat-related injuries. Several had also died during the movement from their ancestral villages and hamlets to Cam Lo. I couldn't even imagine having to move a young mother with a two-day-old suckling baby and four other children, all under the age of six, in the back of a deuce-and-a-half truck. A number of the newborn babies didn't survive. It was very sad.

Captain Nhan also told me that several babies had died because their mothers had stopped lactating as a result of the turmoil and stress of moving. It was a growing problem. There was no source of baby formula in the country. When a new mother stopped lactating, it almost immediately threatened the life of her baby. All the new mother could hope for was a readily available and willing wet nurse. Frequently, that was not the case. Colonel Hamblen gave me permission to bring this problem to General Walt's attention in the staff meeting held the morning of 27 May, General Walt's last such meeting. I was proud of General Walt's response. He sat in the center of the front row in our I Corps classified conference room. After I briefed him about the problem and the lack of baby formula in Vietnam, he turned around, glared at the staff, and growled, "Get 'em some milk. I don't care where you have to go, but get 'em some milk." After the staff meeting, I heard the ARVN G-4 discussing the matter with a couple of other officers. It is my understanding that they had to go to Hong Kong to get the much-needed baby formula.

Image 34. A young boy riding on a water buffalo near the Cam Lo settlement

Photo courtesy of the author

***

On Sunday afternoon, 28 May, I returned to Cam Lo with a small group of advisors to take a look at how the settlement was developing. The U.S. Marines had jokingly started referring to the settlement as "Tin City" or "Camp Low." I was hoping that those somewhat derisive names didn't negatively impact the spirit of the refugees. I knew that Father Co and others in the community were doing everything in their power to create a spirit of optimism and hope for the future. I didn't think we should be undercutting their efforts by using derisive or humorous terms to describe the settlement. While chatting with Father Co, he told me that his greatest challenge was "keeping spirits up and attitudes positive." As

I flew back to Da Nang, I reflected on the many challenges facing Father Co and the men, women and children in the Cam Lo settlement.

That evening, General Lam hosted a farewell party for General Walt. I had been invited to attend. At first, I considered declining. I didn't like having to pull my somewhat musty civilian clothes out of the closet and get dressed up for a ninety-minute cocktail party. But then I thought better of it. Out of respect for General Walt, I decided to go. I genuinely liked and respected the man. He had a gruff exterior, but he also had a big heart for the Vietnamese people and believed in taking care of his marines. I had recently been asked to escort him to the navy hospital, where he affixed Purple Hearts to the hospital pajamas of three severely wounded Army enlisted soldiers, all of whom served on sub-sector advisory teams. While there, he also awarded the Purple Heart to a couple of marines. When we left the hospital ward, I couldn't help but notice that his eyes were misty.

I was pleased that I had decided to attend the farewell party. All of Da Nang's luminaries, military and civilian, were there, as were the top brass of the American military. I enjoyed meeting new and different people. Everyone in attendance seemed to be in a mellow, reflective mood as they recalled the many positive things General Walt had done while serving in Da Nang. General Lam gave a very touching speech about General Walt's service to the Vietnamese people in their quest for freedom. Madame Lam stood alongside her husband as he spoke, looking her radiant best. She really was a beautiful woman. She, too, spoke briefly about General Walt's many contributions, and General Walt reciprocated in a very personal and poignant manner.

***

On Monday morning, 29 May, I had the pleasure of briefing Major General Robert Cushman, the officer who would be replacing General Walt. I was asked to describe for him my role as senior medical advisor. I think he was somewhat taken aback by my highlighting the problem of civilian casualties of war. I told him that I could see no way that we were going to win the hearts and minds of the people unless we could somehow reduce the number of civilians being maimed and killed as a result of the war.

On that same Monday, I had two more visitors from the MACV Surgeon's Office in Saigon. I'll not name them, because one of them is still living and I don't want to embarrass him. I went to the airport to pick them up around noon. It was a scorching hot day. I watched their plane arrive. The tailgate of the C-130 dropped, and I spotted them coming down the ramp. We exchanged salutes and handshakes and were walking toward my jeep when all of a sudden the artillery cut loose. They both hit the tarmac, helmets rolling, rifles clattering, and briefcases flying. I stood there and simply said, "Outgoing." They got up, brushed themselves off, and then realized that everyone nearby was bemusedly staring at them. Both suffered second degree burns on their hands from the scorching hot tarmac.

Also on that day, I received a letter from Charles McNeil, a friend from Texas. He told me that his family had been informed that his nephew had been severely wounded while serving with the U.S. Marines in I Corps. The McNeil family had received no follow-up information about the young man. He implored me to help them obtain a more complete report. Although my time was at a premium, I decided I had to try to find out what I could about the young man.

The young marine was wounded on 15 May up near the DMZ. He arrived at the navy hospital in Da Nang that same day. There, he was stabilized and then, on 18 May, taken to the USAF 22nd Casualty Staging Facility, located on Da Nang Air Base. From there, he was evacuated to the 19th Casualty Staging Facility at Clark Air Base in the Philippines, arriving on 19 May. A Casualty Staging Facility was a holding-type medical unit where patients were maintained and cared for while awaiting an aircraft for further evacuation. The young man was to be taken to Japan, or possibly even right back to the United States. When he left Da Nang, his condition was listed as good. He had multiple shrapnel wounds in both legs and his right arm. He also had a fracture of a limb, but I failed to ask which one. I summarized this information in a letter and sent it to Charles McNeil. I felt certain the McNeil family would be grateful to receive the news that he would fully recover from his wounds.

On Tuesday, 30 May, it was reported that General Walt's next assignment would be in Washington, D.C. as the Chief of Personnel for the U.S. Marine Corps. Most marines were flabbergasted, as were the members of MACV Advisory Team #1. All of us considered the assignment to be a slap in the face—a step down, if you will. As a former combat commander he deserved better than that.

On Memorial Day, 30 May, we had a service at the MACV Interfaith Chapel. It turned out to be a very somber event. The names of all those from Advisory Team #1 who had been killed in action during the past year were somberly intoned, with a bell struck as each name was read. May they rest in peace, and may perpetual light shine upon them.

Later that morning, I returned to Cam Lo. The situation had stabilized and was looking somewhat better. It seemed as though practically all of those slated for evacuation from their previous villages and hamlets had now been moved. There appeared to be decent organization of the new community. They had a centrally-located bulletin board where Father Co and others posted notices of community interest. The water situation had definitely improved. They now had three wells that seemed to be functioning reasonably well, although I doubted that they would fulfill the total water needs of the community. Though the wells might provide enough water for drinking and cooking purposes, I doubted they would be sufficient for hygiene and laundry needs. There was abundant food, primarily stocks of rice and fish, but also a little pork and some leafy vegetables.

My biggest concern was the extreme heat. I tried to encourage Father Co to instruct his community that, when they put side walls on their individual homes, they should not run the siding material all the way to the top. I thought that if they left a foot or two open near the top, at that point where the wall adjoined the roof, it would facilitate cross ventilation. They couldn't leave an open space at the bottom of the wall, at ground level, because of rodents and insect infestations. Overall, I was pleased with the progress they had made, and expressed this to Father Co. He, in turn, passed on my comments to those standing around the circle. They all smiled, obviously pleased that someone had noticed the results of their hard work.

I was very displeased, however, with two of the Americans who were ostensibly there to help. They were insensitive, to say the least. They were disrespectful of the women, especially the teenage girls, going so far as to make obscene gestures toward them. Father Co picked up on this immediately. I could see by his eyes that he didn't like it one bit. It hurt him. The two also displayed ignorance of the Vietnamese culture, suggesting things that would obviously violate the dictates of the culture. I didn't know where the two men had come from. One was a lieutenant colonel and the other a sergeant first class. I had never seen either of them before. I voiced my displeasure, but they seemed to blow it off.

To expand on this lack of cultural sensitivity, I observed it quite often among our American military. I don't wish to imply that it was widespread, but it was prevalent enough so that, in my mind, it constituted a significant problem. As advisors, we worked closely with the Vietnamese military, and most of us, if not all, became culturally attuned. Still, a small percentage, perhaps 1 or 2 percent, of the American combatants were insensitive when dealing with the Vietnamese people. Since their interactions were more on a transient basis, I could partially understand this insensitivity. I felt strongly, however, that all U.S. servicemen and women should receive a few hours of instruction, prior to deployment, on the importance of respecting the values and culture of the Vietnamese people. Theirs was an ancient culture. Ours, by comparison, was very new. There seemed to be a bias on the part of some of our troops toward believing that American culture was far superior to Vietnamese, and that the Vietnamese should always bend to the dictates of our culture. This was, in my mind, ethnocentrism in the extreme. I totally disagreed with that line of thought. At the least, I thought, a small handbook addressing the Vietnamese culture, traditions, and values should be printed and distributed to our officers, non-commissioned officers, and enlisted men and women prior to deployment. The handbook could be given to each person being deployed prior to boarding the chartered planes that carried them to war. The long twelve- to thirteen-hour plane ride could then be used productively.

The more I thought about this, the more convinced I became that the shortcoming constituted a significant impediment to winning and maintaining the support of the people. General Westmoreland continued to talk about "winning the hearts and minds of the people." It seemed to me that that was an impossibility unless we Americans got better attuned to the Vietnamese culture and showed respect. I cringed when I saw some of our officers and non-commissioned officers slap the Vietnamese on the back in a Hail Fellow Well Met gesture that, although totally acceptable in our culture, was insulting to the Vietnamese. I knew that a little cultural sensitivity would go a long way. One senior American officer told me, "Piss on them. If they want to be insulted, let them be insulted." Many said, while laughing raucously, "If you want to win the hearts and minds of the people, grab 'em by the balls and jerk. Their hearts and minds will come along with them." One crusty master sergeant in Quang Ngai told me, "Sir, the ARVN enlisted men are all a bunch of queers." When I asked him why he said that, he responded, "Just look at them, walking down the street holding hands." When I pointed out that that was a cultural thing and had nothing to do with their sexuality, he replied, "You don't really believe that shit, do you, sir?" I couldn't even imagine how ineffective these types of soldiers would have been had they been assigned as MACV advisors. I'm not implying that this type of behavior was typical or widespread, but it occurred frequently enough that I thought it constituted a problem.

***

The northern part of South Vietnam continued to be beastly hot as May came to an end. Saigon was starting to cool off, and its monsoon season was expected to start any day. But their monsoon was a far cry from the one that made life so miserable in I Corps. In Saigon, it rained quite hard two or three times almost every day during the monsoon season, but when it was not raining, the sun usually came out. Also, it didn't get numbingly cold as it did in I Corps.

The last day of May dawned blazing hot. It was my daughter Susan's tenth birthday. Susan had been born in Augsburg, Germany, and my wife and I frequently referred to her as our "payday baby" because in those days, soldiers stood in line to receive their pay, in cash, on the last day of each month. I missed my family so much.

On that night, 31 May, there was again no electricity in my hotel. With temperatures hovering around 100 degrees in the daytime and cooling only into the eighties at night, it was very difficult to sleep. Without cross-ventilation and air movement, my room was stifling hot. During that night, I used a small battery-operated fan that my wife had sent. I clipped it to the headboard of my bed and directed the flow of air straight at my head in order to try to get some sleep, but sleep wouldn't come. At about 0200 hours, the power came back on and the slow-moving overhead fan, with my friend the gecko sitting on one of its blades, produced enough ventilation for me to stop perspiring and get some sleep. I could only imagine what the marines sleeping in the boonies were experiencing. I prayed for them.

CHAPTER 12

JUNE 1967

On 1 June, I received encouraging news from my wife about our still fragile son, Michael. His lungs were now functioning at about 80 to 85 percent capacity. We could finally breathe a bit easier. My wife, Patricia, had done such a good job of looking after not only him, but the other five children as well.

On that same day, I wrote and told her that we had to tighten our belts. Our cost of living allowance of seventy-five dollars per month for service in Vietnam had been taken away. The day prior, 31 May, had been payday, and the change was reflected on my pay voucher.

We were again having medical supply problems. MACV Advisory Team #1 was supposed to receive its medical supplies, used to stock the dispensaries that treated the members of Advisory Team #1, from the navy. But the navy's accounting system didn't make allowances for supporting anyone other than the navy and marines. The navy was threatening to cut us off and force us to get our medical supplies from the nearest U.S. Army supply depot, which was a considerable distance away in Qui Nhon, a city outside of I Corps. This didn't make sense and my commander, Colonel Hamblen, was fuming about it. I met with two navy logisticians that morning to try to hammer out some kind of a deal. I hated to leave my replacement with such a mess.

As previously mentioned, I was very concerned about the lack of overlap with my replacement, Major Stoltz. It seemed so unfair for him to have to struggle while trying to determine the background of some of my decisions, Also, my network of contacts throughout I Corps would be unknown to him. I simply couldn't ask SFC Simmons, my NCOIC, to take on the task of comprehensively orienting him on all the nuances, sensitivities, and complexities of my duties and responsibilities.

What I had been thinking about for several days, and finally decided to do, was seek permission to bring Captain Len Schumacher to Da Nang from Quang Ngai to work with me during the three weeks prior to my departure. He could then orient Major Stoltz upon his eventual arrival before returning to Quang Ngai. I discussed this with Captain Schumacher, and he told me he would welcome the opportunity to work at corps level. He had a very capable NCOIC whom he felt certain could handle matters in Quang Ngai during his absence. I ran this plan by Colonel Hamblen, and he gave it his approval. He volunteered to call Colonel Ulsaker, senior advisor to the ARVN 2nd Infantry Division in Quang Ngai, and explain to him the necessity of having Captain Schumacher in Da Nang for a few weeks.

Bob Helton's replacement, Captain Charles Delane, arrived in Da Nang during the night of 2 June. My first impressions of him were very positive. He was seemingly in excellent physical condition, had done his homework, and had a positive attitude. My impressions were formed while enjoying a bowl of pretzels and a couple of beers after his late night arrival. He had big shoes to fill. I told him that as a newly assigned officer he had only one chance to make a good first impression and that he had done so.

The next day, Saturday, 3 June, Captain Delane was fully engaged in administrative processing and attending briefings on the current tactical situation in the upper two provinces of I Corps, Quang Tri and Thua Tin, his area of responsibility. I spent several hours with him explaining our medical advisory operation and how he and I were to interface.

That afternoon, Captain Schumacher flew to Da Nang from Quang Ngai. I knew that he had a pretty hot temper and that it sometimes got in the way of getting things done. I counseled him about this shortcoming, and he told me that his immediate boss in Quang Ngai had done likewise. I was hoping he could hold down the fort and not ruffle too many feathers until Dick Stoltz arrived and took over.

Our clerk typist, SP-4 Behner, was promoted to SP-5 on Saturday, 3 June. It was quite an accomplishment for a soldier with just a little over two years in the army. His being rapidly promoted could at least partially be attributed to being at the right place at the right time. That always helped, but coupled with that, he had well-developed clerical skills, a strong desire to learn more about the army way of doing things, and a terrific attitude. Also, and of importance, he had never missed a day of work. We could rely on him being there to do his job. I had been encouraging him to go to college after his service obligation was fulfilled. He had an outdoor promotion party early that afternoon and I stopped by for a beer and hamburger, along with Captains Delane and Schumacher. He was pleased that we had come by to meet his friends.

After SP-5 Behner's promotion party, I met with Captains Delane and Schumacher to discuss the Cam Lo settlement. I told them that I was going to take them to the site the next day and that I wanted them to pay particular attention to everything that was said and done, and to ask any and all questions that came to mind. This was to be my last visit to the refugee settlement. I wanted to insure that both of them were thoroughly read in on what was going on up there. We had invested a lot of time, effort, and sweat in trying to insure its success and had developed a fondness for the people. I wanted to do everything I could to ensure that the settlement was properly supported. Father Co had worked long and hard to meet the needs of his people, but I knew in my heart that he alone wouldn't be able to keep it all together without continuing ARVN and U.S support. The U.S. military had insisted, for humanitarian reasons, that the people be relocated so the free fire zone could be established. In my mind, we now owed those who inhabited the settlement our continued support. That was the message I tried to impart to Captains Delane and Schumacher during that Saturday afternoon in the hope that they would accurately and strongly pass it on to Major Stoltz upon his arrival in Da Nang.

That evening, our monthly hail and farewell party was held at the Officers' Club. All of the "newbies," those who had arrived during the preceding month of May, were hailed, and all of those scheduled to depart during the month of June were farewelled. Colonel Hamblen embarrassed me. His words about my work were a little too flowery. The best part of the evening was the floor show. A New Zealand group that was touring the country performed at the club that evening. Six men and one woman put on a terrific show. The woman's violent hip action during a Tahitian dance number caused quite a stir. Everyone enjoyed the entire group, but mostly her.

When I arrived at my office on Sunday morning, 4 June, I received some good news about the Cam Lo settlement. The staff duty officer told me that a decision had been made to dam the Cam Lo River, which was about 1,000 yards from the refugee settlement, and then to run a pipeline from the river to a 32,000-gallon tank that would be placed in the middle of the refugee settlement. The water, although not potable, would serve their sanitation, hygiene, and laundry needs.

Prior to takeoff for Cam Lo, I was able to get a seat on the plane for Master Sergeant Parrish, the man who would serve as Captain Delane's NCOIC. Captain Delane had never met him until we stopped in Hue and Sergeant Parrish climbed aboard the aircraft. Cam Lo was within Captain Delane's and Sergeant Parrish's geographic area of responsibility, and I wanted to make certain they were aware of the continuing support the project would need. Clearly, I was emotionally involved with the project. Precisely why this was the case I wasn't quite certain. It probably resulted from General Walt's strong words to me about the importance of the project.

I was very pleased with the way things had developed at Cam Lo. There had been a sense of shared responsibility among the ARVN, civilian public health officials, and MACV. We hadn't been able to attain this level of cooperation very often during my eleven plus months in country. It was gratifying to see how things were coming along. I was invited into four or five of the newly constructed homes on that day. Although all felt unbearably hot to me, no one seemed to be complaining. When I met with Father Co, I highlighted the progress and praised his efforts, as well as those of the settlement's organizing committee. Captains Schumacher and Delane, who were seeing the project for the first time, did likewise.

The nuns in the dispensary were currently fighting an outbreak of rubella, commonly called measles. The disease that those in the settlement were experiencing seemed more virulent and serious than the one I remembered having as a kid. It was producing very high temperatures, especially among the children. Most of those with rubella also seemed to have conjunctivitis. The eyes of many of the children were inflamed and full of pus. Communicable diseases were a constant threat in a refugee population. The civilian public health officials from Quang Tri Province, who were on the scene, didn't seem overly concerned. They thought the outbreak would soon run its course.

There appeared to be plenty of food and water. We watched an elderly man prepare a feast. A young heifer had been killed before we arrived. The man was just about finished roasting the entire carcass when we got there. When he determined that the flesh was cooked throughout, the carcass was removed from the open fire, and the man started scraping the hair off the hide with a big machete-like knife. When we left, the hide still remained on the carcass. Dozens of children circled the pit while the man was working, fascinated by the carcass and the process of preparing the flesh to eat, as kids would be anywhere.

Image 35. Cam Lo refugee scraping hair off of a roasted heifer

Photo courtesy of the author

That day was quite an introduction to Vietnam for Captain Delane. He told me later that he never envisioned his job would entail the things we were doing. While riding in the helicopter on the way to Cam Lo, we saw several bombing runs, as well as exploding artillery rounds. It almost seemed surreal. We were sitting in a helicopter, 1,500 feet above the earth, and would suddenly see a plane come in, release its payload of bombs, and then accelerate to get out of there. Then we would see the telltale puffs of smoke and knew that something, perhaps a cache of ammunition or other supplies, was being destroyed.

After observing Captain Delane for two days, I felt very good about his serving as an advisor. He asked pertinent questions and didn't pretend to have all the answers, as some newly assigned officers did. He was humble but had confidence in his own abilities. I liked the fact that he kept himself in superb physical condition. I noted that he interacted well with the ARVN officers to whom I introduced him. This was a very good sign.

Starting on Monday, 5 June, I took Captain Schumacher to every nook and cranny of I Corps. I wanted to orient him to the job as thoroughly as I possibly could. I had long thought that the orientation phase of a new assignment was vitally important. Frequently, it set the tone for the future and was especially helpful in the determination of priorities. I wanted him to meet the key players, the decision-makers, face-to-face and in the work environment. It was one thing to meet an officer or NCO socially, but the person was really an unknown entity until you had the opportunity to interact with him or her in the work environment. I found that that was where you could truly take the measure of the person.

That morning, as on all Monday mornings, we had a formation during which we had to listen to a weekly wrap-up of war related news presented over loudspeakers. Only a very few of the advisors spoke Vietnamese, so for most of the Americans the session was boring. I kept thinking of all of the things I should be doing instead of standing there in that formation. It was mandatory for all ARVN officers and enlisted men assigned to I Corps HQ and highly encouraged for American advisors. Colonel Hamblen always insisted that we have good representation at those Monday morning news reading sessions. Apparently, General Lam, the I Corps Commander, thought they were important from a morale and esprit perspective. I thought it ridiculous that we should have to attend. I had expressed my views to Colonel Hamblen but he told me yet again, "Stop your whining."

The intensity of the war had picked up throughout all of South Vietnam. It was especially bloody for the Americans. We were told, on that Monday morning, that the week just past had produced the second highest American casualty count of the entire war. The resolve shown by the VC and NVA seemed stronger than ever. I could see it in the eyes of the enemy soldiers imprisoned in the POW camp across the river. I was hoping that there were diplomatic initiatives being put on the table that I was unaware of. We all sensed that the support of the American people was slipping, and, as casualty counts continued to mount, I knew the downward slope of their support would accelerate. Ever since the Civil War, a war that produced more dead and wounded than all our other wars combined, we as a nation have had a rightful aversion to casualties. The enormous number of casualties produced during that war continued to haunt us as a nation.

On 6 June, I participated in an awards ceremony during which I was awarded an Air Medal. The Public Information Officer asked me to fill out a form allowing him to send information about the award to my hometown newspapers, the *Appleton Post Crescent* and the *Seymour Press*. I declined. I thought the good people in my home village, Black Creek, Wisconsin, had probably read enough about me, as several articles about my work had been published in the local papers. The Air Medal was awarded to those servicemen and women who had over 100 hours of logged flight time over hostile terrain. I had exceeded that criterion by a bunch.

On that day, I had yet another Saigon Cowboy with me while trying to orient Captain Schumacher to my duties. I had decided that the best way to orient him was simply to have him tag along, meeting the people and listening to the dialogue, after which I would attempt to put it all in perspective before we moved on to the next interaction.

The visitor from Saigon was Master Sergeant Cavanaugh, an old and trusted NCO friend. He was sent to I Corps to take a look at all the MILPHAP teams with a view toward assessing logistical and maintenance support. Any help he could provide would be greatly appreciated, for the support they were now receiving from the NSA, although improved, was still below standard. I was very disappointed in the Navy's unwillingness to step up to the plate and fully accept the MILPHAP support mission. Generally, the Navy did an outstanding job in the supply and maintenance areas, but for some inexplicable reason they had rebelled over the assigned MILPHAP mission. They kept telling me that it was not directly related to the war. If the treatment of civilian casualties was not directly related to the war, what pray tell was?

On that same Tuesday morning, Duy Tan Hospital took over two of its newly renovated buildings. I was pleased to see at least a part of the major construction project completed before my departure. Captain Phat, Major Tu and I had put a lot of time and effort into getting the project launched.

The ARVN hospitals remained depressingly crowded. Some of the things I saw on a daily basis were heart-rending, to say the least. While I was at Duy Tan Hospital with Captain Schumacher on 6 June, five U.S. Marine helicopters landed and disgorged their cargo of maimed and wounded. Several civilians were among the wounded, which was fairly typical. Usually, wounded children would just lie there motionless, with their big eyes looking impassively upward. It got to me every time. On that day, 6 June, I observed a young woman, perhaps nineteen or twenty years old, who was holding an obviously dead baby as she was offloaded from a helicopter. The young mother would not concede that her baby had died. She clutched the lifeless body to her chest. A U.S. Navy corpsman gently helped her off the helicopter as she clung to her deceased child. Those were the tragedies of war few Americans ever witnessed, but I saw all too frequently.

On Wednesday, 7 June, I received an early morning phone call from Colonel Hamblen informing me that the *Helgoland* was coming to Da Nang. He was elated, as was I. Colonel Hamblen wasn't certain when the ship would be moved from Saigon to Da Nang, but the Germans had made a firm decision to move it. Colonel Hamblen thanked me for the small role I had played in helping to convince German authorities to move the ship.[1]

Image 36. The German hospital ship, the *Helgoland*, docked in Saigon harbor

Photo courtesy of the author

That day and the next were spent trying, as best I could, to acquaint Captain Schumacher with my responsibilities in Da Nang. We moved throughout the city, visiting the I Corps Surgeon, all the ARVN medical units, public health officials in the city, the U.S. Air Force Casualty Staging Facility, several offices in I Corps HQ, III MAF HQ, NSA HQ, the USAID Hospital, the U.S. Navy Hospital, and several other organizations and individuals. Captain Schumacher told me he was a bit overwhelmed. I insisted he take detailed notes, which we reviewed for accuracy and completeness each night after eating dinner.

On the morning of Thursday, 8 June, I came to the office at the usual time, about 0500. I had just gotten a pot of coffee going when Colonel Beeson, the deputy commander, called from the command suite and asked that I come up. When I arrived in his office, he offered me a cup of coffee and asked if I had a few minutes to talk. Almost two hours later, I finally got out of his office, and then had to hurry over to the

Visiting Officers' Quarters to pick up Captain Schumacher. Colonel Beeson and I had discussed all the medical projects and initiatives we had going. He expressed great concern because he had just seen the letter Colonel Hamblen had received stating that it was not possible to get Major Stoltz to Da Nang before my departure. Colonel Beeson seemed less than convinced that Captain Schumacher could adequately orient Major Stoltz upon his arrival. I tried to reassure him that it would work, but when I left his office, he was still skeptical. I'm sure his concern was partially related to the fact that he was to take command of MACV Advisory Team #1 upon Colonel Hamblen's departure. Colonel Beeson had voluntarily extended his own tour of duty in Vietnam to have the opportunity for a senior-level command position.

Captain Schumacher and I spent the day of 8 June in Quang Ngai and Tam Ky, departing Da Nang shortly after my meeting with Colonel Beeson. The ride to those cities was again almost surreal. Len Schumacher and I were sitting in the helicopter, flying at about 1,500 feet, when all of a sudden we saw shells bursting in the wide mouth of a river at the point where it entered the South China Sea. As we observed and studied the scene below us, we noted that there was a U.S. Navy vessel lying two to three miles offshore. The shelling was clearly coming from that vessel. Then, we noted that there were four sampans on the river, feverishly trying to escape the shelling by heading inland up the river from the coast. Shells continued to fall among the sampans. One sampan pitched violently to the side. More shells exploded nearby, and the sampan that had pitched to the side began to sink. Then, another was partially crippled by the shelling. Simultaneously, an air strike came in. Four jet aircraft start plastering the remaining sampans with all they had. Soon all sampans were crippled and two were sunk. We could actually see people diving from the sampans into the water. What precisely was going on, we did not know. All we could speculate was that the four sampans were trying to run arms and ammunition into Vietnam from the north, but we had no way to verify this speculation.

It was the first and only time I witnessed that type of coordinated combat activity on the part of the Navy and the Air Force. It was almost as if we were sitting in a theater watching a movie. From our vantage point, we could see it all unfold. I was wearing a headset, so I could also hear the dialogue between the pilot and co-pilot as they watched the drama below. They were sitting in the bubble, where they noticed things that I did not, so I appreciated their commentary.

The visits to Quang Ngai and Tam Ky went well. Even though we were in cities that Len Schumacher was very familiar with, his home turf so to speak, he had not met some of the key people in the province hospitals, including one of the newly assigned MILPHAP team commanders. On the way back to Da Nang, we stopped in Chu Lai and met several of the U.S. Army Medical Department officers assigned to Task Force Oregon, a growing presence in I Corps. One of them, an army MSC officer by the name of LTC Anistranski, angered me with his attitude toward our allies, the ARVN. I couldn't understand how some officers, admittedly a very small percentage, could be so callous. The United States had not entered the war because it was compelled to do so, or even because it was invited to do so. We entered of our own volition. We chose to enter the war because we thought it was in our national interest to do so. When President Kennedy committed large numbers of advisors to the war, and President Johnson upped the ante by sending in combat forces, we signaled our clear intent to wage war as an ally of the Republic of Vietnam. Why should we now denigrate our ally? This was, in my opinion, stupidity of the first order. While the ARVN assuredly had shortcomings and deficiencies, I felt duty-bound to help them improve instead of simply writing them off as being an incompetent, unmotivated fighting force.

The day of Friday, 9 June, was spent in and around Hue. As were most trips away from my home base of Da Nang, the trip to Hue was eventful. It was raining as we boarded the aircraft, but not too hard. As we approached the Hai Van Pass, the weather started closing in on us. The pilot thought he could beat the worsening weather through the pass. When we got about halfway through, the weather turned decidedly worse. There was a dangerously low ceiling and not much visibility. After a couple of changes in altitude and direction, the pilot found an opening and we got through the pass, only to find that the weather beyond the pass was equally as bad or worse. The pilot tried to retreat back through the pass to the safety of Da Nang, but that didn't work either. He then headed out to sea and, while flying at a very low altitude, followed the jagged coastline. We had two passengers on board who had to be dropped off at Phu Bai, which lies about ten miles south of Hue. In order to get to Phu Bai we had to fly inland, at a very low altitude, for eight to ten miles.

When we took off from Phu Bai, I showed Len Schumacher the sign on the side of the runway that had an arrow pointing east and a bold hand-lettered inscription reading: Chicago 10,657 miles. He laughed, as did all Americans who saw it. The humor seemed to escape the Vietnamese.

The visit to Nguyen Tri Phuong Station Hospital was a bit disconcerting. Although I had asked Captain Nhan, the I Corps Surgeon, to call in advance and tell the commander we were coming and the purpose of our visit, the hospital commander chose to be away. We were briefed and escorted through the hospital by the hospital adjutant. I told Captain Schumacher that this was the ARVN medical unit that gave me the greatest concern in all of I Corps. As we were returning to Da Nang, I thought more about that troubled hospital and specifically ordered Captain Schumacher to relay my apprehensions to Major Stoltz.

***

One of the programs that pleased me immensely was the children's corrective surgery program, Project Help, that Dr. John Henry Giles and I had spearheaded during our time together in Da Nang. Dr. Giles had returned to the United States by this point, but there were other surgeons who willingly took on the duties implicit in the program. As a measure of the program's success, for the months of April and May, I had been publishing occasional notices in the I Corps Daily Bulletin asking anyone who knew of a child with a harelip, a club foot, an external growth, or a mangled limb to call my office in order to have the child evaluated by a Navy physician. We were now having to advertise in order to keep the surgeons busy. Children with highly visible deformities were becoming difficult to find. As I introduced Len Schumacher to several of the newly assigned surgeons, I remembered clearly my initial meeting with Dr. Giles when he told me that war was episodic in nature. He proved to be absolutely correct. What a good and decent human being he was.

By mid-June, the members of MACV Advisory Team #1 had seen several newspaper articles about General Walt and his new assignment as Director of Personnel for the USMC. We were told that more articles, questioning the assignment even more rigorously, had been published in the United States. His new assignment seemed to be a slap in the face. We had no way of knowing if the Marine Corps was treating him shabbily or if there was something more behind the assignment. All I knew for certain, based on about ten months of observation, was that he was a very compassionate and good man and a respected commander. I personally liked him very much. I found him to be highly moral and a dedicated Marine Corps officer. He cared about his marines. I was told that he was the sixth of thirteen children in the Walt family. I had personally seen, on several occasions, his steel blue-gray eyes moisten up when reports of Marine casualties came to his attention or when he went to the Navy Hospital to pin Purple Hearts on the wounded. I also saw, on one occasion, those same steel blue-gray eyes turn ice cold when he was chewing out an officer whom he thought was derelict in his duties. I didn't know enough about war strategy or tactics to even comment on his performance in those areas, but I did know, with certainty, that he and General Westmoreland did not see eye-to-eye on how to prosecute the war. Whether that was the reason he was seemingly being pushed aside I did not know. But it pained me that he had to go through such a messy ordeal regarding his assignment. He deserved better. I felt as though we greatly needed more military officers with his high level of integrity and dedication. I also felt that history would vindicate him insofar as his disagreement with General Westmoreland.

***

On Monday, 12 June, I received a letter from my wife informing me that our infant son was sick once again. He had a 103-degree fever and a sore throat, and she was very concerned. She had immediately taken him to a military pediatrician at Brooke Army Medical Center, where he was placed on antibiotics. In just a little over a week, he would be two years old, and, since his lungs were still not functioning at full capacity, we knew we had to be careful.

My maid, God love her, gave me a hand-written note on 12 June requesting that before departing I give her an electric fan. It was customary for departing officers and non-commissioned officers, members of our Advisory Team, to give their faithful maids a small gift upon departure. I decided to buy a fan for her, even though it was in violation of a military regulation. When we purchased any item in the BX costing over ten dollars, we had to certify, in writing, that it was for our personal use. Why this regulation was put into effect, I do not know. Practically everyone I knew violated the regulation to some degree. It was an unenforceable regulation and, in my mind, unenforceable regulations should not be published. Bá Vy's note requesting the fan hit me in the soft spot. The note was all about her small, hot home and her ten children.

***

I realized that I had fallen into some bad dietary habits that I had to change. I had been eating only one decent meal a day, the evening meal, plus a cookie or candy bar in the morning and at noon. And I had been drinking far too much coffee. It was a bad combination, a poor diet and too much caffeine. I had lost a lot of weight in the past eleven months as a result of that poor diet and frequent bouts of diarrhea. I came to this realization when I went to the beach on Sunday afternoon, 11 June. My swim trunks were far too big and almost fell off during our touch football game. Then, when I was at the Navy Hospital on 12

June, I stepped on a scale and was startled to see that I was down to 138 pounds from my normal 162.

***

For the past week, I Corps had been comparatively quiet, with virtually no large-scale confrontations. The war planners felt strongly that the VC and NVA had simply backed off to regroup, resupply, and rest their forces before starting another large-scale offensive. God only knew where and when that would happen. They had the significant advantage of being able to choose the place and time to engage our forces. They were able to disengage and withdraw into the hamlets and villages, hide their meager equipment, and blend in with the population. Or they could slip into Laos, or cross into the DMZ, and feel reasonably confident we would not pursue.

On 14 June, I sent my wife several photos taken at a brief ceremony at Duy Tan Hospital. Four additional TV sets had been donated by CARE, the worldwide charitable organization. CARE officials specifically requested that the ARVN Officers' Wives' Club make the presentation to the patients. One photo showed Madame Lam making the presentation with several wives of ARVN officers proudly standing alongside her. My wife commented that all the women in the photo were very beautiful. In another of the photos, I was seated alongside John Frechette, CARE's representative in Vietnam. He was a delightful man. I had spoken with him at several social events and had always enjoyed the lively conversation.

The flambeaus—the Vietnamese called them rain flowers—were all ablaze in Da Nang. I found them to be very enticing. I often wished I could bottle up some of the scent they produced. The aroma of the blooms was most pleasant when sitting on the balcony of our hotel.

On 15 June, I was sitting at my desk, reflecting on the current status of our medical advisory team in I Corps. The team was, at that time, authorized fifty enlisted men and four officers. We had a full complement of officers and were one enlisted man over authorized strength. Upon his arrival, Major Stoltz would have a full complement of men, plus a top-flight NCOIC in SFC Simmons. Also, I knew that Chuck Delane, in Hue, would prove to be a strong replacement for Bob Helton. I felt confident I was leaving Major Stoltz a solid team.

I hearkened back to the previous fall, when at one time, we were at 45 percent of authorized enlisted strength. When the sub-sector advisory teams didn't have an assigned medic, they were exceedingly vulnerable. We had been most fortunate. The NCOIC and I had guessed right in every instance. Without exception, every time an advisor assigned to a sub-sector advisory team was wounded, we had had a medic on the team. How lucky could we get? Someone had to be smiling down on us when we decided which sub-sectors had to go without a medic during the prolonged period when we were so short staffed.

The war had been very quiet in I Corps during the past ten days, giving the ARVN an opportunity to free up some hospital beds and get ready for the next wave of wounded that would assuredly come. The people responsible for studying such things told us that the enemy was simply regrouping and resupplying during that relatively pacific period. When would he choose to strike again? It seemed my guess was as good as anyone else's.

On Friday, 16 June, Captain Schumacher and I flew to Quang Tri. While there, we visited all ARVN medical units in and around the city, as well as the Quang Tri Province Hospital. That visit gave me not only the opportunity to again emphasize to Captain Schumacher the vital role played by the province hospitals, but also to say goodbye to Captain Pittard. Before leaving Quang Tri, we also visited the refugee settlement that was essentially the Buddhist counterpart to the Christian settlement at Cam Lo. I could readily see why the ARVN and U.S. had given relatively little attention to the Quang Tri settlement. The predominantly Buddhist population in the city had set up its own support system and the refugees were seemingly being resettled in a very efficient and effective manner. There was no need for additional ARVN or U.S. support.

In a letter received from my wife on that same day, she mildly chastised me for my less than enthusiastic reaction to having been awarded an Air Medal. I responded by writing to her, "I deserved no special recognition for my hours in the air. All I did was sit in an airplane or helicopter while being transported from one location to another. The people who deserved recognition for flight hours logged over hostile terrain were the pilots, co-pilots and crew members. The passengers did nothing, for the most part, other than sit there and observe." I had long felt, and I still feel, that the Air Medal should be awarded only to pilots, co-pilots, and crew members.

I went on to tell my wife of a fairly common practice of passengers in small aircraft or helicopters while in Vietnam. Many passengers, me included, sat on their flak jackets while flying. Why? Because we thought it would give us some limited protection from ground fire that might penetrate the belly of the aircraft. Although I had no idea how much protection the flak jacket would actually provide, I was certain it would provide some.

That evening, Friday, 16 June, I asked the NCOs who were a part of our medical advisory team, along with my good and faithful ARVN driver/interpreter, Sergeant Thong, to join me on the balcony of my hotel for a couple of beers or sodas, some peanuts, pretzels, chips and dips, and some lively conversation. I hired the Vietnamese chef at the Officers' Club to whip up some special dips for the occasion. I didn't know what the ingredients were, and maybe didn't want to know, but the dips he occasionally prepared for promotion parties and special celebrations were very tasty. Since I owed much to this fine group of non-commissioned officers, I wanted to express my heartfelt thanks and appreciation to them. I would miss each of them. Sergeant Thong told me earlier that day that he "learned many big lesson from Thieu Ta Van Straten." If he only knew how much I had learned from him.

Prior to my departure, I had given a lot of thought to the year I spent in Vietnam, summarizing in my head what I had seen and experienced. I wondered if my viewpoints were commonly held. As a non-combatant, a medic, I probably saw things through a different filter. Be that as it may, I had come to at least one firm conclusion. For the most part, military officers and non-commissioned officers were a pretty honorable group of people. There was a certain bond that caused us to look out for one another. True, there were exceptions. But, based on my limited experience, I had concluded that military officers could be placed in one of three separate and distinct categories.

Category #1 consisted of those officers who went about doing their jobs to the best of their ability. They knew what they were doing. They operated within the rules of land warfare. They were ethical and truthful. They made rational decisions based on the facts available. They looked out for the welfare of their soldiers. In this category I placed about 93 to 94 percent of all the officers I had met during my eleven-year military career.

In Category #2 were those officers who, although good and decent men and women, probably would be better off in civilian life. Their temperaments were such that they would never be good at the decision-making process, a process that was so vital in the military, especially in combat. They were indecisive. They dithered and dathered over even minor decisions. They insisted on volumes of information before making even minor decisions. They were overly concerned that feelings would be hurt if they made decisions contrary to popular opinion. Their indecisiveness frequently had dire consequences and was on occasion deadly. They were good people, but they didn't belong in the military. I could only hope that the "up or out" policies of the military would catch up to these officers and steer them into other professions or occupations. To a degree, I pitied these officers. I had met quite a number of them. I would place about 5 to 6 percent of all the officers I had met in this category. I hoped for the sake of the military that the system would ferret them out and steer them away from a full military career.

And in the last category, Category #3, the smallest but most dangerous category of all, I placed about 1 percent of all the officers I had met, maybe even less than 1 percent. The officers in this category would sell their souls to the devil for military advancement in rank. They were not dumb, in fact they were often quite intelligent, and they did their homework. They understood the military culture and ethos, and they purposely tried to manipulate it to their personal advantage. They were dangerous. Many of them were narcissistic. Self-advancement meant everything to them. Frequently their seniors didn't see through their narcissism, but it didn't take their subordinates long to realize they were dealing with seriously flawed leaders.

During my eleven-year career, I had never worked directly for an officer whom I would place in Category #3, but I knew quite a number of them. I avoided them as much as possible. On two occasions, however, prior to arriving in Vietnam, I had worked for officers that I would definitely place in Category #2. I liked them as people, but not as military officers. In the work environment, they could be most exasperating. I had been thinking of these categories for quite some time, even prior to combat, and had often wondered if others categorized military officers in a similar manner. Maybe it was just me.

On Saturday, 17 June, as I prepared to go to the Saturday morning staff meeting, it suddenly dawned on me that this would be my last weekend in Da Nang. I had sought and was granted special permission to allow Len Schumacher to attend the staff meeting. He was eager to see the differences between a division-level meeting and one conducted at corps level. I was hoping that both Lieutenant General Cushman, who had by that time been promoted and replaced General Walt as the senior American commander, and General Lam would be in attendance, and they were. The presence of a flag-rank officer had a tendency to elevate the conduct and discourse of the meeting.

During the staff meeting, it was reported that problems had arisen at the Cam Lo refugee settlement. Recent heavy rains had washed all sorts of debris into the Cam Lo River. They now depended on water from the river for sanitation and laundry needs. The water had become very muddy, and to compound matters, the wells that had been dug were proving insufficient for meeting their needs for drinking and cooking water. Consequently, despite our warnings not to do so, they had been using water out of the river to drink and cook. The result was that many, perhaps most, were suffering from raging diarrhea. Public health officials and engineers were reviewing the situation to see if there was a safer source of water. The settlement required a huge amount of water to fully meet the needs of its 17,000 to 18,000 inhabitants.

Complicating matters even further for the ARVN and for our advisory team was a growing refugee problem in Nghia Hanh, a district to the south of Quang Ngai City. Almost 10,000 poor souls were expected to pour into that area during the next few weeks. I was told, but was unable to verify, that many of them, perhaps most, were tragically poor family members of the enemy, the Viet Cong. Those who had arrived thus far were in pathetic shape, with all sorts of intestinal parasites and untreated medical conditions. It seemed strange that scarce South Vietnamese resources would have to be expended to meet the medical and nutritional needs of families of the enemy, but humanity itself demanded that they be treated, sheltered, and fed. I had been trying, as John Hennigan had ordered, to disengage totally and let Captain Schumacher be the interface with the ARVN, but it was tough to do when situations such as this arose.

As I sat there in the staff meeting, thinking about my year at war that was about to come to an end, I again realized how fortunate I had been to be in an assignment that had allowed me to see and experience practically all of I Corps. I believed that, at that point, I knew as much or more about the total medical situation throughout the five province area that comprised I Corps as any other person. I had worked with and experienced medical and other humanitarian support efforts offered by Vietnamese civilian agencies, the ARVN, three branches of the U.S. military, the Free World military, USAID, and Catholic Relief Services. I had observed, to a very limited degree, the medical support systems of the VC and the NVA. I had mentioned this to Colonel Hamblen a few days prior and he responded, "I believe you, lad. That's just another reason why we should keep you over here for awhile." I backed off that conversation in a hurry. Colonel Hamblen, by the way, called every officer who was serving in the rank of major or below "lad" if he was pleased with their job performance.

After the staff meeting, Len Schumacher and I spent much of the morning wrapping up some administrative items that were begging for attention. Later that morning, he and I were involved in a couple of first class flaps that gave him a splitting headache. I didn't have the heart to tell him that the types of verbal altercations we had experienced that morning were fairly routine during a typical day's work. At that moment, the tactical situation was calm, but I knew it wouldn't remain that way for very long.

That afternoon, the G-4 Advisory Section threw a going away party for me. I joked that I didn't know if it was to show their appreciation for what I had done to elevate the level of discourse in the office, or to celebrate the fact that I was finally leaving. We were to be treated to grilled steaks, baked potatoes, beer or soft drinks, and combat volleyball—a tough combination to beat. I wrote earlier in this memoir that the only rule for combat volleyball was that there were no rules. That had now been changed. We had established one rule: "It doesn't matter how hard you slam into the net or one of your opponents as long as you make contact with the ball." Making contact with the ball became an end unto itself.

It hardly seemed possible that my year at war was coming to an end. But that reality was hard to escape at the farewell party. That afternoon, people from my section— officers, non-commissioned officers, and enlisted men—were saying goodbye and wishing me Godspeed. John Hennigan gave a very touching speech about me and the contributions I had made. I reciprocated with a speech of my own. I told them that if I were to stand before them and tell them that I was sorry to be going home, I'd be guilty of telling them an untruth. But if I were to stand before them and tell them that I was sorry to be severing friendships with many of them, I'd be telling an absolute truth. That set the tempo of my remarks, which were probably too long but seemed to be appreciated. The steaks were delicious, the beer was cold, and the volleyball game was, as expected, rough. We all had a good time.

Sunday, 18 June, was Father's Day back in the United States of America. I had received cards and thoughtful handwritten notes from my wife and four of our children. The two youngest drew pictures of our family on vacation with a little assistance from their older sisters. I missed them all very much. I had been absent for a year of their lives, and I wondered if the two youngest children, our two sons, would even recognize me.

Shortly after Sunday morning Mass, followed by breakfast, I headed to China Beach for one last swim. Even at that early hour, about 1030, there must have been eight to ten thousand marines on the beach. I was pleased, because God only knew how much they needed a fun-filled break. Since the city of Da Nang was still off limits, there wasn't a whole lot for young marines to do on a Sunday. On many Sundays, they were slogging through the rice paddies or battling the mosquitoes in the jungles. They deserved some time off.

***

The jets were screaming off the runway of Da Nang Air Base early Monday morning, 19 June. As they took off, I always wondered where they were going and what their targets might be. When I arrived at the office, I was saddened by the news that Major Bonnette, a good and respected man, had lost the front half of his left foot when he stepped on an anti-personnel mine near Cam Lo. He was up there trying to help the refugees. While walking toward one of the field latrines, he stepped on the mine. He was somewhat fortunate that the explosion had not cost him his life. The war for him was over.

Later that morning, I had a very important meeting concerning support of the MILPHAP teams. The NSA, Da Nang, officials had gotten turned down by MACV HQ on their request to be relieved of the mission to provide full maintenance and logistical support to the MILPHAP teams.

They had asked me to describe for them how I envisioned that mission being accomplished and how much support was required. John Hennigan said I should let Captain Schumacher handle the meeting by himself, but I just couldn't do that. I knew it would be a tense situation and possibly confrontational. I had been crossing swords with officers in the NSA for about six months over this issue and I thought I'd better be the lead horse at the meeting and let Captain Schumacher be a spectator.

Also on that day, I sent my wife a newspaper clipping showing a picture of Father Co and a brief article presenting basic information about him. The information I had passed on to my wife earlier had been correct. Father Co did indeed flee North Vietnam with his parishioners to escape Communist harassment and religious persecution. The move to Cam Lo had been the fourth that his group had made since leaving their ancestral villages in North Vietnam. How long ago they had left North Vietnam, I could not ascertain. What a courageous man he was, and his parishioners as well. The last time I saw him, I wished him well. I told him that I'd pray for him and the good people at Cam Lo. Being a small man, he reached up to put his hand on my forehead, smiled at me, and then gave me the traditional Catholic blessing. It almost brought tears to my eyes. Here I was about to go home to the land of plenty while he and his parishioners had virtually nothing in terms of material goods. All they had was each other, their faith in God, and a lot of trust in the future.

The few days I had left in country weren't seemingly enough to do all the things that still needed doing. Before the arrival of Captain Schumacher, I had prepared a list of forty-seven people I wanted him to meet. As of Tuesday, 20 June, I had only been able to track down nineteen of them. There was still much to do.

That evening, I had a wonderful time at a farewell dinner in my honor hosted by the Vietnamese military medical community. The cuisine in the Te Gioi Restaurant was quite exquisite and the decor was stunning. It always surprised me to walk into a beautifully decorated

Vietnamese restaurant when the exterior of the building looked so plain and unappealing.

After dinner, Major Tu made a very touching speech, perhaps a little too flowery, but I appreciated his sentiments. During my response, I got a little choked up. I just hated the thought that, as I prepared to go home, they had to soldier on for God only knew how long. They faced a very uncertain future. I couldn't quite understand how they kept their spirits as high as they did.

They then presented me with several mementos. Among them was a figurine depicting a Vietnamese man and woman carved out of the horn of some animal. It was a very attractive piece of craftsmanship and became even more special when I was told that it was carved by Dr. Luong, one of the skilled surgeons on the Duy Tan staff.

In keeping with their social customs, there were no women in attendance. I still had never met Major Tu's spouse. I had worked with him for a year, and we had become trusted friends, but I had never met his wife or any of his six children. Most Vietnamese professionals kept their private lives just that—private.

As I later lay in bed reflecting on the dinner party, the artillery on the perimeter of the city pounded away. It went on for much of the night. I didn't know what was going on, but felt it was probably harassing and interdiction fire. Big artillery guns were located fairly close to Da Nang. They fired at known or suspected avenues of infiltration to deny the enemy access to those routes. What always bothered me was the "what if" question. What if a family or a friendly, old man had not been forewarned and inadvertently decided to use one of those routes? Horror the thought.

On 21 June, John Hennigan showed me a copy of the statistical recap of the war for the months of April and May 1967. During that two-month period, 46 percent of all VC or NVA incidents in all of South Vietnam occurred in I Corps, the smallest of the four corps areas. During those two months, 64 percent of all the enemy dead were killed in I Corps.

And, sadly, 54 percent of all U.S. servicemen who were killed in action in the entire country met their deaths in I Corps. The numbers shocked me. I knew that this corps area had been very active, but I had no realization that the actual numbers were so disproportional. I Corps was indeed the focal point of the war at that point. I couldn't help but wonder what the civilian casualty numbers looked like. I felt those numbers would be even more disproportionate.

I continued to have difficulty tracking down the people I wanted Captain Schumacher to meet before I departed. It was a bad assumption on my part that most of them would be readily accessible. I should have known better, as we all seemed to be leading rather hectic, almost desperate lives. Where we would be at any given time during the day was difficult to predict. As of that day, 21 June, I still had eighteen names remaining on my list. We still had work to do.

That night, the NCOs honored me with a dinner at their club. We had a few beers and then a relaxing meal, along with a lot of lively conversation. We recalled happenings both pleasant and tragic. They were a fine group of men. I told them that I'd be proud to serve with any of them again. I was especially pleased with my NCOIC, SFC Simmons. He was top flight and I felt badly that I had not been able to get him promoted to master sergeant. I Corps simply didn't have an available promotion quota.

I still hadn't been able to get Captain Schumacher to Hoi An to meet key people in that city. Recent skirmishes in the city and surrounding areas had kept us from getting into the MACV compound by helicopter. I was hoping that I wouldn't have to scratch that part of my orientation plan. All I could do was try. I wanted so much for my replacement to have a better first few months than I had had. When I arrived in country I was pretty much, as the old saying goes, flying by the seat of my pants.

Thursday, 22 June, a member of our medical advisory team, SFC Duckworth, was injured. The full extent of his injuries was still to be determined, but it appeared that he suffered significant damage to both his middle and inner ears. Sergeant Duckworth was assigned to Hoi An, which had been a hot spot for the past week. On 22 June, he went to his room after lunch, thinking he had time for a brief nap. He had just laid his head on a pillow when the whole building seemed to explode. A Vietnamese electrician, who had been working in the building, turned out to be a clandestine enemy combatant. He had planted a plastic explosive and a small timing device in Duckworth's closet, then immediately disappeared, leading to the conclusion that he had set off the charge. The explosion lifted a part of the roof off the building. It picked up the bed upon which Duckworth was lying and threw it about twenty feet. Fortunately it threw him out of the way of a part of the roof that collapsed into his room. As a result of the explosion, he couldn't hear anything, but the physician who saw him felt confident he would eventually regain some hearing. How much was anyone's guess. It was indeed a strange and difficult war. You never quite knew who the enemy was. SFC Duckworth was fortunate that the damage to his body wasn't more extensive.

On that same day, 22 June, General Lam pinned another decoration on me, for what I wasn't quite certain at the time. I was given a copy of the citation, but since it was in Vietnamese I didn't have a clue as to what it said. The decoration was the Republic of Vietnam Honor Medal, about which I knew nothing. I was surprised and humbled. The presentation was at Duy Tan Hospital.

The orientation of Len Schumacher continued at a feverish pace on 22 June. I was able to introduce him to most of the remaining people on my list, but not all. I had done my best. I had done what I could to make for a seamless transition. The day was also the second birthday of my son Michael. Although he was still fragile, his lungs were definitely getting stronger. I thought of him often during the day.

On Friday morning, 23 June, the last full day I was in Da Nang, I was about to depart the office with Captain Schumacher to go across the Han River to the U.S. Navy hospital. As I got up from my desk to depart, John Hennigan called me aside and told me to be back in the office no later than 1600 hours in a fresh uniform. I suspected that he was going to present me with an award, but I had no idea what was actually going to transpire. Len Schumacher and I were all over the city on that day, meeting people until about 1500 hours, when I dropped him back at the office and hurried to my room to shower and change uniforms. I got back to the office a few minutes after 1600 hours because I had been held up at an intersection by a lengthy convoy of ARVN trucks. Upon my arrival John Hennigan looked me over and smiled his okay.

A few minutes later, just the two of us got into his jeep, which surprised me greatly, and drove down to the point where we could catch the III MAF ferry across the Han River. We boarded the ferry and, a few minutes later, got off onto the III MAF pier. LTC Hennigan didn't say a word as we walked up the walkway and entered III MAF HQ and made our way to a conference room. Standing there was my Vietnamese counterpart and about 10 other ARVN officers and non-commissioned officers with whom I had worked during the past year. Colonel Hamblen and several people from the G-4 Advisory Section were also there. Everyone smiled, but nobody said a word. A few seconds later, in strode Lieutenant General Robert Cushman, the senior U.S. military officer in I Corps, along with Lieutenant General Lam. All attendees came to attention as the III MAF adjutant read the order awarding me the Legion of Merit. I was stunned. General Cushman then made some overly generous remarks, we shook hands, and he and General Lam left the assemblage. John Hennigan stepped forward and said, "I'll see you all tonight at 1830 hours at the MACV Officers' Club."

The night was wonderful. Being with good Vietnamese and American friends in a casual setting was a nice way to say goodbye. The club did a great job in preparing and serving the meal. John Hennigan gave a short speech, again being overly generous with his praise, as did my good and trusted Vietnamese friend, Major Tu. I kept my remarks short, primarily thanking those in attendance for their support during my year at war. It was a night I would long remember.

***

Image 37. LTG Robert Cushman, USMC, awarding the Legion of Merit to the author

Photo courtesy of the author

I arose on Saturday, 24 June, at 0430 hours with the realization that this would be my last day in Da Nang. The time of my flight to Saigon had been changed once again. I was now scheduled to depart at 1050 hours. It would be tough saying goodbye to the fine men and women in the HQ. I had asked my good and faithful Vietnamese interpreter, Sergeant Thong, to give me a ride to the airport at 0945.

When I arrived at my office at about 0515 hours, I was all alone. I sat at my desk and reflected on the events of the past year while waiting for the coffee to brew so I could enjoy a cup while typing a short letter to my wife. Unexpectedly, the telephone rang, startling me out of my reverie. When I answered, the SDO said, "Jim, Colonel Hamblen would like you to come up for a few minutes." As I hurried up to his office, I couldn't help but wonder what it was he wanted to see me about.

I entered his office, stopped about three paces in front of his desk, saluted smartly, and said, "Sir, Major Van Straten reporting as requested."

He returned the salute and then said, "Sit down, lad. Would you like a cup of coffee?"

From that moment on I knew it would be a pleasant meeting, because for him "lad" was a term of respect and endearment. I sat down, the staff duty officer brought us each a cup of coffee, and we sat there for what seemed an eternity without speaking. There was dead silence. I was becoming uncomfortable when finally he spoke.

"I'm sorry I couldn't make last evening's dinner. You know how it is. I just couldn't get away."

I replied, "I understand, sir."

He then said, "So today's the day you're going home?"

I replied, "Yes, sir."

He then asked, "How's that baby of yours doing?"

I responded, "Thanks for asking, sir. He seems to be doing much better overall, but right now he's battling a sore throat with high fever. There have been anxious periods for my wife, but right now things seem some better. His lungs are now operating at about 85 percent of normal."

He responded, "That's good, lad, that's good." Then he went on, "I'm curious about you. Are you intending to stay in the army?"

I responded, "Yes, sir. Why do you ask?"

He said, "Well, now that you have the doctoral credentials, I would imagine there'd be opportunities for you out there."

I responded, "There are, sir. I've received a few nibbles, but I still have a three-year service obligation, and besides that, I like the army and especially the Medical Service Corps."

He then asked, "Did you ever consider transferring to the combat arms? You'd make a fine infantry or armor officer."

I responded, "Thanks for the compliment, sir, but I'm happy where I am. The Medical Service Corps seems to be a good fit for me."

He went on by asking, "What led you in the direction of the Medical Service Corps?"

I said, "Sir, my faculty advisor in college was a kindly priest by the name of Father Anselm Keefe. He had served as a chaplain in a medical unit in the Pacific during World War II and he steered quite a number of his biology majors into the Medical Service Corps."

He responded, "Biology, huh? That explains the Medical Service Corps. Where did you go to college?"

I answered, "Sir, I graduated from St. Norbert College in 1955."

He then said, "I've heard of that school. It's in Wisconsin, isn't it?"

I replied, "Yes, sir. It's located in West De Pere, a small city about four or five miles from Green Bay."

He replied, "You said you graduated in 1955. That means you've got about twelve years in the army."

I replied, "No, sir, actually I'll have eleven at the end of this coming October. I had a sixteen-month break in service."

He asked, "A break in service, what was that all about?"

I answered, "Well, sir, even though I was given a regular army appointment right out of college, by virtue of being designated a Distinguished Military Graduate from the ROTC program, I never really intended to stay in the army. I served my three years, got out right on schedule, and regretted it almost immediately. I took a job as the principal of an elementary school near Green Bay and, as the year wore on, realized I had made a mistake. I missed the army way of life and the interesting people I was constantly coming in contact with while in the army."

He then asked, "So you applied for recall and came back in the army?"

I replied, "Yes, sir, and I've never regretted that decision."

He then paused a moment before saying, "Well, look, lad, I'll not take any more of your time, but I just wanted to look you in the eye and tell you that you've done one hell of a job. I've been in the army a long time, and I can count on the fingers of one hand, maybe on only one finger now that I think about it, the number of officers with not even eleven years of service who have been awarded a Legion of Merit. You may not be aware, but the LOM is known as a colonel's award, and you're only a junior major. I want you to know that yours was earned. You've done one helluva job. You connected with the Vietnamese people, military as well as civilian, to a degree that few advisors are ever able to achieve. You gained their confidence and their trust, two critical components of being a good advisor." He then paused for a moment, smiled, and said, "Now get the hell out of here before you get too puffed up. I have only one last thing to say before you leave, and that is I'd be proud to serve with you again someday, and Godspeed."

I responded, "Thank you for your kind words, sir. They mean a lot to me."

I stood up and saluted smartly. He returned the salute, then came around his desk and shook hands while patting me on the back. We walked out of his office together and shook hands again at the door before parting. As I made my way back to my office, I couldn't help but think that the year in Vietnam was assuredly the most professionally rewarding of my almost eleven-year army career. Were it not for my family, I most definitely would have extended my tour of duty in Da Nang as Colonel Hamblen had requested.

When I arrived back at my office, I drank a cup of coffee with LTC Hennigan and then took a nostalgic walk around the HQ to shake a few hands and say goodbye to the men and women I had served with and come to respect during the past year. I then called Major Tu at Duy Tan

Hospital to say farewell and to wish him and his family the very best in the future. Sergeant Thong then threw my bags in the jeep, and we were off to Da Nang Air Base and the start of my trip home. As I walked across the tarmac to the waiting plane, Sergeant Thong was still standing alongside the jeep. I would miss him.

The flight from Da Nang to Tan Son Nhut Air Base outside Saigon was uneventful. I was met by an officer from the MACV Surgeon's Office and given an out-processing checklist which outlined all the things I had to do to get ready to leave the combat zone.

On Monday, 26 June, I methodically went about the various steps in the process of clearing. I cleaned and turned in my rifle and all my web gear, was debriefed and reminded of my responsibilities regarding classified information that I possessed, signed a bunch of forms, and accomplished various and sundry other tasks necessary to get final clearance to leave the country. Finally the form was signed and stamped. I was one more step closer to home.

Tuesday, 27 June, was spent in the MACV Surgeon's Office. I communicated as accurately as I could the medical situation in I Corps, highlighting lessons learned, the status of the *Helgoland* hospital ship, and potential and known problem areas.

I spent my final night in Saigon drinking in the sights, sounds, and smells of that exotic city. I had tried to reach Major Phat, my old friend from Da Nang, who now served in an ARVN Airborne Division headquartered just outside of Saigon, but was never able to make contact. I was hoping that he and I could get together for dinner one last time before my departure. I wanted to say goodbye to him, as I respected him greatly. That having failed, I contacted a couple of friends from the MACV Surgeon's Office and went to dinner with them. We ate in a delightful seafood restaurant floating on a boat in the Saigon harbor.

The next morning dawned bright and sunny, so clearly it was going to get blistering hot. I was transported to Tan Son Nhut Airport, arriving about 0900 hours, where I was manifested on a flight scheduled to depart in mid-afternoon. All persons on the flight were then shepherded out onto the tarmac and marched to an area where shade was provided by long sheets of corrugated metal placed atop twelve-foot wooden poles. We were to sit there for five and a half hours. The heat became unbearable, the grumbling was loud, and the discontent palpable. There was nothing to do but sit there and melt. Even reading a book proved impossible because of the heat. Most of the 300 or so men on the flight tried to lie down, using an item of carry-on luggage as a headrest. Soon, all the men's uniforms were soaked with perspiration. Fortunately, several lister bags full of potable water had been positioned around the shaded but scorched area.

The time of our scheduled departure came and went. There was no plane, and the discontent bordered on mutiny. As an officer, I was becoming concerned that things were about to get out of control. Other officers and NCOs were concerned as well. Several of us started mentally exploring the options should matters turn even uglier. Just as things were getting near the boiling point, a plane taxied up to a point near our tin-covered shelter, which by then felt like a sauna. Explosively loud cheering echoed across Tan Son Nhut Air Base. An Air Force sergeant and a representative from the charter airline stepped before us, shouted some instructions, and we started the boarding process.

The cabin of the aircraft seemed even hotter than the outside. Whereas there had at least been a slight breeze outside, no air moved inside the stifling hot cabin. The loading process seemed interminably long. But finally it was finished and the plane was ready to depart. It was jam-packed, not a single empty seat on the aircraft. The cabin doors were closed and the plane started to slowly move when suddenly it stopped. The cabin doors were reopened, a set of mobile stairs rolled up, and an armed MP sergeant climbed up the stairs and into the aircraft with two prisoners shackled together in front of him.

Through the aircraft's PA system, the MP sergeant explained that the two prisoners had been charged with very serious crimes and that they were being returned to the United States for incarceration prior to trial. The names of three boarded passengers were called, and they were ordered off the aircraft to accommodate the MP sergeant and the two prisoners. There were jeers as the three enlisted men, whose names had been called, reluctantly left the aircraft.

Finally, we were ready for takeoff. The pilot taxied to the end of the runway, revved up the jet engines, and took off. As the wheels cleared the ground, despite the discomfort that everyone had suffered for the past several hours, there was raucous cheering. As we were slowly gaining altitude, those of us seated in the cabin heard several snapping sounds. The officer seated next to me said, "Small arms fire. We've been hit by small arms fire." He then told me that he was reasonably certain the plane had been hit and that, while the aircraft was seemingly flying well, and we were probably in no danger, he doubted that the pilot would take a chance that the ground fire had not severed a hydraulic line or damaged some other vital part of the airplane. He said he thought the pilot would take the aircraft to a sufficient altitude to safely turn it around and then return to Tan Son Nhut. Sure enough, within two or three minutes, the pilot or co-pilot got on the intercom and said, "Ladies and gentlemen, we seem to have a mechanical problem. We're going to have to return to Tan Son Nhut to have the aircraft checked out." The pilot never acknowledged that the plane had been hit, but everyone in the cabin felt certain that it had. It seemed to take an interminably long time to gain altitude and get clearance to land from air traffic control. Eventually we were again on the ground.

The plane had to be off-loaded for the inspection process, so we again had to return to the inferno created by the metal roof and the late afternoon tropical sun. The grumbling intensified, but everyone seemed too tired to do anything other than flop onto the withered and downtrodden grass and try to sleep. At about 2330 hours, almost midnight, we reboarded the aircraft and finally departed for Travis Air Force Base in California.

The plane was loaded primarily with young enlisted men. Almost all seemed to be army. I saw only a few officers and non-commissioned officers aboard. The senior officer, a U.S. Navy commander, was designated troop commander. He made a few announcements shortly after takeoff, and we were on our way to Hawaii, where we would refuel before continuing on to Travis Air Force Base.

After what seemed like an interminably long flight, we arrived in Hawaii. The plane was rapidly refueled, and we reboarded. Prior to takeoff, the captain informed us that, because of runway congestion at Travis Air Force Base, we were being diverted to San Francisco International Airport. This was wonderful news for those of us making connecting flights. How good it would be to see the Golden Gate Bridge and the United States of America, the land of the free and the home of the brave.

The pilot eventually landed at San Francisco International and taxied to the gate, but before we were allowed to deplane, an airport representative came onto the plane and made an announcement. "Soldiers, sailors, marines, and airmen, welcome back to the United States of America. We appreciate your service. Thank you very, very much. I need to tell you, however, that these are very divisive and difficult times in our country. The American people are sharply divided over the war in Vietnam. Emotions are running high, especially in San Francisco. Since this is an international flight, you must claim your baggage and clear customs upon deplaning. Because we don't want you subjected to verbal abuse as you walk to the gates for your connecting flights, we strongly recommend that those of you in military uniform change into civilian clothing at the first opportunity. You'll find the bathrooms in San Francisco International Airport to be large and accommodating. Again, thank you for your service, ladies and gentlemen. You may now deplane."

I was shocked. I couldn't believe what I was hearing. But as we deplaned and saw the open hostility in the eyes of a few of the people, it was apparent that our service was not appreciated by all our fellow Americans. As we stood at the baggage claim area someone yelled, "Baby killers!" I couldn't help but feel sorry for the enlisted men and women who were waiting for their luggage, especially the young draftees. What had they done to provoke this hostility? It seemed so unfair. One person, just one unknown loud mouthed person, had lessened the joy of their homecoming.

It seemed a fairly high percentage of those who deplaned had been drafted into the armed forces to fight a war that their elected officials told them was in the national interest of the United States. President Eisenhower and then President Kennedy, after careful analysis and soliciting the best counsel available, had taken the first small steps into the war when they sent military advisors to assist the army of South Vietnam. Then President Johnson, after the tragic assassination of President Kennedy, upped the ante and committed American forces to direct combat roles against the VC and NVA. The "domino theory," cited by many in our Department of State as the reason for the war, held that if South Vietnam fell to Communism other nations would soon follow.

It all seemed so unfair. So many of those who had fought and died had been drafted. They went to war and they served, whereas many others had fled to Canada or enrolled in a university or college to escape the draft.[2] How terribly demoralizing this was for these young men and women, to be denigrated upon returning home after having been drafted by their government to serve. Many of their fathers, grandfathers, and uncles had fought in World War II or Korea and were proud not only of their service, but also of their uniforms. And now being told to remove their uniforms so as not to be verbally abused was hard to understand and for many, me among them, disheartening. I could see the hurt and lack of understanding on the young soldiers' faces. I couldn't help but wonder why the San Franciscans weren't instead protesting to their elected officials. Why should young drafted soldiers be subjected to their verbal abuse?

But those feelings soon dissipated as the warm feeling of finally getting closer to home began to set in. I had done my best and was proud of my service. I accepted the fact that the right to dissent and protest are vital parts of our democracy, even though seemingly unfair and misguided at times. I went to war to protect our way of life, and as a career officer, I couldn't choose the time or the place of engagement. In the end, the decision regarding whether or not to engage in warfare was the solemn burden of our elected civilian officials. Civilian control of the military is a prerequisite of stable government, and the ultimate decision as to whether or not to wage war had to be that of our elected officials. My year at war was over and I flew home to my waiting family.

CHAPTER 13

REFLECTIONS

Upon leaving Vietnam I never imagined that the war would grind on for another seven long and tragic years. I thought there would be a negotiated settlement far sooner than 1975. The longer the war went on the more apprehensive I became. I feared for my former South Vietnamese military colleagues and civilian friends and acquaintances should the North Vietnamese prevail.

As a result of many discussions with ARVN officers and civilian government officials, I knew that many in South Vietnam, especially those in positions of influence and power, feared retribution should Ho Chi Minh and his generals prevail. They felt that once it became known to the captors that they had actively opposed the North they would be punished. This was especially true of those who had befriended the Americans. Later events proved that their fears were justified.

Saigon fell to the Communists on 30 April 1975. I watched with great trepidation, from the sanctuary of the United States, a world away, as the tragic events in Vietnam started to unfold.

An estimated 65,000 South Vietnamese citizens were summarily executed at the end of the war. Many of those killed were government officials and military officers. About one million others were sent to prison or reeducation camps where large numbers perished, perhaps as many as 250,000.[1] Nobody can be certain of the numbers as records were not kept. It seems likely that some of my former Vietnamese friends and colleagues were among those selected for execution, imprisonment, or the reeducation camps.[2]

To escape those horrors, many Vietnamese decided to flee the country, to start a new life elsewhere. Transportation by air was impossible. The Communists rigidly controlled all air traffic. Fishing boats, designed for the coastal waterways and rivers, not for the open seas, were the only viable alternative. The number attempting to flee by boat has been put as high as 1.5 million. The Australian Immigration Ministry reported that deaths among those attempting to flee ranged from an estimated low of 50,000 to as high as 200,000. Again, no one can be certain of the numbers.[3]

People throughout the world were horrified and saddened to witness on television some of the small, over-crowded fishing boats arrive on foreign shores, after many perilous days at sea, only to be rejected and literally pushed back into the open ocean. They were unwelcome and unwanted, even though their lives hung in the balance. The Vietnamese occupants of many of the boats scuttled them near shore to avoid being forced back into the ocean by those who objected to their landing. Piracy of the boat people was commonplace, as was kidnapping and forced prostitution.

As this human tragedy unfolded, I prayed for all of the valiant Vietnamese people who tried to escape the horrors and inhumanity of it all. I prayed especially for those I knew personally. I was anguished. I had so many questions and so few answers.

I was heartened by the actions of President Ford and President Carter, as well as the governments of other responsible nations. President Ford opened the immigration door to accommodate a sizable number who were fleeing, and President Carter opened that door even wider. Both recognized that we, as a nation, had an obligation to help our former allies escape the indignities of being a people without a country.[4] The United

States eventually accepted approximately 823,000 refugees; Australia and Canada each welcomed 119,000; France accepted 96,000, and Great Britain opened its doors to 19,000.[5]

Both South Vietnam and the United States paid a very heavy price in terms of lives lost during the war. About 250,000 members of South Vietnam's armed forces were killed in action while an estimated 465,000 civilians lost their lives as a direct result of the war. Many were assassinated by Viet Cong terrorists. The United States also suffered heavy losses. Over 58,000 men and women, 47,000 as a direct result of enemy action, were killed during the prolonged conflict.[6]

Huge numbers of Vietnamese men, women, and children were driven from their homeland as a result of the war. It has been estimated that over two million fled, over 11 percent of South Vietnam's total population, establishing new homes elsewhere.[7]

Well after this mass exodus was over, I found out that Dr. Tu, my first Vietnamese counterpart, and his family were in Australia. How they got there, I do not know. I have no way of knowing whether they were allowed to emigrate or if they fled the country as "boat people." I had received several letters from Dr. Tu shortly after my departure from Vietnam, the last at Christmas-time 1969. After the war ended, I received one letter from him after he arrived in Australia. I do not know if he and his family were living in some type of resettlement camp or living independently. The letter provided few details. I immediately sent a letter in reply, but I do not know if the letter was delivered for I received no response. I have since sent several email messages to various Vietnamese-Australian professional associations and societies, asking for help in locating Dr. Tu but have never received a response to any of my inquiries.

Major Phat, the former commander of Duy Tan General Hospital, is apparently now living in Denver, Colorado. About four or five years ago, after having had no contact with him for approximately forty-five years, I received an email message from him. He gave no details about his new life, simply telling me he was living in Denver. We exchanged two email messages. In the second message I sent to him, I informed him that my wife and I would be away from home for two months, at our lakeside cabin in Wisconsin, and that I would contact him as soon as we returned. Upon our return, I sent another email but it came back to me as undeliverable. I tried several times to re-send the message, but every time, it came back labeled undeliverable. All I can assume is that Dr. Phat changed internet service providers and we lost contact.

I do know that in the closing days of the war, the United States airlifted to safety about 130,000 Vietnamese who were in grave danger of reprisal for their close ties to the American military. Generally these people were well-educated professionals. It seems plausible that Doctors Tu and Phat might have been among that group.

I worry about Sergeant Thong, my ever faithful and invaluable interpreter and driver. Did he survive? Was he looked upon by the Communists as being complicit with the enemy by virtue of his loyalty and service to me? I do not know.

Bá Vy, my ever cheerful and much appreciated maid, also concerns me greatly. Were she and her large family spared from the Communist onslaught? Was the fact that she worked for the Americans for so many years held against her during the Communist reckoning?

Mr. Khoi, whose life was transformed when Dr. Giles removed the disfiguring nevus from the side of his face, and little Ho Thien, with his ingratiating smile through his surgically repaired upper lip, did they and their gracious and grateful mothers survive? Did the Communist captors look upon those who had life-altering surgeries, performed by American military doctors, with disfavor and decide to punish them? I have no way of knowing whether or not persons we tried to help were dealt with harshly during the Communist purge that transpired at the end of the war.

As for my fellow American comrades in arms, it saddens me to report that both of my immediate military superiors, LTC Fred Mabra and LTC John Hennigan, are now deceased. Colonel Hennigan died in 1987 at age 57, less than twenty years after leaving Vietnam, while Colonel Mabra passed away in 1995.

The commander of MACV Advisory Team #1, Colonel Archelaus Hamblen, was promoted to brigadier general sometime after his Vietnam assignment and died of complications following a stroke in 2005.

I have had no contact with SFC Sanders or SFC Simmons, two of the three fine soldiers who served as the NCOIC of the Medical Advisory Section of the G-4's office during my time in Vietnam. I did, however, receive several letters from SFC Davis, two written while he was a patient in Walter Reed Army Medical Center, and one from New Orleans, where he was visiting his family while on convalescent leave. He again thanked me profusely for saving his life, which I assuredly did not do. I simply got him to the hospital promptly after finding him in a diabetic coma. I wish I could make contact with these fine NCOs, as I respected them greatly and appreciated their fine work.

Likewise, I have had no contact, since leaving Vietnam, with Captain David Stephens, the Assistant G-4 advisor, or SP-5 Behner, the clerk-typist who served our office so capably. I think of them frequently and wish them well.

Captain Bob Helton, who served so heroically, went on to serve a full military career in the MSC and retired with the rank of colonel. He now lives in Marble Falls, Texas. Captain Charles Delane, who followed Bob Helton, also remained in the army and retired in the rank of LTC. He now resides in Plantation, Florida. I feel indebted to both of these fine officers.

Sadly, Len Schumacher, who headed our medical advisory effort in Quang Ngai and Quang Tin Provinces, died in 2011. He, too, served a full career before retiring in the rank of LTC. Before his death he resided in San Antonio, Texas.

Joseph Lutz, my St. Norbert College classmate, who introduced me to Arc Light bombing while standing along the edge of a rooftop restaurant in Saigon on a beautiful summer evening, went on to a very distinguished military career in special operations. He retired with the rank of major general. Sadly, he died in 1999 at the age of 66. Rest in peace, dear friend.

General Lewis Walt, for whom I gained such tremendous respect, died in 1989. I believe his views regarding how to fight the war gained wide acceptance during the intervening years. Clearly, the strategy of attrition and the tactics of "search and destroy," as advocated by General Westmoreland, Secretary McNamara, and ultimately the White House, during the early years of the war, were abhorred by General Walt. This strategy and tactic failed to bring the two parties to the negotiating table and were, in large measure, abandoned when General Westmoreland left Vietnam in 1968. The resolve of the Communist insurgents was simply too strong to be swayed by loss of life, equipment and supplies, and the destruction of infrastructure. I once heard General Walt angrily exclaim, "Dammit, if they think we can kill our way out of this war they're wrong." Upon his departure from Vietnam, most members of MACV Advisory Team #1, me included, thought his assignment as the Director of Personnel for the USMC was a career ending slap in the face. We were obviously wrong as General Walt was eventually promoted to full general, four star rank, and assigned as the Assistant Commandant of the Marine Corps.

The German diplomat, Baron Hermann von Richthofen, who was supportive of moving the *Helgoland* hospital ship from Saigon to Da Nang, went on to a very impressive career. He served as the German ambassador to the United Kingdom from 1989 to 1993. While in London, he became an instant celebrity because of his genealogical linkage to Baron Manfred von Richthofen, the "Red Baron" of WWI fame. After leaving his ambassadorial assignment in London, he was appointed German ambassador to NATO HQ. He remained in that position until his retirement from diplomatic life in 1998.

Although somewhat irritating at the time, I now know and can appreciate why the commander of Advisory Team #1, Colonel Arch Hamblen, steered so many social invitations, off duty teaching responsibilities, and other opportunities to meet and interact with a broad range of Vietnamese people, to include government officials, journalists, students, and high ranking military officers, in my direction. I am convinced it was because of my connections to medicine and education. The mantra voiced unceasingly by American commanders, from General Westmoreland on down, was, "We've got to win the hearts and minds of the people." Medical support was among the most visible and compelling means available for doing that, as was education, but to a lesser degree. Even though I had no clinical expertise whatsoever, the silver caduceus on the lapel of my uniform, coupled with the highly visible medical initiatives we had going in I Corps, spoke loudly to the Vietnamese people throughout the five province region.

The ancient culture of the Vietnamese people was, for me, a treasure to be studied and admired. As I think back upon my experiences, I remember the people as very open and friendly. By their very nature, they were polite and sensitive, never boastful or arrogant. Family relationships and family roles were exceedingly important to them. I found them to be a very proud people. I once had an old man tell me that there is an ancient myth which says, "The Vietnamese are descendants of an angel and a dragon." I assume the myth can be interpreted to mean that the sensitivity and gentleness of the Vietnamese people came from an angel while the dragon was responsible for instilling the fighting spirit that emerges when their freedom or livelihood is threatened.

It heartens me to see that the Vietnamese who emigrated to our country, after fleeing the post-war horrors of South Vietnam, are doing well. They have been rapidly assimilated into our society, and most have become responsible citizens. Practically all, it seems to me, have learned the English language and most have adopted American life-styles while keeping their own culture alive.

For me personally, my service in Vietnam ingrained in me not only a fuller realization of the fragility of life but also a deeper appreciation of family and a keener understanding of the resiliency of the human spirit. I know that, as a direct result of my experiences in that then war torn country, I am now even more appreciative of my family and friends and of my own God-given life. Every day is a blessing.

EPILOGUE

After the first printing of this book was released, a friend living in Pennsylvania, retired Colonel Douglas Braendel, read it and noted that I had lost contact with my two ARVN counterparts and was concerned about their safety and well-being. Colonel Braendel immediately contacted Nguyen-Mau Trinh, a Vietnamese-American pharmacist and former ARVN officer, who lives in the Washington, D.C. area. Colonel and Mrs. Braendel had sponsored the Nguyen family at the time they immigrated to the United States. Colonel Braendel asked for Trinh's help in locating the two officers.

Within days pharmacist Trinh had located both officers. Colonel Braendel sent me their email addresses and I immediately reestablished contact with both. Dr. Pham Viet Tu is now an Australian citizen and lives in Brisbane. Dr. Tran Tan Phat is a naturalized U.S. citizen and lives in Midway City, California.

When we served together in the Republic of Vietnam, MAJ Tu was an internist assigned as the Corps Surgeon (the lead physician) of the First Corps Tactical Zone, the upper five provinces of the country, while Dr. Phat was an orthopedic surgeon who served as the commander of one of South Vietnam's largest and most sophisticated military hospitals, Duy Tan General Hospital in Da Nang.

Their story is instructive and worth telling. Shortly after the Vietnam War ended on April 30, 1975, both Dr. Tu and Dr. Phat were incarcerated and spent three degrading and demoralizing years in a Communist reeducation camp. During this lengthy incarceration, Dr. and Mrs. Tu's six children were denied all opportunities for advanced education. Upon release from the camp, Dr. Tu and his wife made two unsuccessful attempts to get their family out of the country by boat. Both attempts failed, one because of navigational errors on the part of the pilot and the other because the craft was not seaworthy in open ocean waters. It had been built as a fishing boat to be used only on coastal and inland waters. Their money nearly exhausted, the parents decided, almost in desperation, to try and at least get their children out of the Communist country and give them an opportunity for a better life. Boats were thought to be their only viable option for escape. They divided their six children into two groups and gave them instructions to try and make their way to Australia. One group departed Vietnam in 1980 and the other in 1982. Amazingly, both groups were successful in escaping the country. One group landed in Songkhla Province in southern Thailand and the other group reached Bidong Island off the coast of Malaysia. Both groups stayed in refugee camps briefly and then were transported to Australia. In 1990, eight long years after all of their children has been resettled in Australia and 15 years after the war had ended, Dr. Tu and his wife were allowed to leave Vietnam and be reunited with their six children. Sadly, Mrs. Tu died in 2009. Dr. Tu recently sent me an email message describing those anxious and fearful years. His concluding sentence was, "These events occurred a long time ago, but in my mind they feel like yesterday."

MAJ Phat's story is quite different. While I served with him in Da Nang, during 1966-67, he was a bachelor. He married in December 1968, eighteen months after I left Vietnam. He and his wife had three children, two daughters and a son. After his three-year period of incarceration ended in 1978 he was allowed to work as a "paroled medical servant." He worked initially as an orthopedic surgeon and later as a spine surgeon in two different Saigon hospitals, Binh Dan and HCM Orthopedic. In 1992, 17 years after the war ended, he and his family were finally allowed to emigrate to the United States under the "Orderly Departure Program," a program created under the auspices of the United Nations High Commissioner for Refugees. The Phat family was sponsored by relatives already living in the United States. Initially they settled in Mission Viejo, California, but later moved to Midway City where they now live.

Because of differences in medical education, neither Dr. Tu nor Dr. Phat was able to become credentialed as a physician in their newly adopted countries. Demonstrating the tremendous resilience that seems to characterize the Vietnamese people, both went back to school to learn new professions. Dr. Tu earned a Ph.D. in the field of public health, while Dr. Phat studied and was employed in the field of electronic medical records and electronic data processing.

The following photo images show how my counterparts and I looked during the war and how we look now, more than a half century later.

Image 38. MAJ Pham Viet Tu

MAJ Pham Viet Tu served as both the I Corps Surgeon and the commander of Duy Tan General Hospital during the author's tour of duty in Vietnam.

Image 39. MAJ Tran Tan Phat

MAJ Tran Tan Phat served as the commander of Duy Tan General Hospital until his transfer to the Saigon area about midway through the author's tour of duty.

Image 40. MAJ James Van Straten while serving as the Senior Medical Advisor in I Corps

Image 41. Dr. Pham Viet Tu now living in Brisbane, Australia

Image 42. Dr. Tran Tan Phat now living in Mission City, California

Image 43. Dr. James Van Straten now living in Windcrest, Texas

About the Author

After his service in Vietnam, Major Van Straten went on to serve a full thirty-year career in the U.S. Army Medical Service Corps, retiring in 1986 with the rank of colonel. Among the more significant positions he held in the years following his service in Vietnam were Director of Health Manpower Programs in the Office of the Assistant Secretary of Defense for Health Affairs in the Pentagon, Deputy Commander of the Medical Field Service School at Fort Sam Houston, Texas, and Chief of Staff of Seventh Medical Command in Heidelberg, Germany. During his last U.S. Army assignment, he served as the director of a Department of Army-sponsored study aimed at improving the command and control of the Army Medical Department.

Colonel Van Straten graduated from the Army's Command & General Staff College at Fort Leavenworth and was designated an honor graduate. He also graduated from the Army War College, the army's most senior college, at Carlisle Barracks, Pennsylvania. Concurrent with his attendance there, he served on the College's Current Affairs Panel, a small group of officers selected to travel throughout the United States interacting with students and faculty at some of America's premier universities and colleges.

Upon retiring from the army, Colonel Van Straten accepted a position as assistant to the president of Incarnate Word College, now known as the University of the Incarnate Word. Within six months, he competed for and was selected as founding dean of the college's Division of Professional Studies. He remained in that position until September 1990, when he again competed for and was selected as dean of the School of Allied Health Sciences at the University of Texas Health Science Center at San Antonio. In 1992, he was appointed Honorary Colonel of the Army Medical Department Regiment by The Surgeon General of the United

States Army, serving in that honorific position until 1996. In late 1997, Dr. Van Straten retired from the University of Texas Health Science Center at San Antonio and from professional life.

Sadly, his loving wife, Patricia, to whom he wrote the many letters that became the primary source for this memoir, now suffers from Alzheimer's disease. She and her husband, who serves as her caregiver, still try to lead an active lifestyle, despite the difficulties that arise because of the disease. During the year that her husband was in Vietnam, Pat wrote to him almost daily, usually in the middle of the night when the six children were asleep. Unfortunately, Jim did not save her letters. Had he done so, they would have added an interesting further dimension to this memoir.

Jim and Pat's six children are all married and living responsible lives. All have attended college; five hold bachelor's degrees and two have master's degrees. One daughter, Kathy, graduated from her father's undergraduate alma mater, St. Norbert College. Susan and Laurie graduated from the University of Texas at Austin. Susan also earned teacher certification (K-6) and special education certification (K-12) from the University of North Texas. Leslie attended Northern Virginia Community College and San Antonio College.

The two Van Straten sons both attended military academies. Steven graduated from the U.S. Military Academy at West Point. Michael, who was so gravely ill as a baby, graduated from the U.S. Merchant Marine Academy at Kings Point. Both sons also hold master's degrees, Steven from the University of Wisconsin at Oshkosh and Michael from Old Dominion University. Jim and Pat Van Straten also have eight grandchildren and one great grandchild who brighten their lives.

ENDNOTES

NOTES TO CHAPTER 1

1. Stanley L. Kutler, *Encyclopedia of the Vietnam War* (New York: Charles Scribner's Sons, 1996), 48.

2. Robert J. Topmiller, *The Lotus Unleashed: The Buddhist Peace Movement in South Vietnam, 1964-1966* (Lexington: The University Press of Kentucky, 2002), 71-91.

3. Edwin H. Simmons, *The Illustrated History of Marines: The Vietnam War* (New York: Bantam Books, Inc., 1987), 58-61.

4. Jan K. Herman, *Navy Medicine in Vietnam: Passages to Freedom to the Fall of Saigon* (Washington: Naval History and Heritage Command, 2009), 21-23.

5. U.S. Department of Defense, Military Assistance Command, Vietnam, *DA Pam 360-521, Handbook for U.S. Forces in Vietnam* (Washington, D.C. Government Printing Office, 1966), 2-6.

6. George D. Moss, *Vietnam: An American Ordeal* (Upper Saddle River: Prentice Hall, Inc., 1998), 108.

7. U.S. Naval Operations, Vietnam, *Highlights: (No. 10) July 1966,* (Washington, D.C.: Naval History Division), <http://www.mrfa2.org/MRFA%20'Highlights'%20copies/mrfa-10/high-10.htm>

8. Victor H. Krulak, *First to Fight: An Inside Look at the U.S. Marine Corps* (Annapolis: Naval Institute Press, 1984), 205-06.

9. Shelby L. Stanton, *The Rise and Fall of an American Army: U.S. Ground Forces in Vietnam, 1965-1973* (Novato: Presidio Press, 1985), 125.

10. James P. Coan, *Con Thien: The Hill of Angels* (Tuscaloosa: University of Alabama Press, 2004), 43.

NOTES TO CHAPTER 2

1. Michael A. Hennessy, *Strategy in Vietnam: The Marines and Revolutionary Warfare in I Corps, 1965-1972* (Westport: Praeger Publishers, 1997), 93.

2. Edwin E. Moise, *The International Commissions: ICC (ICSC) and ICCS,* June 8, 2011 <http://www.clemson.edu/caah/history/facultypages/edmoise/icc.html> (21 April 2014).

3. Neil Sheehan, *A Bright Shining Lie* (New York: Random House, 1988), 177-78.

4. Stanley Karnow, *Vietnam: A History* (New York: Penguin Books, 1984), 379.

5. Kutler, 339.

NOTES TO CHAPTER 3

1. Kutler, 460.

2. Dieter Nohlen, et al., *Election in Asia: A Data Handbook, Vol. II, South East Asia, East Asia and the South Pacific* (Oxford: Oxford University Press, 2001), 331-34. William C. Westmoreland, *A Soldier Reports* (Garden City: Doubleday and Company, Inc., 1976), 188.

3. Joseph H. Newberry, Colonel, U.S. Army Retired, email messages dated 16, 18, and 19 October, 2013 exchanged with author. (Author initially thought engine oil was being added but Colonel Newberry, a medical evacuation helicopter pilot, informed the author that it was in all likelihood hydraulic fluid.)

4. Willard Pearson, *The War in the Northern Provinces: 1966-1968* (Washington, D.C.: Department of the Army, 1975), 12-13.

5. William C. Gibbons, *The U.S. Government and the Vietnam War: Executive and Legislative Roles and Relationship* (Princeton: Princeton University Press, 1990), 198.

Notes to Chapter 4

1. Herman, 24-25.

2. Hennessy, 65-66.

3. Topmiller, 72-73. Robert D. Schulzinger, *A Time for War: The United States and Vietnam, 1941-1975* (New York: Oxford University Press, 1997), 182.

4. Krulak, 195-204.

5. Bobby K. Helton, Colonel, U.S. Army Retired, myriad email messages exchanged between Colonel Helton and the author during January and February, 2014 to insure accuracy of account.

6. Robert S. McNamara and Brian VanDeMark, *In Retrospect: The Tragedy and Lessons of Vietnam* (New York: Times Books, 1995), 262.

7. Westmoreland, 187.

8. Schulzinger, 193.

9. Westmoreland, 190-91.

Notes to Chapter 5

1. Kutler, 143.

2. Hennessy, 73.

3. Herman, 27.

4. Jeff Dentice and Noonie Fortin, "Entertainer of the Troops," <http://www.war-veterans.org/Maggie.htm> (28 April 2004).

Notes to Chapter 6

1. Anonymous Author, "Marine Corps League Awards," *Marine Corps Gazette*, Vol. 55, Issue 9, September 1971, Front Page.

2. Phillip Knightley, "Part Three, The Role of the Press: Was the Coverage of the War Fair, Vietnam1954-1975," in *The American Experience in*

Vietnam: A Reader, ed. Grace Sevy (Norman: University of Oklahoma Press, 1989), 119-20.

3. Nancy Gibbs and Michael Duffy, *The Preacher and the Presidents: Billy Graham in the White House* (New York: Center Street Publishers, 2007), 148-49.

4. Jean Shellenberger, comp., *The 9th Engineer Battalion, First Marine Division, in Vietnam: 35 Personal Accounts* (Jefferson: McFarland and Company, Inc., 2000), 58-59.

5. Herman, 30-32.

6. Christian G. Appy, *Patriots: The Vietnam War Remembered From All Sides* (New York: Penguin Books, 2003), 333.

7. Dennis Small, *Christmas Story,* <http://www.davtnnorthport.org/wp-content/uploads/2011/06/Christmas-Story.pdf>, (11 April 20014).

NOTE TO CHAPTER 7

1. George C. Herring, *America's Longest War: The United States and Vietnam, 1950-1975* (New York: McGraw Hill, Inc., 1996), 175-76.

NOTES TO CHAPTER 8

1. Robert Sherrod, "A Monstrous War," *Life Magazine,* January 27, 1967, 20-29.

2. Colin L. Powell and Joseph Persico, *My American Journey* (New York: Random House, Inc., 1995), 147.

3. Martha L. Gellhorn, "Suffer the Little Children. . . .," *Ladies Home Journal,* January 1967, 107-110.

4. Third Marine Amphibious Force. Vietnam, Attachment to ICCI 3050-1, "Vietnamese Customs Applicable to Emergency Situations," 27 February 1967.

5. HQ Marine Aircraft Group II, 1st Marine Aircraft Wing, FPO San Francisco, *Subject: Command Chronology, period 1-28 February 1967,*

pt. II, para. 10, 13 March 1967, <http://media.nara.gov/usmc/075/00
004261.pdf> (5 April 2014).

6. William T. Johnson, "William T. Johnson and Charles B. MacDonald,"
<http://www.presby.edu/library/archives/blog/july-2009/> (July
2009).

Notes to Chapter 9

1. George D. Moss, *Vietnam: An American Ordeal* (Upper Saddle River:
Prentice Hall, Inc., 1998), 256-58.

2. Sheehan, 10.

3. *Congressional Record,* Vol. 113 (Washington: Government Printing Office, May 1967), 286.

4. Ibid., 618-19.

Notes to Chapter 10

1. Mike Larson, *Heroes: A Year in Vietnam With the First Air Cavalry Division* (Bloomington: IUniverse, 2008), 148.

2. Bobby K. Helton, Colonel, U.S. Army Retired, several email messages
exchanged with author during February and March, 2014 to insure
accuracy.

3. Sheehan, 620.

Notes to Chapter 11

1. Kutler, 202.

2. Sheehan, 643-45.

3. Maynard Parker, "Report: Hong Kong," *Atlantic Monthly,* Vol. 220, No.
5, November 1967, 14-28.

4. Kathryn M. Talalay, *Composition in Black and White: The Life of
Philippa Schuyler* (New York: Oxford University Press, 1995), 276.

NOTES TO CHAPTER 12

1. H.C. Nonnemann, "The German Hospital Ship *Helgoland* in Vietnam," in *Disaster Medicine: Types and Events of Disasters Organization in Various Disaster Situations,* Vol. 1, eds. Rudolf Frey and Peter Safar (Berlin-Heidelberg: Springer), 225-26.

2. James R. Ebert, *A Life in a Year: The American Infantryman in Vietnam, 1965-1972* (Novato: Presidio Press, 1993), 16-24.

NOTES TO CHAPTER 13

1. Lewis Sorley, *A Better War: The Unexamined Victories and Final Tragedy of America's Last Years in Vietnam* (New York: Harcourt Brace & Company, 1999), 383.

2. Anonymous Author, History Learning Site, "Vietnamese Boat People," 2014, 1 http://www.historylearningsite.co.uk/vietnam_boat_people.htm> Accessed 14 March 2015

3. Ibid., 1.

4. Alicia Campi, "From Refugees to Americans: Thirty Years of Vietnamese Immigration to the United States," 2005, 2 http://www.ilw.com/articles/2006,0313-campi.shtm>Accessed 16 March 2015

5. Anonymous Author, History Learning Site, "Vietnamese Boat People," http://www.historylearningsite.co.uk/vietnam_boat_people.htm> Accessed 14 March 2015.

6. Sorley, 383.

7. Ibid., 383.

Bibliography

Books

Appy, Christian G. *Patriots: The Vietnam War From All Sides.* New York: Penguin Books, 2003.

Coan, James P. *Con Thien: The Hill of Angels.* Tuscaloosa: University of Alabama Press, 2004.

Ebert, James R. *A Life in a Year: The American Infantryman in Vietnam, 1965-1972.* Novato: Presidio Press, 1993.

Gibbons, William C. *The U.S. Government and the Vietnam War: Executive and Legislative Roles and Relationship.* Princeton: Princeton University Press, 1990.

Gibbs, Nancy and Michael Duffy. *The Preacher and the Presidents: Billy Graham in the White House.* New York: Center Street, 2007.

Hennessy, Michael A. *Strategy in Vietnam: The Marines and Revolutionary Warfare in I Corps, 1965-1972.* Westport: Praeger Publishers, 1997.

Herman, Jan K. *Navy Medicine in Vietnam: Passages to Freedom to the Fall of Saigon.* Washington: Naval History and Heritage Command, 2009.

Herring, George C. *America's Longest War: The united States and Vietnam, 1950-1975.* New York: McGraw-Hill, Inc., 1996.

Karnow, Stanley. *Vietnam: A History.* New York: Penguin Books, 1984.

Knightley, Phillip. Part Three, The Role of the Press: Was the Coverage of the War Fair?, Vietnam 1954-1975," in *The American Experience in Vietnam: A Reader.* ed. Grace Sevy. Norman: University of Oklahoma Press, 1989.

Krulak, Victor H. *First to Fight: An Inside View of the U.S. Marine Corps,* Annapolis: The Naval Institute Press, 1984.

Kutler, Stanley I., ed. *Encyclopedia of the Vietnam War.* New York: Charles Scribner's Sons, 1996.

Larson, Mike. Heroes: *A Year In Vietnam With The First Cavalry Division.* Bloomington: IUniverse (ebook format), 2008.

McNamara, Robert S. and Brian VanDeMark. *In Retrospect.* New York: Random House, Inc., 1995.

Moss, George D. *Vietnam: An American Ordeal,* 3rd ed. Upper Saddle River: Prentice Hall, Inc., 1998.

Nohlen, Dieter, Florian Grotz, and Christoff Hartman. *Election in Asia: A Data Handbook: Volume II: South East Asia, East Asia and the South Pacific.* Oxford: Oxford University Press, 2001.

Nonnemann, H.C. "The German Hospital Ship Helgoland in Vietnam." In *Disaster Medicine: Types and Events of Disasters Organization in Various Disaster Situations. Vol. 1.* Berlin-Heidelberg: Springer, 1980.

Pearson, Willard. *The War in the Northern Provinces: 1966-1968.* Washington, D.C.: Department of the Army, 1975.

Powell, Colin L., and Joseph E. Persico. *My American Journey.* New York: Random House, Inc., 1995.

Scales, Robert H. *Firepower in Limited War.* Washington, D.C.: National Defense University Press, 1993.

Schulzinger, Robert D. *A Time for War: The United States and Vietnam, 1941-1975.* New York: Oxford University Press, 1997.

Sheehan, Neil. *A Bright Shining Lie: John Paul Vann and America in Vietnam.* New York: Random House, 1988.

Shellenberger, Jean, comp. *The 9th Engineer Battalion, First Marine Division, in Vietnam.* Jefferson: McFarland and Company, Inc, 2000.

Simmons, Edwin H. *The Illustrated History of Marines: The Vietnam War.* New York: Bantam Books, Inc., 1987.

Sorley, Lewis. *A Better War: The Unexamined Victories and Final Tragedy of America's Last Years in Vietnam.* Harcourt Brace & Company, 1999

Stanton, Shelby L. *The Rise and Fall of an American Army: U.S. Ground Forces in Vietnam, 1965-1973.* Novato: Presidio Press, 1985.

Talalay, Kathryn M. *Composition in Black and White: The Life of Philippa Schuyler.* New York: Oxford University Press, 1995.

Topmiller, Robert J. *The Lotus Unleashed: The Buddhist Peace Movement in South Vietnam, 1964-1966.* Lexington: The University Press of Kentucky, 2002.

Westmoreland, William C. *A Soldier Reports.* Garden City: Doubleday and Company, Inc., 1976.

GOVERNMENT PUBLICATIONS

Congressional Record, Vol. 113. Washington: Government Printing Office, May 1967.

Military Assistance Command, Vietnam. *DA Pam 360-521, Handbook For US Forces in Vietnam.* Washington: Government Printing Office, 1966.

Third Marine Amphibious Force, Vietnam, Attachment to ICCI 3050-1. "Vietnamese Customs Applicable to Emergency Situations." 27 February 1967.

MAGAZINE ARTICLES

Gellhorn, Martha L. "Suffer the Little Children. . . .," *Ladies Home Journal,* Vol. 84, No.1, January 1967, 107-110.

Parker, Maynard. "Report: Hong Kong." *Atlantic Monthly,* Vol. 220, No. 5 (1967): 14-28.

Sherrod, Robert. "A Monstrous War," *Life Magazine,* 27 January 1967, 20-29.

NEWSPAPER ARTICLE

Anonymous Author, "Marine Corps League Awards," *Marine Corps Gazette,* Vol.55. Issue 9, September 1971.

PERSONAL CORRESPONDENCE

Van Straten, James G. Three-hundred-fifty-two letters written by author to his wife while he was in Vietnam. Letters became the primary source for this book.

WEBSITES

Campi, Alicia. "From Refugees to Americans: Thirty Years of Vietnamese Immigration to the United States," accessed 15 March 2015, http://www.ilw.com/articles/2006,0313-campi.shtm

Dentice, Jeff and Noonie Fortin. "Entertainer of the Troops," accessed 28 April 2014, http://www.war-veterans.org/Maggie.htm

HQ Marine Aircraft Group II, 1st Marine Aircraft Wing, FPO San Francisco, "Command Chronology, period 1-28 February 1967, pt. II, para. 10, 13 March 1967," accessed 5 April 2014, http://media.nara.gov/usmc/075/00004261.pdf

History Learning Site, "Vietnamese Boat People," accessed 14 March 2015, http://www.historylearningsite.co.uk/vietnam_boat_people.htm

Johnson, William T. "William T. Johnson and Charles B. MacDonald," accessed 23 April 2014, http://www.presby.edu/library/archives/blog/july-2009/

Small, Dennis, "Christmas Story," accessed 11 April 20014, http://www.davtnnorthport.org/wp-content/uploads/2011/06/Christmas-Story.pdf

U.S. Naval Operations, "Vietnam, Highlights: (No. 10) July 1966, Washington, D.C.: Naval History Division," accessed 14 April 2014, http://www.mrfa2.org/MRFA%20'Highlights'%20copies/mrfa-10/high-10.htm

INDEX

500 A Different Face of War